CITIES OF THE CLASSICAL WORLD

Colin McEvedy (1930–2005) was a psychiatrist, historian and demographer. His many acclaimed books included seven earlier Penguin atlases. *Cities of the Classical World*, the last book he compiled before his death, is the result of a lifetime's enthusiasm for classical history, and of many years spent travelling to major ancient sites from Babylon to Pompeii.

Douglas Oles is a historian, editor and life member of the British Institute of Archaeology at Ankara. He was for many years a friend and colleague of Colin McEvedy and accompanied him on some of his visits to classical cities.

CITIES
OF THE
CLASSICAL
WORLD

*An Atlas and Gazetteer of
120 Centres of Ancient Civilization*

Colin McEvedy
Edited by Douglas Stuart Oles

PENGUIN BOOKS

PENGUIN BOOKS

UK | USA | Canada | Ireland | Australia
India | New Zealand | South Africa

Penguin Books is part of the Penguin Random House group of companies
whose addresses can be found at global.penguinrandomhouse.com.

First published by Allen Lane 2011
Published in Penguin Books 2019
005

Set in 9.35/12.5 pt Haarlemmer MT Std
Typeset by Andrew Barker Information Design
Printed and bound in Italy by Grafica Veneta S.p.A.

A CIP catalogue record for this book is available from the British Library

ISBN: 978-1-846-14428-8

Contents

*Colin McEvedy (right) and Douglas Oles in 1996 at
the ruins of the Roman theatre in Aizanoi, Turkey.*

Introduction

Colin Peter McEvedy, 'psychiatrist, historian, demographer and poly-math' as the *Independent* later described him, was born in Salford, Lancashire, on 6 June 1930, the third son of a surgeon. His father sent him to Harrow, where he fell in love with jazz and ancient history and won a scholarship to Magdalen College, Oxford. There he read Medicine and kept a pet python.

Although history remained his great intellectual passion, McEvedy met family expectations and joined his two brothers in the medical profession. In fact, he achieved a certain degree of notoriety as a psychiatrist. In 1970, while at the Middlesex Hospital, he co-authored two controversial papers on a mysterious epidemic which, fifteen years earlier, had overtaken 300 of the live-in nursing staff at the Royal Free Hospital. Not a single patient was affected, and no causative organism was ever found. The condition had been ascribed to a benign form of encephalomyelitis. McEvedy argued persuasively that it was an epidemic of conversion hysteria triggered by fear of contracting polio. This was not kindly received by the medical profession, and something of a rumpus followed. In 1972 he was appointed Consultant Psychiatrist to Ealing Hospital, where he helped to design a new acute unit in which each patient had an individual room.

As it turned out, Colin McEvedy became much better known as the author of more than half a dozen historical atlases, most of which remain in print. These atlases, illustrated with his own (originally hand-drawn) maps, were translated into many languages and enjoyed by historians and teachers as well as the common reader.

In 1978 McEvedy with Richard Jones published an *Atlas of World Population History,* reflecting his long-time interest in the growth and shifting of populations. He next conceived an atlas with separate entries on every city in the Roman Empire that ever achieved a population of at least 10,000 persons. His idea was to accompany each historical summary by a map, and each map would be drawn to a common scale. This unprecedented approach would allow readers to readily grasp the differences in size between the various cities being considered. At the time of his death, McEvedy was nearing completion of this, in many ways his most ambitious, undertaking, one that he often despaired of finishing and several times put aside, only to take up again.

The development of this atlas was a task of many years, and drew on an enormous number of reference materials, some quite rare and others never translated into English. In researching it, McEvedy had the advantage of his own extensive library; he also spent hundreds of hours delving through infrequently disturbed shelves in the London Library. In his last years he became devoted to the more specialized shelves of the Classics Library at Senate House.

Over time, McEvedy's ambitious design for the book expanded. He added some smaller towns that he thought would be of interest to general readers, even though they didn't meet his initial criterion of 10,000 inhabitants. He also attempted to estimate the populations of each city, based on combining written historical sources with knowledge of the areas enclosed by each city's walls. McEvedy was on the conservative side in his population estimates, arguing that many other modern historians had inferred unreasonably high population densities in ancient cities. As a skilled synthesizer of complex information, he explained his reasoning clearly and convincingly.

As a starting point for his population estimates, McEvedy typically looks at the fragmentary ancient sources. For example, in his chapter on Alexandria, he begins with a census of buildings that dates from the third or fourth century AD. He also considers (e.g. at pages 14 and 51) the fact that many citizens of ancient city-states often lived outside the city walls. His population figures for Athens derive in part from Herodotus' estimate of freeborn males that probably reflects a census of the late sixth century BC. For Constantinople, he begins with known information about the number of Roman wheat rations that were available to be diverted from Egypt in the early fourth century AD. For Rome, he triangulates between several bits of information, including a fourth-century survey of houses and the recorded wheat rations in earlier reigns. McEvedy extrapolates the available data on a few cities to the larger number of communities for which no ancient population records survive, blending his knowledge about the areas enclosed by city walls and the portions of each site that were actually inhabited with archaeo-logical evidence of changes in density of residential architecture over time. He also considers the major reductions in population resulting from wars and plagues, which he discusses in a number of entries. The credibility of McEvedy's population estimates is attested to by the suc-cess of his groundbreaking *Atlas of World Population History* (1978). In June 2001, he was honoured in Florence, Italy, when the International Union for the Scientific Study of Population invited him to speak at its conference 'History of World Population in the Second Millennium'. The IUSSP report of those proceedings referred to McEvedy's population atlas as an 'oft-quoted' reference.

Although McEvedy's researches and maps obviously reflect the work of many other historians and archaeologists, it would be wrong to treat his scholarship as entirely secondary. He visited most of the listed cities himself and took pleasure in tracing the topography and ruined walls at each location. In 1996 I was fortunate enough to accompany McEvedy on a driving tour that included the Thracian town of Perinthos. More than one local inhabitant with a home abutting the old city wall was sur-prised that day to look up and see a determined Englishman in a dark-grey pin-striped suit walking along the top of the wall in an effort to measure its proper dimensions.

I first met Colin McEvedy in the mid 1980s, at the ruins of ancient Aphrodisias in Turkey. I was slowly ascending the cavea of the Roman theatre while he was leading his family up the other side of the same monument. The white marble steps reflected the rays of the hot summer sun, and Colin's wife Sarah could be heard suggesting that the day's quota of ancient ruins might already have been satisfied. When we met at the top of the theatre, the two parties of English-speaking visitors introduced themselves, and it turned out that we were all stay-ing at hotels amid the ancient ruins at Hierapolis. A dinner that evening blossomed into a twenty-year friendship that included many visits and history-laden conversations.

At the time of his death on 1 August 2005, most of McEvedy's city histories were stored on an early-model Macintosh desktop computer from which they proved rather difficult to retrieve. His hand-drawn maps were distributed through stacks of neatly organized folders, where his extensive notes testified to the diligence of his research. The fate of the atlas remained uncertain for some time, primarily because the author was unavailable to tie together the last loose ends. There was a renewed incentive to do so, however, when Penguin offered to publish the book. Some city maps required a little editing to supplement the rough sketches that remained in McEvedy's files, and the reader will still find a few gaps in the text (several cities lack an estimate of the ancient population). It also seems that the author intended to summarize the populations of all the cities on some kind of combined historical graph, but that task was never finished. The book was, however, otherwise close to completion, and readers familiar with McEvedy's brisk and sometimes irreverent style will discover a text consistent with the high standard set in his earlier historical atlases.

Although many will no doubt consult this atlas only in connection with a few cities in which they have a particular interest, it offers additional value to those who find time to read it from cover to cover, as the entries paint a colourful and comprehensive picture of the phases in which ancient cities typically grew (and in many cases declined) across the wide expanse of the Roman Empire. The entries also explain the origins of many well-known place names. There are a number of common themes, but there are also many unique factors that influenced the rise and fall of individual communities, and which help to explain their subsequent rebuilding or abandonment in modern times.

As well as offering a concise introduction to 120 ancient cities, this atlas includes a useful list of further reading for those who are interested in a particular place. In a few instances, the author's bibliography has been supplemented by adding significant works published since his death.

It is rare, perhaps, for a historian to act also as his own cartographer, allowing him to coordinate his maps with the points emphasized in his text. It is even more unusual for a historian to have substantial expertise as a demographer, an essential qualification for producing this work. Moreover, in a time when academic specialization often favours the publication of monographs on narrow historical topics, McEvedy had a rare ability to condense and summarize a vast range of political, military, economic, architectural and cultural information into a text that the general reader can readily comprehend. Happily, he also approached his writing with balanced judgement and a subtle sense of humour. It was no coincidence that McEvedy's historical atlases found a large audience and remain highly approachable introductions to history today.

In admiring McEvedy's scholarship and the elegance of his writing, it would be unfortunate if we lost the memory of his engaging personality. McEvedy drew his maps in a basement office room at his home in Hammersmith, west London. There, his work table was often strewn with sketches and references being used to map the outlines of the particular city then occupying his interest. His sprawling library also included stacks of obscure site plans and brochures that he acquired on visiting the subject cities.

Although McEvedy was certainly able to concentrate on a narrow geographic location when his researches called for it, he remained an omnivorous reader. The broad learning that resulted enabled him to find topics of common interest with almost anyone with a lively mind, and helps to explain the remarkably diverse crowd of people who mixed together on the occasion of his wake. They shared memories of conversations in which McEvedy moved seamlessly from history to art to language to science, and even to the Formula 1 race results or the latest movies that had amused him.

McEvedy could hold forth with authority on almost any history-related topic, but he was also a good listener. He was entirely willing to question established opinions and seemed to enjoy testing new theories by sharing them with anyone who expressed interest. He was immensely learned but also genial and without a trace of condescension. He had a preternatural sense of time passing when away from his books, which made it difficult for him to suffer fools gladly. If he found himself in a place where he was unable to find intelligent conversation or someone to share his irreverent humour, he would sometimes slip away and return to his researches.

That humour was often revealed in the characteristically laconic postcards that he sent to friends while on his numerous travels. Once, when reporting that he had stopped for a picnic lunch in Greece, he simply wrote, 'Et in Arcadia eggo.' In the Acknowledgements at the end of his *New Atlas of North American History*, he wrote, 'I must, however, acknowledge the support I have received from my publishers . . . my secretary, Sandra Cook, and from my wife and children. Particularly the latter, without whom this book would have been finished in half the time.'

Colin McEvedy's three daughters, who have each inherited shares of his wonderful library, reflect in various ways their father's love of art and history, and his tolerant view of the diverse world. This last atlas, which could never have been completed without their support, is a final gift to the readers who learned to value his succinct expositions on the complex threads from which our modern cities have woven their past.

Douglas Stuart Oles

Acknowledgements

The completion of this book reflects a collaborative effort by a number of people. The author's three daughters (Binky, Flora and particularly Allegra) and his son-in-law (Guy Sellers) each played important parts in discovering and assembling the maps and narratives in McEvedy's extensive personal files. William Dorrell, a long-time friend and colleague, together with his wife Jane, provided invaluable editorial assistance. The conversion of McEvedy's hand-drawn maps to scaled digital images reflects an enormous effort by David Woodroffe, the illustrator who worked with McEvedy on other atlases for more than twenty-eight years. The chapter texts were primarily preserved through the kind efforts of Sandra Cook, who volunteered to type and correct the original drafts as a long-time and devoted friend. Dr John Ma of Corpus Christi College, Oxford, kindly read the proofs, made some valuable suggestions and saved us from several errors. At Penguin, the book was seen through to publication by Georgina Laycock, Rebecca Lee, Caroline Elliker and Stuart Proffitt.

ALEXANDRIA

Egypt

History

Alexandria was founded by Alexander the Great during his brief foray into Egypt in 332–331 BC. Although his first act was to have himself crowned pharaoh at MEMPHIS, the country's traditional capital, he had probably already decided that his conquest needed a new capital, Greek in style, population and orientation. Hence the siting of Alexandria at the western tip of the Nile Delta, about as near to Greece as you can get without losing contact with Egypt altogether. In fact Alexandria was to be known as Alexandria-by-Egypt, rather than Alexandria-in-Egypt, and it is not too far-fetched to see it as an extension of Greece for the government of the adjacent Egyptian territory.

Though Greek sailors were notoriously reluctant to venture out of sight of land, the crossing from Greece to North Africa was one open sea voyage that they were prepared to make. They had been doing so since the Bronze Age, and in the seventh and sixth centuries BC had founded a clutch of little colonies on the coast of Cyrenaica, plus a trading post in the Nile Delta at Naucratis. The founding of Alexandria meant a great increase in such traffic, with most of it being channelled on to a single route, the passage from Alexandria itself to RHODES at the south-east corner of the Aegean. The economic and political connections between the two cities became very close and only started to fade towards the end of the Hellenistic era, the period when the Levant was ruled by Alexander's successors.

As far as Egypt was concerned, Hellenism meant the rule of the Ptolemies, a dynasty founded by Ptolemy I Soter ('the Saviour'), the Macedonian general who was governor of Egypt at the time of

Pharos lighthouse

Diabathra

palace district

PORTUS MAGNUS

ISLAND OF ANTIRHODUS

Temple of Isis

Timonium

ISLE OF PHAROS

present-day coastline

Posidium

theatre

Heptastadium

Caesareum

present-day coastline

Royal Library

mausoleum

Paneum

gymnasium

Fort

Moon Gate

RHACOTIS (EGYPTIAN QUARTER)

Serapeum and Pompey's Pillar

stadium

N

0   500 m

intra muros area c. 1,005 ha

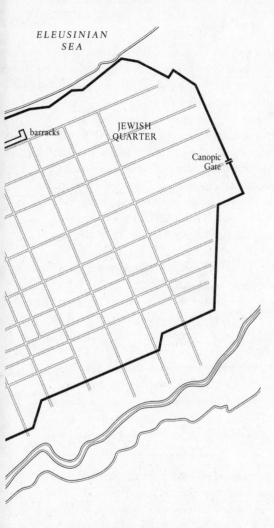

ELEUSINIAN
SEA

barracks

JEWISH
QUARTER

Canopic
Gate

LAKE MAREOTIS

The Pharos

Today no visible trace remains of what was once the most celebrated sight of ancient Alexandria, the Pharos, the name given to the lighthouse on Pharos Island. Completed in the early third century BC, the Pharos is the first building of this type of which we know, certainly the first purpose-built one. For the next six centuries it fulfilled its pioneering function, marking the entrance to the Great Harbour by night and, by virtue of its height, by day too. It became the symbol of the city and as such was featured on its coins; it also makes occasional appearances in mosaics and on intaglios. Then, in late antiquity, all mention of it ceases, presumably because it had been wrecked by the seismic upheavals that so drastically altered the harbour area during this period. But this was far from the end of its story: the memory of it survived its downfall, and, as the years passed, and even its ruins crumbled away, it entered the realm of legend. It wasn't just for its incredible height that it had been accounted one of the Seven Wonders of the Ancient World, said the storytellers. The statue that stood at the top was the real marvel, the work of a master magician who conferred on it the power to spy out ships a day's sail away. If they belonged to an enemy, the statue would utter a warning cry to the city's defenders; they reportedly could then use the great bronze mirror that stood alongside the statue as a burning glass, setting fire to any vessels foolish enough to press home their attack. So long as this strange figure stood on its watchtower, the city was safe from its foes – at least those who came by

Alexander's death. In 313 Ptolemy decided that the building of Alexandria was sufficiently advanced for him to take his court there, and in that year the new capital officially opened for business. However, Ptolemy still went back to Memphis for his coronation as pharaoh. Although he invented a new and ultimately very successful god for Alexandria, named Serapis (see p. 11), he and his successors always remained respectful of Egypt's traditions and beliefs. The idea of Alexandria as a purely Greek city was to suffer a gradual erosion almost from the start.

Nonetheless, purely Greek was the way Alexandria began, both in

sea. But once it was gone, the world would never see its like again.

What lies behind all these tales? A cynic might say not very much, pointing out that the list of the Seven Wonders was drawn up at Alexandria, and that the Pharos' place on it probably owed more to local patriotism than to any special features of the lighthouse. Of the various claims made on its behalf, the one most frequently trotted out is its unrivalled height. Arab sources give figures equivalent to 300, even 400 metres, and even today the favoured reconstruction, published by the German scholar Hermann Thiersch in 1909, proposes an overall height of 120 metres. There are two reasons to be suspicious about this. The first is that the Greeks had no experience of tall buildings and it is most unlikely that, at their first attempt, they managed something nearly twice the height of the towers of Notre Dame (sixty-nine metres). The second is that on the coast at Abusir, thirty-two kilometres (twenty miles) to the west of Alexandria, there is an ancient monument thought to be a scaled-down version of the Pharos that consists of three storeys, the first square, the second octagonal and the third circular. The site of the Pharos itself is now occupied by a Mamluk fort whose central keep is thirty metres square. If, as many think, this incorporates the Pharos' first storey, the complete building would have been about sixty metres high.

There is no doubt about the fame of the Pharos: as a generic word for lighthouse its name still survives in French (*phare*) and Italian (*faro*). And there's no question that the name was first applied to the illuminating structure in Alexandria.

town planning and in population. Immigration from Greece was encouraged by generous subsidies in terms of jobs military and civil, and of land grants. In fact, as is the case with all Greek cities, many of Alexandria's citizens would have visited their nominal metropolis only on rare occasions, content to live out their days on the farms granted to them when they first arrived. Many of these farms seem to have been in the Fayum, where the Ptolemies launched a big programme of land reclamation. About half the named Alexandrian citizens we know of resided there, and although this conclusion has probably been biased by

The Museum and the Library

Ptolemy I's ambitions for Alexandria were not just personal and political; he wanted to see it become the intellectual capital of the Mediterranean world. For advice on how to achieve this ambition he turned to Demetrius of Phaleron, an interesting character who had governed Athens for a decade on behalf of King Cassander of Macedon, been expelled when the city fell to Demetrius Poliorcetes, and eventually ended up as a member of Ptolemy's entourage. Between them, Ptolemy and Demetrius agreed on a two-point programme: (i) to establish a royal library; and (ii) to fund a circle of philosophers, scholars and men of science who would form a permanent academy, to be known as the Museum (named after the Greek muses). The Library would contain a copy of every work of importance to Greek scholarship. The Museum would offer a place to anyone of exceptional status in the world of learning.

There were two possible Athenian models for the Museum: the Academy founded by Plato, and the Lyceum founded by Aristotle. Aristotle's Lyceum was the more influential as far as the Alexandria Museum was concerned. Plato's Academy had become a haunt of pure philosophy and not much else. The Lyceum was still following Aristotle's precept that everything from astronomy to zoology was worth studying and embodied the spirit of inquiry that Ptolemy and Demetrius wanted. The Museum was, after all, a temple of all nine muses.

It is worth stressing that the Museum was a society for scholars, not a museum in our modern sense of the term. Nor was it a university. The members of the Museum could take on fee-paying students if they wanted to, but there was no organized student body. The

the fact that the Fayum is a favourite hunting ground for archaeologists, there is no doubt that many Alexandrians not only lived in the country but lived so far away that they would have been unable to play much of a role in the city's affairs.

Meanwhile, the Greek landowners who chose an urban lifestyle retained the services of native estate managers, something obviously

nearest thing to it today would be a centre for advanced studies, although by present-day standards the Museum would be considered a pretty small affair. It probably had no more than a dozen or so fellows, supported by an equivalent number of clerks and domestics. The premises were certainly simple, with a colonnaded court where the fellows could meet, alcoves where they could chat, and a dining room for communal meals. It is not likely there was any residential accommodation.

The Museum got off to a good start with the appointment of Euclid, the most famous geometrician of his day, who we know was in Alexandria in Ptolemy's lifetime. The Library presented more of a problem because Demetrius' connection with Athens and Ptolemy's provision of funds produced such a huge influx of papyrus rolls that coping with them was almost impossible. Many will have arrived in poor condition, few were labelled adequately and cataloguing them must have been a nightmare. Only then could the real work begin: producing 'standard editions' after collating all the various texts. In the reign of Ptolemy II (285–247 BC) the work was far enough along for someone to produce the following statistics:

> *Catalogued volumes in the Palace Library* 90,000
> *Catalogued volumes in the Outer Library* 42,800
> *Uncatalogued volumes* 400,000

The catalogue itself ran to 120 volumes, the equivalent in today's terms of twelve average-sized books.

Cataloguing was done on a three-tier system, first by subject (law, philosophy, etc.), then by author (arranged chronologically), then by title (arranged alphabetically). Some of the subjects were

much more worthwhile in the case of the larger holdings. Such an arrangement amounted to a transfer of wealth from country to town, and such transfers, combined with the revenues lavished on the capital by the early Ptolemies, provided a powerful engine for growth. Alexandria rapidly became the wonder of the Mediterranean, the biggest, most exciting metropolis the world had yet known. If you are looking for the

probably subdivided – drama into tragedy and comedy, for example. This meant that if you wanted to find Euripides' *Medea* you had to know that this was a tragic drama and that Euripides lived after Aeschylus and before Lycophron. It might seem easier to us to have arranged the whole catalogue alphabetically, but any educated Greek would have known enough about his authors to find his way around the Library shelves without difficulty. In fact, the remarkable feature of the catalogue was that it had any alphabetical classification at all. So far as we know, no one had ever used the alphabet for this purpose before.

The Library catalogue started off with an emphasis on Greek literature that it never wholly lost. However, the presence of many eminent mathematicians and men of science in the Museum led to its becoming a repository for all important work done in these fields too. As such, it was of interest to Greek scientists everywhere. Archimedes, of 'eureka' fame, always kept in touch with the Library even though he spent most of his life in distant Syracuse. Some of his books are dedicated to Alexandrian scholars; all of them would have found a place in the Library.

The head librarian in Archimedes' day was Eratosthenes, perhaps the most remarkable of all those who held this post. He wrote poetry and literary criticism that was considered more than passable by contemporary critics; he did pioneering work in chronology, establishing the dating system based on the four-yearly cycle of the Olympic Games that was used to the end of the classical period; and he made significant contributions to both arithmetic and geometry. He was also the first systematic geographer, beginning by measuring the size of the earth – the first time this had been done – and

first city with a population ever to reach the 100,000 mark, Alexandria is much the best bet.

Why Alexandria? The answer is that at a time when wealth was still almost entirely agricultural, Egypt was an extraordinarily easy country out of which to wring resources. It had an unparalleled highway in the Nile, a river that put every Egyptian farm in direct communication with the wharves and warehouses of the capital. It had already acquired the

working his way through the whole subject, from cartography (he introduced the concept of parallels of latitude) to ethnography.

After Eratosthenes, the calibre of the academic staff of both the Library and the Museum began to decline. Successive Ptolemies had less and less to spend, and although it is not true that later Greek intellectuals had any less to say, they had less to say that was original. By the Roman period, the Museum had become a sort of literary society and the Library was no longer mentioned at all. There was even a story circulating that the best part of it had gone up in flames during the battle between the Alexandrians and Julius Caesar in 47 BC. It is unlikely that this is true, as Claudius Ptolemy (unrelated to the kings), writing in Alexandria at the time of the emperor Hadrian (AD 117–38), clearly had access to a vast number of books.

To later ages, Claudius Ptolemy was the ultimate polymath, an authority on astronomy, astrology and geography. As late as the sixteenth century people still settled arguments by turning up the relevant entries in the *Almagest*, his textbook of astronomy, the *Tetrabiblos*, his astrological compendium, or, perhaps the most frequently consulted of all, his *Geographia*. Today we recognize that little of what Ptolemy wrote was new, that he belonged in fact to that characteristic species of library-goer, the encyclopaedist. And we mark him down accordingly. But we shouldn't be too hard on him because it is through Ptolemy that the work done by earlier geographers and astronomers has come down to us. Because of his writings, the nature of much that was in the famous Library can be reconstructed, even though the place itself has long since perished.

habit of yielding up a percentage of its produce to a foreign administration. And the Ptolemies introduced a more effective administration than Egypt had ever had. As a result, they could feed what was, by the standard of the time, a large mega-city and still have a surplus of cereals to sell overseas. The early Ptolemies are said to have had a revenue of 12,000 talents a year, compared to the 1,000 ATHENS earned in its heyday; and even the later Ptolemies, whose grip on the country was comparatively feeble, could still count on 6,000 talents. Alexandria had more than its share of three-star attractions – Alexander's tomb, the Pharos, the Museum, the Royal Library and the Serapeum (*see* pp. 11–13) – but the first thing that struck visitors was the city's sheer size.

Like most big cities, Alexandria soon acquired minority populations. Most notable in what was supposed to be a Greek city were the Egyptians, who crept in almost from the start. Next came the Jews: it was at Alexandria, and for the local community, that Jewish scholars produced the first Greek version of the Old Testament (traditionally seventy of them, each working independently). In fact, by the first century BC it seems to have been the Greeks who had become the minority. The Romans, who usually had a forgiving attitude towards the Greeks, regarded the Alexandrians as a mongrel lot, and looked on them with a cold eye.

The fall of the Ptolemaic kingdom is a romantic tale, in which the fortunes of Cleopatra VII, the last Ptolemaic ruler, were linked first with Julius Caesar, then with Mark Antony, and then, in a final grim confrontation, with Octavian, the future emperor Augustus. With Cleopatra disposed of, Octavian turned Egypt into a Roman province, a status it was to retain for the next 700 years.

Population

That Alexandria was intended to be a big city from the start is clear from the plan: the four residential quarters that gave it its initial shape cover 186 hectares, considerably more than that occupied by the inhabited area of classical Athens. Moreover, we can be sure that Alexandria exceeded its founder's expectations, for a fifth quarter was added later, bringing the residential zone up to 236 hectares, nearly twice the Athenian total. If densities were comparable to those in Athens, this expanded area indicates an Alexandrian population of 70,000 or so.

In fact densities were probably higher. A twelfth-century manuscript preserves an Alexandrian *notitia* (census of buildings) of the third or fourth century AD that gives the number of houses in each of the five quarters. Manuscripts are often corrupt, but the consistency of these figures (5,058; 5,990; 2,140; 5,515; 5,593) is convincing and overrides the suspicions raised by the miscalculated total (it should be 24,296 but is

New Gods for Old: Serapis and the Serapeum

In the ancient world, religion was bound up with locality. Each community had its deity, each city its god or goddess. Egypt illustrates this particularly well: there was a god for every nome (county), and the main temple in the county town was reserved for worship of that deity.

The foundation of Alexandria meant that Egypt had acquired a major new locus, one that clearly required a matching addition in the heavens. Ptolemy I, who saw this both as an obligation and as an opportunity, announced that he had had a dream in which an anonymous god dwelling somewhere on the shores of the Black Sea had begged to be brought to Egypt. A ship was sent to find this unhappy deity, and the people of the Black Sea port of Sinope were persuaded to part with one of their cult images, apparently a variant of Pluto, god of the underworld. This image was brought back to Alexandria, where Ptolemy received it with due ceremony.

The arrival of the Sinopean Pluto pleased the Greeks of Alexandria but meant nothing to the Egyptians. So Ptolemy charged Manetho, high priest of Ra at Heliopolis, with finding the newcomer an appropriate slot in the Egyptian pantheon. Manetho quickly discovered that Ptolemy's deity was the equivalent of the Egyptian god of the dead, Osiris. Specifically, he identified him with the form of Osiris worshipped at Memphis, the sacred bull Apis. Between them Ptolemy and Manetho had now come up with a god who met the needs of the dynasty, its capital and the native population of the country. He soon became known as Serapis, an amalgam of Osiris and Apis.

The temple in which the new god was installed was constructed in

given as 47,790). If we assume 3.6 persons per house, the number suggested for Athens, this translates into a population of around 87,500 living at a density of 370 per hectare.

If Alexandria had 80,000 to 90,000 people in the fourth century AD, it certainly had more than that in its heyday under the Ptolemies (third to first centuries BC). During that period the island of Pharos had a

Rhacotis, the Egyptian quarter of Alexandria. The site was probably chosen because it already had a temple of Isis, the goddess who was now proclaimed to be the consort of Serapis. Greek architects built a serapeum alongside the Iseum, and erected a vast rectangular colonnade enclosing both of them. Within it a special priesthood conducted elaborate rituals designed to promote the welfare of the Alexandrians in general and the Ptolemies in particular.

Serapis has been described as a god designed by a committee, and that, it must be admitted, is not far from the truth. As such, he might be expected to do poorly compared to deities conceived in more mysterious ways. However, Serapis did very nicely, not just in Alexandria but throughout the Mediterranean world. He was considered to be especially effective in medical matters, and it is common to find models of afflicted limbs and diseased organs as votive offerings at his shrines. The most famous of these was not the original Serapeum in Rhacotis but one at Canopus, modern Aboukir, twenty-four kilometres (fifteen miles) to the east of Alexandria. This was the object of an annual pilgrimage by the Alexandrians, during which, according to some authorities, standards of sexual behaviour were looser than they should have been.

With the rise of Christianity, the Alexandrian Serapeum became a bastion of the old pagan way of life. It reputedly housed the 'Outer Library', the smaller of the two libraries founded by the Ptolemies. By the fourth century it had probably become the main meeting place of the schools of philosophy and classical studies for which Alexandria had always been famous. As such, it was an object of particular hatred for the Christians, who demanded the right to convert the temple of the god into a Christian church. The prefect of Egypt persuaded the patriarch Theophilus to wait for instruc-

considerable population (Julius Caesar took 6,000 prisoners there in 48 BC), and so did the palace quarter on the harbour front where the Ptolemies held court until the dynasty was extinguished by Augustus; both these areas were deserted by the time of our census. The same is probably true of Rhacotis – the area to the south of the city that was the site of the Egyptian settlement which antedated it – as it contained the

tions from Constantinople; the emperor's reply, granting the patriarch's request, arrived in AD 391.

The jubilant patriarch wasted no time; brandishing the imperial rescript, he led his congregation out to Rhacotis, into the sanctuary. There he came face to face with the colossal image of the god created by the sculptor Bryaxis seven centuries before. The confrontation is recounted by Gibbon in his twenty-eighth chapter with appropriate irony. After recalling the legend that 'If any impious hand should dare to violate the majesty of the god, the heavens and the earth would instantly return to their original chaos,' he describes how an intrepid soldier, bearing an axe, mounted a ladder and aimed a vigorous stroke at the cheek of the statue. The Christians held their breath, but as 'the cheek fell to the ground, the thunder was still silent, and both the heavens and the earth continued to observe their accustomed order and tranquillity. The victorious soldier repeated his blows; the huge idol was overthrown and broken in pieces, and the limbs of Serapis were ignominiously dragged through the streets of Alexandria. His mangled carcass [this must have been the wooden armature of the image] was burnt in the amphitheatre, amidst the shouts of the populace; and many persons attributed their conversion to this discovery of the impotence of their tutelary deity.'

So ended the reign of Serapis, although the event was probably less dramatic than Gibbon has it. A contemporary tells us that when the image of Serapis was toppled, the Christians watching let out such a mighty shout that it was heard in the circus nearby – which suggests that, given the opportunity to measure one faith against the other, many Alexandrians had preferred to spend the day at the races.

port. In sum, it is a reasonable proposition that Alexandria's population was well over the 100,000 mark by 200 BC and that it stayed there until the Mediterranean economy fell in the third century AD. Thereafter, the population probably declined, but only slowly, and Alexandria remained the second city of the empire for some considerable period after the foundation of CONSTANTINOPLE.

Many people think that Alexandria's population was much higher than 100,000. Peter Fraser, whose monumental three-volume study of Ptolemaic Alexandria makes him the man to consult on each and every aspect of the classical city, believes that in the first century BC the city's population may well have reached 1,000,000. He gets to this figure by taking Diodorus' statement (of *c.* 60 BC) that the free population of the city was 300,000 and assuming that Diodorus was referring to the number of free males (children as well as adults) resident in the city. Multiply this by two to get the total free population, then add 400,000 to take account of slaves. For AD 50 he thereby suggests a figure of 1,500,000.

There are various troubles with Fraser's calculation, however. One is that, to qualify for the perks that made emigration to Egypt worthwhile, Greeks had to register as citizens in one of the three Greek cities of Egypt: Alexandria, Ptolemais (a modest foundation in Upper Egypt) and Naucratis (tiny). The vast majority opted for Alexandrian citizenship, but that doesn't mean that they all lived there. In fact we know that the citizen rolls (both sexes, and including children) contained the names of many people who resided elsewhere in Egypt. Fraser's global figure itself is fine for the country as a whole – it seems consistent with a papyrus of *c.* AD 40 which gives a total of 180,000 male citizens of somewhere (it surely must be Alexandria), or 360,000 citizens altogether – but what this indicates is the number of Greeks living in Egypt (adding 5 per cent to take account of Ptolemais and Naucratis), not the smaller number of Greeks living in Alexandria.

The difference between residents and citizens was still causing confusion under the Late Empire. In the fifth century AD, Eusebius remarked that the Alexandria of his day had fewer people in the age band 14–80 than it had previously in the age band 40–70; this is a roundabout way of saying that the rolls had fallen by two-thirds. However, it doesn't follow that the city had shrunk by anything like this amount, or indeed that it had shrunk at all, for a fall of this magnitude would have happened automatically once there was no longer any financial incentive for Greeks living away from Alexandria to register as citizens. If it hadn't happened earlier, this certainly became the case in AD 212 when the emperor Caracalla conferred Roman citizenship on everyone except slaves.

AMASYA

Amasya province, north Turkey

Classical *Amaseia; capital of the kingdom of Pontus
and of the late Roman province of Helenopontus*
(formerly *Diospontos*)

The castle of Amasya was the political starting point for the dynasty of
Pontic kings that began with Mithradates I in the third century BC and
culminated in the seesaw career of Mithradates VI, ROME's most
intransigent enemy, in the first century BC. It is situated on top of a cliff
that overlooks the river known in classical times as the Iris, and at the
present time as the Yeşil Irmak, or 'Green River'. Strabo the geographer was born here *c.* 60 BC and describes the triangle of walls that had
the castle at its apex and the river at its base, creating 'both a city and a
fortress'. Calling it a city is overdoing it a bit: the space at the foot of the
cliff is very limited, and it is unlikely that the 'lower town' ever covered
more than twelve hectares or that the lower town and acropolis together
ever held more than 2,000 people.

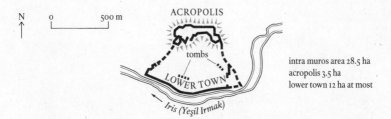

intra muros area 28.5 ha
acropolis 3.5 ha
lower town 12 ha at most

After his capture of Sinope in 183 BC, Pharnaces II of Pontus moved
his court there, but Amasya maintained its royal connections. It was the
birthplace of Mithradates VI. In the Roman period it was looked on
with favour and eventually became a capital again, this time of the late
Roman province of Helenopontus. This dignity it retained until the provincial system disintegrated in the eighth century.

Amasya has been surveyed but not excavated. There are no classical remains to be seen apart from some rock-cut tombs, generally and not unreasonably assumed to be the burial places of the kings of Pontus, and a fine set of defensive walls. The walls are essentially as Strabo described them, although clearly remodelled on many occasions since. The existing castle is entirely medieval.

AMMAN

Jordan

Later *Philadelphia*

The modern capital city of Jordan has traces of settlement as early as the sixth millennium BC. The city's citadel, now known as Jebel Qal'a, bears evidence of inhabitants as early as the Neolithic period. The name Amman derives from Ammon, the son of Abraham's nephew Lot, the purported ancestor of the Ammonites who emerged in the late Bronze Age or early Iron Age. In the ninth century BC, Rabbat Ammon was the capital of a small state that attempted to maintain independence by ally-ing with Syrian cities against Assyrian advances. In the eighth century BC, however, it succumbed to Assyrian control during the conquests of Tiglath-Pileser III.

After Alexander the Great, Amman fell to the Ptolemaic dynasty. Ptolemy II, Philadelphus (285–247 BC), rebuilt the city and modestly named it Philadelphia. It should not be confused with the city of the

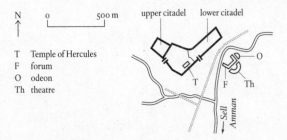

same name in Lydia and presumably will not be confused with the city in Pennsylvania. Philadelphia passed from the Ptolemies to the Syrian Seleucids and was thereafter subjected to Roman rule after the conquests of Pompey the Great.

Later in the first century BC, Mark Antony transferred Amman as a gift to Cleopatra's Egypt. After the Battle of Actium, however, it regained a measure of local autonomy in the Roman East. The city became a member of the Decapolis league, the ten-city Greco-Roman federation, and it achieved substantial prosperity as a trading centre when the emperor Trajan annexed the neighbouring (competing) Nabatean kingdom. Amman became an important stop on the Via Nova Traiana. Under Roman rule, Amman acquired the usual architectural adornments of a prosperous city, including a theatre (with seats for around 6,000 people), a five-apsed nymphaeum and a system of colonnaded streets. The citadel displayed a Hercules temple that was either built or restored during the reign of Marcus Aurelius.

In the Byzantine period, Philadelphia was an episcopal see, and the remains of several churches were recorded when the city ruins were studied in the early twentieth century. By the late 1800s, however, Amman had become an abandoned ruin. Its reoccupation began in 1878, when Ottoman authorities sent a small community of Circassians to live there.

ANTIOCH

Present-day *Antakya, Hatay province,*
south Turkey

Founded in 300 BC, Antioch emerged as the capital of the Seleucid
Empire in the second half of the third century, when Seleucus' original
choice, Seleucia Pieria, proved unsuitable. Annexed by ROME, along
with what remained of the empire, in 64 BC, it continued to serve as the
metropolis of Syria and Palestine for the remainder of the classical era.

There is literary evidence indicating that the county of Antioch contained 200,000 people in the early second century AD and 150,000 in
the late fourth. According to John Chrysostom writing in AD 383, 10 per
cent of the population was on the breadline at that time and the Church
looked after a fifth of these, i.e. 3,000 people. If this was the urban element, and the poor were no more numerous in the city than in the surrounding country, the city's population would have been 30,000 or
about one fifth of the total. If the fall in population after the second century was evenly distributed between city and countryside, it follows that
the city's population at that time would have been around 40,000. These
numbers are of course all far from firm, but the percentage of urban
residents looks about right for a city that had no special arrangements
for its food supply.

The existing walls, which were built by Justinian in the sixth century,
enclose about 590 hectares. This area includes much of Mount Silpius,
the hill overlooking Antioch. The slopes of that hill are too steep to be
easily built on, so the raw figure isn't a useful basis for population estimates. On the other hand, the 375 hectares that were level and readily
habitable do seem to have been fully built up at the end of the third century AD because the emperor Diocletian, who built a palace at Antioch
at that time, did so on a site outside this area and to the north. The implication is that the city had a population of around 37,500 in his day

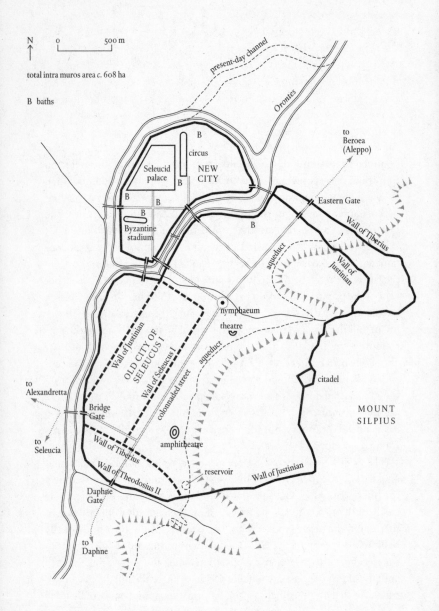

N

0   500 m

total intra muros area *c.* 608 ha

B baths

B

circus

Seleucid
palace

NEW
CITY

B

B   B

B

Byzantine
stadium

to
Beroea
(Aleppo)

Eastern Gate

Wall of Tiberius

B

aqueduct

Wall of
Justinian

nymphaeum

theatre

Wall of Justinian

OLD CITY OF
SELEUCUS I

Wall of Seleucus I

colonnaded street

aqueduct

citadel

to
Alexandretta

Bridge
Gate

MOUNT
SILPIUS

to
Seleucia

Wall of Tiberius

amphitheatre

Wall of Theodosius II

reservoir

Wall of Justinian

Daphne
Gate

to
Daphne

present-day channel

Orontes

(375 hectares × 100 per hectare). The density is unlikely to have been higher than 100 per hectare because we know that Antioch's housing was typically single storey.

There are two other fragmentary bits of evidence that point to a population of about this size. One relates to the special suburb of Ctesiphon, built by the Persian king Chosroes I for the captives taken at Antioch in 538, which was said, admittedly at a later date, to contain 30,000 people. It's not very likely that it did, but the figure could derive from the number of prisoners taken when Antioch surrendered to Chosroes. And then there is the first estimate for the city in modern times: 20,000 in 1927. An aerial photograph of the city taken in 1932 shows that it then occupied about half the level area within Justinian's wall. This suggests that the intramural population in classical times can't have been much more than 40,000.

ANTIOCH IN PISIDIA

Deserted site near Yalvaç, Isparta province, south-west Turkey

Capital of the late Roman province of Pisidia

Pisidian Antioch was founded by the Seleucid king Antiochus I (281–261 BC) to protect the east–west route across Anatolia. It was a genuine colony. The settlers were Greeks from Magnesia on the Meander, although history doesn't relate how many there were or how they fared. In fact we know next to nothing about the place until 25 BC when the emperor Augustus decided to restock Antioch with veterans discharged from the Third Legion. This transformed it from a Greek colony into a Roman one. The break with the past seems to have been complete: the

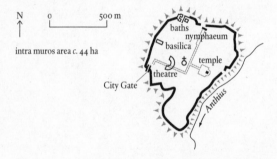

N   0   500 m

intra muros area *c.* 44 ha

baths
nymphaeum
basilica
temple
theatre
City Gate
Anthius

version of the emperor's testament inscribed in the city centre was in Latin, whereas at Ankara, capital of the neighbouring province of Galatia, there were copies in both Latin and Greek.

Strictly speaking, Antioch at this time was not part of Pisidia; it was in either Phrygia (if you took a traditional view of the geography) or Galatia (if you followed the contemporary administrative divisions). The city was therefore properly referred to as Antioch towards Pisidia. However, there is no need to be too pedantic about this, because when

Diocletian reorganized the area at the end of the third century, one of his administrative creations was a Pisidian province with Antioch as its capital.

Antioch remained the metropolis of Pisidia until the seventh century when provinces were superseded by themes. Not long after, in 712–13, a marauding Arab army put it to the sack. That was probably the end of Antioch as a city, although the remains of a small Byzantine church show that the place still had a few inhabitants in the Dark Ages. It has been entirely deserted since the Turks moved into the area at the end of the twelfth century.

In the 1920s the site of Antioch was investigated by a team from the University of Michigan. The expedition produced a map of the town, which shows that it covered some forty-four hectares, suggesting a maximum population of 4,000 to 5,000. They uncovered monuments such as an elaborate city gate of the early third century AD and a pair of public squares, one dedicated to Augustus, one to Tiberius, separated by a monumental propylaea (gateway). Remains from the later centuries include a large fourth-century church and the much smaller Byzantine one.

AOSTA

Valle d'Aosta, Italy

Classical *Augusta Praetorium;*
Roman colony and county
town of the Salassi

An important part of Augustus' plan for tidying up the Roman Empire was the pacification of the areas left behind by earlier advances. Although Caesar had conquered Gaul, the alpine region between Gaul and Italy remained in the hands of often unruly natives, such as the Salassi of the upper Dora Baltea. In 25 BC Augustus decided that the time had come to bring the Salassi to heel, and sent his general Terentius Varro into the area for this purpose. Varro discharged his task with speed and rigour (all Salassi males of military age were rounded up and

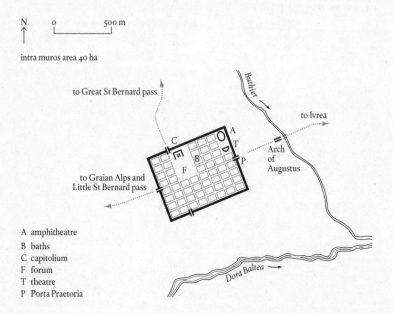

N   0   500 m

intra muros area 40 ha

to Great St Bernard pass

Buthier

to Ivrea

to Graian Alps and
Little St Bernard pass

Arch
of
Augustus

A amphitheatre
B baths
C capitolium
F forum
T theatre
P Porta Praetoria

Dora Baltea

sold into slavery), leaving the way clear for planting a Roman colony. The essentials of this were completed two years later, when a triumphal arch was erected in honour of Augustus by the colonists and the Salassi – although goodness knows what the latter had to celebrate – in conjunction.

The colonists – 3,000 of them – consisted of discharged veterans of the Praetorian Guard, the elite unit of the Roman army. Augustus was clearly determined to do right by them, and he poured resources into the town. Its plan was simple: a forty-hectare rectangle; its military lay-out suggests that it was built on the site of Varro's camp. There was probably more space than the colony needed, which may explain why the amphitheatre was built inside the walls, rather than outside as was usual. The generous treatment of the capitolium and forum complex, which occupies the better part of eight of the sixty-four blocks into which the town was divided, also suggests that there was room to spare. In fact the backwater economy of the Valle d'Aosta had no need of a large urban centre, and it is probable that as soon as Augustus stopped pumping funds into the town, it began to decline.

In the later empire, Aosta all but disappeared. The walls survived, but the street plan was lost. The only sign of life was a huddle of housing along the road that ran through the town. Its one success was in holding on to its bishopric.

Aosta's population, ebbing away from the start, will always have been much lower than its size suggests; perhaps 2,000 to 3,000 in the first century AD, dropping to 1,000 to 2,000 in the fourth century. Even in modern times it has been smaller than you would expect: numbers didn't reach the 5,000 mark until 1823, and the population was still only 7,000 in 1861.

APHRODISIAS

Present-day *Geyre, Aydin province, south-west Turkey*

Capital of the late Roman province of Caria

Around 100 BC two smaller communities, Aphrodisias and Plarasa, joined to form the city now known from its archaeological remains as Aphrodisias. It gets its name from a shrine of Aphrodite that began to attract attention shortly after the Romans took over western Anatolia. In 81 BC Sulla dedicated a golden crown to the goddess; later, Julius Caesar, whose family claimed descent from Aphrodite, followed suit with a golden statue of Eros. What was good enough for Caesar was good enough for the emperors of the Julio-Claudian house. Aphrodisias was singled out for special privileges by Octavian, who made funds available for a major programme of public works. Included in this were a fine theatre, capable of holding 8,000 people, a 'Sebasteion' consisting of a pair of porticos decorated with statuary and dedicated to the imperial cult, and a complete rebuilding of the Temple of Aphrodite. The marble for these monuments came from a quarry only two kilometres (just over a mile) from the city. The high quality and low cost of this material encouraged its use, and the production of official statues – of gods and goddesses, members of the imperial family, local administrators and benefactors – soon became a major industry. So many examples have been found over recent years that they have come near to overwhelming the excavators. Unfortunately few of these pieces rise above their provincial origins, and if the Aphrodisian sculptors ever succeeded in building an export market – and there is some evidence that they did – they must have been competing on cost rather than quality.

Later emperors continued to show Aphrodisias favour. In Hadrian's reign (AD 117–38), the city acquired a commodious set of baths and the Temple of Aphrodite was enlarged and refurbished. Administratively, too, the city fared well. In the middle of the third century, when a new province of Caria and Phrygia was carved out of Asia, Aphrodisias was made its capital, and it continued as capital of Caria when the province was divided by Diocletian. Subsequently, in the mid fourth century, a wall was built around the city. It encloses about ninety hectares, suggesting a population somewhere in the 8,000 to 9,000 range.

Christianity brought important changes. A bishop of Aphrodisias is mentioned in 325; the Temple of Aphrodite was converted into a church in the 440s, and the principal excavator (Kenan Erim) concludes that it was probably dedicated to St Michael. Churchmen also insisted on a change of name for the town, Aphrodisias being too blatant a reminder

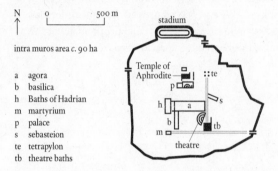

N   o   500 m

intra muros area *c.* 90 ha

a   agora
b   basilica
h   Baths of Hadrian
m   martyrium
p   palace
s   sebasteion
te tetrapylon
tb theatre baths

of the pagan past; they favoured Stavropolis, 'City of the Cross'. The new name is found in some official documents, but the inhabitants seem to have ducked the issue by calling the place Caria, an allowable contraction of its metropolitan title. Geyre, the present-day village on the site, derives its name from this usage.

The history of Aphrodisias comes to an abrupt end in the early seventh century when the city was sacked and its buildings burned by the Persians. No attempt was made to revive it and apart from the theatre, which was turned into a fortified mini-village, the site remained deserted thereafter. As a result, many of the major buildings were still visible when the first European travellers passed through in the eighteenth century. The general opinion was that the stadium was the most impressive, partly because it was essentially intact, partly because the approach to it through the fields north-west of Geyre gave no hint of its presence. The same experience is still available to today's tourist, and there is probably no better way of getting some sense of the showmanship involved in the games of the classical world than to emerge from the darkened vaults of the Aphrodisian stadium into the sunlit arena with its long tiers of seats to either side and, if you use a bit of imagination, the cries of vanished crowds still hanging in the air.

The present series of excavations, pursued regularly since 1961, have exposed and preserved the most important of the city's monuments. This task seems to have absorbed all the available resources; there has been little time to investigate the residential areas or elucidate the layout of the city as a whole. As a result, what is on view today is a series of isolated digs and restorations, few of which stand in coherent relation to one another. A geophysical survey has suggested that the street plan in the still-unexcavated residential areas was a regulation grid, but it seems prudent to wait for a sample area to be uncovered before committing fully to this idea.

APOLLONIA

Present-day *Marsa Suza, Cyrenaica province, Libya*

Port of Cyrene; in the sixth century A D replaced
PTOLEMAIS as the capital of Libya Superior;
diocese: Egypt

Apollonia, the port of the inland city of CYRENE, was recognized as a
town in its own right in the third century BC when the philosophers
Ecdelus and Demophanes of Megalopolis were called in to modernize
the constitutional structures of Cyrenaica. It seems to have achieved a
modest prosperity in the Hellenistic and Roman periods, although with
a walled area that can't ever have been much more than fifteen hectares,
it was always the smallest of the five cities that made up the Libyan
Pentapolis.

Starting in the middle years of the third century AD, marauding Libyan tribesmen made life increasingly difficult for the settled population
of the area. At the beginning of the fourth century, the administration
shifted from Cyrene, which had been the titular metropolis of the

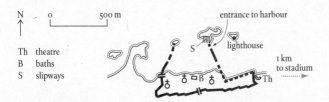

region, to Ptolemais on the coast. But the economy continued to con-
tract, Ptolemais proved too large to be easily defended, and in either the
fifth or sixth century AD the provincial governor transferred his residence to Apollonia. This remained the capital until the Arab conquest
of 642. During this period the sources refer to the city as Sozusa, a
Christianized version of Apollonia derived from the fact that Apollo

was sometimes known as Soter, the Saviour; hence Marsa Suza, the name of the modern village on the site.

The land on which Apollonia was built has undergone considerable subsidence since antiquity, and a significant part of the city, maybe as much as 20 per cent, is now under the sea. The harbour area has been explored by underwater archaeologists; interestingly it includes a set of slipways for warships dating back to the early Hellenistic period. On land, the main remains are of sixth-century churches. The city walls were built *c*. 100 BC.

AQUILEIA

Friuli-Venezia Giulia, Italy

*Capital of the late Roman province
of Venetia et Histria*

Aquileia was founded by the Romans in 181 BC in the territory of the
Veneti, the Italic tribe that lived around the head of the Adriatic Sea. The
Veneti had long suffered at the hands of the Gauls of the eastern Alps,
and they were more than happy to see the Romans establish an outpost
that would put a stop to the Gauls' incursions. In fact, four years earlier,
a Gallic band had occupied the area chosen for the new settlement and

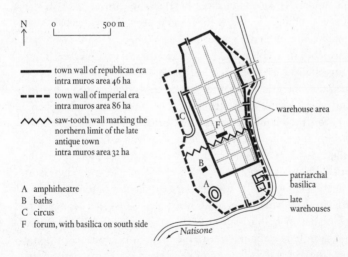

N   0   500 m

━━━ town wall of republican era
      intra muros area 46 ha

━ ━ ━ town wall of imperial era
      intra muros area 86 ha

〜〜〜 saw-tooth wall marking the
      northern limit of the late
      antique town
      intra muros area 32 ha

A amphitheatre
B baths
C circus
F forum, with basilica on south side

warehouse area

patriarchal
basilica

late
warehouses

Natisone

had to be chased away before the colonists – some 3,000 initially, with
another 1,500 arriving twelve years later – could set about building their
farmsteads. Meanwhile the better-off among them built town houses as
well. Aquileia's plan suggests that the founders originally thought in
terms of a rectangular layout that was a bit longer than usual, covering

around thirty-six hectares. The site was on the right bank of the Natisone river at some distance from the sea (about eleven kilometres today, but certainly less than that in antiquity).

Aquileia – both the community and its urban centre – seems to have prospered from the start. By the end of the Republican period in the first century BC, the city walls enclosed an area of forty-six hectares, making it one of the largest communities in the north-east of Italy. In the Augustan reordering of the peninsula, this area became Italy's tenth region, with Aquileia as its administrative centre. The choice of Aquileia followed naturally from Augustus' decision to make the Danube the empire's frontier in central Europe, for Aquileia was a crucial node on the line of communication that ran from north Italy to the armies advancing north and north-east, into Noricum (present-day Austria) and Pannonia (Croatia and western Hungary).

This strategic function continued even after the frontier was achieved. Offensive operations had ceased and the legions had built themselves permanent homes, but Aquileia was still the funnel through which men and goods travelling to and from the Danube provinces had to pass. And so it remained for the better part of 300 years. Then, as ROME's military superiority began to ebb away, the city's role underwent a corresponding change: logistical support for the frontier troops became less important than defence in depth. Aquileia was transformed into a bastion standing guard at the entrance to Italy. A new defensive wall probably dating to this period underlines the new priorities as well as the city's continuing importance. It almost doubled the enclosed area (from forty-six to eighty-six hectares), affording protection, for the first time, to the numerous warehouses that had been constructed along the right bank of the Natisone, as well as to such less essential monuments as the amphitheatre and what looks like a new palace and circus complex of tetrarchical date (late third century AD). At the same time, the position of Aquileia in Italy's administrative hierarchy was confirmed when it was made the seat of the governor of Venetia et Histria, one of the provinces created by Diocletian's reforms. This meant that when Christianity became the officially favoured religion of the empire, Aquileia automatically became the seat of an archbishop.

In the long run, defending Italy proved too hard a task for Aquileia: it was ignored by Alaric in AD 401 and sacked by Attila in 452. Incorporated in Theodoric's Ostrogothic kingdom, it was recovered, along with the rest of Italy, by the East Roman general Narses in the mid sixth century. Narses attempted to resurrect the city, and its defensive function, by building a curious zigzag wall across its waist, a style of fortification that reflects the emphasis placed on archery at this time; but at less than half its previous size (thirty-two hectares, compared to eighty-six), Aquileia was even less able to fulfil its role as guardian of Italy than it had been before. The Lombards, who overran most of the Po valley in 568, simply ignored it, and over the next thirty years the city slowly declined. In 600 the patriarch (a title the archbishop had been using since 554) and what remained of his flock fled to Grado, at the mouth of the Natisone, bringing the urban history of the site to an end.

The later history of the patriarchate of Aquileia has a certain curiosity value. The clergy in the inland areas that had passed under Lombard control elected a new patriarch, so for the duration of the seventh century there were two patriarchs of Aquileia in existence, neither resident in the now-deserted city. At the end of the century the Pope of the time straightened out the situation, recognizing the inland see as Aquileia and the maritime one as Grado. Subsequently the patriarchate of Grado relocated to Venice and evolved into the present-day patriarchate of Venice. The patriarchate of Aquileia developed into an ecclesiastical principality that cut a considerable figure in the medieval period, before falling to Venice in the early fifteenth century. This gave Venice one more patriarch than it needed, and in 1751 the mainland see was eventually suppressed.

The population of classical Aquileia has been the subject of some extravagant conjectures, with one authority proposing a figure of 800,000. Raymond Chevallier in his *Aquilée et la romanisation de l'Europe* thinks 100,000 reasonable, but it is difficult to see how a city that, even with suburbs, can't have covered more than 100 hectares, can have accommodated more than 10,000 people. It seems prudent to assume the lower number, even for the period AD I to AD 350, when Aquileia was at its peak.

AQUINCUM

Present-day *Obuda, 'Old Buda',*
in Budapest, Hungary

Capital of Pannonia Inferior;
diocese: Illyricum

Although the creation of the province of Pannonia was the work of
Augustus (27 BC–AD 14), the line of forts on the Hungarian sector of its
frontier was not fully developed until the time of the Flavian emperors
(Vespasian, Titus and Domitian, AD 69–96). Central to their programme
was the construction of a legionary fortress at Aquincum, to be manned
by the newly raised Legio II Adiutrix. The fortress lies, largely unexcavated, beneath present-day Obuda, near the heart of Budapest. In due
course it acquired the fringe of huts and houses that collected around all
legionary fortresses, but it always remained a military establishment,
and even the term 'garrison town' overstates its civilian function.

In AD 106 the province of Pannonia was divided in two by Trajan,
with Pannonia Superior on the upper Danube retaining the original
provincial capital of CARNUNTUM, and Pannonia Inferior on the middle Danube in need of an administrative centre. The obvious site was
Aquincum, base of the new province's sole legion, and this did indeed
become Pannonia Inferior's capital. But not the existing Aquincum Fortress. As part of the policy of keeping civil and military hierarchies separate, an entirely new town was built some three kilometres (nearly two
miles) to the north. As it was also called Aquincum, we need to be careful (and will be hereafter) in distinguishing Aquincum Town from
Aquincum Fortress.

In Aquincum Town – recognized as a municipium by Hadrian in
AD 124, perhaps promoted to colonial status by Septimius Severus –
excavations have revealed part of the forum, an adjacent set of baths and
a market, as well as some modest housing and a row of shops. The town
wall encloses some twenty-nine hectares. Outside it is a rather small
(fifty-three by forty-six metres) amphitheatre.

Aquincum Fortress had the size and shape (a 'playing card' covering twenty hectares) usual for a legionary camp. At ninety by sixty-six metres, its amphitheatre was much larger than Aquincum Town's; in fact it was the largest in the two Pannonias.

Aquincum had a disastrous time in the second half of the third century, both Town and Fortress being washed away by the tide of barbarian invaders that overwhelmed the frontier provinces during this period. Eventually the area was reclaimed, and a new administration installed, by the emperor Diocletian (285–305). He divided the province of Pannonia Inferior into two, naming the northern half (which included

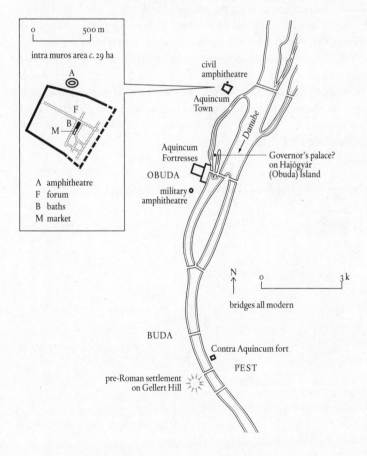

o   500 m

intra muros area *c.* 29 ha

A

F
B
M

A   amphitheatre
F   forum
B   baths
M   market

civil
amphitheatre

Aquincum
Town

Danube

Aquincum
Fortresses

OBUDA

Governor's palace?
on Hajógyár
(Obuda) Island

military
amphitheatre

N

o   3 k

bridges all modern

BUDA

Contra Aquincum fort

PEST

pre-Roman settlement
on Gellert Hill

Aquincum) after his daughter Valeria. The province had its military capital at a revived Aquincum Fortress (subsequently rebuilt on a slightly different site by Constantine the Great), but there was no second coming for Aquincum Town: the civil administration was based at SOPIANAE, 150 kilometres (95 miles) to the south and well back from the Danube.

The final years of Aquincum Fortress saw a steady decline in its size and condition. By the later fourth century, Ammianus Marcellinus (30.5.13) records that things had got so bad that Valentinian I, on a tour of inspection of the Danube frontier in 375, had to give up his plan to winter at Aquincum because the site was too derelict. The Notitia Dignitatum, a Roman army list of the early fifth century, shows Legio II Adiutrix still in garrison, but this must have been a fiction: legion, fortress, indeed the entire Danube defence line in this area, had long since faded away.

Given its limited size, it is difficult to see how Aquincum Town can ever have had as many as 5,000 inhabitants. Something like 3,000 to 4,000 seems far more reasonable. In its heyday Aquincum Fortress may well have had double this number.

ASCOLI PICENO

Marche, Italy

Classical *Asculum; principal city of the Piceni
and capital of the late Roman province of
Picenum Suburbicarium*

Ascoli is situated on a ridge overlooking the confluence of the Tronto and its tributary the Castellano. It was the chief city of the Piceni, the Italic tribal group occupying the Adriatic province known in antiquity as Picenum and today as Marche. In 299 BC the Piceni became allies of the rapidly expanding Roman state, and like many of their contemporaries, they soon found that this was a relationship that was easier to enter into than to leave. Any hopes of recovering their ancient freedoms were finally dashed in 268 BC when the Romans, on some unknown pretext, seized Ascoli, deported its inhabitants to Apulia and repopulated the city with Latin colonists. The region was then tied permanently to ROME by the extension of the Via Salaria from RIETI to Ascoli.

The spotlight of history shone on Ascoli only once, and then briefly. In 91 BC its Latin inhabitants, sick of being treated as second-class citizens by the Romans, rose in revolt, an event that precipitated the Social War – the bitterly fought struggle between Rome and her Italic allies (the socii). Two years later the town was taken by Gnaeus Pompeius Strabo (father of Pompey the Great), bringing the war in this part of Italy to an end, but in victory the Romans conceded what they had not been prepared to admit initially, an effectively equal status for the allied states. Ascoli sank back into relative obscurity, although it remained the chief city of the Piceni, and as such was to act as the centre of the fifth Augustan region of Italy, and, after AD 297, as the capital of the late Roman province of Picenum Suburbicarium.

The city walls of Roman Ascoli underlie at least some parts of the currently surviving circuit, and it is reasonable to assume, given the geography of the site, that the ancient trace was not very different from today's. On this basis we can accept an intramural area of a tad under

100 hectares for the classical town. However, it is clear that not all this space was built up, for insofar as the Roman street plan can be reconstructed it seems to cover only about forty hectares. On general principles it is unlikely that the city's Roman population ever rose above the 4,000 that this size suggests. This lowly position in Italy's urban hierarchy has continued into modern times; as late as 1850 Ascoli had only 11,000 inhabitants.

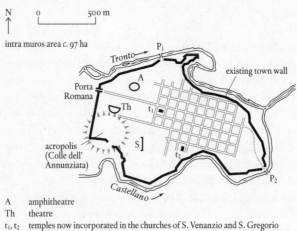

N

0   500 m

intra muros area *c.* 97 ha

A	amphitheatre
Th	theatre
t₁, t₂	temples now incorporated in the churches of S. Venanzio and S. Gregorio
S	monumental Praeneste-type shrine
P₁	ponte di Solestà
P₂	ponte di Cecco

Roman Ascoli contained the usual monuments: temples, a theatre, an amphitheatre and – a necessity given the site – several bridges. It also had one unusual one: a hilltop shrine approached by an elaborate staircase, the whole apparently very similar in design to the better-known example at Praeneste.

ASSUR

On the River Tigris in north Iraq

Capital of Assyria

History

Assur was situated on the upper Tigris, towards the southern end of its dependent territory, the land of Assyria, which, in good times at least, took in most of the north-east quarter of Mesopotamia. The list of its kings stretches as far back as those of any of the south Mesopotamian city-states, but the earliest rulers are noted to have 'lived in tents', and state and city had clearly not come together at this time (the end of the third millennium BC). The nomadic people of the region may have had Ashur as their god, but this Jehovah had still to find his Jerusalem. He seems to have done so shortly after, for an inscription from the city of Assur of *c.* 1950 BC describes work on temples for Ashur, Adad and Ishtar. Assur's subsequent development was rapid. Within fifty years it had become a nodal point in the Near Eastern economy, facilitating the exchange of tin (from some source further east) for silver (obtained from Assyrian merchants resident in Anatolia).

This suggests that, from the start, Assur was a town with unusually strong commercial interests, and that such interests played an important part in shaping Assyrian policies. Annoyingly we have no way of confirming this. Assyrian annals are exclusively military, and exclusively victorious, so we have periods of triumph alternating with periods of silence, neither of them much help in determining what made the Assyrian state tick. It is perfectly possible that, with the ebbing of the special circumstances that had created the tin-for-silver trade, Assur sank back into a situation little different from that of any other Mesopotamian town, its main concern to defend its local interests, its main ambition to grab a slice of its neighbours' territory or possessions. If such was the case it was reasonably successful: for 1,000 years it held its position in the Mesopotamian polity with only brief excursions up or down the ladder of fame.

The reign of Ashurnasirpal II (883–859 BC) marks a break in Assur's typical history. The Assyrian state was transformed into a military machine. Warfare became continuous and the outlook imperial. Part of this programme was the building of a bigger, better capital. Assur wasn't abandoned, it remained the religious centre of the kingdom, and under Shalmaneser III, Ashurnasirpal's son and successor, it was even enlarged, but the energies of the state were now displayed elsewhere. Canterbury could not hope to rival London.

Topography and Population

Assur occupied a tongue of land projecting into the Tigris, which curled around the northern and eastern sides of the city. Subsequently the river shifted away in the north, although it still flows alongside the east side of the site. The area within the original city walls was a bit under fifty hectares; the suburb added by Shalmaneser III brought this up to sixty hectares.

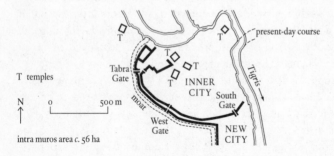

In its final state, Assur must have been an impressive place. The entire northern third was taken up by elaborate public buildings: two separate royal palaces, temples dedicated to Adad, Nebo and Sin, and a massive ziggurat and temple complex for Ashur. But the corollary to this is that not much space was left for people. To get the population up to 10,000 requires densities approaching 300 per hectare in the non-ceremonial space of the original city, and such figures seem improbable, to say the least. An urban population in the 5,000 to 7,500 range seems to be about as high as one could reasonably go.

ATHENS

Attica, Greece

History

The geographical basis of the Athenian state was the peninsula of Attica in Greece. At 2,647 square kilometres this is about the size of a middling English county such as Dorset or Durham, but considerably smaller than Cornwall, the one it most resembles geographically. In the US its equivalent would be Rhode Island. In the early Iron Age, around 900 BC, it may have contained 50,000 people living in a hundred or more scattered communities, most of them coastal. By 600 BC, when the historical record opens, there were probably twice as many people, and all the communities were linked in a political union in which Athens, a hilltop castle with a growing town at its foot, was the agreed centre. This unity was never subsequently questioned.

Sixth-century BC Athens – referring here to the state, not just the town and castle (the 'high town' or acropolis) – suffered from the usual problems of the time, many of which stemmed from a tendency for the rich to get richer and the poor to get poorer. For example, a succession of bad harvests could cause the least well-off to lose their farms and be reduced to serfdom, if not slavery. An answer of sorts was found in the person of Pisistratos, an aristocrat who was prepared to rule on behalf of all the people rather than just his own class, and who ran the state fairly well single-handed from 561 to his death in 527. In Greek terms Pisistratos was a tyrant, but the word didn't have the pejorative connotations that it has now, and the Athenians were sufficiently appreciative of his efforts to allow his sons, Hippias and Hipparchos, to succeed him. Neither of them was up to the job; Hipparchos was assassinated in 514 and Hippias expelled four years later. The question now was what form of government to go for – another, more effective autocrat, or something entirely different?

Famously, the Athenians chose something different, indeed unique. They opted for a democracy. Under the leadership of Cleisthenes, a broad-based populist faction triumphed over both the aristocratic party within the state, and its foreign allies without. Cleisthenes then proceeded to give Athens a constitution that was designed to keep the wealthy in their place, and under which all important decisions, whether political or judicial, would be taken by the people as a whole. The essential elements in the reform were the creation of an assembly, where all males of military age had the right to vote; an executive council 500 strong, with representatives from every community in Attica; and the use of juries that had a minimum of several hundred members, i.e. were too big to bribe. The really cunning thing was that the constituencies that sent representatives to the council were each made up of communities from three separate parts of Attica: one in or near Athens, one on the coast and one inland. That way, the aristocracy, whose influence was usually based on land holdings limited to one sector, couldn't get control of all the individual constituencies and so were unable to dominate the executive.

At the time of Cleisthenes' reforms, in 507–505 BC, Attica probably had around 120,000 inhabitants and Athens town around 7,500. Such figures may seem puny to us but by contemporary standards they most certainly were not. Athens was among the largest of Greek states, and Athens town was easily the biggest place in the entire peninsula. It was probably this exceptional size that led the Persians to misjudge the situation so badly when they launched an expedition against central Greece in 490 BC. The Persians had had no difficulty in conquering the Greek communities on the east side of the Aegean: these were all small, with no more than a few thousand citizens apiece, and the Persians were able to pick them off one by one. They planned to do exactly the same on the west side, where they assumed Greek political structures were much the same. At first it looked as if this was a correct assessment. A Persian task force crossed the Aegean, sailed up the channel between Attica and Euboea and, after the briefest of sieges, took its first objective, the Euboean town of Eretria. Following this successful operation the Persians moved to Attica, disembarking on the plain of Marathon, where they reckoned their cavalry could operate to best effect. The Athenians had no cavalry, but they made a maximum effort as regards infantry and managed to field a force of 9,000 hoplites, armoured spearmen trained to fight in close order. This proved sufficient to rout the Persian army, which was certainly no larger and may have been considerably smaller, than the Athenian. The Battle of Marathon immediately assumed mythic status as a victory of democracy over despotism, the free over the servile, David over Goliath, etc., all of which was near enough true but not much help as regards the longer-term struggle to which both sides, Greek and Persian, were now committed.

The Persian response to Marathon was predictable: if they couldn't support a big enough army by sea then they would have to send one that was big enough by land. It took them ten years to make their preparations, but when King Xerxes was finally ready the army he led across the Hellespont was of crushing size, far bigger than anything seen in Europe before. It was accompanied by a correspondingly large fleet. The Athenians, meanwhile, had made an unexpected decision. Normally when people have had a success they go for more of the same, which in the Athenian case would have meant doubling up on their army. Instead, prompted by the politician and general Themistocles, Athens decided to rely on a Big Navy policy. Themistocles persuaded the assembled Athenians that Sparta was always going to be the number-one land power in Greece, and that if Athens was to be the number one at anything it would have to be at sea. By the time Xerxes entered Greece, in 480 BC, the Athenians had acted on this assessment with such vigour that they had 200 warships at their disposal, as many as all the other states of Greece put together. The first trial of the new navy was a disappointment, a tactical draw that amounted to a strategic defeat. Attica had to be abandoned, and the ships used to ferry the people to the safety of the Peloponnese. The inevitable result was that Athens was ransacked by Xerxes' soldiery, its homes and temples burned. The second sea battle, at Salamis, fully made up for this setback, however: it was a decisive Greek victory that put an immediate stop to Xerxes' advance. The next year the Spartans won a matching victory on land, and such Persians as survived fled back to Asia.

As the Spartans had little interest in the world beyond Greece, it was left to the Athenians to follow up these victories. They quickly destroyed what was left of the Persian navy in the Aegean and liberated the Greek communities along its northern and eastern coasts. These communities were then recruited into a league dedicated to driving home the Greek advantage and attacking the Persians wherever they looked vulnerable, most notably Cyprus (already a predominantly Greek island) and Egypt (always ready to revolt against Persian rule). But both these targets proved tougher than expected. All the league's expeditions failed, many with heavy losses, and eventually Athens had to call it a day. In theory this meant that the league could cut back on its military outlay and its individual members reduce their commitments, but the Athenians didn't see it that way. Contributions continued to be collected at the same level, no one was allowed to opt out, and to underline this new interpretation of the rules, the league treasury, originally situated on the central Aegean island of Delos, was transferred to Athens in 454 BC. What had been billed as a pan-Hellenic coalition had turned out to be an Athenian empire.

Athens' political success transformed the town of Athens itself. Only three years after Salamis, the Athenian statesman Aristides advised his fellow citizens to leave their farms and live in the city. The demands of empire meant that there would be jobs for all. Many would be in the navy, which had its base at PIRAEUS, and others entailed postings overseas, but the lion's share would have been in Athens itself. Just to perform its constitutional functions the city needed a minimum of 6,000 citizens, and with the assembly and the law courts with juries in almost continuous session, it needed them to be there all the time. The influx, which probably quadrupled the city's population, meant extra expenditure, which would have sparked off further growth: the new residents had to be housed, and a new city wall constructed to defend them. On top of this – quite literally – the ceremonial buildings on the hilltop (the acropolis or 'high town'), were now rebuilt in marble, a material rarely used on this scale before. The money for all this came from the league budget, something that caused the Athenians no qualms at all: they fully believed that what was good for Athens was good for its allies, indeed for Greeks everywhere.

Much money was also spent in Piraeus, and on the Long Walls that connected city and port. In fact the situation of Athens in its imperial heyday can only be properly understood if this entry is read in conjunction with the entry for Piraeus. Both places grew as the empire grew, and owed their prosperity to the same maritime strategy, and to the extent the necessary summary of Athenian naval history is given there and not here, it's simply to avoid duplication.

A ballpark figure for the population of Athens around this time – the middle of the fifth century BC, when everything was going Athens' way – would be somewhere around 35,000. This was an unprecedented number of people for a Greek town and it provided the basis for an upsurge in the arts and sciences that made Athens the intellectual capital of the peninsula. It was to the Athenians that Herodotus chose to read his *History*, the first work to deserve that title; it was in the Theatre of Dionysus at the foot of the acropolis that Aeschylus, Sophocles and Euripides presented the tragedies that marked the beginning of western drama. Other Greek communities had their philosophers, but none could rival the reputations of Socrates and Plato, nor could they boast sculptors the equal of Phidias or architects who could match the peerless design of the Parthenon. For the 200 years of the classical period, the fifth and fourth centuries BC, nearly everyone who was of importance in Greek cultural history was an Athenian by birth or adoption.

In the closing years of the fifth century BC, Athens overreached itself militarily and its empire was dismantled by the Spartans in the Peloponnesian War. Both the state and the city of Athens survived this debacle surprisingly well. The Athenians liked the way of life they had assumed in the fifth century, and although the treasury was depleted they proved able to maintain the apparatus of democracy and the festivals and monuments of the city through the fourth century BC. No new glories were added, but just as the Viennese kept up a metropolitan lifestyle after the fall of the Austro-Hungarian Empire, the Athenians long retained the social structure of their imperial era. The citizen body certainly contracted – a census in 312/309 BC returned a figure of 21,000, as opposed to the 30,000 recorded two centuries earlier – but the number of metics (resident foreigners), given as 10,000, made up the difference.

At this point – the end of the fourth century BC – immigration ceased and there are clear signs of decline in every sphere. The city had to submit to the authority of the kings of Macedon, and its subsequent debates were limited to local affairs. RHODES replaced Piraeus as the centre of the Aegean trading network; ALEXANDRIA replaced Athens as the intellectual capital of Hellenism. The population of Attica, as of all Greece, began to seep away to the new lands opened up by Alexander the Great. Athens became a sort of university town, pampered first by Hellenistic benefactors (most notably King Attalus II of PERGAMUM), then by Roman emperors (most notably Hadrian). Indeed, its monuments had never looked better than they did in Hadrian's reign (AD 117–38), and so long as imperial handouts were available, Athens continued in the appearance of prosperity. Underneath this veneer, though, there must have been a steady shrinkage in local resources. Just how low these had fallen became obvious when the town was sacked by the Germanic Heruls in AD 267. A wall built to protect the remaining population enclosed a mere twenty-five hectares, room for no more than a few thousand people. The nadir came with a second sack, by the Slavs at the end of the sixth century AD, after which only the Acropolis seems to have been defended. The story of the city had come full circle. Michael Akominatos, a Byzantine prelate appointed Bishop of Athens in the twelfth century, described it as a godforsaken hole and its inhabitants as uncivilized.

Topography

For a town that enjoyed such high status throughout antiquity, Athens has surprisingly few monuments. However, high quality more than makes up for the lack of quantity, the shining example of this being the Parthenon, the Temple of Athena that forms the centrepiece of the constructions on the acropolis. Built to impress at a time when Athens aspired to be 'an education to Greece', its elegance and opulence ensured that it did so. Now it has become the icon of Hellenism and, in a semi-mystical way, the ultimate statement of classical Greek values. This type of thinking can easily get out of hand, but in this instance there is a real jewel in the heart of the hyperbole.

Originally the acropolis was a simple stronghold, a role it had played since the Bronze Age when there was neither a town at its foot nor an Athenian state. With the political unification of Attica, traditionally ascribed to Theseus, the acropolis became the centre of Athens town, the capitol of the capital, so to speak. And, as Athens town prospered, the existing hilltop shrine to the goddess Athena began to seem unnecessarily humble. Rebuilding began under Pisistratos in the mid sixth century BC, but in the mood of optimism that followed the victory of Marathon, the Pisistratid constructions were swept away as being not grand enough. The top of the hill was levelled, the whole of it declared a ceremonial area, and work begun on a big new temple to Athena the Virgin (Athena Parthenos). This was less than half built when Athens, both

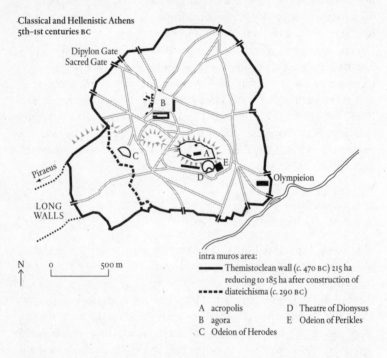

Classical and Hellenistic Athens
5th–1st centuries BC

Dipylon Gate
Sacred Gate

B

C

Piraeus

LONG
WALLS

A

E

D

Olympieion

N

0   500 m

intra muros area:
────── Themistoclean wall (*c.* 470 BC) 215 ha
reducing to 185 ha after construction of
▪▪▪▪▪ diateichisma (*c.* 290 BC)

A acropolis   D Theatre of Dionysus
B agora   E Odeion of Perikles
C Odeion of Herodes

town and citadel, fell to the Persians in 480 BC. Smarting from their earlier defeat the Persians did as much damage as they could, and when the Athenians recovered the city the next year they were so dismayed by what they found that they left the acropolis bare for the next thirty years. Then they began work again, this time with the funds of a sizeable maritime empire at their disposal. The three main buildings that form the present-day acropolis complex – the Parthenon, the Erechtheion (the temple of the city's founding father, Erechtheus) and the Propylaia (the monumental gateway) – were all put up in the period 447–406 BC, before the empire fell and the money stopped. The Parthenon is, of course, the main element, although some classical opinion favoured the Propylaia as the subtler piece of architecture. The Erechtheion, small and in every sense of the word peculiar, is the one with the caryatids (columns in the shape of girls).

In the lower town the main focus of interest is the agora, the open

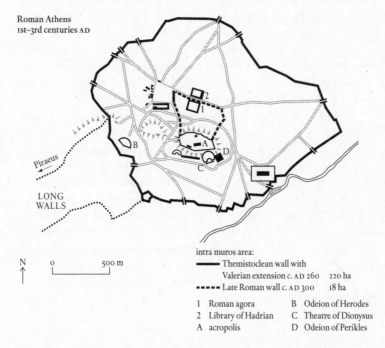

Roman Athens
1st–3rd centuries AD

Piraeus

LONG
WALLS

N

0   500 m

intra muros area:
▬▬▬ Themistoclean wall with
        Valerian extension c. AD 260   220 ha
▬▬▬ Late Roman wall c. AD 300   18 ha

1   Roman agora   B   Odeion of Herodes
2   Library of Hadrian   C   Theatre of Dionysus
A   acropolis   D   Odeion of Perikles

space that served the Athenians as an informal meeting place, and around which were sited the law courts and the buildings of the political executive. It is not, however, where the official assembly of the citizens was held: for this there was a separate open-air site on the Pnyx hill at the western edge of town. The theatre in which the Athenian play-wrights presented their works was at the foot of the acropolis where, in the Greek manner, it could make use of the rising ground for its auditorium.

The Romans added significantly to Athens' amenities. Augustus donated a 'Roman agora' to the city (although this was only a monumentalization of an existing commercial market); his right-hand man Agrippa followed up with a huge, roofed odeon on the south side of the original agora. These were considerable works, but they were overshadowed by the constructions of the philhellene emperor Hadrian and his governor of Asia, Herodes Atticus, who was an Athenian by birth. Herodes Atticus built an unroofed odeon to the west of the Theatre of Dionysus, and turned the earth-banked stadium (athletics track) just outside the city into a gleaming structure of solid marble. Hadrian built a public library just to the north of Augustus' marketplace and completed the Olympieion, a massive temple in the south-east corner of the city that had been started 650 years earlier but never finished. He also laid out a new residential quarter north-east of the Olympieion.

Hadrian's new suburb compensated for the loss of the south-west quarter of the city that had been cut off since a wall had been built to simplify the city's defence line in the Hellenistic period, around 290 BC. When the empire's time of troubles began in the mid third century AD and the emperor Valens ordered the city's defences refurbished, the circuit was extended to include this addition, returning the intramural area to its original size. The line proved too long for the reduced population of Athens to defend. In AD 267 the Heruls, a tribe of Germans who had penetrated the Danube defence line, broke in and put the city to the sack. The late Roman wall built in the aftermath of this disaster, the last significant work of antiquity, is a sad thing, cobbled together from half-destroyed buildings and fallen columns, defending only a tiny area at the foot of the acropolis.

Population

We don't have any direct record of the population of Athens town, but we do have two figures for the number of Athenian citizens – freeborn males of military age. The earlier, 30,000, is given by Herodotus, writing in the mid fifth century BC. It probably derives from a census taken by Cleisthenes at the end of the sixth century BC. Although there is no mention of Cleisthenes conducting a population survey, it is inconceivable that he could have set up his system of proportional representation on the council without finding out how many citizens there were and where they lived. As Athens town supplied twenty-eight of the council's 500 members (5.6 per cent), we can calculate that it had the same proportion of the state's citizens, which suggests that in his day Athens town had a population of 30,000 × 0.056 = 1,680 citizens, and, assuming an average family size of four, a total population of 6,720. This looks reasonable for a town whose great days were yet to come. Figures for the city in its heyday are more contentious. An absolute upper limit is provided by Thucydides' statement that until the Peloponnesian War forced them to retreat to the city, most Athenians lived in the countryside. Subtracting a modest proportion for the residents of Piraeus, this suggests that at the very most 10,000 of Athens' 30,000 citizens lived in Athens town, giving a theoretical ceiling of around 50,000 inhabitants in 431 BC. The preferred figure of 35,000 is based on Xenophon's remark that Athens had 10,000 houses and Dikaiarchos' statement that these were 'mostly mean, few [being] commodious'. Using a low multiplier of 3.5 that squares with this observation yields our ballpark 35,000. John Travlos rejects Xenophon's statement in favour of a calculation of his own based on a built-up area of 120 hectares, fifty (rather grand) houses per hectare and a very grand multiplier of 6: 6,000 houses × 6 = 36,000, a different path to the same result. In 404 BC the aristocratic oligarchy installed by the Spartans invited 3,000 citizens to take part in their government, while expelling 5,000 others from the city. This suggests a citizen population just before the expulsion of around 8,000 × 3.5 = 28,000, to which we can add something of the order of 10,000 non-citizens (metics and their dependants, and slaves), making 38,000. A final pointer to a figure in this general area is the 1861 census, which recorded a total of 42,725 Athenians living in an area of 260 hectares. This could be taken to indicate a population in the region of 42,725 × 215/260 = 35,330 for the city in the fifth century BC when the walled area was 215 hectares.

Until the end of the fourth century BC, figures for Athens town probably held fairly steady. The second census we know of, taken by Demetrius of Phaleron during the 117th Olympiad (312–309 BC) shows a decline in the citizen body (to 21,000), balanced by the addition of 10,000 metics (there would have been almost none in Cleisthenes' day).

Metics probably had fewer dependants than did citizens, but a dispro-portionately large number of them were urban, so the two effects prob-ably cancel out. After 300 BC the course was certainly downhill. By that time and thereafter, there simply can't have been room for a population of more than a few thousand within the late Roman wall.

The Turkish conquest in 1456 ushered in a new phase of growth, but numbers were still short of 10,000 in the year 1500.

AUGSBURG

Bavaria, Germany

Classical *Augusta Vindelicum; county town of the Vindelici,
capital of Raetia in the early imperial period and of
the late Roman province of Raetia Secunda*

Roman Augsburg was situated on a hill overlooking the confluence of
the Wertach and the Lech rivers. The site was chosen in around 15 BC
during the period of the Augustan conquest of the region, when a legion
was stationed at Oberhausen, on the far side of the Wertach. Initially
Augsburg was merely the county town of the Vindelici, one of the more
important of the Celtic tribes inhabiting northern Raetia, but when Raetia was made a province by Augustus in around 22 BC, it was chosen as
the seat of the provincial governor. Although it lost the territory of the
Valais during the reign of Claudius in AD 43, it retained its provincial
government even after Marcus Aurelius, in the 170s, decided to station
one of his new legions (III Italica) there. As the province's senior official,
the legion's commander automatically became its governor, which normally would have meant that the legion's camp at Regensburg (Castra
Regina) would take over the role of provincial capital. This didn't happen: the legion's commander, most unusually, chose to live in Augsburg,
rather than in his legion's camp 130 kilometres (80 miles) to the north.

   Around AD 300 the emperor Diocletian, as part of his mammoth
reorganization of the empire, split Raetia into two halves, Raetias I and
II. He also separated the military and civil administrations, which might
have led to the dux, as the military commander was now known, finally
making the move to Castra Regina. Once again this didn't happen, however, and the dux stayed in Augsburg alongside his civilian counterpart.
This situation continued as long as the empire lasted, which in this part
of the world means the mid fourth century AD.

   Our knowledge of the topography of Roman Augsburg is patchy, to
say the least. The city's outline is reasonably secure: the course of
the city wall is preserved on the west side (along with a gate near the

south-west corner). This, the contours of the hill and the course of the Lech on the east side suggest a perimeter roughly oval in shape, enclosing an area of about sixty hectares. Within this area a fair number of buildings have come to light, but only a set of baths in the north-east quarter of the town has been securely identified. It is permissible to

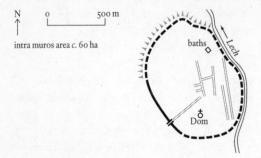

assume that there is an early Christian basilica under the present-day cathedral. Of the theatre, amphitheatre and forum, there is no sign as yet. Nor is there any clearly discernible pattern in the roads and buildings that have been uncovered. Perhaps Roman Augsburg simply developed in an unplanned way within the ramparts of a pre-existing Celtic oppidum, but even so the lack of formality in a place that had a certain importance from its inception is surprising.

AUTUN

Saône et Loire, France

Classical *Augustodunum;*
county town of the Aedui

When Caesar invaded Gaul, the Aedui were one of the area's most important tribes, and their oppidum, Bibracte, one of the most developed of the Celtic 'towns'. It had a considerable range of permanent buildings, including, according to the excavators, houses for the nobility and workshops for artisans. This puts it in a different class from most oppida, which were places where the tribes met in time of peace and rallied in time of war, but didn't have a significant year-round population. It was not, however, the Roman idea of a town, and the emperor Augustus (27 BC–AD 14) decided that the Aedui needed something better. The Romans picked a greenfield site twenty kilometres (twelve miles) to the east, adjacent to the River Arroux.

Augustodunum ('Augustus' town') was laid out within the quadrilateral formed by the Arroux and two small tributaries that flow into it from the south. This very large area, amounting to 200 hectares, was given a girdling wall. Four fine gates, of which two survive, marked the axes of the town, which was constructed on a rectangular grid, though with some irregularities. Outside the grid but inside the walls were the theatre and amphitheatre.

The scale of Roman Autun is a bit surprising. The Aedui may have been one of the largest tribes of Gaul, but most of them would have been simple country folk with no urban ambitions. Perhaps the motive for the extensive circuit was to ensure that the new Roman town exceeded its native predecessor in dimensions as well as function.

The little that is known about the history of Autun begins in the mid third century AD, when it was captured by the separatist Gallic emperor Tetricus in 269 – and presumably by anyone else who attacked it, because the circuit of its walls was far too long to be defensible.

In the medieval period the town was split into two, a 'high town' on the southern hill and a central 'Fort des Marchaux' in the area of the forum. The retreat to the high town is generally believed to have been made in the Roman period, the Fort des Marchaux appearing subsequently, in medieval times, when the secular authorities wanted a base

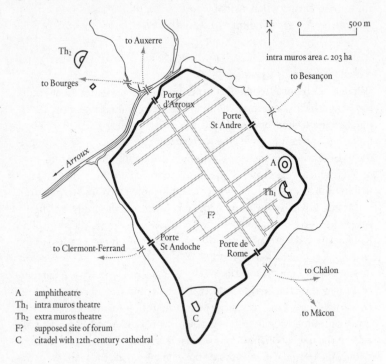

A	amphitheatre
Th₁	intra muros theatre
Th₂	extra muros theatre
F?	supposed site of forum
C	citadel with 12th-century cathedral

independent of the ecclesiastically dominated upper city. If this interpretation is correct, the area of Autun came down with a bang from a nominal 200 hectares at the beginning of the third century to a mere ten hectares at its end. The opposite point of view – that the town was essentially still intact – could be inferred from formal speeches made to the emperor Constantine when he visited the city in AD 311. These are the work of the rhetorician Eumenes, who was principal of the local academy at the time. It is certainly surprising that there was an academy of any sort still in existence given what Gaul had just been through, but it doesn't actually say very much about the state of the town; half a dozen pupils, a master and a servant don't represent much in terms of population statistics. More to the point is the gratitude Eumenes expresses for a reduction in the Aeduan tax roll. Previously this had been based on a figure of 32,000 heads; Constantine agreed to a reduction to 25,000.

Autun's decline may have been stemmed temporarily at the end of the fourth century when, to judge by the list of offices that survives from this era, there were two important armouries in the town. Autun would have had a bit more to it than the *cité de l'évêque* that was emerging in the high town; in fact the future site of Fort des Marchaux may have retained a total population of 3,000 to 4,000. But that would have been the last flourish of a town that had always had more flourish than substance. By the end of the fifth century, numbers would have been more appropriate to the new era – maybe 1,000, certainly no more.

AVENCHES

Vaud, Switzerland

Classical *Aventicum*

In 58 BC the Celtic tribe of the Helvetii lost their independence when Julius Caesar's army defeated them at Bibracte. While visiting LYON between 15 and 13 BC, Augustus reorganized the Celtic tribes, establishing new boundaries. During that time he founded a new city beside the River Braye and just south of Lake Morat to serve as the administrative centre of the Helvetii in the province of Gallia Belgica. It was built on the ancient road between Lake Geneva and the Aar valley and was named after the local spring-goddess Aventia.

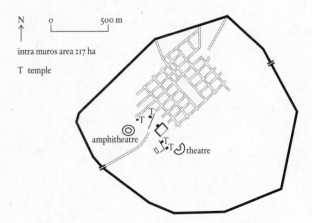

N   0   500 m

intra muros area 217 ha

T temple

amphitheatre

T

theatre

The city's layout followed the traditional Roman model, with rectangular blocks (*insulae*) averaging around 75 by 110 metres in size. Streets varied from around 5 to 9.5 metres in width. It seems that a forum was added under Tiberius, and a theatre decorated with marble statues followed soon after. By the reign of Claudius (AD 41–54), many of the principal houses were being rebuilt in stone.

Although the population suffered from its misplaced support for Vitellius against Vespasian in the confusion of AD 69, the latter showed his magnanimity by restoring the city and designating it as a Latin colony (temporarily renamed Colonia Pia Flavia Constans Emerita Helvetiorum Foederata). Retired Roman soldiers were given plots of land and a share in the responsibility for guarding the important military route from Italy to the Rhine. During the Flavian dynasty, at least two sets of public baths were founded or expanded to keep the ex-legionaries clean and in good company.

Under Trajan the city's wall was upgraded, and the second century AD saw construction of an amphitheatre with capacity for around 8,000 spectators. The city also built a new harbour on the nearby lake that was accessed by a canal.

In AD 212 the Helvetii received a general grant of Roman citizenship, but in 259–60 Aventicum was sacked by the Alemanni. Although the city survived, it seems to have been significantly reduced in size. Ammianus Marcellinus describes it as being in ruins in the second half of the fourth century. In the fifth and sixth centuries, Aventicum was still sufficiently important to be the seat of a Christian bishop. The remains of the city walls and their towers are still impressive today.

BABYLON

Between the Tigris and Euphrates rivers, Iraq

Capital of several Mesopotamian dynasties

History

Mesopotamia, the core territory of modern Iraq, is a very ancient land. It is here that villages first became towns and that writing, the essential tool of civilization, was invented. The surviving king lists show that some of these towns – Kish and Uruk, for example – had histories going back to early in the second millennium BC. Babylon is not as old as that; it is first mentioned early in the second millennium BC, and then only as a dependency of Ur, whose kings were the dominant force in Mesopotamia at the time.

Towns and their territories were not the only element in the political landscape of Mesopotamia; around and between them were pasture lands inhabited by nomadic tribes. Towards the end of the second millennium BC this nomadic component was significantly reinforced by an influx of new tribes from the western desert; these people, the Amorites ('Westerners'), played a significant role in the downfall of the empire of Ur, and their sheikhs took advantage of the resulting confusion to seize control of a whole clutch of towns, including Babylon. There was no attempt to create an Amorite empire; each town remained an independent entity, but now Babylon was a player, not a pawn.

The star of this first (Amorite) dynasty of Babylonian kings was its sixth ruler, Hammurabi. Today he is mainly remembered for his 'eye-for-an-eye' law code, but his contemporaries will have been more impressed by his success in the game of push and shove on the Mesopotamian political ladder. In the course of a long reign (forty-two years, probably 1792–1750 BC) he gradually elbowed his way to the top, and when he died Babylon occupied the position of overall hegemony previously held by Ur. His successors fought hard to sustain this supremacy, although with diminishing returns, until 1595 BC when the Hittite king Mursilis I made a foray into Mesopotamia in the course of which he sacked Babylon and put an end to the dynasty. The city's spell as number one seemed to be over.

As it happened, things turned out differently. Order was restored by another invading group, the Kassites, mountain men from the Zagros. The Kassites, unlike the Amorites, did create a unitary empire, and, having no capital of their own, looked to Mesopotamia to provide one. Babylon seemed to fill the bill better than anywhere else. It was on a branch of the Euphrates, but also close to the Tigris; it was in the Akkadian heartland, Mesopotamia's political centre of gravity. The fact that it hadn't worked well recently wasn't important; the Kassites had the muscle to see that it did. And so it proved. The Kassites ruled Mesopotamia for over 400 years, long enough to make Babylon seem the natural choice for a capital and for the southern half of Iraq to become known as Babylonia; previously it had been called 'Sumer and Akkad'.

The northern half of Mesopotamia was dominated by a separate power, Assyria, which, by the thirteenth century BC, was seriously harassing the Kassites. The Assyrians finally disappeared in the twelfth century, to be replaced by some short-lived Babylonian dynasties whose rulers did their best to keep the Assyrians at bay but often failed. Things became even worse in the time of the ninth dynasty (731–626 BC), which largely consisted of Assyrian monarchs and their deputies. Such resistance as the Babylonians were able to sustain was the work of the region's nomads, the Chaldeans. Eventually the Chaldeans provided Babylon with a new dynasty, its tenth (625–539 BC), which, in alliance with the Medes and the Scythians, turned the tables on the Assyrians and destroyed their state.

The Chaldean kings now found themselves in control of most of the erstwhile Assyrian Empire, a far greater estate than any previous rulers of Babylon had possessed. What is often referred to as the Neo-Babylonian Empire comprised all Palestine (including a derelict JERUSALEM, razed for its defiance), most of Syria and all the useful parts of Mesopotamia. The reign of Nebuchadnezzar, the second king of the Chaldean line, is generally taken as marking the apogee of the dynasty. The same is true of the capital. Nebuchadnezzar built there on a colossal scale, and the remains of the city that a visitor sees today are largely his work.

After Nebuchadnezzar's death in 562 BC, the Neo-Babylonian Empire faltered. There were three short-lived monarchs, followed by a king called Nabonidus who tried to promote the moon god Sin at the expense of Bel Marduk, the patron deity of the city since its earliest days. This created such disaffection that when the Persian king Cyrus invaded Mesopotamia in 539 BC, Babylon fell without a fight. It became the winter capital of the Persian Empire and the year-round capital of the new Persian satrapy (province) of Mesopotamia. There is no reason to believe that its prosperity was in any way reduced by the change of ruler.

Two hundred years later, in 331 BC, Alexander the Great made a similar bloodless entry into the town, which he seems to have envisaged continuing in its existing role. Not so his general Seleucus. When he took over Alexander's Asian conquests he immediately began constructing a new Greek-style capital at a site on the Tigris some ninety kilometres (fifty-six miles) to the north of Babylon. Called SELEUCIA ON THE TIGRIS to distinguish it from the many other Seleucias he founded, the new city was soon draining the life out of Babylon. The transfer of population was effectively completed in 274 BC when Seleucus' son Antiochus ordered the remaining inhabitants of Babylon to move to Seleucia forthwith, excepting only the priests who served in the Temple of Bel Marduk. So Babylon ended its days as a temple town, guarding the old ways, the old religion, the ancient cuneiform system of writing, and the records of astronomical observations compiled each year since 747 BC. In 173 BC a Greek colony called Antioch was installed in the old Mesopotamian city, and its prestige proved enough to keep it going for a couple of centuries after that. Pliny, in the mid first century AD, says it was still there in his day, although the rest of the site had reverted to desert; Diodorus Siculus, writing a generation later, says that the temple was in ruins too. That fits with the last document from the temple archive, dated AD 75, which is also the last example of cuneiform known to us.

Topography

The only Babylon we know much about is the city of the seventh century BC and subsequent centuries, for which we have two sources: the German excavations of the early twentieth century (1899–1917) directed by Robert Koldewey; and the cuneiform text known to scholars as 'Tintir=Babylon', which lists (among much else) the ten wards of the

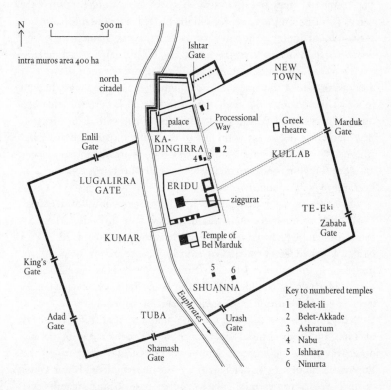

city, giving the position of each in relation to the city gates, plus the names of the top two temples in each ward. Combining both sources has enabled A. R. George to produce a much improved city plan that supersedes the oft-reproduced version based on excavation alone. His work is the basis for the map accompanying this entry.

The most impressive feature of Chaldean Babylon – the city of Nebuchadnezzar – was the six-storey ziggurat situated at its centre. The ceremonial approach to this was from the north, via the Ishtar Gate and the Processional Way. This led to the eastern entrance of the ziggurat's precinct and also, a short way past this, to the eastern approach to the temple of the titular god of the city, Bel Marduk (Bel, an alternative spelling of 'Baal', simply means 'Lord'). These two structures, in their final, much enlarged forms, must have taken up much of the Eridu ward that contained them, because extra room had to be found for two other wards fronting on the river, Ka-dingirra to the north and Shuanna to the south. Intriguingly the three wards with this east-bank frontage are described as lying between the Ishtar and Grand gates (Ka-dingirra), between the Grand and Market gates (Eridu), and between the Market and Urash gates (Shuanna). This can only mean that Babylon had an inner wall enclosing Eridu and its two sanctuaries with the Grand Gate on the Processional Way at the level of the north wall of the ziggurat precinct, and the Market Gate just to the south of the Temple of Bel Marduk. This wall and the Eridu ward within it presumably represent an older Babylon, with an area nearer to fifty hectares than the 400 hectares of Nebuchadnezzar's day.

The guesstimate of fifty hectares includes some or all of the west-bank ward of Kumar, for there was an inner wall on this side of the river too. This can be deduced from the fact that the northern ward on this bank was called the Lugalirra Gate ward and, as there was no gate with this name in the outer wall, the ward must originally have been an extra-mural suburb lying outside a gate of this name in the old town wall. So we have got a glimpse of pre-Chaldean Babylon after all.

Nebuchadnezzar's Babylon had an outer wall, and if you take this into account the intramural area rises to about 850 hectares. Its starting point was Nebuchadnezzar's summer palace on the east bank of the Euphrates, some 2.25 kilometres (1.4 miles) north of the Ishtar Gate. From there it ran on a straight line to a point some 1.6 km (one mile) east of the Marduk Gate, then ran back to the river on a line parallel to, and only a little in advance of, the south wall of the city. It is not at all probable that the extra space it enclosed was ever built over; most likely it was meant to serve as a refuge for country folk and a pasture for animals in the event of a siege.

Population

There are no data on which to base a reliable estimate of Babylon's population. All we can do is look at the likely range of population in comparable places – in particular NINEVEH, for which we have a guesstimate of 30,000. If we accept this as a possible figure for Babylon in its prime (under the Chaldeans and Persians), we then need to address the questions of its earlier rise and later fall. The fall is easy: from 30,000 to below 10,000 in the course of the third century BC. The rise is more of a problem and depends on what view you take of Near Eastern urbanism in the Bronze Age. It seems most prudent to see even the most successful towns of this period, such as ASSUR and Babylon, as having inhabited areas of no more than fifty hectares and populations that topped out at about 7,500 – or, to put it another way, didn't breach the 10,000 barrier.

BENEVENTO

Campania, Italy

Classical *Beneventum* (formerly *Malies*);
capital of the late Roman province of Samnium

Under the name Malies, Benevento was the county town of the Hirpini, one of the four tribes that made up the Samnite confederacy of the south-central Apennines. It fell to the Romans in the course of the Samnite Wars – the wars that transformed ROME from a local into a peninsular power – and it was to cement this success that the Romans decided to turn Malies into a Latin stronghold. They didn't like the name Malies – to them it sounded like Malventum ('Evil Wind') – so they renamed it Beneventum ('Good Wind'). The new colony was established in 268 BC and shortly thereafter linked to the Roman road system by an extension of the Via Appia, the Rome–CAPUA highway. The subsequent extension of the Via Appia to Brindisi enhanced the importance of Benevento as a station on what soon became the main route to Rome's rapidly expanding empire in the East.

Rome's pacification programme in the Apennines was so successful that Benevento has little in the way of history. The colony remained faithful to Rome through the turbulent times provoked by Hannibal's invasion of the peninsula in 218 BC, and through the upheavals of the Social War (91–87 BC), the final vehicle for the expression of Samnite discontents. In the early years of the second century AD, the emperor Trajan built a new road from Benevento to Brindisi on a better line than the one taken by the Via Appia (through Bari instead of TARANTO); he celebrated the completion of this 'Via Traiana' by building a triumphal arch at its starting point on the north side of town in AD 109. The arch survives in surprisingly good order, making Benevento *vaut le voyage* for those interested in things classical. The only other Roman construction to survive is a theatre built by Hadrian and enlarged by Caracalla.

The later history of Benevento is surprisingly upbeat. At the end of the third century it became the capital of Samnium, one of the new provinces set up by Diocletian as part of his administrative reform of Italy. In the late fifth century, when the western half of the empire dissolved, it became part of the Gothic kingdom of Italy; in the early sixth century it was recovered for the empire by Belisarius, commander of the East Roman expeditionary force dispatched by Justinian in 535. In 542, Totila, king of the Ostrogoths, retook the town and, to make sure it could not side against him again, slighted its walls. The collapse of Ostrogothic power in the 550s put it back in imperial hands again, but, not long after, it was seized by the leader of a Lombard war-band who in 571 made it

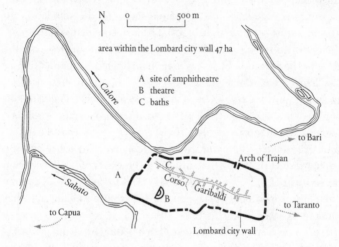

the seat of an independent duchy. This confirmed its importance for the remainder of the Dark Ages, when it must have been one of the few Italian towns to retain a population at the same level it had sustained in the classical period – say 3,000 to 5,000.

Little is known about the topography of Roman Benevento. It is generally assumed that the classical town walls underlie those of the Lombard period (which enclose an area of forty-seven hectares) and that the Corso Garibaldi follows the line of the Roman decumanus. The lie of the land and the distribution of the surviving Roman monuments – the Arch of Trajan on the line of the wall, the theatre within the line, and the amphitheatre outside – support this judgement.

BESANÇON

Doubs, France

Classical *Vesontio;* county town of the Sequani
and capital of the late Roman province of
Maxima Sequanorum

Besançon lies within a loop of the River Doubs, which provides the
town with a ready-made moat on three sides. As the sole landward
approach, on the south-east, is blocked by a steep-sided hill, the position is one with strong natural defences and it is no surprise that the
local Celts, the Sequani, chose it as their main oppidum, nor that Caesar
made it a major base during his conquest of Gaul (for his crisp account
of its topography, see Book One, Chapter 38 in *De bello Gallico*). Following the conquest, Vesontio was Romanized. A bridge – the last
remains of which survived till a flood carried them away in 1953 –
enhanced the town's communications; the line between the bridge and a
triumphal arch at the foot of the hill defined the axis of the lower town
as, in the form of the Grande-Rue, it still does today. The hill, already
fortified in the pre-Roman period, became Vesontio's citadel, another
constant in the town's long history.

These few facts encompass almost all that is known of Roman Vesontio. The only building that has been identified for certain is the amphitheatre, situated on the far side of the river. Within the lower town, a few
sketchy remains support the assumption that the town was laid out with
an orthogonal street plan of the type usual with Roman town planners.
It is unlikely that this grid covered more than eighty hectares, because
the western third of the area within the Doubs meander (about 120
hectares altogether) was used as the town's burial ground.

In the second half of the third century, Vesontio will have shared
in the hard times experienced by the majority of the cities of Gaul. It
is probable that most of the lower town was abandoned at this time,
such population as remained shifting to the area at the foot of the citadel where, possibly around AD 300, a wall was built incorporating the

triumphal arch as a north-facing gate. It was small consolation that the administrative status of this sadly reduced version of Vesontio was to be raised a notch when Diocletian made it the capital of one of the new small-size provinces he set up at this time. Previously, Vesontio had been one of the *civitates* of Germania Superior (along with Nyon, AVENCHES and Basel). Now these four became members of a new jurisdiction, the province of Maxima Sequanorum.

Vesontio was sacked by the Alemanni in 355, recovered by Julian the Apostate and was only finally lost to Rome when it was incorporated into the Burgundian state in the mid fifth century. It had some sort of

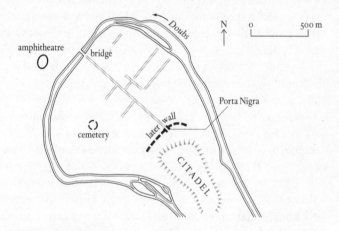

minimal urban life during the Dark Ages, the Magyars finding enough to be worth pillaging when they were in the area in 926. Revival began under the auspices of the remarkable Hugues de Salins, Archbishop of Besançon from 1031 to 1066.

As to population, the general thesis for Romano-Celtic towns of this type is that numbers peaked in the second century, collapsed in the late third century and were under the 1,000 mark by the time the empire fell. The peak in this instance is likely to have been under rather than over 5,000, although there is of course no direct evidence of any sort.

BOLOGNA

Emilia-Romagna, Italy

Formerly *Felsina*; classical *Bononia*; a city of
the eighth region of Italy, subsequently
the province of Aemilia

Nowadays the easiest way to reach the plain of the Po from Tuscany is to take the road that runs due north from Florence to Bologna. In general terms this was equally true in antiquity, so when, in the late sixth century BC, the Etruscans began to establish a presence on the far side of the Apennines, Bologna was the natural place for them to start. Under the name Felsina it became the first – and always remained the foremost – of the Etruscans' trans-Apennine colonies.

Felsina fell to the Celts, specifically to the Boii, in the mid fourth century BC, acquiring the name Bononia either then or when the Romans conquered the region in 196 BC. Its strategic position made it the obvious site for a Roman colony, and in 189 BC, 3,000 settlers were duly dispatched to set one up. Ignoring the existing settlement, the colonists laid out their city in the strictly rectangular form characteristic of *de novo* Roman foundations. In size it was at the upper end of the range for such places, its forty hectares being only a fraction less that PIACENZA's forty-one hectares; the two of them were the only places of this calibre between the Apennines and the Po.

The towns in this valuable territory all lie along the arrow-straight Via Aemilia that runs from RIMINI on the Adriatic to Piacenza on the Po. The road, which eventually gave its name to the region (classical Aemilia, modern Emilia-Romagna) was built, or at least begun, in 187 BC, only a couple of years after the foundation of Bologna. The city already had its grid laid out by the time the Via Appia reached it, with the result that the road is kinked by its passage through the city. In fact it is this kink that provides the main clue to the layout of Bononia, which has otherwise left few convincing traces in the surviving street plan. That the reconstruction is correct is confirmed by the discovery of a theatre in an appropriate spot on the south side of the hypothetical grid. The position of the amphitheatre, of which nothing remains, is given by the title of a little church on the east side of town, S. Vitale e Agricola 'in Arena', but that is too far out of town to be equally helpful.

Bologna is rarely mentioned by Roman historians but seems to have survived well enough until the late imperial/early Lombard period, when the western half of the city was abandoned and a wall built enclosing only the eastern half (and not all of that), plus the theatre. In this reduced form, Bologna survived the Dark Ages, to emerge as a major player again in the high medieval period.

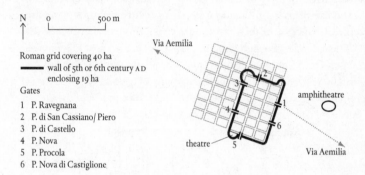

The first surviving population count is medieval: 8,000 hearths in 1371. This within a wall built between 1326 and 1370, enclosing 420 hectares, indicating a density at this time of 8,000 × 4.5/ 420 = 86 per hectare. Numbers had certainly been higher before the Black Death, and 100 per hectare would not be an unreasonable figure for the medieval period as a whole. Taking this as a guide, classical Bologna would have had a population of no more than 5,000 at its best, and no more than 2,000 in the Dark Ages.

BOSTRA

*Present-day Bosra or Busra ash-Sham,
Dar'a province, southern Syria*

*Capital of the Roman province
of Arabia; diocese: Oriens*

Bostra, a town of the Nabataean Arabs, was a small place until Trajan
annexed the Nabataean kingdom in AD 106 and turned the kingdom
into the province of Arabia. This transformed Bostra's fortunes: it was
made the capital of the new province and given a legion (III Cyrenaica,
moved up from Egypt) as its garrison. The civilian side of the city was
eventually recognized as a Roman colony by Elagabalus (218–22). Bostra remained the capital of Arabia until the Arab conquest of the area in

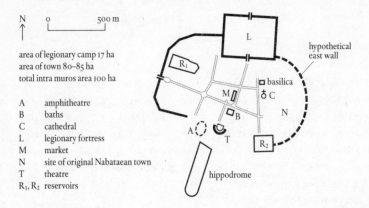

N   0   500 m

area of legionary camp 17 ha
area of town 80–85 ha
total intra muros area 100 ha

A   amphitheatre
B   baths
C   cathedral
L   legionary fortress
M   market
N   site of original Nabataean town
T   theatre
R₁, R₂   reservoirs

637; by then the province was only half its initial size, the southern half
having been given independent status as Arabia II in the early fourth
century.

The considerable remains of Roman Bostra were surveyed by a
Princeton University expedition in the early 1900s. Their team's ana-
lysis suggested that the Nabataean town had been confined to the south-

western area of the site, where there were indications of a street plan with a different pattern from the rest of the city. The far larger area to the west of this, distinguished by colonnaded streets, was attributed to the Romans. The Romans were also clearly responsible for the theatre, the hippodrome and, insofar as it was discernible, the surrounding city wall. What the Princeton team didn't find was the legionary fortress, but air survey has since revealed that it lay on the north side. It covered an area of seventeen hectares, a bit below the twenty-hectare average for legionary camps, but then camps in the eastern provinces do tend to be a bit on the small side.

The northern and western limits of Bostra are easily plotted. The south wall was rubbed out when the theatre was turned into a castle in the thirteenth century, but it appears to have run WSW, paralleling the main street. (If so, the theatre was already acting as a bastion in the Roman period.) The lie of the east wall is entirely unknown, but assuming that it follows the course shown on the map, the city would have had an intramural area of eighty to eighty-five hectares. This relatively large area suggests that in its heyday as a garrison city, Bostra may have had 5,000 or more civilian inhabitants. Even after the rapid rundown of the frontier legions in the first half of the fourth century, it could well have retained something near that number.

CAESAREA MARITIMA

On the Mediterranean coast of Israel

History

Caesarea Maritima (known both as Caesarea-on-Sea and Caesarea of Palestine) was founded by Herod the Great on the site of a Sidonian outpost called Strato's Tower. (Sidon is a Lebanese port about 150 kilometres (100 miles) to the north; Strato was one of its kings.) This outpost dated back to the early Hellenistic period, when increasing traffic

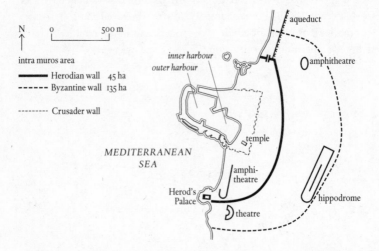

between Syria and Egypt created a need for a safe haven on what was a particularly unwelcoming stretch of coast. Strato's Tower is first mentioned in 259 BC when Zenon, Ptolemy II's finance minister, disembarked there at the beginning of a tour of inspection of Palestine. The town was taken by the Jewish king Alexander Janneus in 103 BC and transferred to the Roman province of Syria by Pompey in 63 BC, then given to Herod the Great by Caesar Octavian, the future emperor Augustus, in 30 BC. Herod, always adept at flattery, renamed it Caesarea in honour of his patron.

Although Herod was king of Judaea, he was only half Jewish, an advantage at a time when ROME's subordinate kings were supposed to be easing their subjects towards the Roman lifestyle. He planned Caesarea as a sort of balance to JERUSALEM, intending it as a purely Roman city that would open up his inward-looking, largely Jewish state to the world of the classical Mediterranean. But it proved too anti-Jewish to fulfil this role. Jews were excluded from citizenship, and the temple that overlooked the harbour was dedicated to Rome and Caesar, not Jehovah. Instead of promoting a shift towards the middle ground, Herod's new city polarized an already difficult situation. Attitudes hardened on both sides.

Built in 22–10 BC as a Roman-style capital for his Palestinian kingdom, Caesarea became the largest place in Palestine when Jerusalem paid the price for the Jewish revolt of AD 66–70.

Population

The only evidence for Caesarea's population is the area enclosed by its walls, but because the site is flat and the plan a simple semicircle, this is more cogent than usual. Herod laid out a grid covering an area of some forty-five hectares, sufficient for a population of 6,000. In late Roman times (fifth century AD) a new wall was built enclosing 135 hectares, indicating that the population had at least doubled in the interim.

The final Roman century may have seen a small decline, and after the Arab conquest in AD 640 there was a complete collapse.

CALAH

On the River Tigris in north Iraq

Capital of Assyria

The spelling Calah is the one used in the Bible; in Assyrian it is Kalhu. The place is often referred to as Nimrud by archaeologists, this being the name of a modern village nearby.

Originally a small town on the Tigris some seventy kilometres (forty-three miles) north of ASSUR, Calah was the site King Ashurnasirpal II (884–859 BC) picked for his new capital. The town had been founded by an earlier Assyrian king, Shalmaneser I, in the thirteenth century BC, but little was left of his predecessor's work by the time Ashurnasirpal was done. He deployed an army of workmen – 47,000 strong by his own account – to build a town that was not only far bigger than Shalmaneser's, but six times the size of the existing capital Assur. It was completed in 879 BC.

In some ways we know very little about Calah. Only the palace (at the south-east corner of the city) and the citadel (at the south-west corner) have been excavated. What we do know is that at the time it opened for business it had 16,000 inhabitants, rather more than can easily have been fed from the surrounding farmlands, even allowing for the fact that some of these were irrigated. Special arrangements must have been made to bring in the extra food needed, presumably by barge, down the Tigris.

What did the people of Calah do? If we assume that a total population of 16,000 implies a figure for economically active adult males of around 4,000, then something like 1,500 may have found employment in the fields and orchards around the city. Perhaps as many as 1,000 worked directly for the king, in the royal bureaucracy, or as palace servants, storemen or craftsmen. Another 1,000, maybe more, would have been hostages forcibly removed from their homelands and placed where the king could keep an eye on them. A few would have been lords and their retainers, people who found it worth their while to be near the king. The rest would have been a mix of petty tradesmen: potters, leather-workers, weavers, dyers, tailors and cobblers. It is probably fair to guess that more than half the people were there purely because this was at once a capital city, a military depot and the place where the Assyrian king spent most of his money. If any of these functions were withdrawn, the population would immediately dip.

What did Calah look like? Here we are well informed as regards the palace and the citadel, both of which were mini-towns with their own

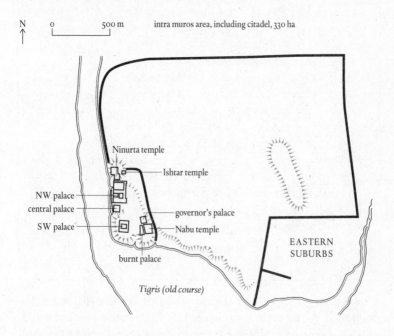

N   0   500 m   intra muros area, including citadel, 330 ha

Ninurta temple

Ishtar temple

NW palace

central palace

SW palace

governor's palace

Nabu temple

EASTERN SUBURBS

burnt palace

Tigris (old course)

walls. Each was a complex of single-storey buildings, each building a labyrinth of rooms and courts, with attached temples and storehouses. These were the Mesopotamian equivalent of China's Forbidden Cities, places where no one was allowed in unless it was their business to be there. About the lower town, constituting 85 per cent of the whole, we know nothing. The general assumption is that a significant part of it was

Versailles

Few later kings have built palace-cities on the same epic scale as the Assyrian monarchs, but one who did was Louis XIV of France, and the statistics for Versailles make an interesting comparison with those for CALAH. In essence, Louis, like Ashurnasirpal before him, transformed a small town (Versailles had about 5,000 people in 1650) into a thriving city (25,000 people in 1700) by making it into the official centre of his government and the permanent seat of his court. But Louis's Versailles was purely a service city: there was no significant agricultural sector, nor any significant military function. Of its jobs, no fewer than 45 per cent were in domestic service of one sort or another, and when the court moved off after Louis's death the population immediately halved.

The lack of an agricultural sector reflects the greater efficiency of transport in the seventeenth century AD compared to the ninth century BC. Louis also seems to have worked his building force to better effect. It is thought that he never had more than 10,000 men engaged in the construction of the actual palace, although the total may have been as high as 20,000 if you include those engaged on the roads and aqueducts that formed part of the grand design. This is still less than half Ashurnasirpal's 47,000. The time taken was probably similar. Louis's building programme was completed in its essentials within ten years. We don't know how long Ashurnasirpal took over Calah, but Sargon built DUR-SHARRUKIN, much the same size as Calah, in eleven years.

a royal park, partly because the area enclosed by the walls, some 360 hectares, is far more than was needed for a population of 16,000, and partly because in the Middle East the tradition of the Paradise Garden, lavishly stocked with plants and animals, seems to be almost as old as the idea of a royal palace. If half the area was park, the built-up half would have had a density of just under ninety persons per hectare, which seems about right.

Calah remained Assyria's capital until 706 BC, when Sargon II moved his court to DUR-SHARRUKIN. Although demoted, Calah retained some administrative functions, and given the expansion in the Assyrian economy, it is likely to have kept an above-average population – say somewhere around the 10,000 level – during the empire's last century.

CAPUA

Campania, Italy; present-day *S. Maria di Capua Vetere*

Capital of Campania throughout antiquity

History

Capua is situated in the middle of the Terra di Lavoro, the famously fertile stretch of land behind the Bay of NAPLES. The site was settled early in the Iron Age, but only became important in the sixth century BC, when the Etruscans made it their main power base in the region. Whatever the nature of the Etruscan hegemony – presumably something similar to the dynastic control imposed on ROME – the period of foreign rule came to an end in the early fifth century BC, when the Greeks defeated the Etruscan forces by land and sea, and the Romans expelled their Etruscan kings. This left Capua free, suspended between the Greek communities of the coast and the Samnite hill folk of the interior. Of the two, the rapidly multiplying Samnites were the greater threat: in 424 BC a Samnite sub-tribe, the Sabelli, took over the town, and by 340 another wave of Sabelli were set for a repeat performance. The Capuans decided to appeal to Rome for help.

The price of Rome's help was a permanent protectorate. The Capuans seem to have been undecided as to whether this price was acceptable, but after they had said yes and then no several times, the Romans imposed a protectorate anyway. To make the point, the Romans built the Via Appia, the first of the many famous highways that underpinned their empire. Begun in 312 BC, the Via Appia would have taken a few years to reach Capua, its initial destination; subsequently, in the third quarter of the third century BC, it was extended via BENEVENTO and TARANTO to Brindisi, its Adriatic terminus.

Although suppressed, Capua's ancient freedoms were not forgotten, as Hannibal's invasion of Italy was to show. Following the Carthaginian general's amazing victory over the Romans at Cannae in 216 BC, the Capuans closed their eyes, deserted the Roman cause and admitted a Carthaginian garrison. But Capua was only one of many towns that Hannibal had to protect; he couldn't be everywhere, and the Capuans weren't capable of defending themselves. In 212 the Romans were back with a vengeance: offers of a negotiated surrender were contemptuously rejected and in 211 the city was forced to yield unconditionally. The citizens who had favoured rebellion were executed, and many of the politically innocent were sold into slavery. The best of the city's land was confiscated and subsequently transferred to Roman colonists.

More Roman colonists arrived in the first century BC – under Julius Caesar (59 BC), Antony (43 BC) and Octavian (36 BC). Capua became a

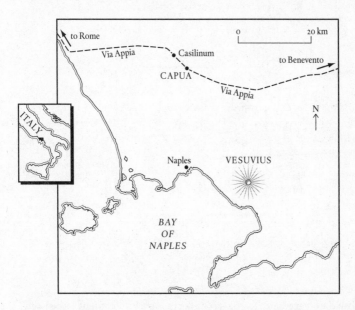

Roman city, and recovered the position it had probably held in earlier times, of standing second only to Rome 'as regards size and opulence' (Livy, 7.31, referring, it is safe to assume, to peninsular Italy). This ranking was confirmed in the second century AD, when the emperor Hadrian presented the city with an amphitheatre only a little smaller than Rome's Colosseum (165 metres on the long axis, compared to the Colosseum's

188 metres). But at the end of the third century the promotion of MILAN as a new imperial capital pushed Capua down a place, and Ausonius, in the late fourth century, represents the city, with its purely agricultural economy, as struggling to hold even this position. The fifth century brought spectacular misfortunes. Capua's perimeter, always too large for easy defence, was readily penetrated by the forces of Alaric the Visigoth in 410 and Gaiseric the Vandal in 455, both of whom sacked the

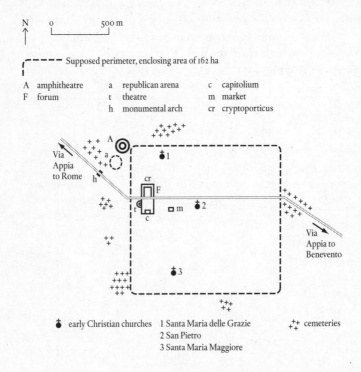

N 0 500 m

⌐---- Supposed perimeter, enclosing area of 162 ha

A amphitheatre   a republican arena   c capitolium
F forum   t theatre   m market
   h monumental arch   cr cryptoporticus

Via Appia to Rome

Via Appia to Benevento

✝ early Christian churches   1 Santa Maria delle Grazie   ⁺⁺ cemeteries
2 San Pietro
3 Santa Maria Maggiore

city but didn't stay; and in 594 it was permanently occupied by the Lombards. The end came in 841, with a sack by Saracen sea-raiders, after which the remaining inhabitants decamped to Casilinum, five kilometres (three miles) to the north on the Via Appia. Rather confusingly they took the city's name with them: modern Capua is on the site of classical Casilinum, while classical Capua lies beneath the present-day town of S. Maria di Capua Vetere.

Topography

Very little work has been done to clarify the topography of ancient Capua. All we have to go on is the kink the city put into the Via Appia, which gives us the city's length west to east (1.3 kilometres). Most of the surviving remains are at the western end, in the area of the city's forum: there is a cryptoporticus north of the main road, and a 'theatre' (surely a council house) and capitolium on the south side. Outside and to the north of the west gate are the republican-era arena, and the imperial amphitheatre that replaced it.

What has not been discovered so far is any sign of a regular street plan. This is a pity for two reasons: first it leaves us uncertain about the extent of the city, and second it deprives us of the information needed to get an idea of its date. As to the first, there's a suggestion, prompted by a kink in a road running north and the position of a burial ground on the north-west, that the distance from the city's mid-point to its north gate was about 440 metres. If the town was symmetrical, this indicates a ballpark figure for Capua's area of $1,300 \times 880$ metres = 114.4 hectares. In fact the consensus is that Capua was not symmetrical, with almost twice as much of it lying south of the Via Appia as north. This would make the city's area something like 160–65 hectares. On the second point, the date of the town's layout, we have Cato's statement that Capua was founded in 471 BC, which, although clearly not true as regards the settlement of the site, will do nicely for a Greek replanning of the town after the expulsion of the Etruscans from the region. In that case the city had at least one more major cross street and a pattern of long, thin city blocks like Naples. It would also have had an irregular circuit, not the rectangular shape shown on the sketch map, and, as a result, a smaller intramural area than the 160–65 hectares proposed above.

Population

As the capital of Italy's most prosperous region, Capua, when not blotting its copybook with the Romans, must have been a cut above the average for provincial centres. Something in the 12,500–15,000 range seems a reasonable guess for its population, and if this doesn't seem much, it is enough to make it the second town in Italy until the end of the third century AD, when it had to yield this position to the West's new capital, Milan. After that, numbers will have fallen slowly but steadily, until AD 856, when the last few hundred Capuans took the decision to abandon the town.

CARNUNTUM

Present-day *Bad Deutsch-Altenburg (Carnuntum Fortress),
Petronell (Carnuntum Town), Lower Austria*

Capital of Upper Pannonia; diocese: Illyricum

Following the conquest of Pannonia by Augustus, units of the Roman army began to move up to the Danube line, which had now become the empire's frontier in central Europe. In AD 15 the first legion to make the move, XV Apollinaris, pitched its camp at Carnuntum, forty kilometres (twenty-five miles) downstream from present-day Vienna. This fortification probably became the administrative centre for the new province of Pannonia, the northern half of what had previously been known as Illyricum.

In AD 103 Trajan divided Pannonia into Superior and Inferior halves. From this point on, there is no doubt as to the status of Carnuntum: it was the capital of Pannonia Superior. This function was not served by Carnuntum Fortress, however, nor by the suburb that had grown up around it, but by a separate town constructed 2.5 kilometres (1.5 miles) to the west. This new settlement, which we can distinguish as Carnuntum Town, was recognized as a municipium by Hadrian (117–38) and as a colony by Septimius Severus (193–211).

By this time, the legions of the Upper Danube were beginning to find it increasingly difficult to uphold the Pax Romana. The emperor Marcus Aurelius had managed to defeat a first wave of Barbarians in the early 170s (years in which he was often resident at Carnuntum), but in the 250s many of the frontier fortresses were overwhelmed and much of Pannonia laid to waste. Eventually the frontier was restored and Carnuntum Town resumed normal life again. But it was no longer a provincial capital in the new administrative order introduced by Diocletian (285–305). He split Pannonia Superior into two halves, Pannonia Prima and Savia, and they had their capitals at SAVARIA and SISCIA, both well back from the frontier. Carnuntum Fortress was still manned by a legion (XIV Gemina, which had replaced XV Apollinaris in the early second century AD), but even legions were not what they had been, with probably no more than two cohorts. So in the early fourth century both Fortress and Town were past their best. Their decline was to continue as the century progressed, and in 375, when the emperor Valentinian II passed through Carnuntum, the Town was described as 'quite deserted now, and in ruins' (Ammianus Marcellinus, 30.5.2). The Fortress was still garrisoned, but by this time XIV Gemina would have been little more than a paper formation.

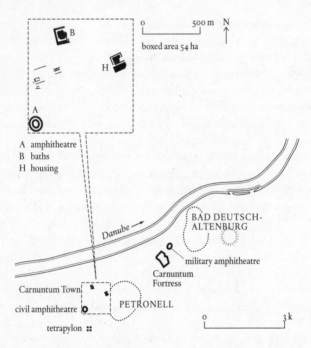

The topography of Carnuntum Fortress is distinct in that it was not only smaller than usual (sixteen hectares, compared to the eighteen to twenty hectares normal for a legionary base) but its plan was oddly skewed. However, it contains barracks for the full quota of ten cohorts, which suggests that its deviations from the norm are of little significance. More to the point is the scale of the surrounding cluster of buildings, considerably larger than most such suburbs. This could perhaps reflect an administrative role for the Fortress suburbs (*canabae*) before the building of Carnuntum Town.

The size and layout of Carnuntum Town are at present little known. With no part of the town wall discovered as yet, any figures must be speculative, but the uncovered remains are spread over an area of about fifty-four hectares, suggesting that the intramural figure was, at a minimum, about sixty hectares. If this is true, it was considerably bigger than its twin, AQUINCUM Town. That this is a real possibility is supported by the fact that the Carnuntum Town amphitheatre rivals the Carnuntum Fortress amphitheatre in size (the civil is 68 by 50 metres, the military 71 by 54 metres) whereas the Aquincum Town amphitheatre is notably smaller (the civil is 55 by 46 metres, the military 90 by 66 metres). Altogether it seems not unlikely that in its heyday, between AD 150 and 250, Carnuntum Town may have had a population of 5,000 or so.

South of the civil amphitheatre stand the ruins of a massive tetrapylon known now as the Heidentor ('Pagan Gate'). It is probably Constantinian, and therefore Christian, but no inscription has survived, and what it commemorated is unknown. It isn't a road-spanning arch of the usual type, because it has a plinth for a statue at its centre; it must be either triumphal, celebrating some victorious but as yet unidentified campaign, or funereal, honouring one of the less important members of the Constantinian dynasty.

CARTHAGE

Deserted site on the east side of the Cape Bon peninsula, Tunisia

Capital of the Carthaginian Empire, and from 29 BC of the Roman province of Africa Proconsularis; diocese: Africa (although technically outside the diocesan system)

History

Carthage was founded by colonists from the Phoenician city of Tyre, traditionally in 814 BC. This date could well be correct, because we know that the Phoenician enterprise in the western Mediterranean began at least two generations earlier than the wave of Greek colonization of the mid eighth century BC. On the other hand, the earliest material found on site is dated 725–700 BC, i.e. 100 years later. Either way, Carthage was a success from the start and by the late sixth century BC was so far ahead of the other Phoenician colonies in the West that it was able to impose its authority on them, creating what was for the time an extremely powerful maritime empire. This included southern Spain, the North African littoral region from TANGIER to LEPTIS MAGNA, the Balearics, Sardinia and the western end of Sicily. The rest of Sicily was Greek, but by the early third century BC the Carthaginians were getting the upper hand in the Greek sector too. Unfortunately, this brought them into conflict with ROME, and as a result of the ensuing war (the First Punic War, 264–241 BC) they lost Sicily, and Corsica and Sardinia to boot.

No longer dominant by sea, Carthage had to rethink its strategy. The result was a decision to transform itself from a maritime power to a continental one by expanding into the interior of Spain and creating a standing army there. This was the force that Hannibal marched across the Alps and into Italy at the start of the Second Punic War (218–202 BC). After many vicissitudes this also ended in defeat for Carthage, and this time the terms imposed by Rome were much harsher: Carthage lost everything except its Tunisian province and was saddled with an indemnity designed to impoverish it for fifty years to come.

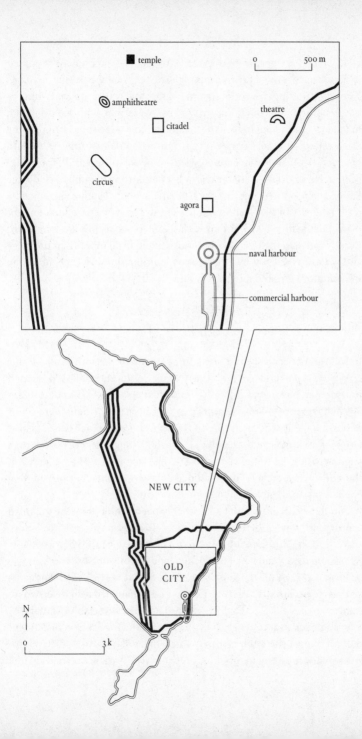

temple

amphitheatre

theatre

citadel

circus

agora

naval harbour

commercial harbour

0   500 m

NEW CITY

OLD
CITY

N

0   3 k

Despite these penalties, the years after the Second Punic War appear to have been the most prosperous in the history of Phoenician Carthage. The city's trading network remained intact and was soon flourishing as never before. The indemnity payments were met without difficulty; indeed it wasn't long before the Carthaginians were suggesting paying the total off at a quicker rate – an offer the Romans testily refused. In fact, the city's booming economy was to prove its downfall, for it suggested that one day Carthage might become strong enough to challenge Rome again, something that the Romans, who had suffered some blistering defeats in the Second Punic War, were not prepared to contemplate. On the flimsiest of pretexts, the Roman Senate initiated the Third Punic War (149–146 BC), which consisted in little more than the siege and sack of Carthage by a Roman expeditionary force. The surviving inhabitants were sold into slavery and the site left desolate.

Population

In its hour of greatest need, in its third and final war with Rome, Punic Carthage seems to have mobilized about 30,000 men. This is around the number ATHENS could raise if it called up all the males of military age in its territory. This suggests that Carthage and Athens were states of the same order of magnitude and maybe, although much less cogently, cities of a similar size as well. The second suggestion receives some support from the figure of 50,000 people said to have surrendered at the end of the siege. This included refugees from the surrounding countryside and implies a lower figure for the city.

A population of 10,000 had probably been achieved by the mid fifth century BC when Carthage acquired control of its hinterland; before that it is difficult to see it having more than the 7,000 to 8,000 people who could feed themselves by farming and fishing locally.

From 146–129 BC the site of Carthage was deserted; then Augustus settled 3,000 families on the spot and a Roman city took over where Punic Carthage had left off. It was probably over the 10,000 mark by AD 1 and back to 30,000 again by AD 150. It remained the second city of the West until the sixth century, when the collapse of Rome's population made it briefly number one. Of course, Carthage too had shrunk by this time, not just because of the general contraction of the Mediterranean economy but because it was losing control of its hinterland. By the time the Arabs arrived in 671, it was barely holding on to city status and it would have been well below the 10,000 mark when it finally fell to the invaders in 697.

Roman Carthage has been the object of an excavation programme sponsored by UNESCO that has gone some way to clarifying the history of the city. The walls of AD 425 enclose 325–50 hectares; if half the area was residential and the density was the same as at Athens, the population would have been near enough 50,600. On the other hand, if the relationship with ALEXANDRIA was similar to the relationship between Tunis and Cairo in the Ottoman period, we should probably look for slightly lower figures: perhaps 40,000 in the third century, falling to 30,000 by AD 400.

CHUR

Graubünden, Switzerland

Classical *Curia; possibly the administrative centre
of the late Roman province of Raetia Prima*

Chur is a small place with a moderately significant position on the route
across the Alps from Como to Lake Constance via the Julier Pass. The
Roman town was situated on the left bank of the Plessur, a tributary of
the Rhine, at the point around 590 metres (1,950 feet) above sea level
where the river emerges from the valley between the Pizokel and Mit-
tenberg hills. The settlement was tiny: its remains are restricted to an
eight to ten-hectare area and there is no evidence of any town wall or any
significant public works.

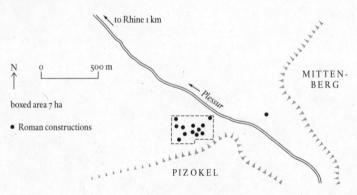

Medieval Chur developed on the opposite bank and was rather larger.
Even by 1900, however, the population only amounted to 11,532.

Chur owes its place in this gazetteer to the fact that it is the generally
favoured candidate for the position of the provincial capital of Raetia
Prima, the western half of the original province of Raetia. A 1991 survey
of Chur in Roman times concluded, however, that this proposition
remained 'neither disproved nor supported'.

CIRENCESTER

Gloucestershire, England

**Classical *Corinium; county town of the Dobunni
and capital of the late Roman province of
Britannia Prima***

The Dobunni, the Celtic tribe that inhabited the Severn Valley, accepted
Roman rule without fuss in A D 43. A generation later they abandoned their
tribal centre at Bagendon in favour of a new foundation five kilometres
(three miles) to the south, which became their 'civitas-capital', to use the
currently favoured term for a Roman county town. The original nucleus
was a pair of Roman forts set up in the 40s and occupied until the late 70s.
The new city quickly acquired a grandiose basilica, the second largest in the
country after L O N D O N's, and a large amphitheatre that can still be seen.

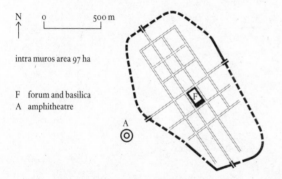

N   0   500 m

intra muros area 97 ha

F   forum and basilica
A   amphitheatre

During the third century A D the city was given a defensive wall. The
area enclosed, ninety-seven hectares, makes it the second largest town
in Roman Britain (London, with 135 hectares, was the largest). In Diocletian's reorganization of the provinces in the early fourth century it
became the seat of the governor of the new province of Britannia Prima.
The forum area was modified at this time, presumably to accommodate
the governor's entourage; the city, as judged by the number of mosaic

pavements installed in the early fourth century, was more prosperous than ever. A reasonable guess at the population would be somewhere in the region of 5,000.

Cirencester's prosperity seems to have lasted into the early fifth century, but the city must have declined rapidly thereafter. It has been suggested that such inhabitants as survived into the sixth century – and we are talking now of a few score, not a few thousand – may have taken refuge in the amphitheatre just outside the city wall. This structure, suitably fortified, is probably the 'city of Cirencester' that fell to the west Saxons after their victory over the Britons at Dyrham in 577.

COLCHESTER

Essex, England

Classical *Camulodunum; initial capital
of the province of Britain*

Colchester was the site of one of the first oppida of Celtic Britain, a proto-town with a small year-round population, but earthworks extensive enough to accommodate the entire tribal levy in times of emergency. Initially it served the local tribe, the Trinovantes, but in 10 BC the Trinovantes succumbed to their more powerful neighbours the Catuvellauni, and Camulodunum, to give the oppidum its Celtic name, became the seat of the Catuvellaunian king Cunobelinus (Shakespeare's Cymbeline). As such, it was the first objective of the Roman army in the invasion of Britain, for the Catuvellauni were sworn enemies of ROME, and determined to maintain both their own freedom and their grip on the other tribes in the south-east of England.

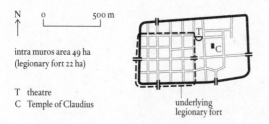

N   0   500 m

intra muros area 49 ha
(legionary fort 22 ha)

T   theatre
C   Temple of Claudius

underlying
legionary fort

The initial phase of the invasion under the emperor Claudius was a resounding success, Camulodunum falling on schedule in the summer of AD 43. Three of the four legions taking part in the campaign then redeployed to the unconquered parts of the country, leaving the Twentieth Legion in garrison at Camulodunum. The legion immediately set about building itself a fortress of standard size (twenty-two hectares) and shape.

In AD 49 or 50, the Twentieth Legion left the area and the fortress was made the nucleus of a Roman colony, initially for discharged veterans of the invasion force. It also became – we think – the seat of the new province's government. The urban area was more than doubled, to forty-nine hectares, and work was begun on a temple to Claudius, the emperor who had given the go-ahead for the invasion and had appeared in southern Britain in time to enter Camulodunum in triumph, on the back of an elephant. But a mere ten years after the Twentieth Legion had left, both temple and town were burned to the ground, when the Iceni of Norfolk rose in revolt under their queen, Boudicca. The revolt was crushed that same year and Colchester was able to start rebuilding almost immediately, but in the interim its capital status had gone for good. LONDON had proved to be a much more convenient base for the province's government, and Colchester, while keeping its rank as a Roman colony, became a backwater, a modest county town with no known history. It is also without significant visible remains of the Roman period, although some of the vaulted underpinnings of the Temple of Claudius survive beneath the town's Norman castle.

COLOGNE

Köln, Rhineland-Westphalia, Germany

Classical *Colonia Agrippinensis; capital of
the province of Lower Germany*

Cologne was built as a tribal centre for the Ubii, a German people who went over to the Romans when Caesar's legions appeared on the Rhine. This made them unpopular with their compatriots, and when the Romans decided not to advance their frontier beyond the river, the Ubii on the far side of it began to find life uncomfortable. Agrippa arranged for them to be resettled on the Roman (left) bank. There, an altar to the imperial cult became the focus of the nuclear settlement, hence Ara Ubiorum, the name under which the place is first recorded. In AD 50, Claudius raised it to colonial status as Colonia Claudia Ara Agrippinensium, which was later shortened to Colonia Agrippinensis, the title from which the modern forms Köln and Cologne are derived.

Cologne originally had two legions camped nearby and the headquarters of the Rhine flotilla a short distance upstream, so it started life with considerable economic advantages. It served as the headquarters of the army of Lower Germany, and when the civil province of Germania Inferior was created (*c.* AD 90) it became the seat of the provincial governor. Its position on the frontier meant that it had to be walled, and in keeping with its exceptional status it was given a splendid enceinte. The circuit measures nearly four kilometres (2.5 miles), and as the plan is not far from square the enclosed area is close to 100 hectares. The wall was reinforced with thirty towers and pierced by five major gates and four minor ones.

Cologne remained equally important under the later empire. Constantine built a bridge across the Rhine and a fort, Divitium, at its far end. One of the thousand-man legions of the period had its base in this fort. Despite this addition to the defences, however, the city fell to the Franks in 355, and it was only after his victory at Strasbourg that the emperor Julian was able to recover the city for the empire. Thereafter, the Romans kept to the left bank. The city finally fell into the hands of the Franks in 456.

Little is known about Roman Cologne apart from the line of its walls. The governor's palace, which included a fine audience hall, lay just inside and to the north of the east gate. The forum was near the centre, with the main baths to the south-west of it. Excavations in the north-eastern insulae have uncovered two fine houses, one embellished with the Dionysus mosaic that is the on-site centrepiece of the Römisch-Germanische Museum. During the Christian era the predecessor of the

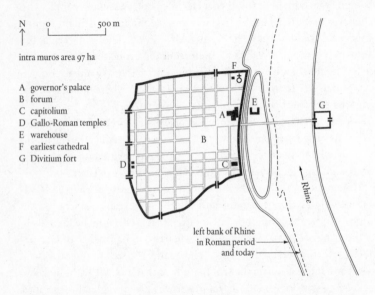

N   0   500 m

intra muros area 97 ha

A governor's palace
B forum
C capitolium
D Gallo-Roman temples
E warehouse
F earliest cathedral
G Divitium fort

left bank of Rhine
in Roman period
and today

Rhine

present cathedral was added, and building in this area continued into the sixth century. By then, however, Cologne had shrunk to a fraction of its former size and the place will have had the character typical of a Dark Age cathedral town, a huddle of ill-kept buildings confined to a corner of the original circuit.

This raises the question of how populous Cologne had been in its classical heyday. The area enclosed by the walls is an uncertain guide, for they were constructed early on when the Romans were full of confidence about their urban programme in Gaul. Nevertheless, what with the guaranteed input provided by the presence of the military and civil authorities, it would be unreasonable to put the population in AD 100 at less than 5,000. Something between 5,000 to 10,000 seems fair for the next two centuries, falling to the lower limit in the late fourth century and declining rapidly to the 1,000 mark in the early fifth century.

CONSTANTINOPLE

Present-day *Istanbul, Turkey*

Formerly *Byzantium*

History

Byzantium, the predecessor of Constantinople, was founded by Greeks, tradition says from Megara, sometime around the middle of the seventh century BC. The site they chose was a small promontory at the southern entrance of the Bosporus, on the left-hand (European) side. This was Thracian territory, and Byzantium is a Thracian name, but there seems to have been little or no friction between the Greek settlers and the Thracians who technically owned the land. If the Byzantines ever paid tribute to a Thracian prince, the sum would soon have become nominal.

The Greek colony prospered from the start, in marked contrast to Chalcedon, the Megaran settlement on the opposite side of the strait. Byzantium had a fine harbour, the famous 'Golden Horn', and the currents at the harbour mouth favoured its fishermen; the result was a prosperous tuna fishery – so much so that tuna were depicted prominently on the early coinage of the Byzantine mint. Chalcedon had no such advantages and was often mocked as a 'city of the blind' because its settlers had been the first to reach the area and yet managed to pick the inferior site.

By Greek standards Byzantium was a considerable place, strong enough to have a serious stab at maintaining its independence, although not quite strong enough to hold out against the real heavies. Incorporated in the Persian and Athenian empires, it recovered its freedom during the Hellenistic period, when it was slightly to one side of the great powers' main areas of interest. This interlude ended with the arrival of Roman troops in the region and the imposition of a protectorate that finally made Byzantium one of the subordinate towns of the Roman province of Thrace. (It was not the provincial capital, a role that was taken by PERINTHOS, ninety kilometres (sixty miles) to the west). Throughout this period – and we are talking of 700 years here, the whole period from the fifth century BC to the second century AD – it retained much the same position in the local urban ranking. The trend was undoubtedly up, moving slowly and steadily, except for a brief downturn when the city fathers picked the wrong side in the Roman civil war of AD 193–7. This was eventually won by Septimius Severus, who, annoyed by the way Byzantium had held out against him, had its leading men executed and its walls slighted. His son Caracalla pleaded the town's case, and eventually Severus relented. In fact he decided to honour it with a new set of walls and, on the south side, a state-of-the-art hippodrome for chariot racing.

Byzantium, even as embellished by Severus, was still a pretty unremarkable place: at the top end of the range for average towns, but without the necessary economic or administrative propellant to get up into the major league. The missing something was supplied by Constantine the Great, who became sole ruler of the Roman Empire in AD 324. By this time the empire had been split into two for administrative purposes – a Latin-speaking west and a Greek-speaking east – and normal practice was for each half to have its own emperor. Constantine didn't intend to share power with anyone, but he didn't dispute the reality of the division and, as he wanted to reside in the east, he decided to create what it had hitherto lacked, a capital of equal standing to ROME. He picked Byzantium as the ideal location for the new metropolis. Building began in 324 and colonists were soon flocking in, attracted by Constantine's offer of free rations for anyone who built a house in his 'New Rome'. Six years after work started, an official ceremony declared New Rome open for business.

After his death in 335, Constantine's city was renamed in his honour and the title New Rome disappeared from all but ecclesiastical documents. A century later, when a survey was made of Constantinople's amenities, it had most of the buildings appropriate for a capital city: an imperial palace; a large number of grand houses for the nobility, the members of the court and the officers of the administration; a cathedral; a senate house; a hippodrome to rival Rome's Circus Maximus; and

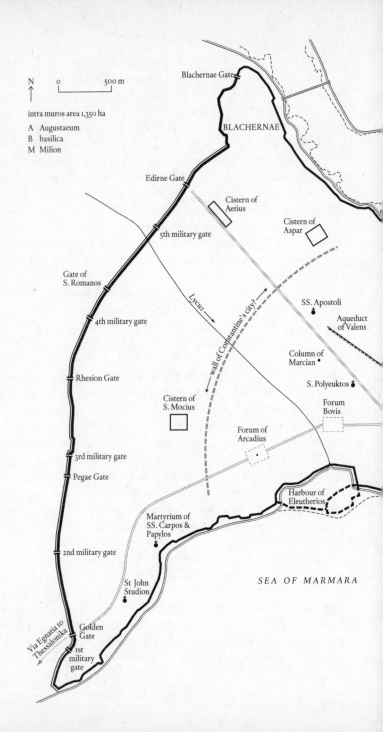

N

0   500 m

intra muros area 1,350 ha

A Augustaeum
B basilica
M Milion

Blachernae Gate

BLACHERNAE

Edirne Gate

Cistern of
Aetius

Cistern of
Aspar

5th military gate

Gate of
S. Romanos

Lycus

wall of Constantine's city?

SS. Apostoli

Aqueduct
of Valens

4th military gate

Column of
Marcian

Rhesion Gate

S. Polyeuktos

Cistern of
S. Mocius

Forum
Bovis

3rd military gate

Pegae Gate

Forum of
Arcadius

Harbour of
Eleutherios

Martyrium of
SS. Carpos &
Papylos

2nd military gate

SEA OF MARMARA

St John
Studion

Vïa Egnatia to
Thessalonika

Golden
Gate

1st
military
gate

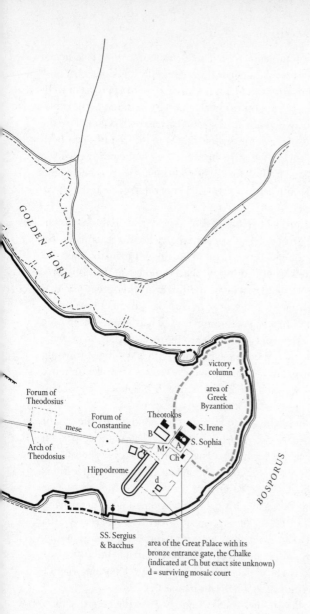

GOLDEN HORN

victory column

area of Greek Byzantion

Forum of Theodosius

Forum of Constantine

mese

Theotokos

B

M

A

S. Irene

S. Sophia

Ch

Arch of Theodosius

Hippodrome

d

BOSPORUS

SS. Sergius & Bacchus

area of the Great Palace with its bronze entrance gate, the Chalke (indicated at Ch but exact site unknown) d = surviving mosaic court

some impressive monumental fora. There was, however, still sufficient open space to allow for further growth, and initially it is somewhat puzzling to find the authorities suddenly deciding to build a new set of walls a kilometre or more west of the original boundary of the city. The explanation has nothing to do with any expected increase in population: the idea was to provide extra resources for the city in the case of siege, both in terms of water (several vast cisterns were built in the newly enclosed area) and grazing land for livestock. The additional area was never built over and in the fifteenth century was still being referred to as the *chora*, meaning countryside.

Constantinople probably reached its classical peak in the sixth century, during the reign of the emperor Justinian, who was responsible for its most famous monument. Early on in his reign, Justinian's rule had been severely tested when rioting by the Hippodrome factions progressed to looting, general mayhem, and finally a widespread fire that destroyed Constantine's cathedral of S. Sophia. Justinian rose to the challenge in splendid style. As soon as order had been restored, he directed his architects to draw up plans not for the usual basilican structure but for a vast, centrally planned edifice with a sky-high crowning dome. No expense was to be spared, no delay tolerated. And within five years the emperor was able to enter the new S. Sophia and say, with every justification, 'Solomon, I have surpassed you.'

S. Sophia was not Justinian's only project; he rebuilt two other major Constantinian churches, SS. Apostoli (the burial place of the emperors) and S. Irene (alongside S. Sophia), and he constructed some new ones of his own. In the political sphere he launched numerous expeditions intended to recover the lost western provinces, even though he was already at war with Persia and his cabinet was unanimous in advising restraint. In the end he seriously overstrained the resources of the empire, and this at a time when they were probably contracting anyway. The end result was an economic collapse, which put an end to any further growth on Constantinople's part. At a local level matters weren't helped by a serious outbreak of bubonic plague in 541.

Worse was to follow in the seventh century. First the Persians, then the Arabs overran Syria and Egypt, and the supply of wheat needed to sustain the capital's population at its existing level came to an abrupt stop. Numbers must have dropped rapidly over the next generations, and the situation continued to deteriorate in the early eighth century. In 717 an Arab army arrived by sea and laid siege to the city; the garrison managed to hold off these attacks and eventually the Arabs withdrew, but they left behind a city that was just a shadow of its once great self. The aqueduct of Valens, the mainstay of the city's water supply, lay derelict, no longer needed by such citizens as remained. Against all Roman practice, graves were being dug within the city precincts, indeed within the inner perimeter drawn by Constantine. Both the empire and its metropolis seemed to be in terminal decline.

Against expectation the empire survived, and its capital recovered. A plague attack in 747 hit Constantinople hard but proved to be the last in the series that had begun 200 years earlier. In 756 new settlers brought in from the Greek islands replenished the city's population, and in 767 the aqueduct of Valens was refurbished for their use. The empire's frontiers stabilized. Slowly the city took on its old imperial role again. There were to be no new buildings on the scale of H.[agia] Sophia (S. changes to H. as Greek replaces Latin), but at least the resources were once again available to maintain the cathedral's structure properly and even add the occasional embellishment.

The years either side of AD 1000 marked the peak of this recovery. The Byzantine Empire, as historians term this revived version of the Eastern Roman Empire, never attained the frontiers of its predecessor – the loss of Syria and Egypt to Islam proved permanent – but its possessions in Europe and Anatolia were considerable and seemed secure; the Arabs, it transpired, had shot their bolt. However, in the 1050s a new enemy appeared in the shape of the Turk. Recent converts to Islam, the Turks brought new enthusiasm and, as a migrating people, a new demographic thrust to warfare on the empire's eastern border. In 1071, at the Battle of Manzikert, they inflicted a catastrophic defeat on the Byzantine army, which opened the way for Turkish tribes to move on to the Anatolian plateau. This movement all but eliminated the Asian half of the empire. Help arrived in the form of the Crusades, but the Crusaders' aid turned to gall in 1204 with the Fourth Crusade's seizure and sack of Constantinople. A westerner was placed on the throne of what became, for a brief period (1204–61), the Latin Empire. Eventually the Byzantines recovered their capital along with most of the remaining parts of the empire, but in the interval the Turks had grown ever stronger. In 1354 a contingent of Ottoman Turks crossed the Dardanelles and began conquering the European provinces. The process was near enough complete by 1401 when the Ottoman sultan Bayezid made preliminary moves against Constantinople, now a capital without an empire. The city was saved when Bayezid was overthrown by another eastern potentate, the mighty Timur, but the respite was only temporary. Within fifty years the Ottomans had rebuilt their position, and in 1453, under the eye of the young sultan Mehmet II, the long-overdue assault on the isolated city began. The land walls, never breached in their thousand-year history, crumbled before the Turkish guns, the elite janissary regiments stormed through the gap, followed shortly after by Mehmet himself – now Mehmet Fatih, 'Mohammed the Conqueror'. H. Sophia became a mosque, and Constantinople one of the capitals of Islam.

Mehmet was determined to restore Constantine's city to greatness. He cleared away the ruined Church of the Apostles and constructed the colossal Fatih Mosque on the site. He built two palaces, the first overlapping the Forum of Theodosius, the second and more ambitious one on the First Hill where Greek Byzantium had stood. The earlier Eski Saray ('Old Palace') has disappeared, but the later complex developed into the Topkapı Palace of today. More importantly, by a mixture of incentive and compulsion, Mehmet raised the city's population from somewhere around 30,000 on the eve of the siege to perhaps 75,000 at the close of his reign in 1481. This makes it not unlikely that by the end of the century the number of Constantinopolitans had reached 100,000, more than ever before. In fact the great days of the city lay in the future, not the past.

Names

Constantinople, present-day Istanbul, has had four names in all. From its foundation in the mid seventh century BC to the beginning of the fourth century AD it was called Byzantium (strictly Byzantion). With Constantine's refoundation it became first New Rome (alternatively Second Rome), then, after his death, Constantinople. Some 1,100 years later, in the early fifteenth century, we find the locals beginning to refer to it as Istanbul. This entirely unofficial name is a contraction of the Greek phrase *eis ton bolin* ('to the city') and was used in a manner analogous to the American term 'downtown'. After the Turkish conquest it became the everyday name, although it did not become the city's official title until 1927. A version of it, Stamboul, is sometimes used to indicate the Old City, the area within the triangle formed by the land walls, the Golden Horn and the Sea of Marmara.

The adjectives used to describe the emperor and his empire are even more various. Historians talk of the Eastern Roman emperor and the Eastern Roman Empire, which is fair enough when there were two halves, but is redundant after the fall of the west in AD 476. As far as the (Eastern) Romans were concerned, the surviving part was the Roman Empire *tout court*. The reason historians like to keep the qualifying adjective is sensible enough – the common language of the east was Greek not Latin – and became stronger with the passage of time. The culmination of this process was the substitution of Greek for Latin in official documents, an event that coincides with the reign of the emperor Heraclius (610–41). Historians mark the changeover by introducing the term 'Byzantine' and applying it to both emperor and empire from the seventh century on. Byzantine is certainly a useful term, but it was never used in this sense by the Byzantines themselves; they continued to call themselves and their empire Roman. (A Byzantine for them was an inhabitant of Constantinople.) Of course, they also recognized the term 'Greek', and in the medieval period westerners were as likely to call them Greeks as Romans. The much reduced empire of this period was usually referred to as Romania.

Walls

The walls as they exist today are known as the Theodosian Walls, because, with the exception of the Blachernae sector and some stretches of the sea walls, the entire circuit was built during the reign of the emperor Theodosius II (408–50). Blachernae was the site of the only bridge across the Golden Horn, and had doubtless come into existence because of that fact. In Constantine's day, when the city wall of New Rome stopped well short of Blachernae, it was a discrete township with its own walls. When in 413 Theodosius decided to build a new set of walls for Constantinople, he made Blachernae the starting point for a land wall that ran south to a point on the Sea of Marmara nearly six kilometres (3.6 miles) distant. The salient at the northern end of the land wall corresponds to the western half of Blachernae's town wall; the rest of the wall follows a near straight line across the peninsula. In 439, with the land wall and its many towers completed, work began on a set of sea walls to protect the shoreline of the city on both its northern face, along the Golden Horn, and its southern aspect, fronting the Sea of Marmara. Shortly after, in 447, an earthquake severely damaged the land wall; it was rebuilt, this time in the form of a double line of walls, in the space of two months. The fact that Attila the Hun was sacking cities throughout the Balkans that year was undoubtedly responsible for the urgency, but the speed of construction didn't diminish the effectiveness of the work. Constantinople's land walls were to remain unbreached for the next 1,000 years.

During this period the line of the sea walls was modified, as silting extended the shoreline, most notably at the mouth of the Lycus on the Marmara shore. This raised the intramural area from the 1,350 hectares of late antiquity to a final figure, on the eve of the Turkish conquest, of some 1,385 hectares. The Blachernae wall was also rebuilt on several occasions, so that from being initially the weakest sector, it became the strongest. Otherwise the walls remained essentially the same. The plan doesn't show the numerous gates in the sea walls that could be supplemented, or bricked up, as occasion demanded. It does, however, show the major gates in the land walls, which were permanent structures. Two sorts need to be distinguished: the city gates, which led to the outside world; and the military gates, which only gave access to the space between the walls. There were six city gates and five military gates. In 1453 the city fell when the Turks bombarded, destroyed and then carried the section of the outer wall opposite the fifth military gate.

The Theodosian Walls were preceded by two smaller circuits of which nothing remains: the wall of late Greek/early Roman Byzantium, and the wall of Constantinople as originally laid out by Constantine the Great. The wall of Byzantium will have followed the contours of the hill that formed the tip of the peninsula – the First Hill of Constantinople's seven (see p. 111) – and though there is no archaeological support for it, the perimeter shown on the plan probably isn't too far from the truth. In that case it will have enclosed an area of seventy to seventy-five hectares.

The line suggested for Constantine's wall is far more problematical. It represents the modern consensus, but an equally good case could be made for a less ambitious circuit crossing the peninsula one to one and a half kilometres further east. This would put the Church of the Apostles, the emperors' mausoleum, outside the city, something that accords better with Roman practice, for although emperors could, if they chose to, ignore the prohibition on burial within the walls, it was considered good manners not to, as with Hadrian's mausoleum in Rome.

Topography and Monuments

The original Greek settlement occupied the part of the First Hill where the Topkapı Palace now stands. As time passed – very slowly, we're talking centuries here – the town spread south until it finally came to cover the entire hill. We read of temples to Athena, Apollo and Poseidon, and of two theatres, large and small, but no trace of any of these buildings has ever been found. Of Byzantium's walls, all that is recorded is the name of one gate (the Thracian Gate), which opened out on to a flat area (the Thracian Field), which can only be the ground on the top of the ridge between First and Second Hills. In fact nothing remains of the Greek city at all. All we can say is that, given the history of slow growth over a long period of time and the sloping edges of the site, its plan was probably pretty much of a jumble; certainly the fifth-century *Description* refers to 'streets and alleys' in this part of the city (First and Second regions) where in the other regions the same item is simply headed 'streets'.

The first significant Roman addition to Byzantium's amenities was the hippodrome donated by Septimius Severus at the beginning of the third century AD. This lay outside the walls of the Greek city, which the emperor had first slighted (following the long siege of the city in 193–6), then restored, maybe even enlarged. But whatever Severus' benefactions were, they were completely overshadowed a century later, when Constantine chose Byzantium as the site of his New Rome. The area immediately north of the hippodrome – presumably part of the old Thracian Field – was laid out as a monumental plaza, the Augustaeum, with, at or near its centre, the Milion, the Golden Milestone from which all distances in the Eastern Empire were measured. A palace for the emperor was built parallel with the eastern side of the hippodrome. And the hippodrome itself was enormously enlarged, which, as the ground fell away sharply at this point, meant that massive substructures had to be built to support its far end. Constantine also monumentalized the first section of the main road that ran west from the Milion, lining it with porticos, and providing it with a focal point in the shape of a circular or oval forum with a colossal porphyry column at its centre. Needless to say, the column was topped off with a figure of Constantine and the forum was named for him too.

Although Constantine was determined to make his New Rome a match for 'old' Rome, he was also keen to emphasize the key difference between the two: his capital was to be a Christian city from the start. So he built a senate house on the north side of his forum, and a basilica just north of the Augustaeum, but no equivalents of the great temples of pagan Rome. Instead there was a vast cathedral, S. Sophia, not finished until 360, in the reign of his son Constantius, and an equally large church on the edge of town, SS. Apostoli, intended to serve as a mausoleum for the emperor and his dynasty.

The last of the Constantinian emperors was Julian the Apostate, who died while campaigning against the Persians in 363. A successor, Valens, had time to build one of the major monuments of Constantinople, an aqueduct spanning the valley between the Fourth and Third Hills, before he too lost his life – and, more importantly, his army – battling against the Goths in 378. The empire made a reasonable recovery from this disaster and the soldier-emperor Theodosius the Great (379–95) was able to pass it on to his sons Honorius (who got the West), and Arcadius (who got Constantinople and the East). Arcadius was succeeded by Theodosius II (408–50). Between them the Theodosians brought the plan of the city to its final form, for although subsequent emperors added new buildings and rebuilt old ones, they didn't change the city's essential plan. The main road running west from the Milion has already been mentioned; some way beyond the forum of Constantine it divided into two, a northern branch running along the crest of the Fourth, Fifth and Sixth Hills, and a southern branch running parallel to the Marmara coast and crossing the Seventh Hill. The elder Theodosius' contribution to the city plan was a very grand Forum at the site of

Hills and Regions

Constantine wanted his New Rome to have everything 'old' Rome had, and that included seven hills and fourteen regions. Regions – administrative districts – were simple enough to organize, but natural features are a bit more difficult to conjure up and Constantinople's seven hills don't exactly leap to the eye. What the city certainly has is a central ridge, running from Seraglio Point at the Bosporus end, to the Edirne Gate. Six of the nominated hills are simply high points on this ridge, with the First overlooking the Bosporus and the Sixth just inside the Edirne Gate, the highest point in the city. The Seventh Hill occupies the south-west quarter of the city, separated from the Fourth, Fifth and Sixth Hills by the valley of the Lycus. The hills along the crest of the ridge are defined not so much

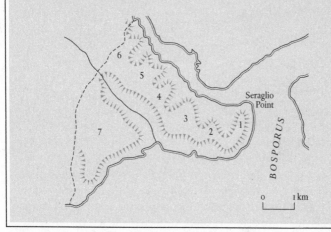

the bifurcation. It was a conscious imitation of Trajan's forum in Rome, and had a similar column with narrative reliefs as its centrepiece, plus a triumphal arch of idiosyncratic design at its western entrance. He also built another, more orthodox arch on the southern road, at a point where it left the city limits and became the Via Egnatia, the military highway that ran across the Balkans to the Adriatic. This arch was later incorporated into the Theodosian Walls, of which it became the Golden Gate. Theodosius' son Arcadius built a forum too, on the southern

by the saddles between them, which are often barely perceptible, as by the valleys running up to the ridge, particularly on the north side.

The main interest of the regions is that they show the way the population of the city was distributed. To judge by the number of streets in each region, more than 80 per cent of Constantinopolitans lived on the First, Second and Third Hills, i.e. in the eastern

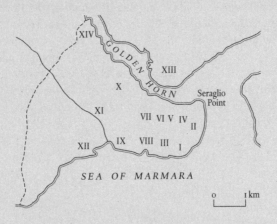

third of the intramural area. Looking at the same data in a north versus south sense (as opposed to west versus east), a similar percentage lived in the regions that bordered the Golden Horn, compared to 20 per cent in the regions fronting the Sea of Marmara. The *Description of Constantinople* from which these statistics are derived dates from the reign of Theodosius II (408–50), but so far as we can tell the pattern was pretty much the same when the city fell to the Ottomans 1,000 years later.

branch of the main road; like his father's it had a column with spiral reliefs, although, unlike his father, Arcadius had no real victories to celebrate. Add the wall of Theodosius II, and the enterprise on which Constantine had embarked 124 years earlier was effectively complete.

How much remains of the early Christian city? Very little from Constantine's day. The outlines of the Augustaeum and of his forum have

The *Description of Constantinople* gives the names of the important buildings, the number of streets, of substantial houses, and of officials for each of the fourteen regions of the city. Two of the regions were on the edge of the Constantinian city, eleven on the Fourth Hill and twelve on the Seventh. Two more were certainly beyond it: the settlement of Sycae on the northern side of the Golden Horn (Region 13) and, on the south side but much further west, the enclave of Blachernae (Region 14). Blachernae, which had its own walls, was the site of the only bridge across the Horn, and had doubtless come into existence because of that fact. The remaining ten regions were situated on the first three of the city's hills, with extensions to the west along the Marmara and Golden Horn shores. Judging from the number of its streets, this area contained nearly 90 per cent of the city's population; on the other hand it contained only just over 60 per cent of the houses of the better off, who clearly preferred the less crowded suburbs.

The *Description* is more than somewhat maddening, as it doesn't use the same categories as the Roman *Notitia Dignitatum*, ignoring the basic housing units (*insulae*) and only giving figues for the superior sort (*domus*). Even they must be defined differently because there are far too many of them by comparison with Rome (4,388, compared to 1,790). In fact, it is very difficult to wring any population data out of the *Description*, although as previously noted the number of streets in each region does give a picture of the population's distribution. Perhaps there is an order of magnitude to be obtained from the probability that Regions 1 and 2, the old Greek city of Byzantium, contained about 10,000 people and that therefore the other twelve regions between them may have contained 60,000 people, making 70,000 in all.

been lost in the many rebuildings the city has undergone; no trace remains of his city wall. His Great Palace on the First Hill was abandoned by the later Byzantine emperors, who preferred Blachernae; it was in ruins long before the Turkish conquest, and there is nothing to be seen there today except for a few mosaic floors. All three of his major churches, S. Sophia, S. Irene and SS. Apostoli, were replaced by new versions in Justinian's reign. His column is still standing, but as a forlorn stump. In fact the most impressive relic of Constantine's building programme is the eroded brickwork cliff that holds up the southern end of the hippodrome.

The Theodosian works have survived considerably better. Theodosius the Great's Golden Gate is still there, embedded in his grandson's wall. Fragments of his other triumphal arch are scattered by the side of the road that runs across the site of his forum, and there are a couple of reliefs from his column built into a neighbouring Turkish bath. The base of Arcadius' column remains *in situ*. And the walls of Theodosius II still gird the city, the one feature of the New Rome that is a genuine match for the 'old'.

Population

When he started work on his new capital, Constantine the Great had at his disposal a supply of wheat sufficient for 80,000 people, this being the amount that Egypt had previously shipped to Rome and was now, because of the decline in Rome's population, available for alternative use. Constantine diverted the Egyptian grain fleet to his New Rome, where he offered free rations – in perpetuity – to anyone who was prepared to set up house there. As a result the population of Constantinople had reached 40,000 within a few years of his death. His son Constantius seems to have decided that this was enough, and cut the number of rations accordingly. Theodosius I raised the total by a trifling amount (perhaps 400 rations), but we have no record of the figure of 80,000 being restored in full, although it is quoted by several later authors as if it had been. So for the heyday of Roman Constantinople – the fifth century and the first half of the sixth – we have alternative population figures of 40,000 and 80,000. The lower figure is surely preferable, for if Egypt was still shipping out 80,000 rations – a dubious proposition given that the country was probably experiencing the same contraction of resources suffered by other provinces during this period – then the two *praesental* armies (the forces stationed in the immediate vicinity of the capital, probably numbering about 15,000 each) will have had first call on whatever was available.

Certainly, later emperors had no interest in boosting the city's population, Justinian going so far as to employ a special officer to ensure that provincials returned home as soon as they had completed their business in the metropolis. By this time the contraction of resources already alluded to was really beginning to bite. A fall in numbers began, initiated by the plague of 542, but continued after its passing. Early in the next century the loss of Egypt, first to the Persians, then to the Arabs, meant that there were, after 618, no more free rations. Population figures will have slumped accordingly, to somewhere in the region of 15,000 to 20,000. This was just enough to mount a successful defence against the small armies fielded by the Avars and Persians in the early seventh century and the maritime expeditions launched by the Arabs in the seventh and early eighth centuries.

From the mid eighth century on, things began to get a bit better, and we can accept a slow recovery to 30,000 by the year 1000. As 30,000 or thereabouts is the figure for the city's population when it fell to the Turks in 1453, the corollary is that the trend towards larger urban populations characteristic of the later medieval period (the eleventh to fifteenth centuries) compensated for Constantinople's rapidly diminishing political clout.

In 1477, a quarter-century after the Ottoman conquest, Mehmet II ordered a house count to find out whether his drive to increase the population of his new capital was succeeding or not. He was reassured to find that it had more than doubled, to a total of 65,000. If it continued to grow at the same rate – and we have no reliable figures for the sixteenth century – it would have been well over the 100,000 mark in 1500. Across the Golden Horn on its northern shore, the district of Galata was growing much faster than Stamboul during this period, and it continued to do so subsequently. The first proper census, taken in 1927, showed 691,000 in the city as a whole, but only 200,000 in Stamboul. This figure, incidentally, makes it exceedingly unlikely that late classical or medieval Constantinople ever held anything like this number, for by the 1920s Stamboul was almost entirely built over, something it had never been in its earlier incarnations.

CORDOBA

Cordoba province, Spain

Classical *Corduba; capital of the province of Far Spain,
and of its successor Baetica; diocese: the Spains*

In the closing years of the Second Punic War, control of eastern and southern Spain passed from CARTHAGE to ROME, the east becoming the province of Near Spain (Hispania Citerior), and the south the province of Far Spain (Hispania Ulterior). Cordoba, in Far Spain, is first mentioned in 152 BC when the Roman general Marcus Claudius Metellus wintered there. In the course of the second half of the century it emerged as the administrative centre of the province.

Roman Cordoba has little recorded history. Its position as a provincial capital was confirmed by Augustus when he reorganized the peninsula sometime around 15 BC, although the name of its province was changed from Far Spain to Baetica (after the River Baetis, today's Guadalquivir). It was to retain this status to the end of the empire. As to topography, it is clear that the town was built in two stages: the first set back from the Guadalquivir, with its street grid on a north–south axis; the second filling in the area between the original town and the river, its streets following the line of the riverbank. The extension, covering thirty hectares, compared to the forty-six hectares of the original town, is generally ascribed to Augustus. The forum was, as might be expected, at the centre of the old town: the theatre and amphitheatre, extramural in their original forms, will have become intramural when the town was extended. The original circus, on the east side of town, was always extramural. It seems to have been abandoned in the second century, and replaced by a new one on the west side.

In the late third century there were signs that Cordoba was declining. The theatre was no longer in use and the temple by the east gate had been abandoned. But the imperial administration remained powerful, and resources were found to build a very grand palace to the west of the town. This presumably became the seat of the provincial governor, depriving Cordoba town of part of its economic *raison d'être*. In fact by the late fourth century Roman Cordoba's population had effectively split into two halves; the palace on the north-west and an urban element now limited to the riverside sector. The upper town – the original foundation – seems to have been entirely abandoned.

An interesting aside: early Arab sources indicate that an interior wall separating the upper and lower towns, of which no trace has yet been discovered, was still standing in their day. This could be the south wall

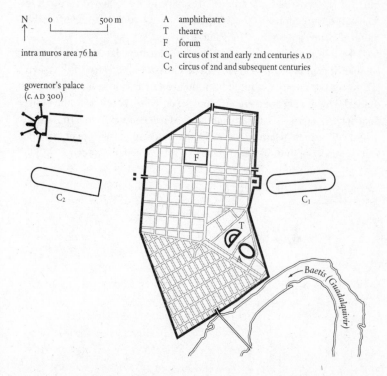

N   0   500 m

intra muros area 76 ha

governor's palace
(*c.* AD 300)

C₂

C₁

F

T

A

Baetis (Guadalquivir)

A   amphitheatre
T   theatre
F   forum
C₁ circus of 1st and early 2nd centuries AD
C₂ circus of 2nd and subsequent centuries

of the original town, brought into use again as the north wall of the riverside settlement, or – perhaps more likely – it could be a new structure serving the same purpose.

Cordoba fell to the Visigoths in the fifth century AD. It was briefly recaptured by the emperor Justinian in the mid sixth century, only to be lost again in 584. It is unlikely to have fared well under Visigothic rule, and was probably a poor place when the Arabs invaded the peninsula in the early eighth century. Nonetheless the Arabs were sufficiently impressed by its site, its remains and its reputation to make it their capital in 720. A new period of prosperity began, eclipsing anything experienced in the Roman period. Twenty-one suburban districts brought the total inhabited area up to near 300 hectares, almost four times the Roman figure. The Great Mosque, originally built to hold 5,000 worshippers, was progressively enlarged until, by the year 1000, it had room for five times as many. While the rest of Europe dragged through its Dark Age, the caliphs of Cordoba could boast a capital that comfortably outranked any city in the Christian West.

The first population figure we have for Cordoba dates from the early sixteenth century, 300 years after the Christian recovery of the town. This puts the number of inhabitants at around 25,000, a total that grew only slowly during the sixteenth and seventeenth centuries. The figure may have been much the same in the eleventh century, when the star of Islamic Cordoba began to wane. That would imply (with many ifs and buts) a peak population for Roman Cordoba of around 5,000.

CORINTH

Corinthia, Greece

History

In the early classical period, the eighth and seventh centuries BC, Corinth was regarded as the leading place in Greece. Few commentators have been able to resist the idea that this exceptional status was linked to its position on the nipped-in waist of the Greek peninsula; traffic through and across this isthmus must surely have been the factor that gave Corinth its head start. In support of this thesis is the fact that around 600 BC the Corinthians built a paved road across the isthmus, and the assumption that they would have made this investment only if there was already a useful transit trade in existence. Maybe so, but by every other indication Corinth, far from facing both ways, always looked westwards. It was in the west that Corinthian merchants sought the wheat they needed to support the homeland's population, it was there that they founded colonies – including such famous examples as Corcyra (Corfu) and SYRACUSE – where they could decant their surplus population. And it was to western markets, sometimes as far afield as CARTHAGE and Etruria, that they sent the export wares that balanced the city's budget. Corinth's position at the head of the Corinthian gulf made it the starting point for the swiftest, safest journey between Old Greece and Great Greece (Sicily and southern Italy); the fact that the Aegean lapped the Corinthians' back door seems of little relevance in their history.

In the middle of the sixth century BC, Corinth town was displaced from its position at the top of the Greek urban hierarchy by ATHENS. As Athens probably had no more than 5,000 people at the time, this is the ballpark figure for Corinth too. It fits with what we know about the tiny scale of urban life in early classical Greece, and if Corinth got a little bigger as the Greek economy expanded in the course of the next half century, it is unlikely ever to have had 10,000 inhabitants. In fact, Corinth played only a modest part in the dramas of the fifth century BC. By this time, incidentally, the Diolkos, the paved road across the isthmus, had clearly lost whatever significance it may have had previously. Ships had become bigger and their captains more confident, taking voyages around the south of the peninsula.

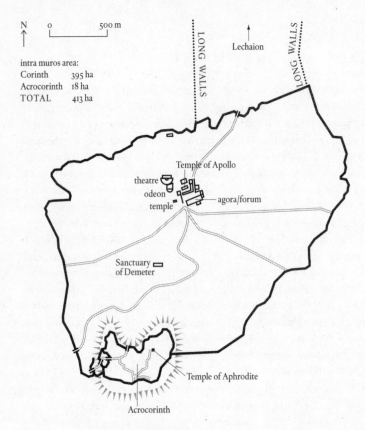

Corinth's isthmian position now conferred on it another role. Philip of Macedon aspired to rule all Greece, and in 338 BC, by winning the Battle of Chaeronea, he was able to fulfil this ambition. Corinth, lying at the entrance point to the Peloponnese, was the obvious place to plant a

Macedonian garrison. Consequently, Acrocorinth, the citadel on the hill overlooking Corinth proper, became one of the three 'fetters of Greece', the strong points that ensured Macedonian control of the peninsula. (The others were PIRAEUS and Demetrias, the latter a castle in Thessaly.) The Romans, after defeating the Antigonid kingdom and inheriting its hegemony, made Corinth the meeting place of the Achaean League. It was at the nearby Isthmus that the Roman general Flaminius proclaimed Greek freedom. The following decades saw uneasy coexistence between the Achaeans and Roman hegemony, or at least influence, in Greece. The ultimate outcome was a revolt by the Achaean League against the Romans. The war ended in disaster for the league, and for Corinth. In 146 BC the Roman general Lucius Mummius not only sacked the city, he razed it and left it an uninhabited ruin.

Exactly 100 years later, Julius Caesar decided to rebuild Corinth. The task was taken over by his heir, the future emperor Augustus, who justified the expenditure by making the restored city the capital of his new province of Achaea (central and southern Greece, previously part of the province of Macedonia). Although Greece was not what it had been in its classical heyday, the focusing of its government on a single city meant that Roman Corinth quickly outstripped its Greek predecessor. The town gained the series of buildings needed for its administrative functions, plus temples for the imperial cult, baths, theatres and Greece's only amphitheatre. With the arrival of Christianity it also acquired the appropriate complement of churches. Corinth appears to have survived the troubles of the later empire reasonably well – there is no sign of the sudden collapse that occurred at Athens in the late third century AD – and it probably retained much of its population until well into the fifth century. The sixth century saw a rapid dwindling, and although Corinth became the capital of the Byzantine theme of Hellas, by then the population was numbered in the tens rather than the hundreds and confined to the hilltop fortress of Acrocorinth. The site of the town itself was deserted by this time, and remains so today.

Population

There are no useful data for Corinth town, although there are a few pointers for the population of Corinthia, town and country taken together. The main evidence is the Corinthian contribution to the Greek army at Plataea in 479 BC, presumably a maximum effort; this consisted of 5,000 hoplites, half the number contributed by Athens, and implying a total population of around 60,000. As Corinthia was less than a third the size of Attica, the density will have been considerably higher (roughly seventy, compared to forty-five, per square kilometre), which would explain why the Corinthians had difficulty feeding themselves at this period. As for Corinth town, as it had no special inputs, there is no reason to attribute anything out of the ordinary to it as regards numbers. A figure of around 5,000 is a reasonable guesstimate for the period 500–146 BC.

Roman Corinth was certainly more populous. The inputs associated with the business of administering Achaea may well have sustained a population on or over the 10,000 mark. In support of this are the public buildings, which are on a considerable scale and are spread over a wide area. But perhaps the most convincing evidence for a population of this exceptional order is the extensive perimeter of the late Roman wall (possibly built *c.* AD 300). This encloses 145 hectares, making Roman Corinth nearly two-thirds the size of classical Athens. Walls are not normally a very good way of judging the number of inhabitants in a place – classical Greek towns often had tiny populations nestling inside walls that ran up the surrounding hills and across empty valleys (witness Corinth itself) – but in the late empire the Romans usually built tight circuits, defending what had to be defended but not much more. No one is suggesting that Corinth town contained two thirds of Athens's fifth-century BC population, i.e. 23,000 people, but, given the town's administrative status and physical remains, 10,000 seems acceptable for the period AD 1–300, and maybe on to AD 500.

CTESIPHON

On the River Tigris, Iraq

History

When the Parthians took Mesopotamia from the Seleucids in 141 BC, the provincial capital was the Greek town of SELEUCIA ON THE TIGRIS. The Parthians, who were a pastoral people, had little interest in towns, and none at all in disturbing the status quo, so Seleucia carried on as if nothing had happened. History was repeating itself here: the previous Iranian rulers of the region, the Achaemenids (Persians), had let Babylon continue as the local metropolis; indeed they had made it their winter capital. Attracted by Mesopotamia's mild winter climate, the Arsacid (Parthian) monarchs did the same as regards Seleucia, except that they didn't actually move into the city. They stopped opposite it, on the eastern bank of the Tigris. That way they were able to benefit from the support systems of the capital, while still enjoying the open-air lifestyle that was the hallmark of the Iranian ruling class. This east-bank encampment was known as Ctesiphon. Most of the year it was no more than a village.

By the second century AD, the Arsacid dynasty was in decline, no longer able to stand up to ROME or protect Mesopotamia from Roman incursions. The Romans annexed the northern half of the country and on three occasions stormed through the south, sacking both Seleucia and Ctesiphon. By the end of this period, both sites lay derelict. However, the Iranians were far from finished. A new lineage, the Sassanids, replaced the Arsacids in AD 224, and they immediately began a vigorous counter-offensive. For the next 400 years, Roman and Sassanid traded blows across their Mesopotamian frontier, doing great damage to each other and to the region without achieving much in the way of permanent gains.

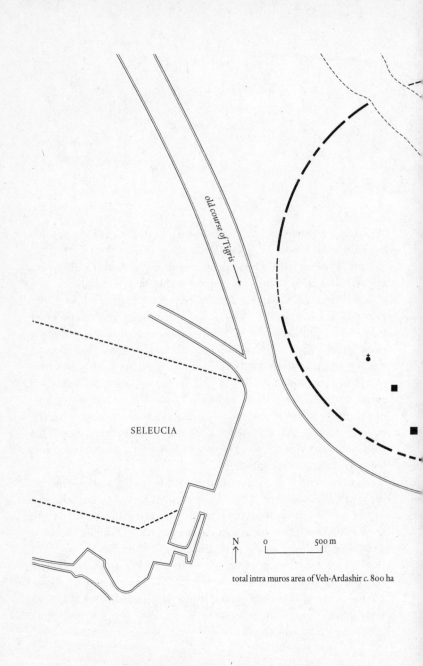

old course of Tigris →

SELEUCIA

N

0   500 m

total intra muros area of Veh-Ardashir *c.* 800 ha

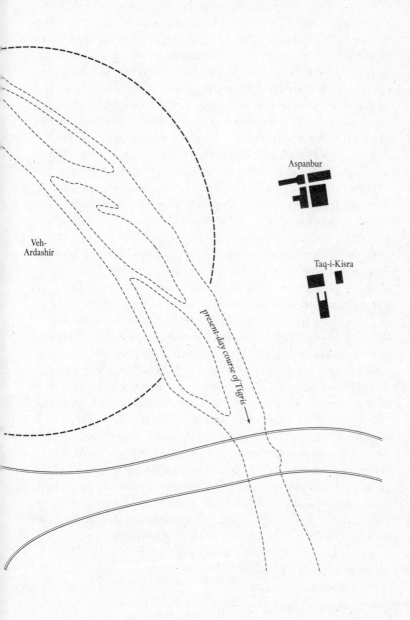

As part of his programme for re-establishing Iranian prestige, Arda-shir I, the founder of the Sassanid dynasty, refounded Ctesiphon under the name of Veh-Ardashir, 'Glory of Ardashir'. He surrounded it with a huge circular rampart, enclosing an area of around 700 hectares, far more than can have been needed for any settlement it may have contained. In fact his version of Ctesiphon seems to have been no more successful than the original in attracting a permanent population, and by the sixth century it too was deserted. Not that the Sassanids had run out of steam, for by this date there was a respectable settlement outside the east gate of Veh-Ardashir. This town, known as Aspanbur, was ornamented by a pair of palaces, of which one, called the Kasr al-abyad ('White Palace') by Arab historians, was later demolished to provide materials for the building of Baghdad, while the centrepiece of the other, the Taq i-Kisra ('Arch of Chosroes') still stands, the sole surviving monument of Ctesiphon's imperial past.

In 637, not long after the Taq i-Kisra Palace was built, the Sassanid Empire was overthrown by the Arabs. The newcomers named Ctesiphon 'al-Mada'in', meaning 'the cities', and Arab chroniclers later claimed that there were no fewer than seven distinct settlements scattered across the area when they first entered it. One of these, the town of Veh Antioch i Khusrau, was really a separate entity. Constructed by the prisoners taken by Chosroes I at the capture of ANTIOCH in 540, it was Roman in style, right down to the baths and hippodrome. It lay five kilometres (three miles) to the east of Aspanbur, made its surrender to the Arabs independently and shouldn't really be counted as part of a 'Ctesiphon complex'. Another distinct settlement that was given a place in the Arab list was Sabat, five kilometres to the south. There may also have been a village within the perimeter of Veh-Ardashir. Even so that only makes four. But maybe the hunt for seven contemporary 'cities' is misguided. Perhaps the real reason for the name al-Mada'in was the vast field of ruins spread out on either side of the Tigris at this point: Seleucia, with the still-standing ziggurat of its predecessor Opis on the right bank; and Parthian Ctesiphon surrounded by the immense rampart of Veh-Ardashir on the left. This sequence must surely have seemed a more impressive testimonial to the capital status of Ctesiphon than the number of its satellite villages.

Al-Mada'in dwindled rapidly after the Arab conquest, its place usurped by the army camps set up at Kufa and Basra. The foundation of Baghdad in 762 all but finished it off. Renamed Bahurasur, Aspanbur was still listed as a small town in the tenth century; by the fourteenth century it was being referred to as a village.

Topography

The area of Ctesiphon has been surveyed, but there has been very little excavation of any sort. At present, Parthian Ctesiphon hasn't been located but is presumed to lie immediately opposite Seleucia. That would place it within the ramparts of Veh-Ardashir, which have been both defined and dated. The eastern half of the perimeter has been destroyed by the Tigris, which now runs through the site. Immediately to the east lie the roughly rectangular remains of Aspanbur, which have not been investigated but are reasonably assumed to be late Sassanid. A kilometre to the south of these ruins is the undoubtedly late Sassanid Taq-i-Kisra, or Arch of Chosroes. The arch is what remains of the central iwan – half-covered reception hall – of a grandiose palace. Such signs as remain in its immediate surrounds suggest that its setting was rural rather than urban.

Population

It seems clear that Parthian Ctesiphon had only a small permanent population, and the same is probably true of early Sassanid Veh-Ardashir. This means that the only period in which Ctesiphon is likely to have been a city in the full sense of the word is during the sixth and early seventh centuries AD. If its main function, even in this period, was as a winter residence for the Sassanid kings, then it probably never had 10,000 year-round inhabitants and can't be accounted much of a city. If it also served as the provincial capital of an administratively centralized Lower Mesopotamia, however, then it may well have held 10,000 for the duration of the sixth century.

CUMAE

Campania, Italy

*The first Greek colony
in peninsular Italy*

History

In the eighth century BC, the Greeks made contact with the Etruscans, who turned out to have exactly what the metal-poor Greeks were looking for: abundant supplies of copper and iron. A lively trade sprang up, mediated by a Greek trading post that was established around 750 BC at Pithekoussai on the island of Ischia. A generation later, this Greek outpost founded a settlement at Cumae on the mainland opposite.

Cumae was a hilltop site overlooking a shallow bay; in other words, an easily defended acropolis with a just-about-adequate harbour. In due course, a lower town was to grow up on the ground below the east side of the acropolis. It was defended by a wall built at a date that archaeologists are still arguing about, and could be anywhere in the fifth or fourth centuries BC.

In the late sixth century BC, relations between the Cumaeans and Etruscans soured, and the Etruscans tried to take the town. In 525, under the able leadership of Aristodemus, the Cumaeans rebuffed the initial Etruscan attack; they then went over to the offensive and, in alliance with the Latins, won a significant victory at Aricia in Latium in 505. A last attempt by the Etruscans to interfere in Campania was defeated by the Cumaean and Syracusan navies in 474, after which Cumae could justifiably claim to be the leading place in the region.

The Cumaeans were not to enjoy their enhanced status for long. First, at a date variously given in sources as 438 or 421 BC, the town was taken over by a local people, the Sabellians. Then came the Romans, whose protection was extended over this part of Campania in the 330s. By 318, the Cumaeans were under the jurisdiction of a Roman-appointed prefect of Capua and Cumae. Greek was replaced first by Oscan (the language of the Sabellians), then by Latin; the buzz of international trade was replaced by the bickering of purely local interests.

This sounds like the end of Cumae as a place of note, but it was to have a couple of unexpected revivals. One came in 37–36 BC, when Octavian, the future emperor Augustus, was at war with Sextus Pompeius, who had taken control of Sicily and made himself a naval power to be reckoned with. Octavian gave his right-hand man, Marcus Agrippa, the task of building a fleet capable of taking out Sextus Pompeius, which Agrippa set about doing in his usual methodical way. The new fleet was to be based at Portus Julius, a purpose-built dockyard on Lake Avernus, on the eastern side of the Cumaean peninsula. Supply was from the north, via Cumae, and to make sure the flow of material was uninterrupted, Agrippa had tunnels excavated connecting the port of Cumae with the centre of Cumae town (the Crypta Romana), and the centre of Cumae town with Lake Avernus (the one-kilometre-long Crypta Cocceia, Lucius Cocceius being the architect responsible for the two constructions as well as various other similar tunnels in the Naples region). These were considerable undertakings, and while they were in progress the Cumaeans must have felt that the town was getting a new lease of life. But once the war was won, the limelight moved away and Cumae's decline, gentle in the last centuries BC, seems to have accelerated in the first century AD. The emperor Domitian built a coast road, the Via Domitiana, which ran through Cumae to Pozzuoli, but as this exits the town via a large ornamental arch (the Arco Felice) this indicates that the defences of the lower town were no longer being maintained. Juvenal, writing during Domitian's reign, describes the town as empty (Juvenal, 3.2) and his contemporary, Statius, notes the peaceful nature of Cumae, perhaps implying that it was a bit too peaceful (Statius, Silvae, 4.3.65). In fact, it is clear that the lower town was progressively abandoned during the period AD 1–400, and that whatever population remained at the latter date was in, or in the immediate neighbourhood of, the acropolis.

The end of Cumae, accordingly, echoes its beginning: it had started out as a fortified hilltop, and that is how it finished up. In the mid fifth century AD, Procopius described it as one of only two strongholds worthy of note in Campania (the other being NAPLES), and in this guise Cumae plays a prominent part in the Gothic war of which he was the historian. Garrisoned by Belisarius in 536, captured by King Totila in 542, it was recovered by the East Roman general Narses in 553, an event that Procopius takes as marking the end of the war. It remained technically Roman for a long time, although in this, its final phase, it was merely one of the outlying castles held by the increasingly independent dukes of Naples. Sacked by the Saracens in 915, it lost even this function, becoming instead a haven for outlaws and small-time pirates. This vipers' nest was extirpated in 1207, since when the site has been deserted.

Topography

The plan of the acropolis is straightforward: it contained the town's two Greek temples, subsequently reshaped into Christian basilicas, plus a rectangular cistern, which is possibly where the famous Sibyl of Cumae uttered her prophecies. Protecting this nucleus are fortifications of all periods from archaic Greek to early Byzantine. As to the lower town, its outline is reasonably secure, although as already remarked, experts disagree as to its dating. The most intriguing section is that overlooking the harbour: it has massive substructures that appear to be the cryptoporticus described by Virgil as the Grotto of the Sibyl (*Aeneid*, 6.42–4). Although his attribution is not now accepted, the construction has an odd, alien feel to it that stirs imaginings it is surely allowable to enjoy. Further east are the buildings that constitute the civic centre, arranged around what may have been the Greek agora and certainly became the Roman forum. Most of them were started in the Sabellian period and remodelled on many subsequent occasions – Republican, Augustan, even Flavian. The amphitheatre outside the south gate dates, in its original form, from *c.* 100 BC.

Population

Cumae can only have had a significant population when the lower town was in existence, between 500 BC and 400 AD. Juvenal's aside implies that there wasn't much to the lower town *c.* AD 90. This, together with the fact that the port of Cumae was slowly silting up throughout antiquity, suggests that, as far as numbers over 2,000 to 3,000 go, we can ignore the years after AD 1. Similarly, we can be reasonably confident that after the Sabellian capture of the town in the late fifth century BC, Cumae will have ruralized in much the same way as PAESTUM after its capture by the Samnites. So if we are looking for figures of the order of 5,000 we need only consider the earlier fifth century, after Cumae had become strong and determined enough to defeat the Etruscans by land and sea. It is possible that in these years, Cumae had a population base

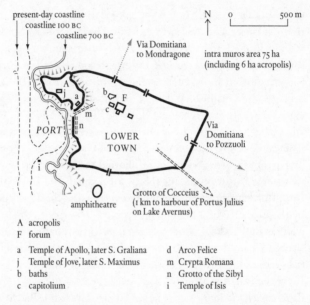

A   acropolis
F   forum

a   Temple of Apollo, later S. Graliana
j   Temple of Jove, later S. Maximus
b   baths
c   capitolium

d   Arco Felice
m   Crypta Romana
n   Grotto of the Sibyl
i   Temple of Isis

this large, but very unlikely that it was exclusively urban. If we remember that ATHENS town, much the largest place in the Greek world in the fifth century BC, only had a population of 7,000, anything over 4,000 for contemporary Cumae looks exceedingly improbable. The reasonable conclusion is that Cumae never had a population of more than 2,000 to 3,000, even in its best days.

CYRENE

Cyrenaica, Libya

*The leading city of Cyrenaica from its foundation
in the late seventh century BC to the mid
third century AD; diocese: Egypt*

Cyrene is a textbook example of colonization as a response to population pressure. The Aegean island of Thera (modern Santorini) has
strictly limited resources: with the rise in numbers that occurred
throughout the Greek world in the eighth and seventh centuries BC, the
islanders' future looked increasingly grim. Sometime in the late seventh
century – the traditional date is 631 BC – the Therans dispatched an
expedition to the stretch of the North African coast due south of Greece
and settled some of their surplus citizens on an offshore island named
Plataea. Conditions there proved to be no better than at home, but the
native Libyans were friendly and showed the newcomers an inland site
that seemed more promising. The position finally chosen by the settlers,
some thirteen kilometres (eight miles) from the coast, was determined
by the presence of an abundant spring. This spring, the locus of the
water nymph Kura, gave its name to the city the Therans founded on the
site and, from the city of Kurene, conventionally Latinized as Cyrene,
the surrounding territory acquired the name of Cyrenaica.

By the time the Romans took over the area in 74 BC, Cyrene and
Cyrenaica had a long history behind them. The region had lost its political independence early on, first to the Persians and then to the Ptolemies, but a steady stream of Greek immigrants had sustained the Greek
character of Cyrene and led to the foundation of three similar cities on
the coast: Eusperides (renamed Berenice by the Ptolemies), Taucheira
(similarly renamed Arsinoe) and PTOLEMAIS, the last being a Ptolemaic foundation. Add APOLLONIA, the port of Cyrene, which had
become a city in its own right, and you have the five cities that gave
Cyrenaica its alternative title of Libya Pentapolis.

The Ptolemies had administered Cyrenaica from Ptolemais; the

Romans preferred Cyrene, giving it the title of metropolis and rejecting Ptolemais' claims to precedence. Under their rule Cyrene prospered until the end of Trajan's reign when there was a rising by the city's Jewish community led by a local firebrand whose name is variously recorded as Lucas or Andreas. His success indicates that Cyrene's Jewish population had increased to a significant level in the Ptolemaic and early Roman periods and that, conversely, its elimination in the course of the conflict (which lasted from AD 115 to 117) left Cyrene with serious gaps in its economy and demographics, and a lot of damaged buildings. Hadrian (117–38) did his best to get the city back on its feet, drafting in new

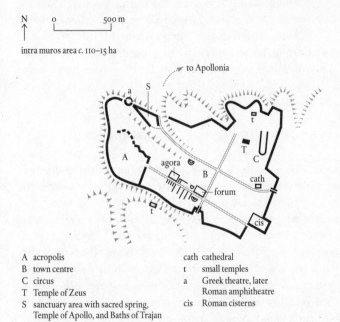

N   0   500 m

intra muros area *c.* 110–15 ha

A   acropolis
B   town centre
C   circus
T   Temple of Zeus
S   sanctuary area with sacred spring,
    Temple of Apollo, and Baths of Trajan

cath   cathedral
t   small temples
a   Greek theatre, later
       Roman amphitheatre
cis   Roman cisterns

settlers, including 3,000 veterans, although some of these may have been earmarked for a new foundation of his named Hadrianopolis, on the coast. He also made funds available for rebuilding the city's major monuments. But the work went slowly, some of the repairs being still incomplete seventy years later, and it seems likely that Cyrene never again achieved the level of prosperity it had enjoyed before the revolt.

By the later third century, there are definite signs of a downturn. There is a report of a war with the tribes of the interior in 268 which required the attention of the prefect of Egypt. Perhaps reflecting continuing unrest, Diocletian made Cyrenaica a province in its own right in 297, under the name Libya Superior (previously it had been the junior half of the province of Cyrenaica and Crete). At that time, he installed the new provincial administration in Ptolemais. Clearly the goodwill of the Libyans, which had been fundamental to Cyrene's well-being from its foundation, had been lost, and, as a result, what had been Cyrenaica's largest city rapidly dwindled. Ammianus Marcellinus, writing towards the end of the fourth century, describes the site as deserted. He may have been overdoing it: archaeology suggests that in his day, and for some while after, it was garrisoned by an army unit that had turned the forum into a fortress, but as far as civic life is concerned, he was absolutely right – the story of Cyrene was over. In the Arab period it isn't mentioned at all.

Topography and Population

The ruins of Cyrene stand on the edge of an escarpment that overlooks the coastal plain. The town is divided by a wadi, which, as it ascends to the plateau, becomes the town's main street. One third of the town's area is north of this axis; the other two-thirds, the site of the earliest settlements and of the acropolis, lie to the south and west. The spring that had attracted the original settlers to the area is situated at an intermediate level, below the acropolis but above the mouth of the wadi; this triangular-shaped area was subsequently monumentalized with shrines and temples, fountains and baths. The main street lies under the present-day Arab village and its buildings are mostly hidden from view, but the parallel street to the south has been excavated. This was Cyrene's civic centre, with the original Greek agora at one end and the Roman forum at the other. No fewer than four theatres have been found: a Roman one facing the forum, a smaller one (an odeon?) next to it, and a third facing the main street. The fourth, north-west of the sanctuary, was hollowed into the hillside in the Greek manner; the Romans converted it into an amphitheatre by building supporting arches on the downward slope.

The north-eastern hill seems to have been reserved for the largest monuments: the Temple of Zeus, the circus and, in the late period, the city's cathedral. The colossal columns of the Temple of Zeus were all thrown down in antiquity – by the Jews in the revolt of 115–17, according to current archaeological opinion, although the jumble (now reconstructed with original materials by an anastylosis) looks more like the work of an earthquake. The circus – as it dates back to Greek times we ought to call it a hippodrome – was a prominent feature, as might be expected given the Cyrenaicans' prowess at chariot racing. They had a string of Olympic victories to their credit and many ancient authors comment on the excellence of the horses bred on the Cyrenaican plateau, and the skill of the drivers.

Cyrene's population can only be a matter for speculation. With an intramural area of 110–15 hectares the town had room for 10,000 or more people, but that would be a very high figure for a colony at the margin of the Greek world; something like 5,000 is a more likely guess. A figure of this order could have been sustained throughout the city's Hellenistic and early Roman history, say from 300 BC to AD 250, with the terminating date (the crash of the later third century AD) more established than the point at which the population first reached the 5,000 mark. The suggested date for this reflects the generally accepted supposition that the Greek economy moved up a gear at the start of the Hellenistic period.

CYZICUS

Deserted site on the Kapı dağı peninsula,
Balikesir province, on the Marmara coast of Turkey

Capital of the late Roman province of Hellespontus

History

Cyzicus was founded in the eighth century BC by seafarers from MILE-
TUS exploring the route to the Black Sea. Needing a base on the Asiatic
side of the Sea of Marmara, they picked the offshore island of Arcton-
nessus (Bear Island, modern Kapı Dağı) and built their settlement on
the south side of it, facing the mainland. A pair of sandbars reaching out
from the coast of Asia isolated the harbour area from the open road-
steads to either side. It seemed an ideal spot.

The traditional foundation date of Cyzicus is 756 BC, with a second
group of colonists arriving in 675. By the mid fifth century the settlement
had clearly developed into a prosperous community, for when the Athenians enrolled it in the Delian League its contribution was assessed at
nine talents. This was far more than any other place on the south side of
the Marmara; the nearest cities of comparable size were Lampsacus in
the Hellespont (twelve talents) and Chalcedon in the Bosporus (nine
talents). And, thanks to its island site, Cyzicus fared better than either of
these when the league was finally defeated: the Persians recovered the
mainland cities in 387, but Cyzicus preserved its freedom. This favourable outcome is a key reason why the city was at its most prominent – and
probably its most prosperous – during the fifth and fourth centuries BC.

Eventually Alexander the Great freed all the cities of Asia from the
Persian yoke. In Cyzicus his name is associated with the building of a
causeway from the island to the mainland. However, the actual engi-
neering works carried out at that time are likely to have had the opposite
aim, for the truth behind the tale is surely that the causeway was formed
naturally, by the extension of the sandbar on the east side. The task fac-

ing the Cyzicenes was to keep a usable channel open so that the harbour could be approached from either direction. Initially they seem to have been successful in this, but soon the western sandbar started giving trouble too. The local geography, which had initially been an asset, was now becoming a disadvantage.

Perhaps because of this problem, Cyzicus never really lived up to the promise it had shown in the classical period. It retained its successful political touch, however, first as an ally of the king of PERGAMUM, then as one of the 'free' cities of Roman Asia with an extensive mainland territory. Augustus reduced its privileges but Hadrian recognized it as a metropolis and Diocletian made it the capital of the province of Hellespontus, one of the units into which he split the over-large province of Asia. Nevertheless, the city seems to have been barely holding its own, and as regards the harbour the battle was now definitely lost. The island became what the French call a *presqu'île*, attached to the Asiatic mainland by a sandy isthmus.

As is so often the case with cities in decline, the sources blame the final demise on an earthquake. In the case of Cyzicus, the earthquake occurred in the seventeenth year of Justinian's reign (AD 544) and is said to have destroyed half the city. The emperor's agents were soon on the spot but brought no succour for the survivors: what they were looking for were marbles that might be used to decorate the new cathedral Justinian was building in CONSTANTINOPLE. Subsequently, Cyzicus seems to have been abandoned in favour of Artace, a small town seven kilometres (five miles) to the west. The timescale is uncertain: Cyzicus appears, although low down, in a Byzantine list of places in the Obsician theme; by the eleventh century it was deserted.

Topography and Population

The site of Cyzicus has been surveyed but not excavated. The layout is typical of a Greek city of the fourth century BC, with widely flung walls taking in much of the hill overlooking the city. There is a theatre set into this hillside and signs of a rectangular grid of streets in the western quarter. On the south side the various constructions pose problems of interpretation, for the existing walls clearly date from the final phase of the city's existence when the harbour had silted up and the sole requirement was the defence of the isthmus. For this purpose, the Cyzicenes built walls across the sandbars that formed the flanks of the isthmus and then linked these together with a simpler wall that follows the quayside of the abandoned harbour. Such ships as still came to Cyzicus during this period put in at small harbours either side of the city; the basins of these have subsequently silted up too.

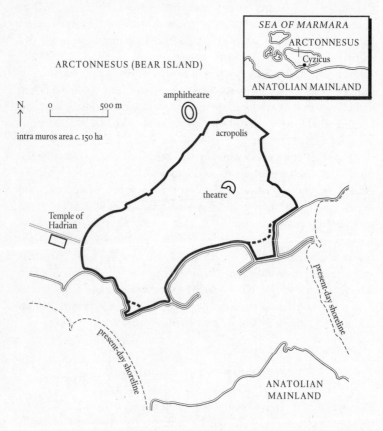

Outside the walls lie the remains of two major monuments: an amphitheatre on the north side and a large temple, completed by Hadrian, outside the west gate. The temple was visited by Cyriac of Ancona in the fifteenth century when thirty-three of its columns were still standing.

Today there is nothing to see except the tunnel vaults that formed its substructure.

The walls of Cyzicus enclose an area of about 150 hectares. Some ninety hectares seem to have been built upon at one time or another, which suggests a possible population for the city in the 6,000 to 7,000 range.

DOCLEA

Present-day *Dukljia, Montenegro*

Capital of the late Roman province of
Praevalitana; diocese: Dacia

Doclea was founded sometime after the conquest of the region by Octavian in 35 BC, as a tribal centre for the Illyrian Docleatae, who had previously managed to make do without any such thing. It was recognized as a municipium *c.* AD 80, by which time it had overshadowed its two closest rivals, Epidaurum, a minor Greek colony on the coast, and Scodra, the capital of the original second century BC kingdom of Illyria. In the late Roman period, *c.* AD 300, it became the capital of the newly created

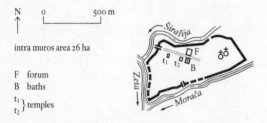

N   0   500 m

intra muros area 26 ha

F   forum
B   baths
t₁ } temples
t₂

province of Praevalitana. This makes it sound more significant than it was: Praevalitana, which amounted to little more than a poor and backward collection of mountain villages, ranked among the least important provinces in the empire.

Its undistinguished history was ended by the Avar invasions of the early seventh century.

DUR-SHARRUKIN

'Fort Sargon'; present-day Khorsabad, north Iraq

CALAH retained its metropolitan status until 717–706 BC when King Sargon II built a new capital, Dur-Sharrukin, forty-five kilometres (twenty-eight miles) further north. It was a little smaller than Calah (320 hectares as opposed to 360) but had the same basic layout, with separately walled palace and citadel areas, and a lower town constituting 85 per cent of the whole. Once again excavation – mostly a matter of hunting for bas-reliefs and man-headed bulls – has been confined to

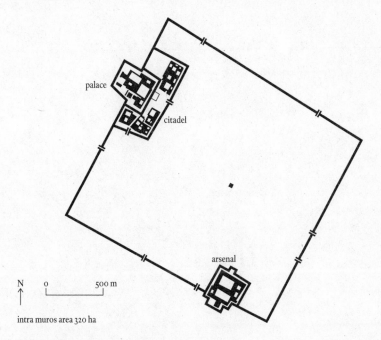

palace and citadel, so we have to fall back on the same conjectures we made about Calah as regards the lower town: was housing scattered all over it, or was half of it a royal park? Given the similarity of the plans, what was true of one was probably equally true of the other.

Echoing this observation, it is safe to assume that Dur-Sharrukin's population was much the same as Calah's, perhaps 14,000 given its slightly smaller extent. The Assyrian Empire was, after all, doing at least as well in the late eighth century as it had done in the early ninth. Sargon II himself, though, wasn't so fortunate, losing his life fighting against the Cimmerians in 704 BC. Subsequently his son and successor, Sennacherib, turned his back on Dur-Sharrukin (perhaps because it had proved unlucky, perhaps because, being at some distance from the Tigris, it was more difficult to supply). It immediately sank to minor rank, with a population appropriate to its much-reduced status. So if, in its best days, numbers were of the order of 14,000, it would only have been at this level for the few years either side of 706.

EDIRNE

Edirne province, west Turkey

Formerly *Adrianople, in Thrace*

History

Edirne, in Turkish Thrace, was founded by the emperor Hadrian, from whom it took its original name of Adrianople or Hadrianopolis. Apparently, it had a predecessor in the form of a Thracian settlement named Uscudama, but if so the layout of the Roman town ignored it, having the standard rectangular shape. This is, however, unusually skewed in execution, with corners deviating by seventeen degrees from the typical right angle. The town was tucked into a bend of the Tunca River, just above its junction with the Maritza, a situation of some strategic importance, as became increasingly apparent after CONSTANTINOPLE had become the capital of the eastern half of the empire. Lying as it does about a third of the way along the main road from Constantinople to the Danube frontier, Adrianople acted as a sort of outer bastion for the defence of the capital.

Adrianople had a narrow squeak in AD 378 when the Goths won a famous victory nearby, slaughtering the emperor Valens and most of his army, but it managed to survive this and the many other vicissitudes that beset the empire at the time. Then in 615 the Danube frontier totally collapsed, and migrating hordes of Slavs descended on Thrace, displacing its previous inhabitants and settling on their lands. We may imagine Adrianople's population reduced to a fearful huddle of uncertain political status. Yet the town survived, to be liberated by Constantine V in 751 and have its previous position in the provincial hierarchy restored (since AD 300 it had been the administrative centre for Haemimontus, one of the four provinces into which Thrace had been split by Diocletian). It became the capital of a theme, the term used to describe the rehashed provinces of the later (Byzantine) empire. Subsequently its standing was enhanced when, following the conquest of Bulgaria in the 970s, it was made the seat of the duke responsible for the defence of the lower Danube.

The years either side of AD 1000 probably marked the apogee of Byzantine Adrianople. Over the next 300 years the fortunes of both empire and town steadily declined. Among the many enemies Adrianople faced, the most persistent and successful were the Ottoman Turks, who crossed over to Europe from Anatolia in 1354 and were soon carrying all before them. By the 1360s (the exact date is disputed) they were in possession of Adrianople, which Sultan Murad I (1359–89) made the base for his European operations. Under the new name of Edirne, Adrianople entered on a phase of rapid expansion.

An unexpected additional impulse to Edirne's growth came with the catastrophic defeat suffered by the Ottoman sultan Bayezid I at the hands of Timur the Lame at Ankara in 1402. This threw the Anatolian half of the Ottoman Empire into confusion and led to Edirne, previously capital of the European half, replacing Bursa as capital of the empire as a whole. For the next fifty years Edirne was the sultans' principal residence, and as such the beneficiary of the funds available for building metropolitan mosques, palaces, caravanserai and bazaars. Most notably it was at Edirne in 1452/3 that the young Mehmet II tested the great guns that he was to use to batter down the walls of Constantinople. The capture of the city, of course, brought with it a diminution in Edirne's status. Constantinople was now to become the sultan's chief residence and the main seat of his administration. But Edirne remained a favoured retreat, playing Versailles to Constantinople's Paris. It became a place where successive sultans came for rest, refreshment and a spot of hunting. It was not until the seventeenth century that it began to lose its appeal and its special status in the Ottoman scheme of things.

Topography

The Kaleiçi ('Old City'), occupying the south-western quarter of the modern town, retains the outline of Roman Adrianople, but the outline is about all that remains from the period. Apparently there were once

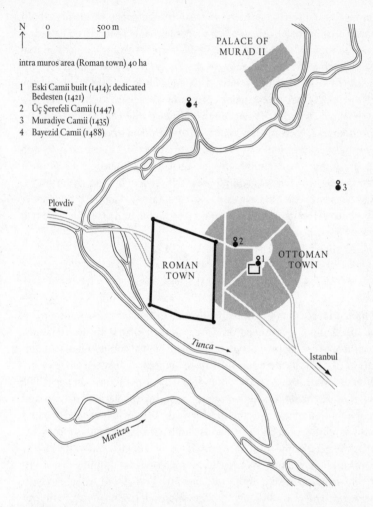

N   0   500 m

intra muros area (Roman town) 40 ha

1 Eski Camii built (1414); dedicated
   Bedesten (1421)
2 Üç Şerefeli Camii (1447)
3 Muradiye Camii (1435)
4 Bayezid Camii (1488)

PALACE OF
MURAD II

Plovdiv

ROMAN
TOWN

OTTOMAN
TOWN

Tunca →

Istanbul →

Maritza →

twelve square towers on each side, plus a round one at each corner, but the only one still visible is the north-east corner tower, which, much rebuilt, now serves as a clock tower. It is the source of one of the city's few pre-Ottoman inscriptions, a plaque commemorating a renovation by the emperor John Comnenus in 1123.

The Ottoman monuments are more numerous and more impressive. The first mosques were simply conversions of some of the small churches in the Roman town, but these were soon superseded by purpose-built structures in the Ottoman town that was rising alongside. The oldest still standing is the Eski Camii (Old Mosque) of 1402–14. Its running costs were met from the rents of the Bedestan (covered market) built nearby. More mosques followed, some of the grandest outside the city proper. The earliest major palace, the Eski Saray of Murad II, was constructed way out of town, on the far side of the Tunca.

Of course, what most people who visit Edirne have come to see are not these examples of early Ottoman architecture, interesting though they are, but the Selimiye, the masterwork of Sinan, Turkey's most famous architect. It was completed in 1574, when he was seventy-nine, and he is supposed to have said that here, rather than the many bigger and better-known mosques he built in Istanbul and elsewhere, he had finally got it right.

Population

There is no reason to believe that Roman or Byzantine Adrianople had an unusually large population. It seems clear that it always remained confined to its original forty-hectare plan, which would suggest a population of no more than 6,000 at best, and half that when things were difficult. With the arrival of the Ottomans, the picture changes. The town more than doubled in size, not counting the various palaces and religious foundations on the outskirts. By 1525, when we get our first hard data, the town had 4,061 households. If we take four as our multiplier, we get a population of 16,244. If we include the staff of the suburban buildings, 18,000 is a not unreasonable total. Numbers were to grow further in the course of the sixteenth century and are said to have been much higher subsequently. The first modern census, taken in 1927 after the city had been through the vicissitudes of the Balkan and First World Wars, yielded a figure of 34,528.

EPHESUS

Present-day *Efes, near Selçuk, Izmir province,*
Aegean Turkey

Metropolis of the Roman province of Asia

History

The history of Ephesus is a tale of two cities, Old Ephesus (modern Aya-soluk), and the much larger Hellenistic and Roman city 2.5 kilometres (1.6 miles) to the south-west. Today both are far from the sea, but when the Greeks first arrived in the area around 1000 BC, the geography was very different, with both sites positioned on the shores of a now-vanished gulf – the retrospectively named Gulf of Ephesus. The agent responsible for obliterating this gulf feature is the River Cayster, which over two millennia has brought down enough silt to fill it in completely. The process was slow, but throughout antiquity the Cayster worked on, pushing the shoreline further and further away from the Ephesian settlements until they ended up completely landlocked.

All this lay in the future when the first Greeks disembarked at the foot of the hill known today as Ayasoluk, but to the locals of the time as Apasa, which the Greeks heard as Ephesus. The colonists were Ionian Greeks, and Ephesus became one of the dozen communities on the stretch of the Turkish coast that constituted the Ionia of the classical period.

Ephesus was first settled as part of the colonizing movement of the eleventh century BC that took Greeks from peninsular Greece to the Aegean coast of Anatolia. In the case of Ephesus the colonists chose a spot overlooked by the twin peaks of Mount Pion, a feature that, according to the locals, was especially favoured by Cybele, the Anatolian mother goddess. This spot became home for the few hundred farmers and fishermen who constituted the original Ephesian polity, and, as numbers grew, the market and meeting place of a more extensive rural community. Eventually something that can reasonably be called a town emerged. So far as we can tell it consisted of a refuge on Mount Pion and a straggle of housing down its northern slope to the bay, where the fishermen kept their boats. A mile to the east was the altar of the mother goddess, now identified with Artemis.

Whatever the size of Ephesus town, the community as a whole didn't lack ambition. This became apparent in the sixth century BC when the Ephesians decided to build a temple to Artemis that would put all the other temples of the Greek world to shame. It was to be 115 metres long, having a double colonnade at each side and a triple one at the front and back. It was also to be built of marble

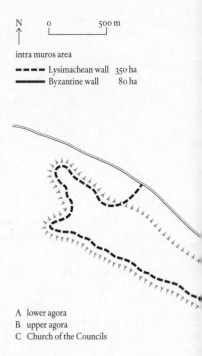

N   0   500 m

intra muros area
- - - - Lysimachean wall 350 ha
———— Byzantine wall   80 ha

A lower agora
B upper agora
C Church of the Councils

throughout. These were all record-busting attributes. No temple had ever been built of marble before, and although later on others were, none ever matched the Ephesian temple's dimensions. The Artemision was to join the Great Pyramid of Giza as one of the Seven Wonders of the Ancient World.

Among those who contributed to the costs of the Artemision was Croesus, king of the inland state of Lydia. A few years later, around 550 BC, he showed his other face, making himself master of Ephesus, and forcing the Ephesians to abandon their acropolis on Mount Pion and live exclusively in the lower town, where he could keep an eye on them. But Croesus' moment of glory was brief: in 547 the Lydian kingdom was overthrown by Cyrus the Great, and Ephesus became part of the Median satrapy (provincial government) of SARDIS. Subsequently the Medes gave way to the Persians, under whose rule Ephesus remained

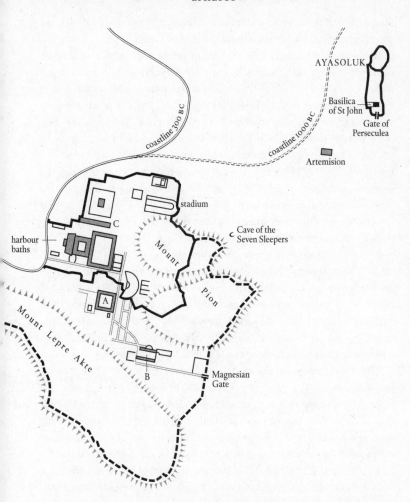

until the Athenians liberated the town, along with the rest of Ionia, in the 470s BC. After the collapse of the Athenian Empire the Persians resumed control, only to be forced out again by Alexander the Great in 334 BC. On his death this particular bit of his empire passed to Lysimachus, one of his generals, who carved out a kingdom for himself that covered Thrace and western Anatolia.

Alexander had vastly enlarged the Greek world, and the successor kings like Lysimachus and, more famously, Ptolemy and Seleucus, thought in much bigger numbers than earlier Greek rulers. This is particularly true of the cities they founded or remodelled, which were much nearer to being cities in our sense of the term than the very modest settlements at the heart of the traditional Greek polis. Ephesus was one of the places chosen for a makeover of this type. First Lysimachus folded two neighbouring Ionian communities, Colophon and Lebedus, into the Ephesian polity, which gave him the increased numerical base he wanted; then he revived Ephesus town by shifting its centre from the northern slopes of Mount Pion, where the harbour was slowly silting up, to the western slopes, where the bay was still usable. Finally he built a new city wall that took in Mount Coressus as well as Mount Pion so that Lysimachean Ephesus would have plenty of room for further growth.

Although Lysimachus' constitutional changes didn't last – both Colophon and Lebedus soon recovered their independence – his remodelling was a success in all other respects. Ephesus grew steadily throughout the Hellenistic (post-Alexander) period, and when the Romans took over in 133 BC, it had become the leading city in Anatolia, eclipsing both MILETUS, the traditional Greek number one, and PERGAMUM, the current political capital. It was to retain this position, although not without some sniping from SMYRNA, to the end of antiquity.

The most important social change between early and late Roman periods was the defeat of paganism by Christianity. At Ephesus the transition seems to have occurred rapidly, in the course of the second half of the third century AD. The symbol of the old ways, the Artemision, was sacked by a roving band of Goths in 262, and the fact that repairs were half-hearted suggests that pagan beliefs were already weakening. Public funds speeded the changeover from old to new, and under the Constantinians Ephesus became a bulwark of the Christian faith. The Third Ecumenical Council of the Church was held in the city in 431, and it was in the curiously elongated basilica near the harbour that the assembled bishops issued the first official doctrine concerning the special status of the Virgin Mary. Subsequently the tradition spread that she had spent her last years in the city, cared for by St John, and the processions around Mount Pion, once held in honour of Artemis, were now resumed in honour of the Virgin. A tomb of St John was discovered on the nearby hill of Ayasoluk (this Turkish name derives from Aya Theologos, 'Holy Evangelist'), and a basilica built there to mark the site for pilgrims. In the sixth century Justinian, looking for a suitable church to rebuild, chose this Basilica of St John as a showcase for the new style he was bringing to ecclesiastical architecture.

Up to this point Ephesus seems to have remained an impressive example of classical urbanism. Major monuments like the stadium, the theatre and the harbour baths were expensively refurbished in the fourth century. Both the main streets were improved in the fifth century, the road up from the harbour by the emperor Arcadius (it was subsequently called the Arkadiane) and the road at right angles to it by a local bigwig named Eutropios. But, as is so often the case in the Eastern Empire, Justinian's contribution marks the last flourish of civic confidence, and even that was off-centre, a mile outside Ephesus proper. The next major structure to be built, probably by Constans II (641–58), was a new, much shorter town wall. Only the north quarter of the city was protected (80 hectares, compared to the 350 hectares enclosed by the Lysimachean circuit). Even within this restricted area signs of social collapse were soon apparent, with crude dwellings being constructed in what had previously been public spaces. The decline seems to have become terminal after 668 when Ephesus was pillaged by an Arab fleet en route to Constantinople.

By the ninth century, Ephesus was an empty ruin. The sole remnant of its population was to be found on Ayasoluk, clustered around the Basilica of St John. The hill had been fortified in the seventh century, and when later historians mention Ephesus it is this small settlement, covering only nine hectares, to which they are referring. In the manner of the time it was called a city, but in demographic terms it cannot have been more than a village.

Many towns of Anatolia collapsed in the seventh century AD, but few so completely as Ephesus. The reason it did particularly badly was that its harbour silted up, depriving the place of one of its basic functions. As previously noted, the River Cayster (modern Kuçuk Menderes) was steadily filling in the bay on which Ephesus was sited, and Lysimachus' change of orientation could only postpone the day when coast and town parted company. By 903 Byzantine naval operations were being conducted from Phygela (modern Kuşadası), indicating that the harbour at

Ephesus was no longer in use. At the present time the site is something over five kilometres (three miles) from the sea.

Topography

The Austrians have been excavating Ephesus on and off since 1896. They have done a good job, and the archaeological zone is now a compulsory stop for tourists visiting western Turkey. In the summer months the heat, the crowds and the activities of the touts get a bit oppressive, but the site is well worth seeing even under these circumstances. Ephesus is, after CARTHAGE, the largest classical city to have remained uninhabited to the present day, and it's not short on either monuments or memories. To stand in the great theatre where St Paul tried to preach, only to be howled down by devotees of Artemis (Diana in the Latin-based Bible, hence the cry 'Great is Diana of the Ephesians'), is to get some measure of the task the early Christians set themselves. Egging the devotees on, of course, were the many Ephesians who made their living selling spin-offs from the cult of Artemis: charms, statuettes, amulets, and so on.

Today Ephesus is an inland site and tourists arrive by car or coach, but in antiquity most visitors came by boat and disembarked at the harbour in the heart of the city. A triumphal arch on the quay marked the beginning of the city's main east–west street, a wide colonnaded thoroughfare leading to the foot of Mount Pion where it formed a T-junction with the main north–south street. Overlooking both was the huge theatre, hollowed out of the side of the mountain in the Greek manner. A left turn would take the visitor past the stadium (a gift from Nero), then out of the north gate of the city and eventually to the site of the Artemision and Ayasoluk. A right turn would take him to the lower agora, the business centre of the city. From the lower agora a road led up the valley between Mount Pion and Mount Lepre Akte to the upper agora, the city's administrative centre, then to the Magnesian Gate from where the traveller could proceed to Magnesia or turn left and follow the processional way that skirted the eastern slopes of Mount Pion and took the devout to the Artemision or, in later times, the Basilica of St John.

During a walk through the city the traveller would see the usual monuments of classical urbanism: half a dozen public baths (including a particularly magnificent set near the harbour), temples to the gods (including the Egyptian deities, Isis and Serapis) and to the emperors (notably Domitian and Hadrian), several elaborate fountains and a library. On the processional way from the Magnesian Gate to Ayasoluk the Christian pilgrim could visit the Cave of the Seven Sleepers, where seven Christians had hidden from the Decian persecution in AD 250 and woken 200 years later, to find themselves in the safety of a converted empire.

Population

There is no direct evidence as to the size of the city's population in its heyday, but we can get a fairly good estimate for that period. Its exceptional status clearly begins with the refounding of the city by Lysimachus in 288 BC, and just as clearly ends with the building of the constricted Byzantine defensive circuit in the mid seventh century AD. So as regards points on a graph, we can limit ourselves to the years 250 BC–AD 600.

As to the peak population, all we can say is that the Romans seem to have rated Ephesus a bit below ANTIOCH. On the ranking we have adopted, this would put it somewhere around the 25,000 mark. It seems reasonable to allow the town a population of this order from AD 1 to 250. One may therefore tentatively assume steady growth from 10,000 in 200 BC, and a drop to 20,000 in the fourth century AD, to 15,000 in the fifth and 10,000 in the sixth.

If you want to query the statement about pre-Lysimachean Ephesus being a relatively unimportant place on the grounds that only a sizeable community could have committed to a project on the scale of the Artemision, take a moment to think about medieval Canterbury, which put up a major cathedral with a population base of only 3,000 to 4,000. In fact we know that c. 450 BC the Ephesian community, i.e. the sum of its rural and urban elements, was paying six to seven talents a year into the coffers of the Delian League, the coalition that Athens had set up to finance the war with Persia. According to the historian N. J. G. Pounds, this suggests a total population of no more than 5,000 to 6,000.

GENOA

Liguria, Italy

Classical *Genua; capital of*
the Byzantine province of Liguria

Genoa gets its first mention in 218 BC, when it was already under Roman control. Thirteen years later it was sacked by the Carthaginian general Mago, Hannibal's brother, but that is the sole excitement we know of until AD 569, when the Lombard invasion of Italy forced the governor of the province of Liguria to abandon MILAN, his normal residence,

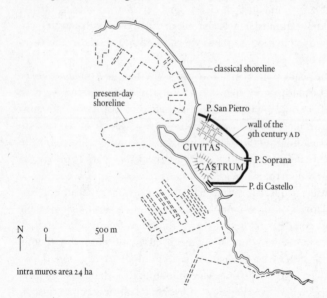

classical shoreline

present-day
shoreline

P. San Pietro

wall of the
9th century AD

CIVITAS

P. Soprana

CASTRUM

P. di Castello

N   0   500 m

intra muros area 24 ha

along with the rest of the Po valley, and take refuge in Genoa. From there he ruled all that was left of his province, which amounted to its sub-Apennine coastal strip, Liguria in the modern sense of the word. This province finally succumbed to Lombard attack in 640.

Genoa was not an important place in the classical era. Its immediate hinterland is a geographically isolated part of Italy, hemmed in by Alps and Apennines. The town handled such exports as the area produced – timber, and cattle and hides – and imported the minor luxuries the locals could afford: wine and oil. But Roman Genoa never rose above this parochial role, playing no part in the wider Mediterranean world either politically or economically.

In keeping with this assessment we find that Genoa was always a small place. The original settlement, which pre-dates the Roman occupation, was on a hill overlooking the harbour. At some stage the Romans laid out a new town at the foot of the hill, where traces of rectangularity are visible in the modern street plan. In the final, Byzantine phase there was – to judge by the remains of a typically Byzantine pentagonal tower that have been found there – a movement back up to the hilltop. The contrast between a citadel on a hilltop and a lower town at its foot, and the movement from one to the other and back again, is echoed in many a town history throughout the Roman Empire. As to scale, the hilltop *castrum* and the lower town *civitas* taken together can't have covered more than twenty-four hectares, for that is the intramural area of a wall built in the ninth century AD that encloses both. In light of this it seems improbable that Roman Genoa ever had a population of more than 3,000 to 4,000. Incidentally, the discontinuity between Roman and medieval towns is unusually well defined in Genoa's case. When the town finally fell to the Lombards, the Lombard king Rothari was so irritated by the unexpectedly sharp resistance that the Genoese had put up, that he not only ordered the walls of the town razed, but decreed that in future it was to be referred to not as a municipium but as a village.

HERCULANEUM

Campania, Italy

*Small town on the Bay of Naples buried by
the eruption of Vesuvius in A D 79*

The name Herculaneum – 'Hercules' town' – suggests a Greek foundation, and historians have always accepted that a Greek settlement provides the most likely starting point for the town's history. The date could
be as early as the late seventh century BC; if so, the numbers involved
would have been tiny, maybe no more than a few families. Subsequently
there would have been an Etruscan input, followed by renewed Greek
influences, before the little community was taken over by the Samnites,
the locals who probably already provided the bulk of its population in
the late fifth century BC. In the late fourth century, Herculaneum, like
the other Campanian communities, became politically dependent on
ROME; its attempt to repudiate this status in the Social War of 91–89 BC
was unsuccessful. In the final phase of its existence – from 89 BC to
AD 79 – Herculaneum was transformed into a purely Roman town, and
a very prosperous one too, as upper-class Romans built villas all around
the Bay of Naples, bringing a flush of wealth to the already existing
communities.

The eruption of Vesuvius that ended the story of classical Herculaneum in AD 79 began in the early afternoon of 24 August. As the wind
on this fatal day was blowing from the north-north-west, it carried the
ash cloud away from the town, which received only a light dusting of
pumice – twenty centimetres, as compared to POMPEII's 2.8 metres.
That was the good news. The bad news was that Herculaneum, being
only seven kilometres (four miles) from the volcano's crater (compare
Pompeii's ten kilometres) was within reach of the first in the series of
pyroclastic flows that began around midnight. A huge mass of glowing
rock, lava and pumice, riding on a cushion of poisonous gas, thundered
down the mountainside and extinguished all life in the town. Other

flows followed throughout the night, until the town was buried under twenty to twenty-five metres of volcanic material. Unlike Pompeii, where the second storeys of the larger houses still poked up through the mounds of debris, Herculaneum simply vanished from human view.

Our sources describe Herculaneum as being built on a bluff overlooking the sea, its flanks defined by two small rivers. This makes it unlikely that the town covered more than fifteen hectares, with the centrally planned area accounting for a little under half of this. On the north side there was a theatre; on the south, a palaestra. The theatre was the first building discovered, during the sinking of a well in 1709. By tunnelling laterally the layout and nature of the building was determined, and its marble veneers and honorific statues brought to the surface. Further tunnelling resulted in a surprisingly good understanding of the town,

N   0   500 m

V   Villa of the Papyri
T   theatre
M   monumental portico
P   palaestra (athletics
    ground)

———— hypothetical 15 ha perimeter

———— coastline in antiquity

Villa of the Papyri, theatre, monumental portico and western quarter known from tunnelling.

Southern quarter and palaestra fully excavated.

Northern and eastern quarters hypothetical.

and to the north of it, the discovery of the sumptuous Villa of the Papyri. But the fact that the pyroclastic material had hardened into rock made work much more difficult than it was at Pompeii, where the overburden was less and most of it only light earth. Tunnelling ceased in 1765, and although the nineteenth century saw an attempt at uncovering the town, progress was slow, the results meagre and the enterprise soon abandoned. We have Mussolini to thank for the quarter of the town that has been exposed, an achievement that has fully justified the expense, and whetted everyone's appetites for further work. Well, not quite everyone: the inhabitants of Resina, the town built on top of Herculaneum's lava covering, are understandably reluctant to be displaced.

And, as at Pompeii, the local directorate wants to be sure that what has been exposed is properly cared for, before approving plans for new work. As a result, what has been done in the last sixty years has been limited to tidying-up operations in the 25 per cent of the town already brought to light.

The tidying up, concentrating on the seafront, has been surprisingly productive. It has not only confirmed that Herculaneum overlooked the sea in much the same fashion as Sorrento does today; it has at least partly solved the problem of what happened to the town's inhabitants. As only a couple of skeletons had been found in the original excavations, it used to be thought that nearly all of them had managed to get away. But work on the seashore, and on the adjoining arcade, has uncovered a huddle of 150 unfortunates who never made it to safety. Multiply this by the still-unexcavated proportion of seafront and it is clear that a substantial minority – maybe a majority – of Herculaneans perished in the disaster that overwhelmed their town. There were too few boats to take them all.

The usual figure quoted for Herculaneum's population is 4,000. Given that the town is very unlikely to have covered more than fifteen hectares, this looks too high. Something in the range 1,500 to 2,000 seems preferable.

Although the Villa of the Papyri remains unexcavated, the tunnellers' work there produced a sufficiently good plan for J. Paul Getty to make it the model for his Villa Museum in Malibu, California. If often-announced plans for uncovering the original Villa ever come to anything, it will be interesting to see how original and replica compare.

HIERAPOLIS

Present-day *Pamukkale, Denizli province, Aegean Turkey*

*Second city of Phrygia Pacatiana, seat of an
archbishop in the late Roman period*

Hierapolis' unique selling point is its hot-water spring, which emerges
near the edge of the plateau on which the town is situated. As the water
cools, it deposits the calcium salts it contains in a series of stalactite-
fringed basins. The result is an extraordinary, brilliant white cascade
extending from the city to the plain below. To the Turks this looked like
a length of cotton, which is why they call the place Pamukkale, 'Cotton
Castle'. The ancients were more intrigued by another aspect of the
spring: a cave near its centre which was deadly to enter. We know now
that this was because it acted as a trap for the carbon dioxide with which
the spring waters are loaded, but to the classically educated there could
only be one explanation: this was an entrance to the underworld. The
devout, the superstitious and the curious were attracted to the site in
sufficient numbers to support a shrine (named the Plutonium, after
Pluto, god of the underworld) and a priesthood (hence Hierapolis, 'city
of priests').

History

Hierapolis was founded by the Seleucid successors of Alexander the
Great sometime in the third century BC. From them it passed to the
kings of PERGAMUM (188 BC), and from them to the Romans (133 BC).
It became a prosperous place, partly because of its fame as the site of the
Plutonium, and partly because it lay within a district renowned for the
high quality of its wool. These two sources of income boosted Hierapolis into second place in the urban hierarchy of Phrygia, outranked
only by the provincial capital, LAODICEA AD LYCUM.

Hierapolis survived the advent of Christianity better than most places that were celebrated for pagan shrines. The reason is that it contained a Christian shrine too, the burial place of the Apostle Philip. Local lore was unclear as to whether Philip had simply retired to Hierapolis and died of old age, or been apprehended while visiting and suffered martyrdom for the faith. The sanctity of the grave, however, was certain, and in the fifth century a fine martyrium was constructed over it. Pilgrims continued to come to Hierapolis just as they had done before; they simply diverted from the Plutonium to the martyrium. It was probably because of his function as guardian of the Apostle's tomb that the bishop of Hierapolis was raised to metropolitan status by Justinian in the mid sixth century.

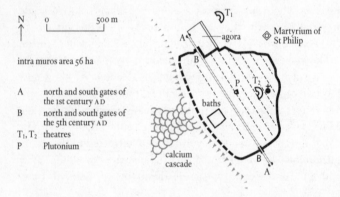

N

0   500 m

intra muros area 56 ha

A   north and south gates of
     the 1st century AD
B   north and south gates of
     the 5th century AD
T₁, T₂   theatres
P   Plutonium

T₁
agora   ◈ Martyrium of
              St Philip
A
B
P. T₂
baths
calcium
cascade
B
A

The decline of Hierapolis is undocumented but was probably initiated by the Persian invasion of the early seventh century. Earthquakes also played an important part in the degradation of the public monuments, many of which were subsequently occupied by squatters. By the eighth century, Hierapolis was no more than a village. Even this was not to endure: we know that the site was deserted when elements of the Third Crusade passed this way at the end of the twelfth century, and it may well have been abandoned long before.

Topography and Population

Hierapolis was a tourist town and had all the amenities appropriate to this function: a fine set of baths, a couple of theatres and a large agora. What it didn't have until late in its history was a town wall. There may have been a move to build one in the latter part of the first century AD, for monumental gates were erected at either end of the main north–south street (by Frontinus, the aqueduct man, serving at that time as proconsul of Asia). The positions of this pair of gates (A on the plan) suggests that in this period Hierapolis covered an oval about seventy-five hectares in extent, but this can only be a rough estimate, for, even if planned, no wall was ever built. Three hundred years later, when times were more dangerous, a wall became a necessity, but the town's resources were not what they had been, and the new city gates (B) were set well in from the first pair. Assuming that its western sector followed the line suggested on the map, this early fifth-century wall enclosed some 56.5 hectares.

A reasonable estimate for the population of Hierapolis would be of the order of 5,000. Many citizens were laid to rest in the necropolis outside the north gate, which is well worth a visit: the field of jumbled sarcophagi, many of impressive size, is a poignant reminder of the investment classical society made in funerary art.

Like Hierapolis before it, Pamukkale is usually packed out with tourists who until recently were able to stay in hotels built around the natural hot-water pools. Not many of them visit the museum (in the old baths) or the theatres and other monuments, but if you feel overrun, there is always the cemetery.

IOL-CAESAREA

Cherchell, 100 kilometres (62 miles) west of Algiers, Algeria

Capital of the Roman province of
Mauretania Caesariensis; diocese: Africa

Iol was founded in the sixth century BC as a trading post and naval station, part of the network of such places that the Phoenicians used to establish their grip on the south-western Mediterranean. By the end of the century it had been absorbed into the Carthaginian Empire; then, at the beginning of the second century BC, it was handed over by ROME to the kingdom of Numidia, its ally in the struggle against CARTHAGE. At this time, excavations suggest that the town covered eight to ten hectares, which in turn implies a population of no more than 1,000 or so.

After quarrelling with Rome at the end of the century (in the Jugurthine War of 118–106 BC), Numidia lost Iol to its western neighbour, Mauretania. The town was looked on with favour by the Mauretanian kings and probably served one of them, Bocchus II (died 33 BC), as his capital. Briefly annexed by Rome on his death, the kingdom was revived for Juba II, a scion of the Numidian line, in 25 BC. Juba is remembered for two things: he married Cleopatra Selene, the daughter of Antony and Cleopatra, and he rebuilt Iol as a purely classical town, renamed Caesarea in honour of his patron, Augustus. Iol-Caesarea is in fact a twin of Herod the Great's CAESAREA MARITIMA at the other end of the Mediterranean. Where Juba's Caesarea differs from Herod's is that although it was named in honour of the Roman emperor, it was not architecturally a Roman town; rather it reflected the passionate philhellenism of the king. A patron of Greek intellectuals, he was honoured as such at ATHENS. Juba undoubtedly used a Greek architect to lay out the new, much-enlarged version of Iol. The city wall snaked over the hills behind the town in typically Hellenistic fashion; the amphitheatre is a weird compromise between the standard Roman form and a Greek stadium. Incidentally, the currently accepted date for the wall is mid second century AD, but the picture it presents is so clearly Hellenistic that it is very difficult to agree with this. Perhaps it was refurbished during this period.

Juba was succeeded by his son Ptolemy, who died in AD 40. Shortly after this, the emperor Claudius decided to absorb the kingdom into the provincial system, making of it two provinces, Mauretania Tingitana in the west (capital, Tangier) and Mauretania Caesariensis in the east (capital, Caesarea). The Roman element in Iol-Caesarea was reinforced by a contingent of veterans, after which the city was officially titled Colonia Claudia Caesarea.

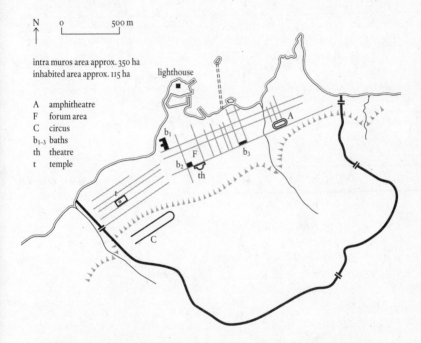

N   0   500 m

intra muros area approx. 350 ha
inhabited area approx. 115 ha

A   amphitheatre
F   forum area
C   circus
b₁₋₃   baths
th   theatre
t   temple

Classical authors have very little to say about Iol-Caesarea's subsequent history, and archaeologists not much more. Hadrian gave the city a fine set of baths (b1 on the plan). Severus added a triumphal entrance to the circus. Economic activity seems to have reached a peak in the early third century AD; the fourth was an era of decline, with no new buildings, just modifications to existing ones. By the time the Vandals arrived in 429, the town was clearly in a poor way, and although the East Romans did succeed in recovering it in 534, they were unable to revive its fortunes. By the late sixth century the site was derelict.

As is so often the case with Greek circuits, the intramural area is an unreliable guide to Iol-Caesarea's population; even the area between the hills and the shoreline – about a third of the total, say 115 hectares out of 350 – generates a suspiciously high figure, something in the region of 12,000 to 15,000. Perhaps 10,000 is allowable for the city's best years, which cover the period AD 1 to 250.

JERASH

North of Amman, Jordan

Classical *Gerasa, a city of the Syrian
Decapolis; diocese: Oriens*

Jerash, a Greek city in present-day Jordan, was probably founded by the
Seleucid king Antiochus IV (175–163 BC) and not, as the city fathers
later came to believe, by Alexander or his immediate successor, Perdic-
cas. Its official title was Antioch on the Chrysorhoas, but it soon reverted
to its original Semitic name of Garshu, Latinized as Gerasa, present-
day Jerash.

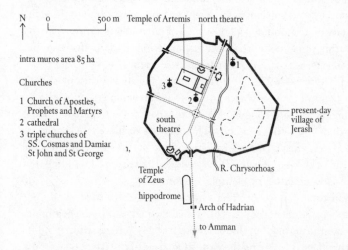

N   0   500 m   Temple of Artemis   north theatre

intra muros area 85 ha

Churches

1 Church of Apostles,
   Prophets and Martyrs
2 cathedral
3 triple churches of
   SS. Cosmas and Damian
   St John and St George

south
theatre

present-day
village of
Jerash

Temple
of Zeus

R. Chrysorhoas

hippodrome

Arch of Hadrian

to Amman

   The city gets its first mention at the end of the second century BC
when the Seleucid Empire was disintegrating. It then formed part of a
mini-principality centred on AMMAN. After briefly falling to the Jewish
king Alexander Jannaeus, it was finally 'liberated' by the Romans. In 63
BC, Pompey included it in a group of ten cities in southern Syria/north-

ern Jordan that subsequently became known as the Syrian Decapolis. This lasted until AD 106 when Trajan transferred Jerash and three of the other towns to his new province of Arabia.

The nucleus of the Hellenistic city of Jerash is thought to have lain just inside the present south gate. If so, it consisted of little more than a temple of Zeus facing a settlement on a low hill opposite. Given its restricted area – of the order of five hectares – the population can't have been more than 500 to 600. Under the Romans there was a dramatic change in scale. A whole new city was laid out on the north side of the Hellenistic town, with a main street 800 metres long. This and two cross streets were lined with colonnades. A temple of Artemis formed the centrepiece of a monumental complex at the city's heart; a wall around the whole, completed in AD 75, enclosed an area of eighty-five hectares.

The prosperity of this part of the world reached its peak in the second century AD when Trajan advanced the eastern frontier of the empire to the edge of the desert. Jerash was able to put on a brave show for the visit of his successor, Hadrian, in 129, erecting a triumphal arch to the south of the city in his honour. The full range of monuments appropriate to a city of this rank was now nearing completion: huge baths, a circus, enlarged versions of the existing temples and a theatre.

But plans to extend the city to the south (indicated by the open bonds on the flanks of Hadrian's arch) were never implemented, and such new monuments as were completed after this date reflect changing needs rather than additional demands. The majority of these late structures are churches, most of them small and poorly built. An exception is the cathedral of the late fourth century which is a fair-sized building, but then it is an adaptation of a temple of Dionysus.

The history of the town effectively came to an end with the Arab conquest of 635. Some of the churches remained in use until the beginning of the eighth century, but there is no sign of any activity after 750. The modern village, occupying the eastern quarter of the Roman city, only came into existence in 1878.

The long period in which Jerash lay abandoned and its relatively remote position – it only received its first western visitor, the German Seetzen, in 1806 – mean that the city is one of the best preserved in the Roman Empire. Although its remains are not as dramatic as those of

PALMYRA or PETRA, it probably gives a better impression of how a city of the middle range looked than those more famous sites.

The population of Jerash in its best days has been estimated, somewhat optimistically, at 13,000 to 16,000. A figure of more than 5,000 but less than 10,000 seems a better guess.

JERUSALEM

Israel/Palestine

History

Jerusalem has the unenviable distinction of being a holy place in three different religions: it's holy for the Jews who built it, for the Christians whose faith was born there, and for the Muslims for whom it is the setting of the Isra and Mi'raj, the Prophet's magical overnight journeys from Mecca to the Temple Mount and from the Temple Mount to Paradise. As a result Jerusalem has had a lot of history – more at times than it might have chosen – but its frequent spells in the limelight don't mean that it was ever a big place. In fact its usual position in the Near East's urban hierarchy has been quite lowly.

Jerusalem's story begins around 1000 BC with King David's capture of what had been, until then, a Canaanite village situated on a hilltop in the rolling, dusty landscape of Judaea. David built his palace there, and his son Solomon picked an area further north on the same ridge for the site of what is now termed the First Temple, a permanent dwelling place for the Jews' hitherto peripatetic totemic deity, Jehovah. Between them, father and son had created a centre that could serve both the political and religious needs of the Jewish people. Alas, after Solomon's death only two of the ten Hebrew tribes continued to recognize Jerusalem's primacy. This meant that the town's growth was slower than might have been anticipated, and it was not until 300 years later, in the reign of King Hezekiah (715–687), that it needed anything extensive in the way of a city wall. The immediate stimulus was probably in 722 BC, when the Assyrian king Sargon II conquered Samaria, the breakaway state founded by the ten northern tribes. Refugees from Samaria will have pushed up Jerusalem's numbers, and the threat from Assyria will have encouraged Hezekiah to look to his capital's defences. The result was Jerusalem's most ambitious secular project yet, a defensive circuit that took in both the initial (east) ridge and the parallel ridge to the west (Mount Zion in current terminology).

Hezekiah's wall served the city well, preserving it through the alarming years of Assyrian supremacy. But the kings of Judah were less successful when it came to dealing with the Assyrians' successors, the Neo-Babylonians, and in 587 BC Nebuchadnezzar of BABYLON took Jerusalem by storm. The temple was destroyed, the walls razed, the inhabitants dispersed or deported, and the site left desolate. The first phase in Jerusalem's history was over.

The second phase began half a century later in 539 BC with Babylon's capture by the Persians. The Persian king Cyrus gave the exiled Jewish leadership permission to return home and begin the rebuilding of their shattered state. The better part of another century was to pass before the walls were rebuilt (under Nehemiah, c. 445 BC) and even then the scale was pretty paltry: the traces seem confined to the east ridge, meaning that the town was little, if any, bigger than it had been in Solomon's day. But slowly population growth resumed and by the time the Persians were replaced by the Macedonians, and the Macedonians in their turn had begun to lose their grip, the city was back to the size it had attained under Hezekiah. This was the situation – a Jerusalem that was once again the comfortably populated capital of a fairly prosperous mini-state – when the Romans, in the form of Pompey and his legions, appeared on the scene.

Pompey made short work of the Jews' political pretensions, taking Jerusalem by assault in 63 BC and drastically reducing the size of the Jewish state. What was left he entrusted to Antipater of Idumea, an Arab from the Negev who, after various vicissitudes, was succeeded in power by his son, Herod the Great. Nobody likes Herod much, but equally nobody questions his shrewdness. He was ruling a largely Jewish population at a time when Jewish fundamentalism was a growing force, in the name of a Roman emperor having little patience with people who rejected Rome's 'civilizing mission'. His solution to this dichotomy was to have two capitals: one, CAESARAEA MARITIMA, entirely Roman; one, Jerusalem, entirely Jewish. At both he was to build feverishly – indeed the idea may well have come to him because he enjoyed building so much – as well as at the various country palaces such as Masada and the Herodium which served as places of retreat (both socially and militarily). The major construction at Jerusalem was, of course, the Temple, its platform and the colonnades that surrounded it, a far more magnificent ensemble than the one it replaced. At the north-west corner of the platform he built a fortress, named the Antonia after one of his Roman patrons, Mark Antony. Running from the Antonia to the existing north wall of the city was a 'Second [north] Wall', which added a new quarter to the city, although we have little idea of its extent. On the opposite side of the city from the Temple, Herod built another fortress, the Citadel, with three immensely strong towers. To the south of the Citadel lay the royal palace. Augustus boasted that he had found Rome brick and left it marble; Herod could have said much the same as regards Jerusalem.

Herod's work was completed by his grandson, Herod Agrippa, who extended the city still further to the north and replaced the Second Wall with a new 'Third Wall'. With this addition the classical city reached its maximum extent, an intramural area of 110 hectares. Its population was presumably also at a new maximum: it was certainly increasingly turbulent and hostile to Roman rule. In AD 66 the First Jewish War broke out, with the city successfully repelling the attack of the Twelfth Legion which had marched down from Syria to sort out the troublemakers. It was a misleadingly good start to an impossible project. By AD 70 there were four legions encamped around the city, which was reduced sector by sector over the course of the next five months. As in Nebuchadnezzar's day, Temple and walls were destroyed, and what was left of the population scattered. The Tenth Legion was left behind to garrison the ruins.

The next change in Jerusalem's status is associated with another Jewish war, the Third, starting in AD 130. It is unclear whether the war was provoked by the emperor Hadrian's decision to refound Jerusalem as a Roman colony or whether the emperor decided on the makeover out of exasperation at Jewish intransigence. Either way, the end result was the same: Jerusalem was renamed Aelia Capitolina (Aelia being Hadrian's family name; Capitolina after Jupiter Capitolinus, the titular god of the Roman state); pagan temples replaced the long deserted synagogues; and Jews were no longer allowed to set foot in the town or live in its territory.

Aelia was not intended to occupy a prominent position in the roster of Palestinian towns; its colonial status simply reflects the need to provide the veterans discharged by the Tenth Legion with a local retirement home. It did, however, gain increasing prestige with the rise of Christianity. When, in the reign of Constantine the Great, Christianity became the officially sponsored religion of the empire, the town became an economic beneficiary too. Pilgrims began to visit, among them Constantine's mother, the empress Helena, who in 326 was lucky enough to find the True Cross, only yards away from the True Tomb of Christ. Constantine immediately ordered the construction of a huge rotunda-cum-basilica covering both sites. This structure, the Church of the Holy Sepulchre, bits of which are still standing today, was only one of a number of buildings funded by public or private donations. At a time when most of the towns in the empire were shrinking, Aelia enjoyed an Indian summer. Jews were allowed back in, at first only one day a year, later as residents.

In the early seventh century, Palestine was lost by the Romans, first to the Persians (temporarily, in 614–30), then to the armies of the Prophet Muhammed (more permanently, in 637). As Jerusalem features in the lore of Islam, the city continued to receive special treatment under the new regime, gaining two major buildings in the first century of Arab rule, the Dome of the Rock and the al-Aqsa mosque. Both are on the Temple Platform that had lain bare since the sack of the city in AD 70, and which was the focus of interest for Islamic scholars. As a result there seems to have been little conflict between new and old religions, and the city was able to continue in its now-habitual role, a target for pilgrims but in other respects a provincial backwater. In fact Jerusalem always seems to have done poorly when Palestine was part of a major empire. It was off the main routes, and imperial administrations typically preferred to base themselves nearer the coast. In the Arab period Palestine was run from a new town at Ramla, halfway between Jerusalem and the sea.

Jerusalem continued in its modest existence until the latter part of the tenth century when, along with Palestine, it passed under the rule of the Fatimids of Egypt. Under threat from the Turks, the Fatimids refurbished the city wall, but despite this they lost it to them in 1078. They recovered it twenty years later, just as the Crusaders were closing in on the city. The next year the Crusaders took the place by storm, massacring all those unable to pay a ransom, and many of those who had. The Christian pilgrims who followed in the Crusaders' wake found the city and its holy places in a sorry condition. Some consolation was obtained by turning the Dome of the Rock into a Temple of Our Lord, and the al-Aqsa mosque into a palace for the Crusader kings, and some new construction followed during the eighty-eight years that the city remained in Christian hands. Then, in 1187, the Muslim hero Saladin, founder of the Ayyubid dynasty, retook the city and expelled its Christian population. Thirty-two years later, another Ayyubid sultan, doubtful of his ability to hold Jerusalem against a Christian counteroffensive, pulled down much of the city wall so that no one else could hold it either. Deprived of security, the population drifted away. For the rest of the medieval period Jerusalem was, for all its famous monuments, a very minor place indeed.

Topography

Jerusalem has been destroyed and rebuilt so many times that it is extremely difficult to recover the city's earlier layouts. The first securely placed item is Herod's Temple Platform, but that, and the approximate outline of the city wall on the eve of the catastrophe of AD 70 (i.e. including the Third Wall in the north) is about all we have for sure as regards the Herodian city. We know a little more about Aelia because we have significant remains of two major monuments, Constantine's Church of the Holy Sepulchre and Justinian's Nea Basilica, plus the Madaba map, a pictorial map of Palestine that contains a vignette of Jerusalem. This vignette clearly shows the main north–south street and a parallel street to the east, both with full-length colonnades. It also shows a semicircular plaza inside the north gate with an honorary column at its centre; this explains why the Arabs call the gate – the present-day Damascus Gate – the Bab al-Amud, or Gate of the Column. The city walls seem to have followed the Herodian trace.

By the Ayyubid period the south wall had been rebuilt on a new, shorter line. This gave the city the shape it has today, although the present walls are an almost entirely Ottoman construction (specifically of 1536–40, during the reign of Suleiman the Magnificent). They do not

1 **Old Testament Jerusalem**

   A City of David   1000 BC
   B City of Solomon 950 BC
   C City of Hezekiah 700 BC

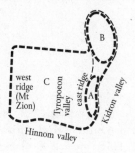

2 **Herodian Jerusalem**

   ✝ supposed site of crucifixion

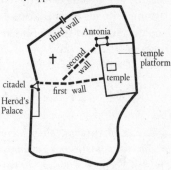

3 **Roman and Byzantine Aelia**

   1 Holy Sepulchre (replacing Temple of Venus)
   2 Nea Basilica
   3 Holy Zion

4 **Ottoman al-Kuds**

   A Dome of the Rock
   B Al-Aqsa Mosque

N   0   500 m

intra muros areas, in ha

1 A 5 B 15 C 60
2 first wall 60 third wall 110
3 110
4 82

stray far from the Ayyubid course. As a result, the intramural area was reduced from 110 to 82 hectares, i.e. by 25 per cent. It would be interesting to know exactly when this contraction took place; the best bet is the Fatimid era, for the fortifications were certainly renewed then (in 1033 and again in 1063), after what was certainly a very long period of neglect.

Names

The name Jerusalem (alternatively spelled Hierosolyma) served the city from its foundation by David to its refoundation as a Roman colony by Hadrian, a period of over 1,000 years. The name conferred by Hadrian, Aelia Capitolina, was soon shortened to Elia. This remained the official designation of the city for the next five centuries and, with the spelling Iliya, for the first three centuries of Arab rule. In the course of the tenth century the local Muslim population began referring to it as al-Kuds, meaning '[the town of] the Sanctuary', the Sanctuary being the Temple Platform. This became, and remains today, the standard Islamic usage.

All the serious monuments of Jerusalem have multiple names too. This is inevitable given the different languages used by the different faiths, but has been compounded by the Arabic delight in synonyms, especially strong in the case of much-venerated objects, where there is a rule that the holier something is, the more names it deserves. The end result is that Herod's Temple Platform is variously known as the Temple Mount, Mount Moriah, the Haram al-Sharif ('Noble Sanctuary'), and the Bait al-Maqdes ('Holy House'). The first Arab rulers called it al-Aqsa ('the Furthest [of the three Holy Places]'), a name now reserved for the mosque at its southern end.

Population

The first run of figures we have, a set of five early Ottoman counts, falls just outside our period. The first four of these counts are preserved in full and, if we apply a multiplier of four, yield the following population totals:

	Households	× 4	Plus Bachelors	Total Population
1525	934	3,736	3	3,739
1538	1,528	6,112	196	6,308
1553	2,614	10,456	309	10,765
1562	2,451	9,804	364	10,168

An incomplete register for 1592 indicates that by then the population had fallen to about 75 per cent of the 1562 total, i.e. to somewhere in the region of 7,500, completing a picture of rise and decline in the course of the sixteenth century that is mirrored in many other cities of the Ottoman Empire and can be accepted as genuine. The 1592 figure is consistent with the next reliable estimate, a figure of c. 8,750 in 1800.

What these data suggest is that early modern Jerusalem usually had a population a bit short of 10,000, and that in earlier periods it would have taken very special factors to push numbers to, let alone above, this level. There are really only three periods when such special factors were operating. The first is the Herodian era, when the city's population was boosted by Herod the Great's building programme and the city itself showed a dramatic increase in size (from 60 hectares to 110 hectares, or by 80 per cent). On this basis it seems reasonable to accept figures of 10,000 for AD 1 and something in the range of 10,000 to 15,000 for AD 50. The second is the early Christian era, when the Constantinian building programme and the start of pilgrim traffic will surely have set the previously half-derelict town on the road to recovery. Unfortunately, this boost coincides with hard times for the empire generally, and if the city doubled its population in the course of the fourth and fifth centuries AD it would have been doing very well indeed. That, on my reckoning, won't have been enough to bring it up to the 10,000 mark, for its baseline population once the Tenth Legion had left can hardly have been more than 4,000. Crusader Jerusalem is difficult to assess. However, we have just one point on the graph to consider because the city was only in Christian hands from 1099 to 1187, and in 1100 it will hardly have had the time to recover from the slaughter that accompanied its capture the year before. Was the influx of Christians enough to push numbers up to 10,000 by 1150? It is a very dodgy proposition, but, as I'm perhaps too inclined to lean to more conservative figures, let's be generous for once. No more than 10,000, though.

About the final medieval phase there can be little doubt. According to Rabbi Nachmanides, the thirteenth-century city contained 1,700 Muslims, 300 Christians and two Jews, of whom he was one, i.e. a total population of around 2,000. This will have slowly built up to the 3,750 recorded in the first Ottoman census some 300 years later.

LAODICEA AD LYCUM

Deserted site, seventeen kilometres (10.5 miles) south of Pamukkale, Denizli province, south-west Turkey

Capital of the late Roman province of Phrygia Pacatiana

Laodicea was founded as a strong point guarding the highway through Phrygia by the Seleucid king Antiochus II. It is named after his wife Laodike, which puts its foundation somewhere between 261 BC when he came to the throne and 253 BC when he divorced her. The town passed to PERGAMUM in 188 BC and was incorporated in the Roman province of Asia in 129 BC.

When the Romans first set up their administration for western Phrygia, they recognized Kibyra as the regional centre. However, Laodicea soon replaced it as the de facto centre of the Kibyrate judicial district, and in the third century it was officially recognized as the local metropolis. This status was confirmed at the end of the century when Diocletian divided the old province of Asia into smaller units, Laodicea becoming the capital of western Phrygia (Phrygia Pacatiana, 'Peaceful Phrygia').

Laodicea's monuments reflect its position in the administrative hierarchy. Its theatre is one of the largest in Asia; its stadium is twice the usual length. There are two agoras and two sets of public baths, as well as various other structures whose purposes have not yet been determined. Unfortunately, apart from a nymphaeum (public fountain) investigated by a Canadian expedition in the 1960s and a theatre, none of Laodicea's surviving edifices have been excavated and we have little idea of how the city developed or declined. A few hints come from inscriptions. The stadium, which apparently doubled up as an amphitheatre, was built in the reign of Vespasian (AD 69–79); the gymnasium with public baths just to the north of it was dedicated to Hadrian (AD 117–38). Other than these two instances we have no firm dates and only a few identifications. Even the line taken by the city wall is uncertain: its western half certainly ran along the edge of the hill, but there is some doubt as to its course on the east.

Laodicea's later history is essentially a blank. In the fourth century AD it was clearly an important place: its woollen goods were famous throughout the empire (they are specifically mentioned in Diocletian's tariff); and it stood high in the civil and ecclesiastical hierarchies (it was the site of an ecumenical council in 380). After that it gradually faded out. Most likely, the decline paralleled that of the other cities of Anatolia, with the really steep fall coming in the early seventh century as a

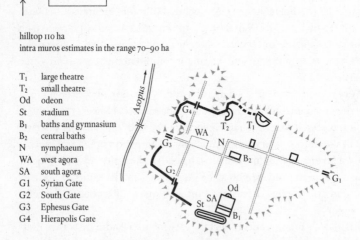

N 0 500 m

hilltop 110 ha
intra muros estimates in the range 70–90 ha

T₁	large theatre
T₂	small theatre
Od	odeon
St	stadium
B₁	baths and gymnasium
B₂	central baths
N	nymphaeum
WA	west agora
SA	south agora
G1	Syrian Gate
G2	South Gate
G3	Ephesus Gate
G4	Hierapolis Gate

result of the Persian invasion. However, one has to be careful not to get into a circular argument on this topic. What is certain is that the site was deserted when the crusading King Louis VII passed through in the winter of 1147–8, the last inhabitants having supposedly fled at his approach.

The site of Laodicea is easily visited from Pamukkale-Hieropolis, which is only 9.5 kilometres (six miles) to the north. In contrast to Pamukkale it attracts few tourists, which is understandable as, apart from the great theatre, there isn't much to see.

LEPTIS MAGNA

Lebda, Libya

*Phoenician colony, capital of the late
Roman province of Tripolitania*

Leptis was founded by the Phoenicians as part of their colonization programme in the western Mediterranean. No foundation date is recorded;
it could be as early as the late eighth century BC, although the oldest
material found so far is of the late seventh century BC. The initial focus
was on the north bank of the Wadi Lebda, whose mouth provided the
colonists with a relatively safe anchorage on what was, in general, an
unwelcoming coast.

Leptis was incorporated in the Carthaginian Empire at the end of the
sixth century BC. Subsequently it emerged as the leading city of its
Tripolitanian sector; indeed it was accounted by some as the most prosperous place in the empire after CARTHAGE itself. This prosperity
seems to have been based on the development of olive farming in the
town's hinterland. In the Roman period Leptis paid its taxes in oil,
exporting large quantities – the figures given are so vast that they must
be exaggerated – to the city of ROME. It is not unreasonable to project
the beginning of this agricultural success story back to earlier times.

Leptis became free – sort of – when Rome dismantled the Carthaginian Empire in 202 BC. The freedom included obligations to Rome, which
the Leptitans were hardly in a position to dispute; the difficulty was that
the kings of Numidia, Rome's allies in the recent contest, believed that
there were obligations to them too. The situation was only resolved in
III BC when the Numidians broke with Rome and Leptis was able to
come out wholly in favour of the Roman connection.

In the Augustan era, Leptis began to add to its hitherto modest stock
of public buildings. First up were a splendid market and a theatre, both
donated by a local magnate, Annobal Tapapius Rufus. The dedicatory
inscriptions (dated 8 BC in the case of the market, AD I in the case of the

179

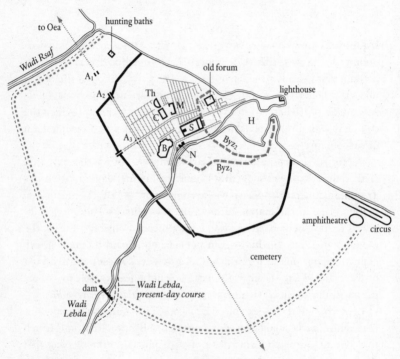

N   0 ———— 500 m

:::::::::: bank, early Roman, enclosing 425 ha
———————— wall, late Roman (*c.* A D 325), enclosing 130 ha
— — —Byz₁ unfinished wall, mid 6th century, intended to enclose 35 ha
— — —Byz₂ completed wall, late 6th century, enclosing 18 ha

to Oea
hunting baths
Wadi Rsaf
A₁
A₂
Th
old forum
lighthouse
D
C
M
S
H
A₃
B
N
Byz₂
Byz₁
amphitheatre
circus
cemetery
dam
*Wadi Lebda,
present-day course*
*Wadi
Lebda*

C   chalcidium
B   Hadrian's baths
H   harbour (now silted up)
M   market
N   nymphaeum
S   Severan forum and basilica
Th   theatre

A₁   Arch of Marcus Aurelius
A₂   Oea Gate = Arch of Antonius Pius
A₃   Arch of Septimius Severus

theatre) are, as might be expected, in both Latin and Punic. Tiberius' reign (AD 14–37) saw the building of the Temple of Rome and Augustus in the (old) forum; Nero's (AD 54–68) the creation of an amphitheatre out of what had been the city's main quarry. These powerful commitments to Romanity maybe prompted Vespasian's recognition of Leptis as a municipium and, forty years later, Trajan's raising it to colonial status. Hadrian (117–38), as was his wont, added a colossal set of baths, Marcus Aurelius (161–80) a circus between the amphitheatre and the shoreline. But all these works pale beside the building programme undertaken by Septimius Severus (193–211), who had been born in Leptis and was determined to honour his home town. A massive new forum, a fine basilica, extensive harbour works and an over-elaborate triumphal arch testify to his imperial largesse.

As far as buildings are concerned, Leptis was now as grand as it was going to get, though the city did obtain an enhanced administrative standing in 303, when Diocletian separated Tripolitania from Proconsular Africa. As Leptis was much bigger than the other two cities in the new province (Sabratha and Oea-Tripoli) it automatically became its capital. But the only new construction that followed this promotion was the building of a city wall, which can only be a sign that all was not well in the surrounding countryside. And sure enough in 365 the local tribesmen, the Austuriani, went on the rampage. Their destruction of Leptis' agricultural base was a blow from which the city never recovered. Very probably, given the contraction of the Mediterranean economy in the fourth century, this agricultural base was already in decline, but without security in the hinterland, the city could not be expected to function properly. When the Romans ceded Tripolitania to the Vandals in 455, they were handing over an asset that was fast wasting away.

When the emperor Justinian's troops recovered the province in 532, the East Roman troops found the site of Leptis deserted, with sand dunes covering most of the city. The Romans rounded up the inhabitants in the immediate environs, and made them resume a similacrum of city-centred life, but the attempt to row against the tide of history had only limited success. Leptis was gradually abandoned to the sands again; when the Arabs conquered Tripolitania in 643–5 the city doesn't even get a mention.

The only available indicators of Leptis' population are the various circuits drawn around the city. The first – of early imperial date – is of no help; it consists of a simple bank enclosing a vast area (approximately 425 hectares) and is clearly defining a city limit, presumably for customs purposes, not an inhabited area. The main wall, probably Constantinian, encloses an area of 130 hectares, which, in the excavated half of the city that lies to the north of the Wadi Lebda, is congruent with the built-up area. Within the Constantinian wall are two smaller circuits, one probably begun at the time of the Roman recovery of Tripolitania but never finished; the other, presumably somewhat later, complete and enclosing an area of eighteen hectares. Very roughly, these circuits suggest a large population for the imperial heyday (AD 1– 350), maybe as much as 10,000, and a very small one, less than 2,000, during Justinian's attempt to revive the city.

Unencumbered by modern buildings, present-day Leptis provides a perfect showcase for Roman urbanism at its most impressive. The major buildings, well preserved by the dunes that once covered them, have been tactfully restored and are easy to read. And, at the time of writing, tourists are still relatively few.

LINCOLN

Lincolnshire, England

Classical *Lindum; Roman colony, probable capital of
one of the late Roman provinces of Britain*

Lincoln has its origins in a legionary camp laid out by IX Hispana some-time around AD 60. The layout was standard, but the scale is a bit smaller than usual, the enclosed area being seventeen hectares, compared to the typical twenty hectares. When IX Hispana moved north to YORK, II Adiutrix took its place at Lincoln (early 70s to late 80s), and following the departure of II Adiutrix for the continent it became a colony for discharged veterans.

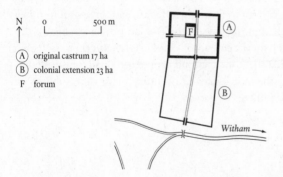

N 0 500 m

Ⓐ original castrum 17 ha
Ⓑ colonial extension 23 ha
F forum

Little is known about Roman Lincoln except that it was reasonably successful. Whereas the comparable Roman foundation at Gloucester remained confined to the pre-existing legionary camp, Lincoln soon boasted a suburb as big as the city itself. At the end of the second century the city wall was extended to take in the suburb; together, the old and new towns had an area of forty hectares, a figure that puts Lincoln in the middle rank of British cities. Two things suggest that it occupied a rather higher position in the ranking than its area would indicate. The first is that it had outgrown its original perimeter; some towns of comparable size, like SILCHESTER, had arrived at the same figure by a process of contraction. The second is that it seems to have been chosen as the capital of one of Diocletian's new British provinces when the two existing ones were divided into four, c. AD 300. This isn't absolutely certain, but the balance of probabilities is in favour and makes it likely that Lincoln achieved a larger population and held on to it longer than most British towns. Something of the order of 4,000 in the third century, and 2,000 at the beginning of the fifth, seem reasonable guesses. The end of Roman Lincoln is therefore likely to have been precipitous even by British standards, for no one would claim that it contained a significant population when the fifth century ended.

Lincoln didn't exist as an urban unit during the Dark Ages, but the late eighth and early ninth centuries saw the site repopulated and by the time of the Domesday survey in 1086 it had a population of about 5,000, enough to give it a respectable fifth place in the Norman kingdom's urban hierarchy. In the later Middle Ages Lincoln slipped down a couple of places, despite an increase in its population to 6,000 to 7,000. These fairly reliable figures, from a time when Britain had three or four times the population it had in the days of the Roman province, suggest the proposed maximum for the colonia of Lindum is not ungenerous. It also fits with the fact that the Roman circuit proved too small for the medieval population: by the mid fourteenth century there were suburbs of varying size outside all the city gates.

LONDON

England

Classical *Londinium;*
provincial capital of Roman Britain

Caesar's account of his raid into Britain (54 BC) and the record of the
Claudian invasion (AD 43) make it clear that there was no pre-Roman
settlement in the London area; for the disunited Celts the lower Thames
was an inter-tribal boundary, not a highway. Rome's military engineers
took a different view. Within a few years of the start of the conquest of
the province, they were using a crossing (whether ford, ferry or bridge is
not certain) at a point within yards of present-day London Bridge, and
had developed port facilities on both banks. A civil settlement grew on
the north side, and by AD 60 London could be compared in size to the
colonies and tribal centres on which the Romans were intending to base
their administration.

Romanization in general, and London in particular, suffered a sharp
setback as a result of the revolt of Boudicca, queen of the Iceni, who
burned down COLCHESTER, London and St Albans before her ultimate defeat in AD 60. London showed its vitality by making a quick
recovery. By the end of the first century AD it had become easily the biggest place in Britain, and its practical advantages as a communications
centre had led the governor of the province to make the city his official
residence. Not much is known about the topography. It rather looks as
though there was a formal settlement east of the Walbrook, and an
unplanned one west of the brook, between the Cripplegate fort and the
Thames. The formal settlement had a regular plan with a large forum
and basilica complex as its centrepiece. This is the best known feature
of Roman London, deservedly so as it was much the largest building in
the province. The Cripplegate fort and its attached amphitheatre seem
to have been constructed at much the same time as the official buildings
east of the brook (in the late first century/early second century AD),

which is a bit odd given the apparent lack of a single administration over the two settlements. Even more mysterious is the assumed bridge over the Thames, which everyone believes in, but for which there is not yet any clear evidence, and only eye-of-faith archaeology.

The city wall was built at the end of the second century AD, probably as part of the preparations made by Clodius Albinus, a governor of Britain who saw himself as a contender for the imperial throne, against the impending invasion of his more successful rival, Septimius Severus. A hundred years later – possibly at the time when another local man, Carausius, was trying something similar – the circuit was completed by the construction of a wall along the river front. The final Roman refurbishment of Londinium's defences was carried out in the third quarter of the fourth century, when bastions were added to the land wall.

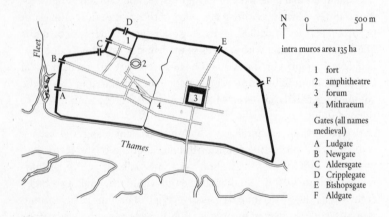

N   0   500 m

intra muros area 135 ha

1   fort
2   amphitheatre
3   forum
4   Mithraeum

Gates (all names medieval)

A   Ludgate
B   Newgate
C   Aldersgate
D   Cripplegate
E   Bishopsgate
F   Aldgate

The surprising thing about the city wall is its extent. Archaeologists consider that Roman London was well past its best at the time the wall was built, and the built-up area, which even at its maximum fell far short of the 135 hectares enclosed by the wall, was contracting, not expanding. It seems that the scatter of buildings along the river, plus the presence of the Cripplegate fort, made a semicircle the most economical line to defend. As for the shrinkage in London's population and pretensions, there is no doubt about that. The basilica had turned out to be a white elephant, and was to be demolished at the end of the third century; a triumphal arch built in earlier, more optimistic times was broken up and its stonework used in the construction of the river wall. London, like the other places on the provincial list it headed up, had failed to reach the Mediterranean-inspired targets set for it.

Eventually, in AD 410, the Romans withdrew their troops to meet more pressing needs elsewhere, and Britain reverted to the pre-conquest Celtic polity of tribal cantons. As such, it had no need of a capital, even so humble a one as late Roman London. Within fifty years of the departure of the last Roman soldier, the city was completely deserted.

What was Roman London's population when the city was at its best, at the beginning of the second century AD? All we have to go on is the intramural area of 135 hectares, indicating a potential population, at 100 per hectare, of 13,500. Clearly actual numbers fell far short of this figure, but a peak population of 6,000 to 7,000 seems possible. This is enough to put it at the top of the demographically challenged roster of Romano-British towns, but not enough to enable it to qualify as a city in our numerically defined sense of a place with a minimum 10,000 inhabitants.

LUCCA

Toscana, Italy

Classical *Luca; capital of the late Roman
province of Tuscia et Umbria*

The Roman colony of Luca was founded in 177 BC, twenty-two kilometres
(fourteen miles) north of the Arno and thirteen kilometres (eight miles)
from the sea. Its history, at least as known to us, is uneventful, although it
did have its moment in the spotlight in 56 BC, when it was the setting for a
famous meeting between Caesar, Pompey and Crassus. Four years earlier
these three men had shouldered the senate aside and taken over the running of the Roman state. Now they needed to meet up and iron out the
differences that had arisen between them since then. The difficulty was
that Caesar, who was in the middle of his conquest of Gaul at the time,
couldn't return to ROME without laying down his command; however,
Lucca, which was not on Roman territory as defined at the time, he could
manage. The three met, cemented their alliance and departed, leaving
Lucca once again to the obscurity of provincial life. A decade later, Lucca
lost its special geographical status as the nearest town to Roman Italy
when Caesar abolished the province of Cisalpine Gaul in which it had previously been situated. It was now fully Roman, and in due course became
the administrative centre for the seventh (Etruscan) region of Italy.

Another three centuries passed without anything to record, then
Diocletian, around AD 300, abolished Italy's privileges and divided the
peninsula into provinces of the standard late imperial type. Regions
seven (Etruria) and six (Umbria) were combined to form the province
of Tuscia et Umbria, and Lucca was made the provincial capital. It was
a surprisingly enduring choice: Lucca was to remain the most important place in Tuscany throughout the Dark Ages and only lost out to
Florence in the eleventh century. Even after Florence had overtaken it
in wealth and population and was political master of the Arno valley
– and more – Lucca retained both its independence and its prosperity.

Roman Lucca was not a very large place. From the street plan it looks as if the original grid covered just under forty hectares. The streets were straight but somewhat irregularly spaced; the forum was on the north-west side of the central intersection. A theatre and amphitheatre were built on the town's northern boundary, the amphitheatre probably in the Flavian period (AD 69–96). Eventually a wall was built that roughly coincided with the outline of the original rectangle, although on the north-east it curved inwards so as not to be overlooked by the amphitheatre. Because of this curve, the intramural area was reduced to 37.5 hectares. All that remains today are a few segments of town wall and the ghost of the amphitheatre, preserved in the layout of the buildings surrounding the central arena.

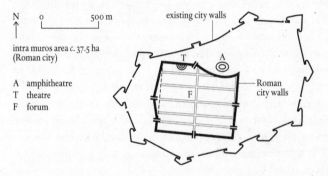

The first population figure to survive from Lucca is 4,736, this being the number of males who swore fealty to King John of Bohemia and his son Charles in 1333. By that time, the town had grown and a new circuit of walls had been built that raised the intramural area to seventy-five hectares. The implication is that Roman Lucca, with 37.5 hectares, could have had a population of 7,500. The next reliable figure is 20,770 in 1744, but by then a third set of walls – those visible, to such impressive effect, today – had pushed the intramural area up to 120 hectares. On this basis the Roman town would have held 6,500 people. Both figures are probably too high. The fourteenth-century count reflects the peak of medieval Lucca's prosperity, when the city's residents would have been more tightly packed together than ever before. And by the eighteenth century, buildings were much taller than they had been in Roman times. Something nearer 5,000 seems a more likely population figure for Roman Lucca.

LYON

Rhône, France

Classical *Lugdunum; Roman colony
and provincial capital*

History

Lyon was founded as a Roman colony, Lugdunum, on a greenfield site,
in 43 BC. It was clearly intended to be the administrative centre for the
part of Gaul recently conquered by Julius Caesar – Gallia Comata
('long-haired Gaul') as opposed to the already Romanized Gallia Nar-
bonensis (modern Provence). Its position, at the junction of the Saône
and Rhône, was well chosen: it lay just inside the new territory, in easy
communication with both the pacified south and the more problematic
north. Munatius Plancus, the governor of Gallia Comata responsible
for Lyon's foundation, had every reason to be pleased with his creation,
and it is given pride of place in the inscription on his gravestone, which
still survives in his home town of Gaeta.

The new colony was situated on a bluff on the right bank of the Saône,
fractionally to the north of its confluence with the Rhône. Most maps of
the Roman town show a wall running around the top of the hill (now
known as Fourvière), and it is more than likely that Lugdunum had a
wall, or at least a rampart, of this shape and size. Unfortunately no trace
of any such thing has been found in any of the many excavations conducted in and around the hill. The most that can be said is that the lie of
the land and the distribution of the cemeteries, which had to be outside
the city limits, indicate that these limits – the *pomerium* in the legal jar-
gon of the time – can't be very different from the line suggested for the
wall. This gives us an area for the city of around sixty to sixty-five hectares, not a large amount for a place intended to be the administrative
centre for most of Gaul.

There was, however, a bit more to Lyon than the Fourvière settlement. A considerable commercial suburb grew up on the right bank of the Saône, under the bluff of Fourvière. In time it was matched, if in a weaker form, by a settlement known as Canabae ('the huts') on the opposite bank of the river. Further north on the peninsula between Saône and Rhône was the ceremonial centre of Condate ('Confluence'), where delegates from the Sixty Tribes of Gallia Comata met in a specially built amphitheatre to discuss – within limits – matters of common interest, and pass – without dissent – decrees honouring the emperors. Condate is unlikely to have had much in the way of year-round population (and was anyway legally distinct from Lyon), but the gatherings held there will have entailed some economic benefit for the colony. In the years immediately following its foundation, the future of Lyon as one of Gaul's major urban centres must have seemed assured.

These expectations were never really fulfilled. In part this may have been due to the fact that Augustus split Gallia Comata into three separate provinces – Aquitania, Belgica and Lugdunensis – of which only the last was ruled from Lyon (although Lyon did retain some overall supervising functions as regards Aquitaine). Probably more important was the colony's lack of a tribal base – it seems to have had only the most minimal territory. Then there is the town's purely civil function. The big spender in the Roman scheme of things was the army, and Lyon was a long way from the Rhine frontier and its legions. All it had to bolster its economy was a single cohort.

Lyon's prosperity was confined to the first and second centuries AD, when it was the seat of an important imperial mint. But the third century saw its original site abandoned, with the remaining population concentrated in a strip of land between Fourvière and the Saône. The turning point is usually taken to be the city's decision to back Albinus' unsuccessful challenge to Septimius Severus in the civil war of AD 197. However, despite the fact that the decisive battle between the two was fought nearby, there is no direct evidence, either literary or archaeological, that Severus torched Lyon, and archaeologists think that the move away from the hilltop was already in progress in the late second century. Be that as it may, the significant fact is that Lyon could not recover from whatever bad experience it may have had. In the course of the third century it became a small place, not really deserving its status as the capital of a major province.

This melancholy fact was recognized in the provincial reorganizations that took place in the late third and mid fourth centuries, when Lugdunensis was split, first into two, then into four parts. Lyon, which had started out as the master of sixty cities, ended up as the capital of a mini-province that consisted of only three (including Lyon itself).

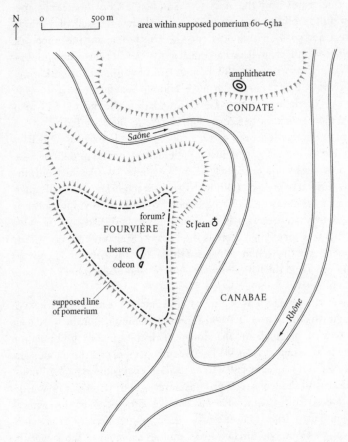

Condate was abandoned at much the same time as Fourvière. The last recorded act of the 'sixty cities' is dated to *c.* 260, and reused material from the meeting place has been found among the late Roman constructions bordering the right bank of the Saône. The main focus of these was the cathedral of St Jean, with its associated baptistry of St Stephen.

Topography and Population

Aside from tombs, present-day Lyon has only three Roman monuments to show: a theatre and an odeon in Fourvière, and the amphitheatre where the delegates of the sixty cities met in what was then Condate and is now Croix-Rousse. The theatre (Augustan) and the odeon (Hadrianic?) have been carefully excavated and restored. The remains of the amphitheatre (built by Tiberius) are relatively scanty. Lyon also has excellent museums including, for those who are interested in that sort of thing, a superb lapidary collection.

Population is an interesting topic, if only because it shows how ideas can change. Nineteenth-century estimates ranged from 400,000 to 200,000. By the twentieth century the figure had come down to 35,000. Given that the settlement on Fourvière was comparable to POMPEII in area, and that the consensus nowadays is that Pompeii had a population of around 6,000, anything over 10,000 seems improbable. More likely the density was below, not above, Pompeii's, and that Lyon's population, even including the riverside suburbs, was never more than 6,000 to 7,000. And that only during the first and early second centuries AD; by the third it will have been well on its way down to the 500–1,500 band characteristic of Gallic towns in the Dark Ages. Curiously, when Lyon began to revive in the ninth century, the focus was at Condate (the medieval Bourg), not the late Roman enclave around the cathedral (the Cité).

MAINZ

Rhineland-Palatinate, Germany

Classical *Moguntiacum;*
capital of Upper Germany

History

Moguntiacum was named for Mogon, a Celtic god who presumably had a sanctuary of some sort in the vicinity. What interested the Romans about the site was its geographical position, as it overlooks the Rhine just downstream from the point where the river is joined by the Main. This made Moguntiacum an obvious command-and-control centre for the upper Rhine, and Augustus posted two legions there as early as 13 BC. The legions set up their camp on a hill a bit back from the river. As the camp's perimeter follows the contours of the hill, its plan is less regular than the general run of legionary fortresses. It covers twenty-eight hectares, a somewhat smaller area than one would have thought was needed for two legions, but then there was a satellite camp four kilometres (2.5 miles) upstream at present-day Weisenau. Some troops will also have been detached to man the fort at the head of the bridge across the Rhine. The bridge, of course, was the military establishment's *raison d'être*, and its construction must have been one of the first tasks that the legions undertook.

As one of the empire's biggest military bases, Mainz soon attracted a considerable civilian population. The whole left bank of the Rhine, from the harbour area a couple of kilometres downstream from the bridge, to an area opposite the junction with the Main a kilometre upstream, was dotted with the houses of traders and shopkeepers, and the shacks and lean-tos of less-respectable camp followers. The second century AD saw a theatre built at the southern end of this straggling town; there must already have been an amphitheatre somewhere, probably close to the legionary fortress, but it hasn't been located as yet.

In AD 90 the garrison of Mainz was reduced from two legions to one, and Upper Germany became a civilian province (as opposed to a military command). This did not result in any loss of status for the town, where the provincial governor simply replaced the previous general in command – the two were anyhow not all that different in the Roman scheme of things. The only significant result was a shift in the centre of gravity from the legionary fortress on the *Hochplateau* to the as-yet-undefined town between the fortress and the river. Just how far this shift had gone by the third century is apparent in the drastic revision of the defences that took place after the near collapse of the empire in the 250s. All but the eastern end of the *Hochplateau* was abandoned, and a new wall built running in an arc from the river to the eastern end of the legionary fortress and then back to the river again. The focus was now entirely on the town, and whatever garrison remained was accommodated within the new circuit. This enclosed a tad under 100 hectares (assuming the missing corners have been filled in correctly), a very considerable area for this period, when the urban element was generally contracting rather than expanding.

The final century of Roman Mainz is ill-documented. The garrison was placed under the command of a 'Dux Moguntiacum', but he seems to have had very few troops at his disposal: neither in 368, when there was a serious German invasion, nor in 406, when a second incursion began the downfall of the Western Empire, did the town manage a successful defence. All that survived this debacle was the town's ecclesiastical function, and Mainz soon joined the ranks of Dark Age 'towns' that consisted of nothing more than a few dozen poor dwellings clustered around a modest-sized cathedral. Things only began to pick up again in the ninth century AD.

Population and Topography

Garrison towns – towns where the soldiers outnumber the civilians – aren't real towns, so the idea that by AD 90 Mainz is likely to have had a population of around 15,000 (certainly 10,000 soldiers, and perhaps as many as 5,000 civilians) isn't of much interest to the urban historian. But if, as is perfectly possible, Mainz hung on to the majority of its

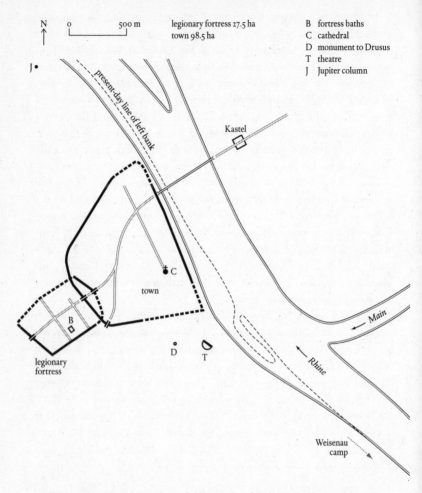

N

0   500 m

legionary fortress 27.5 ha
town 98.5 ha

B   fortress baths
C   cathedral
D   monument to Drusus
T   theatre
J   Jupiter column

J•

present-day line of left bank

Kastel

C

town

B

Main

legionary
fortress

D   T

Rhine

Weisenau
camp

civilians after the reduction of the garrison to a single legion, the town
would have acquired a viability that it hadn't had before, and by the second century, with imperial prosperity at its peak, a half-military, half-
civilian population of 10,000 would have given it a significant, if still
slightly ambiguous, place in the urban hierarchy of the Gallic provinces.
After AD 300 its relative position will have improved, even if absolute
numbers fell. Decline will have accelerated with the rundown of the
frontier defences that took place in the mid fourth century: by the mid

fifth century, population is more likely to have been under than over the 1,000 mark.

Other than the (excellent) Landesmuseum Mainz and the Römisch-Germanisches Zentralmuseum there is not much to be seen of Roman Moguntiacum. There is the stump of a large monument to Drusus, Tiberius' younger brother, and a replica of a Celtic 'Jupiter-column' put up in the wrong place. The other remains are foundations only. An interesting non-material survival is the name Kastel, still applied to the bridgehead suburb across the Rhine.

MALATYA

Eski Malatya, 'Old Malatya', Malatya province, East Turkey

Classical *Melitene;*
capital of the late Roman province of Armenia 2

Malatya has its origins in a legionary fortress constructed by XII Fulmi-
nata as part of Vespasian's reorganization of the eastern frontier in
AD 71–2. The same legion continued in garrison at the site until the system of fixed defences was abandoned in the fifth century, a period of
some 400 years during which Malatya acquired a considerable civilian
population. The settlement was raised to municipal status by Trajan and
eventually, in the fourth century, became the capital of the late Roman
province of Armenia 2. It retained this role until provinces were replaced
by themes in the eighth century.

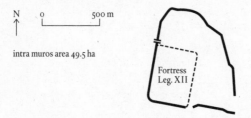

N   0   500 m

intra muros area 49.5 ha

Fortress
Leg. XII

Although no excavations have been carried out at Malatya, the line of
its walls is still visible. On the west and south they are completely
straight and clearly derive from the original fortress, the implicit dimensions of 500 by 360 metres and area of 18.5 hectares being normal meas-
urements for a legionary camp of the early imperial period. The part of
the circuit enclosing the adjacent civilian quarters (which brings the
total intra-mural area up to 49.5 hectares) is ascribed to the early sixteenth century. This seems very unlikely, although a wall of earlier date
could have been remodelled at that time.

MARSEILLE

Bouches-du-Rhône, France

Ancient Massalia, or Massilia

In around 600 BC, colonists from Phocaea in Ionia founded a settlement, Massalia, on three low hills overlooking the Gulf of Lyon. It was close enough to the mouth of the Rhône to serve as a point of transshipment for trade up that river, but it was far enough away to avoid the river's steady build-up of silt. Another attraction was a readily available source of fresh water. In Massalia, Greek colonists traded the amphorae and luxury goods of their homeland for such products as grain, amber and tin. As the city grew, it founded its own colonies, notably at Nice, Antibes and Ampurias.

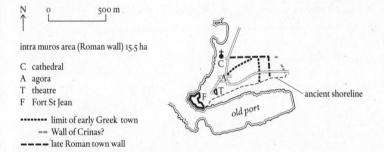

N   0   500 m

intra muros area (Roman wall) 15.5 ha

C   cathedral
A   agora
T   theatre
F   Fort St Jean

- - - - - - - limit of early Greek town
       Wall of Crinas?
— — — — late Roman town wall

ancient shoreline

old port

When attacked by Hannibal in the Second Punic War, Massalia remained true to ROME. Massalia was less prescient, however, when it backed Pompey in the civil war against Caesar. When Caesar took the city after a six-month siege in 49 BC, he spared it from destruction out of regard for its venerable past, although Caesar felt it prudent to relieve the city of its fleet and war machines.

Over the years, the city's importance did not improve to the same degree as the local wines. Politically and in connection with the Rhône trade, it was overshadowed by growth of the imperial administrative centre at LYON. The defences of Massalia were again tested when the emperor Maximian took refuge there after falling out with Constantine I. Maximian was besieged, however, and compelled to surrender.

Built on a promontory above the Vieux Port, the city was well protected against both hostile Segobrigii Gauls and enemies who might arrive by sea. It has always been a polyglot city of sailors and a melange of cultural diversity. The historian Tacitus, in the fourth chapter of the biography of his father-in-law (Gnaeus Julius Agricola) who studied in Massalia, wrote that it was 'a place where Greek refinement and provincial frugality meet in a happy blend'.

For years, it was difficult to determine the features of the ancient city because it had been covered by the great modern port. Common wisdom taught that the city had declined severely after the siege in 49 BC. More recent excavation in the port area suggests, however, that Massalia remained an active centre of trade well into the late Roman period. More than fifty ancient wrecks have been discovered in the Bay of Marseille, and many of the artefacts are displayed on the site of a former Roman warehouse (the Musée des Docks Romains).

MEMPHIS

Egypt

History

Memphis, like Cairo, lies close to the junction between Upper Egypt, the land watered by the undivided Nile, and Lower Egypt, the Delta. This transition area is the country's natural communication centre, the northernmost place from which land journeys can be made with the minimum number of river crossings, and the nodal point for river journeys of any description. Its advantages were quickly appreciated by King Menes, the ruler who unified Egypt and became its first pharaoh around 3000 BC. As soon as his command over the country was complete, he moved his court here (from Thinis, far to the south), making Memphis the seat of his administration. We don't know exactly where he built his palace but it will have been somewhere near the Temple of Ptah, which lay on the left bank of the Nile at the centre of the southern part of the Memphite tell. Alas, there's nothing to be seen of Old Kingdom Memphis today, not even the river, which has been shifting steadily eastwards over the centuries and now lies three kilometres (two miles) to the east.

What does remain is the string of pyramids and funerary temples that stretches along the desert edge, marking the burial places of the Old and Middle Kingdom pharaohs. The sequence starts eighteen kilometres (eleven miles) to the north with the three great pyramids of Giza, runs south on the escarpment overlooking Memphis, where the Saqqara cluster includes the prototype monument, the step pyramid of Zoser, and finally terminates some sixty-five kilometres (forty miles) further south with the al-Lisht group and the bent pyramid of Sneferu. In total this fantastic linear necropolis spans some eighty kilometres (fifty miles), the entire length of the Memphite nome. In it, the Egyptian preoccupation with the afterlife and taste for the colossal finds its earliest expression; it is also, and more relevantly from our point of view, an homage to the rituals prescribed by the mummiform god Ptah, and the first work of the death industry that was to underpin the Memphite economy throughout the city's history.

During Old and Middle Kingdom times (roughly 3000–1700 BC), Memphis was probably not a very impressive sight. There is no reason to believe that the Temple of Ptah was significantly larger than other temples of the time, or that the village that lay outside its precinct walls was of more than modest dimensions. But when grandeur finally arrived, it did so with a bang. As is so often the case in Egypt, the man responsible for construction was Rameses II, the ruling pharaoh in the middle years of the New Kingdom. During his sixty years on the throne, Rameses II (1300–1240 BC) built on an unprecedented scale, as witness the great hypostyle hall at Karnak and the Temple of Abu Simbel in Nubia. Because almost nothing remains of it, his work at Memphis is less well known, but his reconstruction of the Temple of Ptah was clearly of a magnificence to match anything he achieved elsewhere. The best measure of this is the size of the temple precinct, which he enlarged to nearly twenty-five hectares. Whether or not he also built a new palace is unknown, but his successor Merenptah did, in the area between the south-east corner of the precinct and the Nile. It covered about five hectares. From this time, Memphis will have had all the trappings needed for a ceremonial capital. The 'Temple of the Ka [soul] of Ptah', pronounced like 'Egypt', became synonymous with the government of the country, and thereafter was the term usually used by foreigners when referring to it.

The reign of Rameses II marks the apogee of the New Kingdom, which subsequently drifted out of Near Eastern politics and into a centuries-long state of somnolence and backwardness. A rude awakening came with the Assyrian invasion in 675 BC, and although this particular intrusion was brief, Egypt had to live with the threat of invasion by one or other of the great powers for the next 150 years. As the Egyptian military was too far gone in decline to be of much help in this situation, the pharaohs had to look abroad for their troops. They looked to the Aegean, and specifically to the 'bronze men', the armoured spearmen of Greece and Caria. Some of these mercenaries were stationed at Pelusium, the gateway to Egypt, but many were installed at Memphis, in a camp to the north of the Temple of

Ptah. Here the pharaohs of the time built a palace and citadel, within a precinct that matched the scale of the temple. It's a situation reminiscent of the split that existed in so many French medieval towns between the secular ruler's *ville* and the separate *cité* centred on the cathedral.

The pharaoh's mercenary army drove off the Babylonians but succumbed to the Persians (525 BC), who in due course were beaten by Alexander the Great (332 BC). Alexander made Memphis, which had retained its capital status under the Persians, his first stop, and it was in the Temple of Ptah and according to ancient ceremonial that he was crowned pharaoh. However, Alexander had plans for Egypt that were anything but traditional, including the construction of a new capital on the coast called – surprise, surprise – ALEXANDRIA. This was still being built when, nine years later, he died, and as a temporary measure his general Ptolemy placed his body in the Temple of Ptah. Mummified by the god's priestly undertakers, Alexander's corpse lay there until 313 BC, when Ptolemy – now de facto king of Egypt – declared Alexandria officially open. He moved his court there from Memphis, and Alexander's body along with it.

The building of Alexandria necessarily meant demotion for Memphis, but it continued to be the second city of Egypt during the Ptolemaic and early Roman periods. The early Ptolemies (up to Ptolemy VII in 171 BC) were crowned there, just as Alexander had been, and pilgrims continued to come in large numbers to the Temple of Ptah. But now it was not Ptah who was the object of their veneration, but Osiris, the god of resurrection. Since the time of Rameses II, this cult of Osiris had focused on a sacred bull – the Apis – kept in the southern part of the temple precinct. When the bull died it became Osiris, and was treated as such, being mummified and buried in a special catacomb in the Saqqara necropolis. It was then replaced by a new Apis, found after a nationwide hunt somewhat like that for a new Dalai Lama, its identity confirmed by a special set of markings. All Egypt contributed to the bull's upkeep, and the cult became the country's closest approximation to a national religion. The Ptolemies actively encouraged it, merging their own, entirely synthetic deity Serapis with Apis-Osiris, which is why the catacomb of the bulls is referred to as the Serapeum. Egyptians had no objection to this sort of thinking; in fact it is clear that many of the pilgrims visiting Memphis used the sanctified site to pay homage to

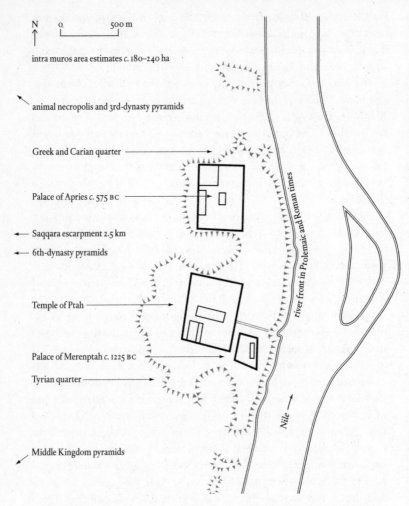

N

0   500 m

intra muros area estimates *c.* 180–240 ha

animal necropolis and 3rd-dynasty pyramids

Greek and Carian quarter

Palace of Apries *c.* 575 BC

Saqqara escarpment 2.5 km

6th-dynasty pyramids

Temple of Ptah

Palace of Merenptah *c.* 1225 BC

Tyrian quarter

Middle Kingdom pyramids

river front in Ptolemaic and Roman times

Nile

their home-town gods. For example, a common object of worship was the ibis, the bird sacred to Thoth. At Memphis the believer could buy an ibis and for an appropriate fee have it embalmed and buried in an ibis catacomb. There are literally tens of thousands of ibises, each individually wrapped and potted, in galleries tunnelled into the western escarpment. And there are other galleries for hawks and cats.

If, as seems likely, this obsession with mummification as a preliminary to rebirth had become the main prop of the Memphite economy in the early Christian era, so the rise of Christianity, with its own vision of immortality, put the city's continuing existence into question. The end came with extraordinary speed. So far as we can tell, in AD 200 Memphis was still functioning much as it had done for the previous several centuries. Yet by AD 302 when the future emperor Constantine the Great passed by, the place had already become a deserted tumble of ruins. The old gods and their worshippers had fled; the ibises were just birds and the cats just cats.

Topography

The known elements in the plan of Memphis are few and simply listed. They are, from north to south: the quarter of the Greek mercenaries; the quarter of the Carian mercenaries; the palace and citadel of the 26th-dynasty pharaohs; a low-lying area dividing the northern and southern halves of the town; the temple of Ptah; some minor temples; and the quarter of the Tyrians. The outlines of the palace/citadel and of the Temple of Ptah were established by Flinders Petrie in six seasons of excavation at the beginning of the twentieth century; Petrie also uncovered the short-lived palace of Merenptah, east of the Temple of Ptah, which burned down within a few years of building. The other items are only known from literary references.

Recent investigations have filled in some details regarding the west gate of the Ptah precinct and the minor temples on its south side. More important are the results of soundings taken by the Egypt Exploration Society's team, which have greatly improved our understanding of the history of the Memphite tell.

Population

As there are no surviving data about the population of Memphis, estimates of its size have to be derived from the archaeology of the site. This is not quite such a disheartening prospect as you might think, because it is clear that until about 600 BC the city was confined to the southern half of the tell. This has an area of about 110 hectares, which in theory is enough room for a population of 10,000 or so, but there are cogent reasons for believing that the actual number was considerably lower than this. Firstly, twenty-five hectares were taken up by the precinct of the Temple of Ptah, which will have had a population of a few hundred at most; secondly, there are only Middle Kingdom remains on the western side of the tell, which suggests that the town was shifting eastwards with the Nile, and that the area inhabited at any one time was never as large as the tell might seem to tell you.

After 600 BC, the case for a population of 10,000 plus is much stronger. Not only did the total area of the site double, but the fact that Egypt was under threat meant that the country needed much stronger administration than before. The armies had to be paid for, which could only be done by wringing more of the cereal crop out of the peasantry. Circumstances like these favour metropolitan growth.

It seems reasonable to posit that Memphis' population first reached 10,000 in 600 BC, and that it had increased to something like 15,000 by 550 BC. This level may have been sustained as long as Memphis remained the capital of the country, i.e. until the administration moved to Alexandria in 313 BC. It will then have dropped back to around 10,000, a figure maintained until AD 150 (pretty certainly) or AD 200 (maybe), when a catastrophic decline set in, leaving the site effectively depopulated by AD 300.

Figures given for the area of Memphis vary from 100 hectares to 365 hectares, which is not so surprising given that there was no city wall and what is being measured is an irregularly shaped tell. Rounding out the existing perimeter yields a pear-shaped area of about 240 hectares. Intruding into this are three low-lying areas which the locals refer to as lakes (singular *birka*) because they used to flood during the Nile's annual inundations. The north birka represents the gap between the northern and southern halves of Memphis; the middle birka the Ptah precinct. What the south birka signifies is disputed, but it seems safe to assume that it was an area with little in the way of habitation. Subtracting these three zones yields a potential inhabited area of about 180 hectares. Figures larger than 240 hectares suppose that there has been significant erosion of the tell, but too much shouldn't be made of this idea: the tell appears to have almost exactly the same topography now as when it was first surveyed by Napoleon's savants 200 years ago.

MÉRIDA

Badajoz province, Spain

Classical *Emerita Augusta; capital
of the province of Lusitania, and later the seat of
both the count and the vicar of the Spains*

Mérida, on the right bank of the Guadiana, was founded by Augustus, supposedly in 25 BC although the archaeologists say that serious work on the town only began some ten years later. It had two functions, the first of which was to provide a home for discharged legionaries, the second to act as the administrative centre for the newly created province of Lusitania. Money flowed freely to make the city worthy of its purposes. It was given two forums, one to serve the townsfolk, another to provide a venue for the delegation that the Lusitanian peoples were obliged to dispatch from time to time to demonstrate their loyalty to the Roman state. There was also a theatre and, somewhat later, probably in the Flavian period (AD 69-96), an amphitheatre and a circus. Just outside the town are another two constructions of early imperial date: a bridge across the Guadiana (with fifty-seven of its original sixty-four arches still standing), and the terminal section of an aqueduct now known as Los Milagros, 'The Marvels' (of which thirty-seven piers and ten three-tiered arches survive).

Mérida seems to have weathered the transition to late antiquity better than the great majority of Roman towns. An element in this better-than-average performance was certainly the provincial reorganization carried out under Diocletian in the last years of the third century AD. In the course of this, most provinces were halved in size; however, Lusitania not only retained all its territory, but its administrative centre, Mérida, had its area of responsibility widened to include all Spain and part of Morocco. The creation of this 'Diocese of the Spains' will have brought a new flow of funds to Mérida, and that this was actually the case is proved by the restoration work carried out in the 330s on the theatre, amphitheatre and circus. These structures make one wonder if there may be a palace to be discovered in this suburban sector comparable to the one recently excavated outside CORDOBA. Something of the sort could be expected to have been provided for such a high-ranking official as the civil vicar of the Spanish diocese, and for his military opposite number, the count of the Spains, who contributed to the restoration of the circus, along with the governor of Lusitania, in 337–40.

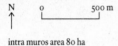

intra muros area 80 ha

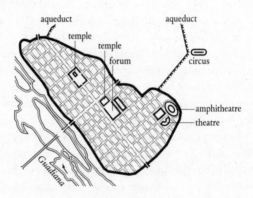

This brings us to the question of Mérida's walls, also substantially refurbished under the later empire, which enclose an area of eighty hectares. Some sections, most notably the riverside stretch, presumably follow the line established in the Augustan period, and it is claimed that much of the rest of the perimeter also has its origins in the Augustan–Flavian era. But it is by no means unlikely that the Augustan foundation was limited to the central core of the town – a rectangle of perhaps thirty-three hectares – and that the theatre and the amphitheatre were originally extramural. If so, Mérida, defying the secular trend, was a bigger place in the late empire than it had been in the imperial zenith.

Mérida remained the titular capital of the Spains through the fifth century, despite being occupied by barbarian invaders – first the Suevi in 439, then the Visigoths in 456. An interesting inscription of 483 has the city's bishop Zeno and the Visigothic nobleman Salla combining forces to repair both the walls and the bridge. But in the sixth century the city declined substantially, and it has never been of much importance since. In the seventeenth and eighteenth centuries its population hovered around the 5,000 mark and was still only 6,000 in 1850. The physical limits of Roman Mérida suggest that numbers in the classical era were probably of the same order.

MILAN

Italian *Milano, Lombardy, Italy*

Classical *Mediolanum; capital of the late Roman
province of Liguria, of the diocese of north Italy and, in
the fourth century* AD, *of the West Roman Empire*

The first settlement on the site of Milan is usually credited to the Etruscans, who in the course of the fifth century BC entered the Po valley and founded a dozen or so 'cities' there. One of these, Melpum, has traditionally been recognized as the forerunner of Milan. There is no real evidence for the identification, and if any form of Etruscan colony did exist where Milan stands today, it would have been swept away in the Celtic invasion of the early fourth century. The Celts who subsequently settled the area were the Insubres, and it was as their tribal capital, under the classical (but Celtic-derived) name of Mediolanum, that the town gets its first certain mention. This is only some thirty years before the Romans imposed their rule on the Insubres, which they did in 196 BC.

Subsequently, Milan grew in a slow and steady way until it emerged, some 500 years later, as the second city of Italy. The legal stages of its development are well known: Milan was officially deemed a Latin town in 89 BC and a Roman one in 49 BC; from being a municipality under the republic it became a colony under the empire. Unfortunately, far less is known about the city's physical growth. At the heart of modern Milan there is a small area distinguished by a rectangular grid of streets. This suggests that at some stage the Romans laid out the city anew. The area involved was only eight hectares, which would indicate an early date (second century BC?) and a tiny population (1,000–1,500 ?). By the geographer Strabo's day (around AD 1) the town had obviously grown a lot, for he puts it in the same category as VERONA. Strabo isn't 100 per cent reliable about Italy, but we can accept the implication that Milan was now in the fifty-hectare class, because the few topographical clues that we have point in that direction.

The next phase, during which Milan outstripped all its rivals in north

Italy, is associated with Diocletian's reform of the imperial administration in the closing years of the third century AD. As far as Italy was concerned, this involved a demotion, for the peninsula lost its special status and was split up into smaller provinces like those in the rest of the empire. Milan, as the largest city in the new province of Liguria, automatically became the seat of the provincial governor. In fact, the neighbouring province of Aemilia was usually lumped together with Liguria, and the governor of Liguria was made responsible for both regions, having larger responsibilities than most of his colleagues. But this enhanced local status was only one element, and a minor one at that, in Milan's

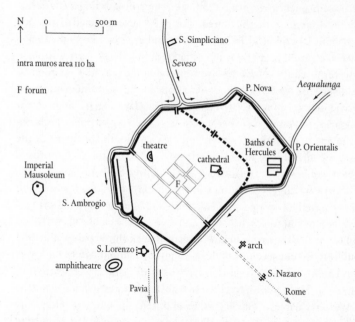

promotion. Diocletian had decided to divide the empire into eastern and western halves, and the colleague he chose to rule the west, Maximian, established his court at Milan.

Maximian brought with him a large retinue, including, on the civilian side, the officials responsible for the next administrative tiers, the prefecture of Italy and the diocese of north Italy. To house them, he embarked on a major building programme, the result of which was the addition of new quarters on both the western and eastern sides of the city. The western side contained a palace and a circus: on the east there was a luxurious set of baths, the 'Baths of Hercules' – Maximian identified himself with Hercules just as Diocletian did with Jove. Milan also became the seat of an imperial mint. As befitted its enhanced size and status, the city was given a new set of walls, enclosing a total of 110 hectares. Ausonius describes these walls as 'doubled', which has been interpreted to mean parallel sets of fortifications like the land walls of CONSTANTINOPLE, but there is no sign of any such doubling in the surviving remains and it is possible that all Ausonius meant is that there were significant elements of an earlier circuit still standing in his day.

For the remainder of the fourth century, Milan continued to function as an imperial capital, although, as the number of emperors fluctuated between one and four at any one time, it didn't always have a resident emperor. What it did have towards the end of the period was a remarkable bishop, St Ambrose, who ranks as one of the most important early church fathers. Ambrose arrived in Milan in a lay capacity, as governor of Liguria and Aemilia. He became the city's bishop by public acclamation in 374 and subsequently emerged as the dominant figure in the Western church hierarchy. He is remembered today for his opposition to the Arian heresy, his introduction of chanting and hymn singing into the liturgy, and his excommunication of the emperor Theodosius I, who had permitted his troops to massacre the inhabitants of THESSALONIKI. His fame, however, has been somewhat overshadowed by that of his disciple, St Augustine, whom he baptized in the baptistry attached to St Tecla, the predecessor of the present-day Duomo, in 387.

St Ambrose died ten years later, as the storm clouds were gathering around the Western Empire. Five years after that, the generalissimo of the Western armies, Stilicho the Vandal, told the emperor Honorius that he couldn't guarantee his safety if he remained in Milan. Honorius sensibly, if not very courageously, thereafter removed his court to RAVENNA. The predicted indignities were not long in coming. Northern Italy was overrun by the Visigoths a few years later, and Milan itself was sacked by Attila the Hun in 452. Major disaster, though, was postponed until the sixth century when the city was recovered for Rome by Justinian's expeditionary force, only to be recaptured and subjected to a merciless sack by the Ostrogothic king Uraia in 539. According to the historian Procopius (*c.* 500–*c.* 562) in his account of the Gothic War, the city was reduced to ashes and its 300,000 male inhabitants slaughtered. As exaggerations go, this alleged death toll must be something of a record, probably being off by something like two orders of magnitude. It is unlikely that the city held more than 15,000 people for the Goths to put to the sword, and there are always some survivors of every massacre. But by the second half of the sixth century, Milan had certainly been reduced to a very low ebb. The Lombards, the final wave of Germans, who took the city in 569, thought so little of it that they chose neighbouring PAVIA – not previously a town in the same class as Milan – as their capital.

Aside from Procopius' lunatic figure, we have no direct statement as to the population of Milan. However, his account (7.21) does make it clear that, despite the loss of the court, the city on the eve of the Ostrogothic sack was still the biggest in north Italy. If we allow 10,000 for Ravenna, this suggests a population of not much less than 15,000. At its peak in the fourth century it may have had a few thousand more. Ideas as to when Milan began to grow into a significant city remain speculative, but 5,000 in AD 1 is a believable starting point.

MILETUS

Present-day *Balat, Aydin province,*
Aegean Turkey

History

Miletus was the most important place in Ionia during the eighth to sixth centuries BC, a period when Ionia – the central sector of Anatolia's Aegean shore – was one of the key centres of the Greek world. It was the mother city of more than thirty colonies, most of them in the Black Sea (Milesian patriots later claimed that the real number was nearer ninety); it was also the focus of the 'Ionian awakening', the initiating phase of classical Greek civilization, and, in the political sphere, the leader of the Ionian revolt, the first in the long series of wars between Greeks and Persians.

Ionia was colonized by Greeks from the ATHENS region in the fifty years either side of 1000 BC. They founded a dozen 'cities' (meaning mini-states), two of them on the offshore islands of Chios and Samos, the rest of them on the corresponding stretch of the mainland. Miletus, the southernmost Ionian settlement, was the only one with a significant previous history, having been an outpost of the island culture of the Aegean in the Bronze Age. But the settlements of that era were tiny: the story of Miletus as an urban centre begins with the Iron Age Ionian community.

Miletus town was built on a peninsula that jutted into the Gulf of Latmos. A hill at its root, present-day Kalabaktepe, served as an acropolis; a wall extending from this defended the peninsula. These defences proved sufficient to ward off a series of invasions by the Lydian king Alyattes at the beginning of the sixth century BC, but subsequently the Milesians succumbed to Lydian pressure, and by the time of King Croesus they had become tributaries of the Lydian state. When Croesus was overthrown by Cyrus, the king of Persia, Miletus was automatically incorporated in the Persian Empire (546 BC). The terms were not harsh and Miletus gained a place in Persian councils.

At first the relationship seemed to work well. Miletus demonstrated its loyalty by faithfully guarding the bridge of boats built across the Danube by King Darius I for his Scythian campaign of 513 BC. This was a significant contribution because the campaign was a failure, and if the Ionians had burned the bridge – as some of them wanted to – Darius' forces would have been in serious trouble. Yet barely fourteen years later, Miletus was to raise an Ionian revolt in an attempt to throw off Persian control. The rebellion was hastily conceived, ill thought out and ultimately doomed. Persian forces closed in on Miletus in 494 BC, broke through the city's defences and razed it. For fifteen years the site lay deserted; then the Greek counteroffensive spearheaded by Sparta and Athens liberated Ionia, and such Milesians as survived began the long task of rebuilding their city. A second Persian occupation (404–334 BC) must have delayed the work, which only really got going after Miletus' final liberation by Alexander the Great.

The revived Miletus grew into a reasonably prosperous place. It never regained its position at the top of the roster of Ionian cities, but it eventually reappeared as number three, after EPHESUS and SMYRNA. In Roman times it retained enough importance to be made the provincial capital of Caria when the original province of Asia was subdivided *c.* AD 300. But this was the city's last bit of good news, for the fourth century was to mark the beginning of a severe decline. This had two components, of which the first was the Mediterranean-wide economic contraction that set in at this time. The second, specific to Miletus, was the silting up of its ports, as the Meander gradually filled in the Gulf of Latmos. In AD 343 the vicar of Asia supervised the construction of a canal that had apparently become necessary for continuing access to the sea. It couldn't solve the long-term problem; by the sixth century the Lion Harbour had been abandoned and a new city wall was built straight across its mouth. This wall, traditionally ascribed to Justinian, protected only the upper town, reducing the intramural area from more than ninety hectares to barely forty. It seems likely that the next century saw a complete collapse in the city's population, although some would argue for a gentler decline. All we know for sure is that by the tenth century AD the only remaining habitation was a castle built on the ruins of the Roman theatre. Here the Byzantine governor of the region had his 'palace', the word for which led the site to be named Balat. In village form Balat survived until 1955 when it was wrecked in an earthquake; the villagers then decided – much to the relief of the archaeologists – to rebuild on a new site, some distance away from the remains of the classical city.

Topography

The few data known for archaic (pre-494 BC) Miletus can be simply stated. There was a fortified acropolis on present-day Kalabaktepe and there were settled areas on the peninsula around the temples of Athena and Apollo. And that's about it. The line of the city wall is unknown, apart from a partially excavated ring wall around the top of Kalabaktepe and a spur from this leading off towards the east side of the peninsula. If this wall took the course suggested in plan I below, the town would have had an intramural area of about 120 hectares.

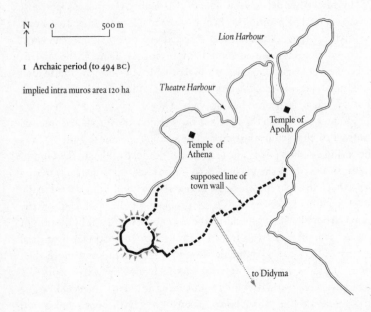

N 0 500 m

I Archaic period (to 494 BC)

implied intra muros area 120 ha

Lion Harbour

Theatre Harbour

Temple of Apollo

Temple of Athena

supposed line of town wall

to Didyma

Considerably more is known about classical Miletus. This is largely because it was built to an overall plan prepared by one of the city's most famous sons, Hippodamus, the 'father of town planning'. Hippodamus' name immediately conjures up a picture of a regular street plan, with housing arranged in rectangular blocks, and Miletus certainly shows this. However, this was only part of his system, which also involved a clear segregation between public and private areas. At Miletus, the public zone lies across the centre of the peninsula, the trademark grids (on slightly differing orientations and patterns) occupying the areas to north and south.

Classical Miletus was smaller than its archaic predecessor. Any reoccupation of Kalabaktepe was short-lived, and the new city wall took a simple line across the base of the peninsula. This reduced the intramural area to some ninety to ninety-five hectares. Aside from the temples inherited from the archaic town, the public buildings included a theatre, a huge agora and a stadium. The Romans greatly enlarged the theatre, remodelled the stadium and built several sets of baths (one donated by Faustina, the wife of Marcus Aurelius). They also built a

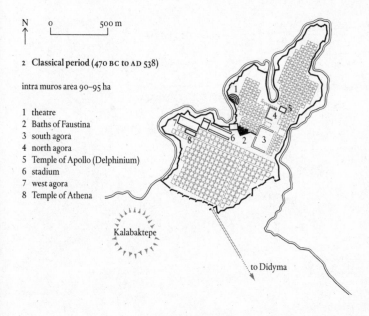

N   o   500 m

2   Classical period (470 BC to AD 538)

intra muros area 90–95 ha

1 theatre
2 Baths of Faustina
3 south agora
4 north agora
5 Temple of Apollo (Delphinium)
6 stadium
7 west agora
8 Temple of Athena

Kalabaktepe

to Didyma

huge monumental gateway to the agora, which German archaeologists moved to Berlin in 1908; it can be seen in the somewhat confusingly named Pergamon Museum. Several churches and an episcopal palace survive from the period of the later empire.

Population

There are no ancient figures on which to base a population estimate for Miletus town; the best we can do is to make an informed guess at the population of the Milesian city state. This can be done in two ways: first by using the number of ships that they manned at the Battle of Lade in 494 BC; secondly by attempting to calculate the 'carrying capacity' of the Milesian chora (countryside). The Battle of Lade represents an all-out effort by a Miletus that was fighting for its life, just as Salamis represents a similar all-out effort on the part of a cornered Athens. The Athenians, with a citizen body of 30,000 adult males, managed to equip

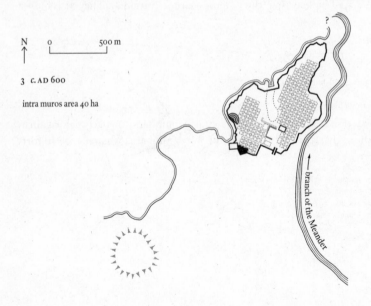

N   0   500 m

3 c. AD 600

intra muros area 40 ha

branch of the Meander

180 ships, the Milesians 80, suggesting that the number of adult male Milesians was about $30,000 \times 80/180 = 13,333$, and, using a multiplier of four, that the total population of Miletus state would have been around 50,000 to 55,000. This is considerably more than the 'carrying capacity' calculations, which fall in the range 23,000 to 34,000. Either way, archaic Miletus was clearly a large polity by the standards of the Aegean world at the time. This solves the main question raised by the colonization programme of the seventh and sixth centuries BC: did Miletus have the numbers to sustain this on its own? Given that only a few hundred settlers were needed to start a colony, the answer is clearly a yes. Even a population at the lower end of the suggested range would be enough to do it.

As to Milesian city proper, all one can say is that on the eve of its destruction in 494 BC it may have housed about 5,000 people. It is unlikely to have had many more because Athens, undeniably the Greek number one at the time, had fewer than 10,000. Recovery from the Persian sack was undoubtably slow, and numbers are unlikely to have reached the 5,000 mark again before the Hellenistic era. In late Hellenistic/early Roman times, the archaeological record shows that the city was adding to its amenities, and it is reasonable to believe that population reached a new peak in the second century AD, the heyday of the classical world. What this peak was is a matter of personal judgement. I would propose a figure of 7,000 to 8,000, while recognizing that there was room for twice that number within the walls. On any view the contraction that then set in will have taken numbers down to 5,000 again by the early sixth century when the intramural area was reduced to forty hectares.

MYRA

Deserted site near Demre, Antalya province, south-west Turkey

Capital of the late Roman province of Lycia

History

No later than the fifth century BC, the Lycians had an important city at Myra. On the west bank of the River Myrus (Demre Çayi), it was built around five kilometres (three miles) upstream from its port at Andriace (Kocademre).

When a Lycian league was formed in 168 BC, Myra became one of its six leading cities. The harbour at Andriace served as a base for part of the league fleet, which was protected by an iron chain hanging between two towers. The second-century AD historian Appian records that the army of Brutus and Cassius broke that chain and expropriated the city's gold and silver treasure when fighting against Octavian and the Second Triumvirate. This may help to explain why the city later welcomed both Augustus and his successor Tiberius as 'benefactors and saviours of the entire universe'. In AD 60, St Paul changed ships at Andriace while en route to ROME.

Early in the fourth century AD, the city's most famous inhabitant was its bishop, Nicolaus Orphanos. He was said to perform various miracles, later being revered as St Nicolaus. His cathedral was dedicated to St Irene. After his death, the saint was buried in a Byzantine church that stands at the west end of the Turkish village of Demre. His bones were not, however, destined to rest in peace. In 808, a Saracen commander attempted to destroy the tomb, but he was reportedly misled into destroying another tomb in the same church. In April 1087 a band of adventurers from Bari broke open a tomb under the floor of the church and carried what they understood to be the saint's bones back to their home city. Not to be outdone, the Venetians later claimed to have stopped by and recovered the saint's bones while on their way to the First Crusade. As if that weren't enough, the museum in Antalya has also displayed bones it claimed to have been taken from the tomb of St Nicolaus. As if to compensate for the plundered bones, the churchyard is now adorned with a large metal statue of Baba Noël, inexplicably dressed as Santa Claus.

Under Theodosius II (AD 408–50), Myra became the capital of the Roman province of Lycia, and it seems to have prospered during the Christian era.

Topography

Romans often measured distances in terms of stades, a unit based on the length of a chariot-racing track (around 185 metres or 625 feet). The geographer Strabo described Myra as standing at a distance of twenty stades from the sea. Today the distance is closer to thirty stades, due to the masses of silt that have been carried down into the alluvial plain of the River Myrus. Much of ancient Myra remains covered by this silt.

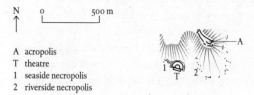

N   0   500 m

A acropolis
T theatre
1 seaside necropolis
2 riverside necropolis

From the pre-Roman time, the most notable visible monuments are two groups of rock tombs dating from the fourth century BC. They are cut into the face of a cliff and reproduce architectural elements from temples and wooden houses of the time. They bear inscriptions in Lycian and Greek. Nearby is a well-preserved Roman theatre, measuring around 120 metres in diameter.

At the port of Andriace, one can still see a granary constructed during the reign of Hadrian (roughly sixty by thirty metres). The front wall was carved with a Roman inscription listing standard weights and measures.

NAPLES

Italian *Napoli, Campania, Italy*

Classical *Neapolis*

History

The settlements the Greeks established in and around the Bay of Naples
are among the oldest of their Italian colonies. The first, on the island of
Ischia (Pithecusae to the Greeks), dates to *c.* 750 BC; the next, at CUMAE
on the mainland, was probably founded about twenty-five years later.
Inside the bay proper the Cumaeans may have set up a trading post on the
island of Megaris (present-day Castel dell'Ovo) by the early seventh century BC. By mid century, however, they were certainly established on the
promontory opposite. Here, on the hill that overlooks the much-roman-
ticized harbour of Santa Lucia, they founded a small *polis* that later
sources say was called Parthenope. At the time it was still unclear whether
this stretch of coast was going to be Greek or Etruscan, and the issue
remained undecided till the early fifth century, when the Cumaeans and
Syracusans won a series of victories that forced the Etruscans out. The
Greeks then decided to consolidate their position by founding a new
polis alongside Parthenope. They called it Neapolis, 'New Town', with
the result that Parthenope became known as Palaeopolis, 'Old Town'.

Palaeopolis can never have been more than a village; Neapolis was a
more ambitious foundation, and it prospered. A lot of this can be put
down to good political judgement. The Neapolitans opted for an alliance with ROME almost as soon as the Romans appeared in the region
(*c.* 327 BC), and they never wavered in their allegiance. The Palaeopoli-
tans, on the other hand, started to quibble about this and that and had
their homes burned over their heads. Neapolis struck coins declaring its
solidarity with Rome; Palaeopolis was never heard of again.

From the fourth century BC to the fourth century AD, Naples has very little recorded history. There was one bad moment, in 82 BC, when the town was sacked by Sulla – picking the right side in a civil war was a nightmare for local governments – but for the rest the Neapolitans were able to enjoy the fruits of the Pax Romana. It is true that the town never received the level of patronage that the emperors lavished on its neighbour Puteoli, which had been founded as a Roman colony in 192 BC, and which imperial decree made the premier port of the region, but Naples jogged along comfortably enough. And by the high point of the empire, Naples became the frontrunner, the most important place in the bay. So far as we can tell, this was almost entirely due to Vesuvius. A catastrophic eruption in AD 79 had already eliminated POMPEII and HERCULA-NEUM, Naples' rivals in the eastern half of the bay. Thereafter a slow

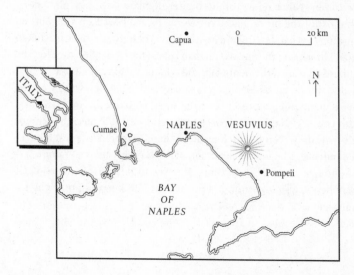

seismic movement in the western half began to pull Puteoli down below sea level. And as Pozzuoli's harbour works flooded, so Naples took over its functions.

Politically speaking, Naples managed to hold the stage even when the Western Empire was losing the plot. Fearing a seaborne attack by the Vandals, the emperor Valentinian III (425–55) ordered the Neapolitans to refurbish their city wall, but he couldn't prevent the Vandals sacking Rome itself. Still, Naples seems to have been rendered safe enough to receive the last Emperor of the West, Romulus Augustulus, who was forced to abdicate by his Gothic guard in 476. This aptly named 'Little Augustus' lived out his last days in a villa overlooking Santa Lucia. Naples, now under Gothic rule, did as well as any place could at a time when the Mediterranean economy was weakening with each decade.

In 535 the Eastern emperor Justinian attempted to recover Italy from the Goths, entrusting the task to his general Belisarius and what looked like an inadequate army. The next year, after a surprisingly easy conquest of Sicily, Belisarius marched up the Italian shin and called on the Neapolitans to resume their imperial allegiance. The Neapolitans refused, not fancying Belisarius' chances against Gothic forces, but Belisarius' troops managed to seize the city by slipping in along its aqueduct. Seven years later a Gothic counteroffensive retook Naples, along with most of the other places recovered by the East Romans, but ten years after that Naples, together with the rest of Italy, was back in Roman hands. This wasn't the end of German rule in Italy – in 568 a new lot, the Lombards, invaded the peninsula and conquered almost all of it – but it was decisive as far as Naples was concerned. So long as the Eastern Empire maintained a presence in the west, which it did until the mid eighth century, Naples was part of that empire, and when the empire finally withdrew, Naples, under a line of hereditary dukes, preserved its independence. The final incarnation of the classical city was, appropriately enough, as a city-state ruling the bay. In this form it lasted until 1140, when it was incorporated in the Norman kingdom of Sicily by King Roger II.

Topography

Although there is scarcely a stone to be seen of Greek Neapolis, the city's plan is still clearly visible at the heart of modern Naples, an extraordinary example of an urban pattern persisting over a period of nearly 2,500 years. The orthogonal grid consists of four reasonably broad streets (*plateiai*) crossed by at least twenty, maybe twenty-three, narrow lanes (*stenopoi*). As a result the city blocks are long and thin. This is in striking contrast to standard Roman town planning in which the blocks are typically square, as for example at PAVIA, PIACENZA and

VERONA. The city's walls also lasted a long time, until the period of rapid growth that began in the thirteenth century rendered them obsolete, and they began to be quarried away. Now there is very little left except their foundations, and even these have been found only on the north and east sides; their course on the west and south can only be guessed at, using the street plan and the lie of the ground as guides.

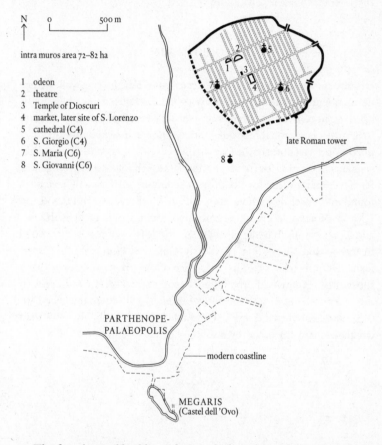

N   0   500 m

intra muros area 72–82 ha

1 odeon
2 theatre
3 Temple of Dioscuri
4 market, later site of S. Lorenzo
5 cathedral (C4)
6 S. Giorgio (C4)
7 S. Maria (C6)
8 S. Giovanni (C6)

late Roman tower

PARTHENOPE-
PALAEOPOLIS

modern coastline

MEGARIS
(Castel dell 'Ovo)

The few classical buildings that can be located on this grid are in the area of the forum, in the centre of town. They amount to a theatre, an odeon, a temple of the Dioscuri (the heavenly twins, Castor and Pollux) and a market, all of early imperial date. An amphitheatre and a stadium are documented but not located. In the fourth century these buildings were neglected as attention turned to the provision of churches for the increasing number of Christians. In or soon after AD 355, Constantius II built a basilica that became known as Santa Restituta, the precursor of the present-day cathedral; other churches were added under later Roman emperors, by the Goths and, after the reconquest, by Justinian. In the seventh century all building ceased.

Population

Despite the uncertainty about the exact course of the city wall, we can be confident that the intramural area will have fallen somewhere in the 72- to 82-hectare range, which suggests a maximum population of 7,000 to 8,000. It is reasonable to believe that numbers reached this level during the imperial noon of the first to third centuries AD, and that the subsequent decline was, by the standards of its neighbours, relatively gentle. Partial compensation for the drop in economic activity will have been found in the well-documented reception of refugees from Puteoli and CAPUA. Nonetheless, contraction could not be avoided and by the seventh century must have been severe. A telltale layer of black earth dated to this period shows that previously built-over land was now being farmed. On the other hand, persistence of the street grid shows that a substantial fragment of urban life was still preserved. A community of the order of 2,000 to 3,000 would be enough to maintain the necessary continuity, and if that doesn't sound much, it was probably more than could be said of any other town south of Rome.

NINEVEH

On the River Tigris in Iraq

Capital of Assyria

History

It appears that the earliest occupation of the citadel mound of Nineveh (Tell Kuyunjik) dates from around the seventh millennium BC. By the second millennium BC, it was already an important city with a well-known temple dedicated to the goddess Ishtar. At the end of the eighth century BC, after the rapid rise and sudden fall of his father's capital at DUR-SHARRUKIN, Sennacherib (704–681 BC) decided to construct a new capital city on the site of Nineveh. His residential complex had an impressive length of around 500 metres, and he modestly called it the Palace Without a Rival. Sennacherib's grandson Ashurbanipal (669–627 BC) built a second palace, which contained the famous lion-hunt reliefs that may now be seen in the British Museum.

The city ultimately expanded to the point where its double walls covered a distance of around twelve kilometres (7.5 miles). These walls were pierced by at least fifteen gates, guarded by giant stone winged figures. As an indication of the city's size, the Old Testament prophet Jonah records that it took 'three days' journey' to cross it (Jonah 3:3). Of course, Jonah also recorded having spent three days and nights in the belly of the great fish, suggesting that reference to three days may have been a literary device used to describe a long time.

In the summer of 612 BC, Nineveh was sacked by Medes and Babylonians. Although thereafter greatly reduced in importance, Nineveh survived as a Hellenistic, Parthian and Roman city for another 1,000 years.

The well-published excavation of Nineveh by Austen Henry Layard, which began in 1846, is a milestone in the history of archaeology.

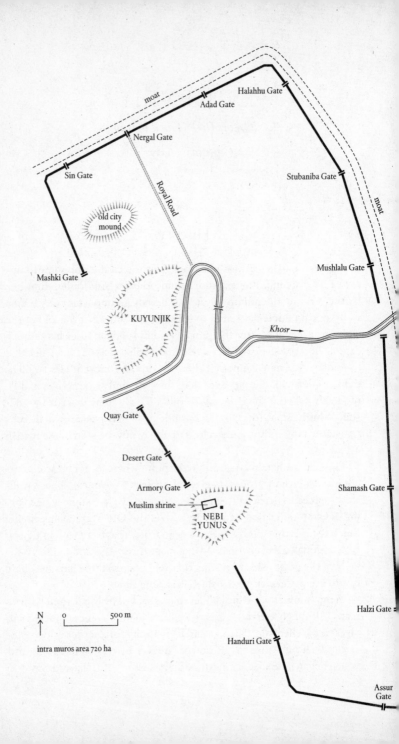

moat

Halahhu Gate

Adad Gate

Nergal Gate

Sin Gate

Stubaniba Gate

moat

old city mound

Royal Road

Mashki Gate

KUYUNJIK

Mushlalu Gate

Khosr →

Quay Gate

Desert Gate

Armory Gate

Shamash Gate

Muslim shrine

NEBI YUNUS

N

0   500 m

Halzi Gate

intra muros area 720 ha

Handuri Gate

Assur Gate

Population

At 720 hectares, Nineveh was twice the size of CALAH, and as it ruled an empire twice as big, it could well have had twice the population. The prophet Jonah, who wanted the Lord God to destroy Nineveh, reports that one of His reasons for refusing was the multitude of people in the city: 'more than six score thousand' (Jonah 4:11). It is just possible that this figure derives from a stele like Ashurnasirpal II's at Calah and represents the number who attended a feast celebrating the city's dedication. If so, it would double Ashurnasirpal II's figures in each category, i.e. a city population of 32,000 and a guest list of 120,000. We know that both Sennacherib and his son Esarhaddon held such feasts.

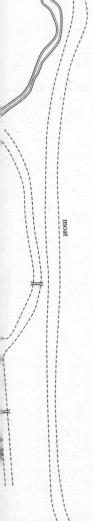

moat

OSTIA

Lazio, Italy

The great port of ancient ROME was located thirty kilometres (sixteen miles) away at Ostia, at the mouth (from which it derives its name) of the River Tiber. The Romans attributed their acquisition of this site to their semi-legendary king Ancus Marcius in the second half of the seventh century BC, who may have expanded Roman territory in that

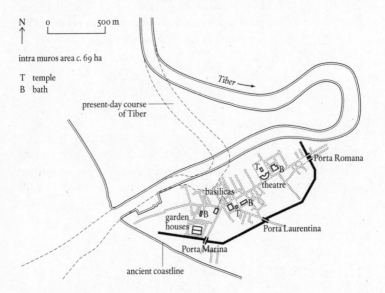

direction in order to gain control of nearby salt beds. Ostia was important to Rome for various reasons. In addition to providing salt, it served as a point of defence against enemies who might arrive by sea, and as the centre of trade for products being trans-shipped into or out of the Tiber.

During the First and Second Punic Wars (264–201 BC), Ostia became an important Roman naval base. Later, the military fleet gave way to a crowded harbour of merchant vessels, especially those carrying grain from North Africa.

Under Agrippa in the second decade BC, the city received its first permanent stone theatre. As Rome increased its demand for imported products, the original harbour proved too small. Claudius (AD 41–54) therefore built a large artificial harbour three kilometres (two miles) to the north. It was formally inaugurated by Nero (54–68), who depicted it on the reverse of a famous sestertius. Trajan (98–117) added an impressive hexagonal dock area, which remains largely intact today. A community grew up around the artificial port, and Constantine I (306–37) recognized it as an autonomous entity under the name Portus Augusti Ostiensis, or 'Portus' for short.

Foreign trade brought great wealth to Ostia. Three public baths, large granaries and multi-floored apartments survive to bear witness to this prosperity. Over time, however, Ostia tended to lose both business and population as visiting vessels came to prefer the newer harbour facilities in Portus.

The size of Ostia has been reckoned at around sixty-nine hectares. Based on its relatively dense settlement pattern, Jonathan Reed has applied an average of 435 persons per hectare to derive an estimated population of 30,000 at the city's high point. Russell Meiggs has estimated more than 50,000, but that figure seems excessively high.

Trade continued to decline as the Pax Romana gave way to conditions in which the Mediterranean became increasingly unsafe for commerce. After Arab marauders sacked the Vatican in 846, Pope Leo IV responded by blessing an Italian coalition fleet led by Duke Sergius I of NAPLES. At the Battle of Ostia in 849, with assistance from a well-timed storm, Sergius succeeded in scattering the Arab fleet so that it never again threatened Rome.

Over the centuries, the Tiber deposited enough silt so that Ostia is today around three kilometres from the sea.

OVILAVA

Present-day *Wels, Upper Austria*

Capital of the late Roman province of Noricum Ripense;
diocese: Illyricum

Ovilava, a small settlement on the north bank of the Traun, prospered
after the Roman takeover of Noricum, the Celtic kingdom of which it
was a part, in 15 BC. It was recognized as a municipium by Hadrian
(AD 117–38), and as a colony by Caracalla (211–17). Its status was further
enhanced when Diocletian, *c.* 300, divided the province of Noricum into
two, Noricum Mediterraneum ('Inland Noricum') and Noricum Ripense (the part bordering the Danube). Ovilava became the capital of
Noricum Ripense, a position it held until the barbarian invasions of the
early fifth century that swept away the Roman order of things in this
part of the world.

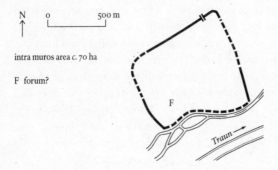

N
0   500 m

intra muros area *c.* 70 ha

F forum?

Ovilava is buried deep beneath modern Wels, so very little is known
of its topography. Enough has been found of the town wall to indicate
that it enclosed a roughly square area of some seventy hectares. The
forum has been tentatively placed in the south-west quarter, but not one
of the public buildings that must have existed in a town of Ovilava's

exalted rank – leaving aside its metropolitan status, it was the only Roman colony in the whole of Noricum – has been identified so far.

Its size and its administrative function suggest a peak population for Ovilava of 5,000 to 6,000, putting it on a par with the Inland Norican capital of VIRUNUM.

PADUA

Italian *Padova, Veneto, Italy*

Classical *Patavium; a city in the tenth region of Italy,*
subsequently the province of Venetia et Histria

Padua, the county town of the Venetic Patavi, is first mentioned in 302 BC when the Spartan condottiere Cleomenes sailed up the Po estuary looking for some easy pickings. The Patavi soon showed that they were well capable of looking after themselves, and after suffering more damage than he had inflicted, Cleomenes withdrew in some haste. The Gauls' entry into north Italy proved more of a problem; it was the need for a counter to their pressure that led the Patavi to form an alliance with the Romans. The Patavi were to remain faithful to this alliance even in the darkest days of the Hannibalic war.

Friendship with ROME, as ever, led to absorption in the Roman sphere, and to the reconstruction, probably in the first century BC, of Padua as a Roman town. It quickly became very prosperous: the geographer Strabo brackets it with VERONA as one of the two most important places in Transpadana after MILAN. And although we know very little about Roman Padua, what we do know matches Verona's topography to an extraordinary degree. Both were situated within a loop of river (the Adige in Verona's case, the Brenta in Padua's); both had an amphitheatre and a theatre at opposite ends of town, outside the formally planned area. As to the street grid itself, we can't say too much because at Padua, unlike Verona, no trace of it remains today, and although something can be hazarded as to its siting and scale (on the basis of the surviving set of Roman bridges, the spacing of which presumably corresponds to the spacing of the main streets), it has to be admitted that the reconstructed plan is a fairly fanciful exercise. Nonetheless, there is only a limited amount of space within the Brenta loop (113 hectares to be exact) and it is not easy to fit in a square of much more than the suggested forty-three hectares. This is much the same as Verona's forty-one hectares.

Where Padua and Verona part company is in their later history: Verona becomes more important, whereas Padua seems to have faded. It survived as a place of some significance, however, until 601, when it was subjected to a brutal sack by the Lombards and was abandoned by such of its inhabitants as survived. They re-established themselves on the far side of the Venetian lagoon, at Malamocco, where they were out of reach of any mainland enemy.

To judge by the chaotic jumble of streets at the heart of medieval Padua, it owed nothing to its Roman predecessors except for the six little bridges shown on the plan. But once refounded it grew rapidly, and by the thirteenth century had become one of the most prosperous places in the Lombard plain. In 1254 the number of adult males taking an oath of allegiance

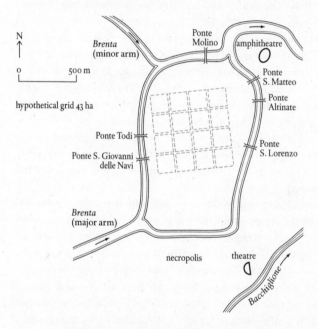

was recorded at 2,606, equivalent to a total population of about 11,000. Of these, about half lived within the loop as defined by a wall enclosing seventy-six hectares. The implied density of 5,500/76 = 72 per hectare suggests a population for Roman Padua of 3,000 to 4,000, although it may have touched 5,000 at its most prosperous in the first century AD.

PAESTUM

Campania, Italy

Formerly *Poseidonia; in classical times, Paestum
was numbered among the cities of Lucania,
the province next to Campania*

Poseidonia, on the Italian shin, was founded around 600 BC by Greeks
from Sybaris, a colony on the instep, and one of the earliest Greek settlements in Italy. The motivation may have been to strengthen contacts
between Sybaris and Etruria, the main trading partner of the Italian
Greeks, and Poseidonia was well suited for this purpose, being halfway
between the two. But if any such benefits accrued to the mother city they
were short-lived, because Sybaris was attacked and destroyed by its
neighbour, Croton, in 510 BC. Poseidonia on the other hand quickly
became an exceptionally prosperous town, the period 550–450 BC seeing the construction of the three major temples (two dedicated to the
city's patron goddess Hera, and one to Athena) that have given the town
its lasting fame. No one would dispute that they constitute the most
impressive testimony that remains to the scale and sophistication of the
Greek enterprise in peninsular Italy.

As was often the case with Greek colonies, there was no trouble initially between the colonists and the native people, who in this case were
an Italic tribe, the Lucanians. They were hill folk, whereas the Greeks
were only interested in the coastal plain. But in the fifth century BC a
rapid increase in the native population – part of a demographic upsurge
that was taking place throughout Italy – brought the Lucanians down
from the mountains and on to the Poseidonian *chora* (rural territory).
The movement was too strong for the Poseidonians to resist, and some
time between 420 and 390 BC (there is no exact date in our sources) the
town passed under Lucanian control. Apart from a brief 'liberation' by a
Greek condottiere, Alexander the Molossian, in 332–326, it remained
Lucanian until it was absorbed into the expanding Roman state in the
early third century BC. By then the use of Greek had ceased and only

one of the many Greek festivals was still being celebrated. Even the name had changed, Poseidonia being replaced by the Italic form, Paestum.

To the Romans, Paestum looked like an ideal site for a colony, and this status was duly established in 273 BC. To mark the occasion, the town was completely revamped. The original Greek plan (as evinced by the three surviving temples) had been oriented at right angles to a line connecting the north and south gates. Now, a new grid was laid out at a six-degree angle to this. (The style is still Greek, with the housing in long narrow blocks, so maybe the surveyors were brought in from

N 0 _____ 500 m

intra muros area 115 ha

P. Aurea
P. Sirena
P. Marina
P. Giustizia

A   Temple of Athena   c. 500 BC [Temple of Ceres]

B   Temples of Hera   c. 450 BC [Temple of Poseidon]
C   c. 550 BC [basilica]

D   agora

E   amphitheatre

F   forum

NAPLES, which has a very similar layout.) At the same time, the eastern half of the city wall must have been relaid in a more rectilinear fashion, as it conforms to the new grid. In fact, the makeover was so extensive one can only assume that under Lucanian rule the town had all but died. This fits neatly with the archaeologists' observation that whereas in the Greek period habitations in the *chora* are rare, in the Lucanian years they are the norm.

The resources the Romans poured into their colony of Paestum (technically Latin, at least until the imperial period) suggest that they had high hopes of it developing into a place of some importance. These hopes were never fulfilled. A second colonization – of discharged sailors from the fleet at Misenum in AD 71 – failed to remedy the situation, and after the town received a damaging coat of ash during the eruption of Vesuvius in AD 79, some of the housing seems to have been abandoned. In fact, the seismic activity around Vesuvius seems to have been the root problem, not because it erupted but because decades of subterranean movement tilted the terrain and raised the shoreline. As the shoreline lifted, the rivers around Paestum no longer flowed directly into the sea, with the result that the Paestan *chora* was turned into a malarial swamp. More than half a century before Vesuvius' great eruption, the geographer Strabo had already observed that the site was waterlogged and unhealthy, and this was doubtless the reason for the town's ultimate failure.

The last phase of Paestum's history saw a remnant population clustered around the Temple of Athena, now a church. The bishopric of Paestum is mentioned in AD 652, but in the next century the site was abandoned in favour of Capaccio five kilometres (three miles) inland, in the relatively healthy foothills. There, a church was built to 'Our Lady of the Pomegranate', the goddess Hera remade in Christian guise, for the pomegranate had always been Hera's attribute.

PALMYRA

Central Syria

History

Palmyra is an oasis in the Syrian Desert, near enough halfway between Homs (ancient Emesa) on the west and Dura-Europos on the eastern, Euphrates side. As such it was a convenient stopping place for caravans using the desert route as a short cut between the two arms of the Fertile Crescent. This caravan traffic doesn't seem to have been very important before the first century BC, but Palmyra was doing well enough by then to attract the attention of Mark Antony. He mounted a raid on the place in 41 BC, hoping for easy pickings. The Palmyrenes thwarted the Romans in the simplest possible way, by abandoning the oasis and disappearing into the desert. For the following fifty years the Romans appear to have left Palmyra alone.

This particular fifty years seems to have been a very prosperous period in Palmyra's history. Perhaps because of the opening of the trans-Asian Silk Road, caravan traffic was increasing rapidly throughout the region. As a result, Palmyra grew in both wealth and population. However, it was no longer possible for the Palmyrenes to abandon their oasis homes and hide in the desert when danger threatened – they had too much to lose. This meant that sooner or later they would have to accept formal incorporation into the Roman imperial system. The accommodation seems to have been made during Germanicus' eastern tour, in AD 14–17. Not long after, Roman-style buildings began to go up in the town and, as the years passed, Palmyra took on more and more of the trappings, both architectural and social, of a Roman provincial town. By the mid third century it had become very grand indeed.

At this point the Roman Empire ran into serious trouble. In 251 the emperor Decius was killed fighting the Goths; in 252 the Persian king Sapor broke through the Roman defences in Mesopotamia and put ANTIOCH, the capital of the East, to the sack. As the higher levels of command failed, power devolved on the provincials. One local noble-man who rose to the occasion was Odenathus, the leading figure in Palmyra, who, operating on the flank of the Persian advance, managed to restore the situation on the eastern front. In 260 the emperor Vale-rian arrived, hoping to build on Odenathus' success, only to lose every-thing by letting himself be captured during a parley. Valerian's son Gallienus, fully occupied in Europe, now gave Odenathus official recog-nition as Rome's commander in the East, and Odenathus once again drove the Persians back, this time as far as the gates of CTESIPHON. His position was so strong that when he died in 267 his widow Zenobia decided to proclaim their son emperor. She even managed to take over most of the eastern half of the empire. But Aurelian, the new Emperor of the West, gave her no time to consolidate her rule, and by 272 nothing was left of her empire except Palmyra itself. The town surrendered on terms only to revolt again the next year and be sacked for its pains. It was never of more than local significance thereafter.

Topography

The ruins of Palmyra constitute one of the most impressive panoramas bequeathed to us by antiquity. This is partly because the remains are relatively well preserved, with, for example, nearly half the 350 columns lining the main street still standing, but more particularly because of the desert setting, which encourages romantic musings on the rise and fall of empires and, indeed, the fleeting nature of life itself. The majesty of ROME conjured the city out of the sands, and when the legions departed, to the sands it returned. And so on.

This line of thought is no doubt aided by the uncompromisingly clas-sical language of Palmyra's architecture. In the land of the Arab, the city seems particularly exotic. It was probably less so in its heyday, for the classical elements often conform to older, purely Mesopotamian ideas. Nowhere is this more apparent than in the town's focal monu-ment, the Temple of Bel. This appears at first glance to be a typical, if rather larger than usual, classical temple, but it was entered via an asymmetrically placed door in the side, and contained statues of its gods at either end.

After the Temple of Bel (and its matchingly outsized precinct), the most impressive of Palmyra's remains is the colonnaded main street. This runs along the central axis of the town, from the Temple of Bel in the south, to the camp of the Roman garrison in the north. On or near it are the public buildings: fountains, baths, a theatre and a fine public market. The Roman camp probably occupied the original nucleus of Palmyra, from which the town gradually spread out southwards. It is always referred to as Diocletian's camp, because it was in his reign that the major building work was done, but presumably the garrison was put in place by Aurelian.

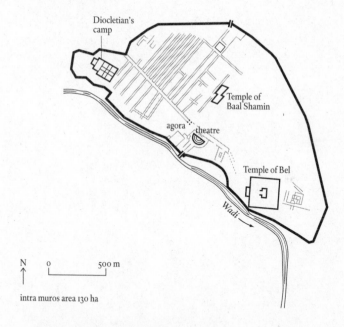

As well as the city wall, assumed to date from Odenathus' day, there is a rampart running roughly a kilometre (0.6 miles) further out. It's either a line representing some jurisdictional boundary of the city or, less likely, a siege-work of Aurelian's day.

Population

Did Palmyra ever reach a population of 10,000? The walls built by Odenathus are extensive, enclosing 130 hectares, and, so far as we can tell, most of this area was inhabited. So it was big enough. The scale of its public buildings suggests that it was also rich enough to attract an above-average population, as does the confidence with which it stepped into the breach created by Valerian's defeat. Its failure to gain a place in the official administrative hierarchy can be explained by its peripheral position and relatively early downfall. On the whole it seems reasonable to put it over the 10,000 line in the mid third century.

PARIS

France

Classical *Lutetia Parisiorum;*
county town of the Parisii

Like the other Celtic tribes of Gaul, the Parisii of the Seine valley had an 'oppidum', a place where they held their tribal gatherings and which, by the last century BC, may have acquired a small permanent population. Caesar (in *De bello Gallico*, VII.58) mentions that this meeting place, known as Lutetia, was on an island in the Seine with bridges to either bank, and it is always assumed that the island concerned was the Île de la Cité at the heart of present-day Paris. There is no direct evidence for this, but the island has the right relationship with the town of the same name that the Romans subsequently laid out on the left bank of the river, so it is a reasonable as well as an emotionally satisfying thing to believe. The new town was officially called Lutetia Parisiorum, 'Lutetia of the Parisii'. In due course it acquired the usual features of Roman urbanism: a forum, a theatre, an amphitheatre and several sets of baths.

In the mid third century AD the good times came to an end as far as the cities of Gaul were concerned. Many of them went up in smoke as barbarian armies roamed through the defenceless territory much as they pleased. What exactly happened to Paris is unknown, but when the fogs of war cleared, the settlement on the left bank was derelict and the population had taken refuge on the Île de la Cité. This was the much-reduced Lutetia of which the emperor Julian spoke so affectionately, praising the climate, the water and the local produce, when he made Paris his headquarters in the winters of AD 358–60.

The Roman town on the left bank of the Seine was never walled, so estimates of its extent (forty to fifty hectares?) and population (3,000 to 4,000?) are matters of choice. The size of the fourth century AD town on the Île can be determined more certainly at nine hectares, indicating that the population at this stage can't have been more than 1,000 to

1,500. This fits with Lutetia's lowly position in the administrative hierarchy: the capital of the province in which it was situated, Lugdunensis IV, was SENS, a town of more than twice the size. In fact, Paris owes its place in this book to its later greatness; it never rated very highly in the Roman scheme of things.

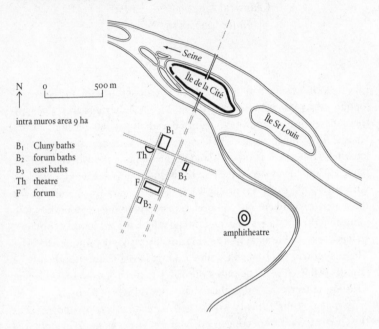

Paris fell to the Franks in 486, and Clovis, king of the Franks, made it his residence in 508. But other kings favoured other places – Charlemagne ruled Western Europe from Aachen – and Paris's position at the top of France's urban hierarchy was not firmly established before the reign of Philippe Augustus (1180–1223).

PATARA

Antalya province, south-west Turkey

*Port city to Xanthos in the late
Roman province of Lycia*

Just east of the mouth of the Xanthus river in ancient Lycia (south-west
Anatolia) lay the port city of Patara. After XANTHOS, Patara was the
second largest city of the region.

Patara followed the fate of the mountainous district where it was
located. The Lycians seem to have originally inhabited the west coast of
Asia Minor. Faced with increasing Greek colonization in that area, the
Lycians migrated to the southern Anatolian coast. There they fiercely
maintained their independence until forced to accept Persian rule in
around 540 BC. They briefly regained independence with Athenian help
around 468 BC, but Persian rule resumed and they were also temporarily subject to Mausolus of Halicarnassus (377–353 BC). After most of
Lycia submitted to Alexander the Great, the district passed to Antigonus I (315 BC), who used it as a naval base. Demetrius seems to have
utilized it for the same purpose during his siege of RHODES in 304 BC.
In the third century BC, Ptolemy II acquired and restored the city, briefly
renaming it Arsinoe in honour of his wife.

By AD 197 the city had returned to the Seleucid Empire under Antiochus III. After Antiochus lost the Battle of Magnesia in 189 BC, however, Rome compelled him to accept a disarmament treaty under which
he agreed to give up his elephants and ships of war. In 188 BC a Roman
commander enforced the treaty by burning the Seleucid fleet at Patara.
The Romans then handed Lycia over to their Rhodian allies. After a long
rebellion, however, the Lycians managed to regain their autonomy and
established a Lycian league. By the time of Augustus, twenty-three cities of Lycia elected a collective leader (the Lyciarch) and issued coins on
behalf of their confederation.

In the Pontic Wars, Mithradates VI was unable to take Patara by siege in 88 BC, perhaps because he committed the sacrilege of cutting timber for his siege engines in the precincts of the nearby shrine to the goddess Leto (Letoon). However, in 42 BC, Brutus was successful in a siege after releasing certain female prisoners to the city. Plutarch suggests that the released women persuaded the leaders of Patara that Brutus was indeed an honourable man; although Dio Cassius reports that Brutus added the incentive of setting up an auction outside the city walls where the citizens of Patara could see their captured men being sold one by one into slavery. In either case, Patara was persuaded to hand over all its gold and silver, which were the objects of Brutus' siege.

In around 30 BC, Augustus issued a decree confirming Lycia's freedom, but in AD 43 under Claudius, the territory was annexed and joined to the Roman province of Pamphylia. Patara served as an administrative centre for the Roman governor.

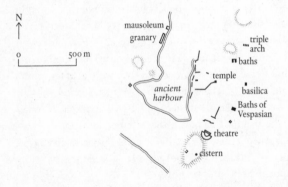

Patara was particularly known for its oracle of Apollo, which seemed to keep surprisingly regular hours. Herodotus reports that the prophetess could not be visited at night, and Apollo was away throughout the six summer months (visiting Delos). Although once highly respected, the oracle of Patara seems to have fallen into disuse by the early years of the Roman Empire. Patara is later famous as the birthplace of St Nicholaus, and a large basilical church was built in the western part of the city during the period of late antiquity. The main commercial attribute of Patara was its port, where St Paul stopped and changed ships on his way back to JERUSALEM at the end of his third missionary journey. Today the former port is an abandoned marshy field separated from the sea by a broad sand dune.

The remaining ruins include a fine triple-arched gateway with inscriptions from Mettius Modestus, the governor of Lycia-Pamphylia around AD 100. The site also offers a well-preserved theatre, in which the cavea has largely filled with drifting sand. The proscenium bears an inscription from the reign of Antoninus Pius (AD 138–61), but another inscription mentions the theatre being repaired as early as the reign of Tiberius (AD 14–37).

PAVIA

Lombardy, Italy

Classical *Ticinum, a city in the eleventh region of Italy,
subsequently the province of Liguria*

Pavia seems to have been a lot more successful at maintaining its identity than in getting into the history books. Its origins are obscure, but it must have been founded as part of the Roman programme for nailing down the Transpadane lands in the second, or, at the latest, the early first century BC. However, the first firm date we have for it is provided by a dedication to Augustus (27 BC–AD 14), implying the existence of a

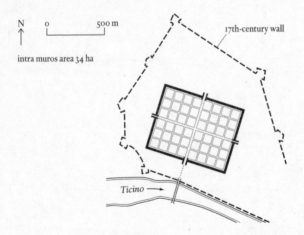

monumental gate in honour of the emperor. The town plan will already have been established by then; to judge from the run of the existing streets it consisted of an array of 6 × 8 = 48 square blocks, covering thirty-four hectares.

In late antiquity, with north Italy under threat of barbarian invasion, Pavia started to attract more attention. The emperor Aurelian installed a mint in the town in AD 274, and a significant body of household troops must have been stationed there in 408 because it was their mutiny that led to the downfall of the Western generalissimo Stilicho. Theodoric the Ostrogoth used it as a winter headquarters and his successors as a stronghold for their treasure. Under the Lombards, who captured the town in 570, it became a capital city, although that is a distinction that has to be seen in the context of the time: the towns of Western Europe were approaching their nadir and, more specifically, MILAN had been knocked off its perch by the Ostrogothic sack of 539. The name 'Pavia' is Lombard; the classical name, Ticinum, is retained by its river, the Ticino.

The first reliable figure for Pavia's population dates from the late fifteenth to sixteenth centuries when it had about 17,000 to 18,000 inhabitants. The intramural area by then was 160 hectares, giving a density figure of 106 to 112 per hectare. Applying this to the Roman area of 34 hectares produces a figure of no more than 3,800, so at its best in the fifth to eighth centuries AD, Pavia's population is unlikely to have been much over the 5,000 mark.

PERGAMUM

Present-day *Bergama, Izmir province, Aegean Turkey*

Capital of the Roman province of Asia

History

In the days when Asia Minor was part of the Persian Empire, Pergamum was the seat of the Gongylides, a dynasty of expatriate Greeks that ruled the Caicus valley on behalf of Alexander the Great (336–323 BC). At this time, Pergamum was no more than a hilltop fortress with a small settlement attached to its southern side, and it was in this form that it submitted to the great king. Subsequently it became part of the territory held by Lysimachus, one of the generals who carved out kingdoms for themselves in the decades following Alexander's death. In 282 BC, on his way to confront Seleucus, the most important of his rivals, Lysimachus parked his war chest in Pergamum, to be watched over by a trusted lieutenant, Philetaerus of Tieium. When Lysimachus was killed in the subsequent battle, Philetaerus found himself sitting on 9,000 talents that had no obvious owner, in the middle of a fortress that had no obvious master other than himself.

Philetaerus played his hand cautiously and cleverly, acknowledging Seleucus' overlordship on the understanding that nothing much was done to implement it. When he died, in 263 BC, he was able to leave what was in effect a little kingdom to his nephew Eumenes, whom he had adopted as a son. Officially, however, it is the next ruler, Attalus I (241–197 BC), who is credited with founding the dynasty, as he was the first to use the title of king. He had three successors, Eumenes II, Attalus II and Attalus III, the last of whom died in 133 BC.

The most important of the Attalids was Eumenes II, who transformed his mini-kingdom into a middle-ranking state – at least as regards territory – by choosing exactly the right moment to become a friend and ally of the Roman people. In 190 BC the Romans expelled the Seleucids from Anatolia; they did not, however, want to rule it themselves, so they gave nearly all the land that the Seleucids had claimed there – roughly the west and south-west of the country – to Eumenes. This made him very rich indeed, but it had its downside, for what ROME had given Rome could take away; the kingdom of Pergamum might be a lot bigger, but it was also a lot less independent. Eventually the business of staying on the right side of Rome proved too much for the royal nerves, and Attalus III decided to bequeath his state to the care of the Roman people. The kingdom was transformed into the Roman province of Asia, with Pergamum as its initial capital.

After a shaky start, the area settled down under Roman rule and the city of Pergamum was able to enjoy the benefits of the Pax Romana. Its capital status was soon lost – EPHESUS was much more convenient from the Roman point of view – but even when Augustus made the administrative transfer official in 28 BC, he allowed Pergamum to keep its seniority in matters ceremonial. Under Hadrian (AD 117–38) the city was the recipient of remarkable imperial favours. It was granted the title of metropolis, and if this was a somewhat meaningless use of the honorific – as part of the same deal Ephesus was promoted to 'first metropolis' – the building programme that the emperor initiated ensured that Pergamum kept its place among the leading cities of Asia. An entire new quarter was laid out at the foot of the hill, with the full range of amenities appropriate for a major Roman town: impressive temples, a huge forum, a theatre, an amphitheatre and a stadium. Nearly a kilometre (0.5 mile) outside the city limits a shrine to Aesculapius, the god of healing, was expanded into a lavish spa, which soon became a Mecca for wealthy Roman hypochondriacs.

Some of the prosperity created by these developments would not survive the downturn in imperial fortunes that marked the second half of the third century. In Pergamum's case the empire's 'time of troubles' was worsened by an earthquake in AD 262, and a sack at the hands of a marauding band of Goths. The arrival of Christianity also had negative impacts: the monuments of the old gods, of which Pergamum had a plethora, were no longer an asset; invalids ceased to come to the Aesculapion, and the site was abandoned. Nonetheless, urban life continued. In the mid fifth century the vast Temple of the Egyptian Gods was converted into a cathedral, a remodelling that looks as if it cost almost as much effort as the original building. Pergamum's economy may have been damaged, but it clearly wasn't defunct.

The end came in the early seventh century, with the Persian invasion that laid waste to so much of Anatolia. When the Persians were finally evicted, there seems to have been little left to restore, and the emperor Constans II (641–68) limited himself to refortifying the acropolis. For the next 500 years this tiny (ten-hectare) area was all there was to the once-proud city of the Attalids. In the eleventh and twelfth centuries there was a partial revival as refugees from the Turkish wars arrived in the area. Manuel Comnenus (1143–80) settled them in the Old Town immediately below the acropolis, cobbled together a defensive wall and declared this revived Pergamum the capital of the new theme of Neokastra. It seems to have been a spare settlement. The emperor Theodore Lascaris II (1254–8) commented bitterly on the contrast between the classical buildings and the 'mouseholes' in which the current generation of Pergamenes were living. The area passed to the Turks in the early fourteenth century – apparently without a fight – which meant that the hilltop town lost its purpose; such inhabitants as chose to remain relocated to the foot of the hill, among the ruins of the Roman town, where water was more readily accessible. This shanty town was to become the nucleus of Ottoman Bergama.

Topography

The original nucleus of Pergamum occupies the top of its hill, with an extension down the southern face, which has a relatively gentle slope. Even there the ground had to be terraced before it could take buildings, and as a result the city steps down this side of the hill, making the site fairly challenging for many tourists. The more feeling guidebooks advise you to take a taxi to the acropolis and walk down into the later city.

Pergamum seems to have had the same set of walls from the fifth to the third century BC, with an interior division between a 4.5-hectare fortress/citadel/acropolis at the northern (highest) end of the hill, and a 15.5-hectare town below it. The acropolis contains a series of rather grand Hellenistic houses that are usually taken to be the palaces of the

Attalid monarchs (although everyone has different ideas about which king lived in which palace), together with a sanctuary of Athena, and a very grand temple that Hadrian dedicated to Zeus and his predecessor Trajan, as well as to himself.

The acropolis also contained the famous Attalid library, said to have held 200,000 books and to have rivalled the Library of ALEXANDRIA until Mark Antony gave its contents to Cleopatra as a wedding gift. The word 'parchment' (*pergamenum* in Latin) was named after the city of Pergamum, where its use was perfected under the Attalids – reportedly during a time when Egypt was withholding papyrus from its rival library.

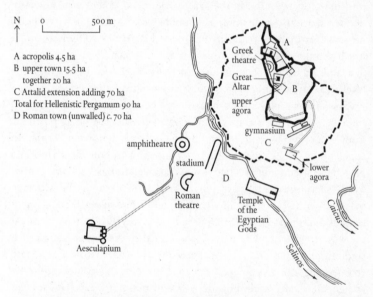

N o 500 m

A acropolis 4.5 ha
B upper town 15.5 ha
  together 20 ha
C Attalid extension adding 70 ha
Total for Hellenistic Pergamum 90 ha
D Roman town (unwalled) *c.* 70 ha

Greek theatre
Great Altar
upper agora
gymnasium
amphitheatre
stadium
Roman theatre
lower agora
Temple of the Egyptian Gods
Aesculapium
Caïcus
Selinus
A
B
C
D

On the west side the slope of the hill was adapted to form a theatre; this has the steepest rake recorded for any Greek theatre and provides a memorably dizzying experience, no play needed.

Immediately below the acropolis lie the remnants of Pergamum's most famous monument, the Great Altar. This was built by King Attalus I to celebrate a victory over the Asian Gauls (St Paul's Galatians) in 230 BC. The battle was presented as the triumph of the Olympian gods over the netherworld giants (i.e. order over chaos) in a long frieze encircling the altar. What has been recovered is now in Berlin, where, painstakingly reconstructed, it forms the centrepiece of the Pergamum Museum; all that has been left onsite are the foundations. The other public buildings in this part of town are relatively minor: a heroon (a shrine for the cult of Hera favoured by the Attalid monarchs) and a small agora. It is safe to assume that most of the rest of the available area – a very cramped 15.5 hectares – was residential.

In the early second century, Eumenes II extended the town to the bottom of the hill and ran a new wall around the hill's base. This increased the intramural area more than fourfold (from twenty hectares to ninety), but given the nature of the ground it is most unlikely that the built-up area increased in the same proportion. There was, however, enough space for some impressive public buildings: a three-level gymnasium (for men, boys and children), a sanctuary of Demeter and a much grander agora than the one in the upper town.

Under the Romans the focus of activity moved from the hill to the level area on the south-west, on the far side of the Selinos river. Here an extensive area – perhaps as much as 125 hectares – was surveyed and then divided up into the sort of urban grid beloved of Roman planners. They stuck to this layout so rigidly that when a major project ran up against the Selinos, they covered over an entire section of the river and placed the large serapeum (also known as the Red Basilica) on top of it. This structure, a temple to the Egyptian Gods, still stands today, a huge mass of brickwork straddling the Selinos, which flows through twin tunnels underneath it. In front of the temple was the Roman forum; on the western side of town there was the usual entertainment complex: a stadium, an amphitheatre and a theatre (the latter able to accommodate 30,000 spectators, as compared with the 10,000 that could fit into the Hellenistic theatre on the hillside). All these buildings seem to have been erected in the reign of Hadrian, and the amphitheatre is particularly interesting. Built over a river, its arena could be filled with water to stage mock naval battles. As there is no reason to believe that the population of Pergamum had suddenly doubled when these buildings were added, the assumption has to be that this Hadrianic programme represents a relocation of the town from hill to plain, not the addition of a suburb.

In the Byzantine period the movement was reversed. Most of the remains of this recolonization of the hill have been removed by archaeologists eager to get at the classical levels, but the walls built around the acropolis in the seventh century, and around the lower town in the twelfth (some say the end of the thirteenth) are still standing. In each case they enclose a slightly larger area than their Hellenistic equivalents (nine hectares plus 16.5 hectares, making a total of 25.5 hectares).

Population

Pergamum under the early Attalids can only have had a small population: there simply wasn't room on the hilltop for more than a few thousand souls. With the extension of the city by Eumenes II the increase in the intramural area to ninety hectares means that, in theory at least, there was space for a population of 10,000 or more, but the reality is that much of the ground is too steep to be of use without extensive terracing, and only the southern face of the hill shows significant traces of that. A population of 10,000 requires an extramural spillover, something for which there is no evidence before Roman times.

This brings us to Roman Pergamum, the unwalled town on the west bank of the Selinos. As is almost always the case with classical sites, considerable knowledge of public buildings is balanced with an almost complete lack of data about the humdrum dwellings that made up the bulk of the development. The amphitheatre, Roman theatre, stadium and Temple of the Egyptian Gods poke up through the Turkish town, but the houses of the people are still buried beneath it. As a result we can't be sure how far the new town extended, although something of the order of seventy hectares is probably a reasonable guess – certainly this is enough to contain all the known remains of the Roman period (bar graves). As regards population, this suggests a figure of around 7,000, putting it in the same ballpark as Hellenistic Pergamum. Add a few thousand for those left behind in the Greek town – priests and servitors for the temples, pedagogues and pupils for the gymnasia – and the population total is somewhere around the 10,000 mark. At a stretch this could apply to the whole Roman period from 150 BC to AD 250.

By 1900 the Ottoman town, after centuries of slow and irregular growth, covered an area of about ninety hectares. It was then thought to have about 15,000 to 20,000 inhabitants, but the first census, taken in 1927, counted only 13,000.

PERGE

Deserted site near Aksu,
Antalya province, south-west Turkey

Capital of the late Roman province of Pamphylia

Perge was one of the half-dozen settlements planted by the Greeks on the Pamphylian (south Turkish) coast during the period immediately following the Trojan War (*c.* 1100 BC). Presumably it started out as a citadel, perched on the hilltop behind the classical town. In the seventh century BC the settlers were reinforced by a Peloponnesian contingent, but Perge attracted little attention before the Hellenistic period when it became prosperous enough to relocate to the foot of the hill. This lower

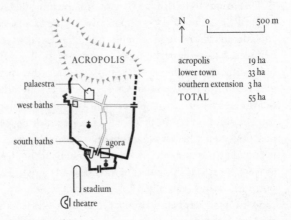

acropolis	19 ha
lower town	33 ha
southern extension	3 ha
TOTAL	55 ha

town was protected by a fine set of walls that enclosed a rectangular area, thirty-three hectares in extent. Curiously, no trace of this or any other circuit has been found on the acropolis, but the archaeological investigation of Perge is still in its early days and there can be no doubt about the hill being fortified. It would have been unthinkable for Perge's citizens to have allowed themselves to be overlooked by an undefended hill, and cisterns atop that hill testify to the city being prepared to hold out at that place.

In the Roman period, Perge did well. A fine palaestra (open-air gymnasium) was erected in the north-west quarter of the town during the reign of Claudius (AD 41–54), and in the Severan era (193–211) a grandiose set of public baths went up outside the south gate. Concurrently the city wall immediately to the east of this gate was torn down to make room for a new agora. A new wall was then built to bring both the agora and the baths within the city. This increased the area of the lower town from thirty-three to thirty-six hectares, a figure we can translate into a population of 4,000 to 5,000.

In the early empire, Perge vied with its near neighbour SIDE for the title of first city of Pamphylia. Eventually the issue was decided in Perge's favour, for when Pamphylia was raised to provincial rank (by Diocletian in AD 297) Perge became the residence of the governor. From this time on there is no doubt that it was the more important of the two. It also seems to have lasted longer, for although the lower town was abandoned in the late Roman period, the acropolis provided a refuge for the more steadfast inhabitants. This remnant held out for a period that can only be guessed at but may have lasted until the eleventh century when Attaleia, modern Antalya, emerged as the leading town of the region.

Perge is well worth a visit. The theatre and the stadium, both situated on the southern approach to the city, make a fine pair of monuments, better preserved than most, and the walls and the original south gate are interesting specimens of Hellenistic military architecture. But there should be more to see than there is. The city's famous Temple of Pergaean Artemis (a variant of the Anatolian mother goddess) hasn't yet been clearly located, and the town plan needs elucidating. It is hoped that the site will soon be adopted by an institution capable of sustaining a long-term programme of excavation.

PERINTHOS

Present-day Marmara Ereğlisi, Thrace, Turkey

*Capital of the Roman province of Thrace and
subsequently, under the name Heraclea, of
the late Roman province of Europa*

Around 602 BC, colonists from Megara in Greece founded a new settlement in Thrace, along the shore of the Sea of Marmara. Known today as Marmara Ereğlisi, it was founded in a strongly defensible position on a high-banked peninsula.

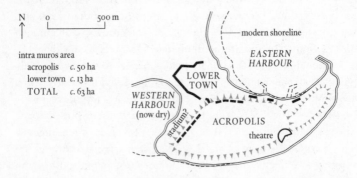

N   0   500 m

intra muros area
  acropolis   *c.* 50 ha
  lower town *c.* 13 ha
  TOTAL   *c.* 63 ha

modern shoreline

EASTERN
HARBOUR

LOWER
TOWN

WESTERN
HARBOUR
(now dry)

stadium?

ACROPOLIS

theatre

Like many Greek cities, Perinthos shifted alliances as the prevailing winds appeared to change. After joining the Delian League, it attempted to break away in 411 BC (during the Peloponnesian War). In 377 BC it joined the Second Athenian Confederacy but later shifted to an alliance with Byzantium that led to brief autonomy in 357 BC. It allied with Philip II of Macedon in 352 BC, but broke away when Philip attacked ATHENS.

In the spring or summer of 340 BC, Philip II laid siege to Perinthos. His troops attacked from the land, while the city continued to receive supplies by sea. Athens reportedly sent 120 ships with arms, hoplites and grain. The Persian satrap from Phrygia also sent soldiers, munitions and gold to aid the defenders. After months of frustration, Philip moved most of his troops away to attack Byzantium (*see* CONSTANTINOPLE), and the siege had been fully lifted before the middle of 339 BC.

Despite its valiant defence, Perinthos was forced to join Macedonia after the Athenian defeat at Chaironeia in 338 BC. Following Alexander's death, the city's alliances continued to shift. Between 255 and 220 BC, it joined with Byzantium in wars against Antiochos II of Syria. At the end of the Second Macedonian War (196 BC), the Romans compelled Philip VI to recognize the independence of certain occupied Greek cities, including Perinthos. By around 188 BC, however, the city became subject to PERGAMUM. It later passed back to ROME in 133 BC to become part of the province of Macedonia. In AD 46 it became part of the newly formed Roman province of Thrace.

When civil war broke out in AD 193 between Septimius Severus and Pescennius Niger, Severus used Perinthos as a base from which to conduct his ultimately successful military operations in Asia Minor. The emperor spent the winter of 193–4 in the city.

By tradition, Perinthos had been founded by Heracles. In around AD 300, Maximian changed the city's name to Heraclea, honouring both the legend and himself (he claimed Heracles as his patron deity). Under Diocletian, who visited the city in AD 286 and again in 293, it became capital of the province of Europa.

In AD 359, Heraclea joined Constantinople and Nicaea in suffering substantial damage from a major earthquake. In AD 378 the Goths threatened to do additional damage, following their victory at the Battle of Adrianople. The city was well served by its defensive walls, however, which again provided effective protection when Attila plundered the region in AD 450.

In AD 514, the Byzantine emperor Anastasius convened an episcopal synod in Heraclea. Justinian improved the municipal water system and the imperial palaces. He also reportedly considered fleeing to Heraclea during the worst of the Nika riots in AD 532. Belisarius moored his fleet there for five days while en route to fight the Vandals. A year after the Avars damaged a church in AD 591, the emperor Maurice visited the city and contributed funds for its restoration. Over the years, however, it was a challenge to keep up with the damage done by recurring earthquakes. Serious damage was recorded in AD 824, 1037–8 and again in

1063. Around 1155 Heraclea became a trading colony of the Venetians, who took full control of the city after their sack of Constantinople in 1204.

Substantial ruins of the city wall are still to be seen, and the grass-covered Roman theatre commands a fine view of the Propontis along the city's southern shore.

PETRA

Deserted site in Ma'an province, southern Jordan

*Capital of the Nabataean kingdom, and subsequently
of the late Roman province of Palestina III Salutaris
(originally Arabia II); diocese: Oriens*

Hidden away among the hills bordering Jordan's southern desert, Petra
is more famous for its site than for its recorded history. It is the classic
'lost city', forgotten by all but a few locals for more than a thousand years,
approached through a winding cleft in the rocks, and ringed by curious
monumental facades that have no real parallels elsewhere. It is clearly
pre-Islamic, but it's not straightforwardly Greek or Roman either.

The Swiss traveller Johann Burckhardt came this way in 1812 after
hearing talk of remarkable ruins at the far end of the Wadi Mousa. He
wasn't able to admit to any interest in antiquities; to have done so would
have put at risk his disguise as Ibrahim ibn Abdallah, a merchant travelling from Damascus to Cairo. Instead he justified the detour by saying

N   0   500 m

intra muros area 19 ha,
reducing to 15 ha in the
Byzantine period

× 'Treasury' (mausoleum facade)
th theatre
m markets
b Qasr el-Bint (main temple)
p palace

the Siq

that he had promised to sacrifice a goat at the tomb of Aaron, which
local tradition identified with a grave on one of the hilltops overlooking
the wadi. This satisfied the locals, who provided a goat and a guide, and
the guide led Burckhardt along the wadi and into the channel it has cut
through the hills, the famous Siq.

As must be the case with a watercourse, even one that is dry for all but a few days of the year, the Siq cuts deeper into the rock the further it goes. The red sandstone walls mount higher, while the path is reduced to the bed of the wadi and the sky to a matching slit overhead. The traveller plods on until, just as expectation is ebbing away, the ravine opens up to reveal, straight ahead, the 'Treasury', looking like the facade of a Hellenistic palace, apparently in a perfect state of preservation.

The drama of this approach proved too much for Burckhardt. Abandoning his carefully cultivated air of indifference, he insisted on dismounting and inspecting the monument. Only when he had satisfied himself that it was a purely funerary structure, a rock-cut framework for some relatively modest tomb chambers, did he remount and allow his guide to lead him through the remainder of the Siq. A few hundred metres further on, the ravine opened up again. There were more tombs, a theatre and finally a sunlit valley across which were strewn the remains of the long-lost city of Petra. Carved into the rock of the surrounding hills were dozens of funerary facades similar to the one he had seen in the Siq. This time Burckhardt managed to retain his composure. His guide was already eyeing him suspiciously; it was time to sacrifice his goat and go home.

Burckhardt's discovery stirred the imagination of Europe. It is the inspiration of the famous couplet

> *Match me such marvel, save in Eastern clime –*
> *A rose-red city – half as old as Time!*

which everyone knows, even if very few remember that the author was John William Burgon (1813–88). He hadn't seen Petra when he wrote it, and when he did get there, many years later, he remarked ruefully that it wasn't as rosy as it had been in his youthful vision.

For a long time Petra remained very difficult to get to, and provided a suitable goal for the more enterprising tourist and a lifetime talking point for those who made it. Today much of the magic has gone. Access is relatively easy, and once you have seen a few of the famous tombs they become rather monotonous.

The town itself is tiny and has little to show: there is a colonnaded street alongside the wadi, with a temple at its end (the Qasr el-Bint Faroun [House of Pharaoh's Daughter] to the locals), and that's about it.

Nor is Petra's history very exciting. It is first mentioned as a stronghold of the Nabataean Arabs in 312 BC. Originally a purely nomadic, Bedouin people, the Nabataeans became progressively more involved in the caravan traffic that criss-crossed the Syrian and North Arabian deserts, acquiring in the process some of the characteristics of a settled state. As such it was included in the political system that Pompey imposed on the Near East in 64–63 BC, becoming a client kingdom attached to the province of Syria. In the years that followed, Petra received the trappings of a classical town, the reign of King Aretas IV (8 BC–AD 40), who was responsible for the Qasr el-Bint, the main street, the theatre and probably the 'Treasury', marking the high point of the process.

The ultimate fate of all client kingdoms was annexation, and this befell Nabataea in AD 106, when Trajan turned it into the province of Arabia. The new province was administered from BOSTRA; Petra had to be content with the title of metropolis, in this case in the literal sense of 'mother city' (of the Nabataeans). But in the late third century AD, when the province of Arabia was divided in two, Petra recovered its original status, becoming capital of the southern half, Arabia II, subsequently renamed Palestina III Salutaris. Petra retained this role until the Arab conquest of the region in the seventh century.

Petra's population may have had seasonal peaks as high as a thousand or two, but it is unlikely to have had a year-round population of more than a few hundred.

PIACENZA

Emilia-Romagna, Italy

Classical *Placentia; administrative centre of the
eighth Augustan region of Italy, subsequently
the province of Aemilia*

We know a considerable amount about the first thirty years of Piacenza's history, but almost nothing about how it fared for the seven centuries after that. Founded in 218 BC, the town was one of a pair of Latin colonies – the other being Cremona – intended to give the Romans a firm grip on the central section of Cisalpine Gaul. The timing couldn't have been worse. That summer, Hannibal crossed the Alps, descended on the Lombard plain and defeated the Roman army charged with its defence. The would-be settlers had to abandon whatever they had managed to build of their town, and escape as best they could, but in dogged Roman fashion they were back onsite again as soon as Hannibal had moved on. By 207 BC they had put together enough of a town wall to make a successful defence against Hasdrubal, Hannibal's brother. In 200 BC, however, they were forced out again, this time by the Boii, the local Celtic tribe. Maybe some colonists hung on in there despite all these setbacks, because in 195 BC Ligurian raiders are said to have reached, but not breached, the walls of the town. But if one had to describe the life and achievements of the first generation of Piacentines, it is difficult to avoid using words like 'uncertain' and 'precarious'.

The second generation had a much easier time of it. With Hannibal disposed of – and the monarchs of the Hellenistic East to boot – in 190 BC, Rome was able to dispatch a new tranche of colonists and, more importantly, connect up the colony to the strategic road network. In 187 BC, the consul Marcus Aemilius Lepidus laid out a road that ran straight as a die from RIMINI on the Adriatic to Piacenza on the middle Po; this, the famous Via Aemilia, determined the geography of Roman settlement in the area between the Apennines and the Po. The string of little towns along the route – Forli (Forum Livi), Faenza (Faventia),

Bologna (Bononia), Modena (Mutina), Reggio (Rhegium), Parma and Fidenza (Fidentia) – became the axis of Augustus' eighth district, more familiarly known as Aemilia (now Emilia-Romagna). Piacenza, its largest town, was its administrative centre throughout the Roman imperial period.

This brings us to the end of what the sources tell us about Piacenza, and as the Roman town is entirely hidden beneath the buildings of the modern city, archaeology has very little to add. This is not to say that all trace of Roman Piacenza has been lost. Almost the entire layout of the Roman town is still visible at the centre of the modern street plan, where

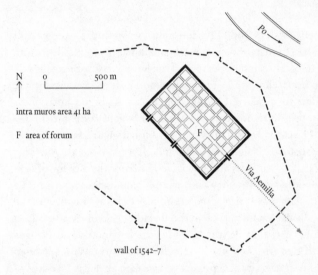

only minimal touching up is needed to restore a 41-hectare rectangle made up of sixty square blocks. All but twenty have survived the 2,200 years since the Roman surveyors first drew their outlines.

As to population, the earliest datum is a figure of 27,000 in 1550, when a new wall had just been completed enclosing 290 hectares. On this basis, Roman Piacenza would have had a population in the region of 3,500 and certainly no more than 5,000.

PIRAEUS

Attica, Greece

History

Piraeus, at the western end of Phaleron Bay, was – and is – the port of
ATHENS, the city itself being some four kilometres (2.5 miles) from
the sea. In the early classical period, up to about 500 BC, the place was
completely undeveloped. Athens' maritime interests were marginal:
it had no fleet to speak of, and little use for a port of any sort. Ships
were probably as likely to be drawn up on the beaches of Phaleron Bay
as dock at Piraeus. This situation changed totally with Athens' adoption of Themistocles' 'Big Navy' policy in 482 BC (*see* p. 44). Warships
needed protected harbours and special facilities for the storage of oars
and sails. Building an Athenian navy meant building a naval base. The
only possible site was Piraeus, the promontory closing the bay on the
west, which had splendid natural harbours either side of its waist: a big
one on the north-west side (the Grand Harbour) and two small ones
on the south-east (the Zea and Mounychia Harbours). With a Persian
invasion threatening, the new project was pushed ahead as fast as possible, but although the navy was ready in time for the invasion of 480
BC, Piraeus was not; the port, its fortifications barely begun, had to be
abandoned along with the rest of Attica. The interruption proved only
temporary. The following year, with the epic victories of Salamis and
Mycale under its belt, the fleet returned in triumph to a liberated Attica,
and the Athenian government was able to reinstate and then expand its
plans for the naval station. This time there was no let-up in the work,
and within a couple of decades Piraeus had become the busiest port in
the Aegean.

The first task was to make Piraeus defensible, and this was done in the 470s BC by building both land and sea walls. But by itself this local circuit fell far short of meeting the strategic need, which was to secure communications between port and city. It was no good Athens ruling the waves if an invading army could position itself between the two, cut off all supplies to the city and starve it out. What was needed was a system of fortifications that would prevent a hostile force from occupying this space. The problem was addressed in the 450s BC, when two Long Walls were built, one from Athens to Piraeus, and one from Athens to the eastern end of Phaleron Bay. Adequately manned, these walls would deny an enemy the use of the entire triangle of land between Athens (at the apex of the triangle) and Phaleron Bay (forming its base). But no sooner was this grand design finished than its flaw became obvious: the two Long Walls were so far apart that they would need separate garrisons. This contradicted the basic premise of the Big Navy policy, which was that Athenian manpower was more profitably deployed by sea than by land. The correct solution to the problem was a wall that ran parallel to the Athens–Piraeus Long Wall, with enough space between the two for the easy passage of carts carrying supplies to the city, but close enough together for one garrison to do for both. This third Long Wall (the 'Middle Wall') was constructed in the 440s BC, and it and its immediate companion are the Long Walls that feature in subsequent events.

Piraeus meanwhile had grown into a considerable place, second only to Athens itself in the urban hierarchy of peninsular Greece. Because the primary business of the town was the construction, equipment, maintenance and repair of warships, we can be sure that most of the male population worked in the dockyards. The next largest group would have been employed in the building trades. The harbours and defences were constantly being remodelled and, with the population expanding, there would have been a sustained demand for new buildings of all types, both public and private. Third would have been the commercial-industrial sector, easily exaggerated in most towns of the time, but undoubtedly of genuine importance here. Athens was no longer capable of feeding itself and had come to depend on wheat imports from the Black Sea. This state-sponsored traffic attracted traders of all sorts to Piraeus, which, in the second quarter of the fifth century BC, became the natural hub for the exchange of the various goods circulating through the Aegean region. With harbour dues forming a significant proportion of Athenian revenues, it seems likely that an equivalent number of jobs were to be found in commerce-based activities. As to manufacturing, the fact that Piraeus was the focus of Athenian military activity, and that all the necessary raw materials were readily available there, would surely have led Athenian entrepreneurs to site their arms factories in the town. If so, this would have raised the numbers working in this sector to exceptional levels. On the other hand, the numbers engaged in food production of any sort would have been nugatory. Each of the harbours would have had its quota of fishermen, but there would have been very few farmers. All this adds up to a most unusual employment profile for a Greek town, one that could only be sustained in the context of a continuing Athenian thalassocracy.

The limits of this thalassocracy were to be severely tested in the war with Sparta that began in 431 BC. The Spartans invaded Attica and the Athenians, as planned, did not resist, but abandoned their farms and took refuge within the perimeter defined by the fortifications of Athens and Piraeus, and the Long Walls connecting the two. A predictable consequence – predictable to us, although not to the Athenians – was an epidemic caused by the overcrowded and unsanitary conditions in which these refugees were forced to live, but despite the many thousands of deaths that resulted, Athenian morale remained firm and Athens' maritime empire was maintained. There were even attempts – misguided, as it turned out – to enlarge it. It was only when the Persians joined the fray, and gave the Spartans the money for a fleet, that Athens' position began to crumble. The end came surprisingly suddenly. In 405 BC, the Spartan admiral Lysander won a crushing victory at Aegospotami in the Hellespont, effectively destroying the Athenian navy. Lysander then used his fleet to blockade Piraeus and force the surrender of Athens in 404 BC. The Long Walls were demolished, and a Spartan-style oligarchic government replaced the Athenian democracy. Piraeus seemed to have lost its purpose.

Well, not entirely. Piraeus' population actually increased in the aftermath of the surrender because the citizens expelled from Athens by the new aristocratic regime took refuge there. Both the original residents, who were now largely jobless, and the newcomers, who had lost everything, were by reflex hostile to the oligarchs, and it wasn't long before there was open warfare between port and city. And the port won. In 403 BC democratic government was restored, and within a few short years, by around 393, a new navy had been created and the Long Walls rebuilt. But although the democracy was real enough, the naval revival was a bit of a sham: the money had come from Persia, now quarrelling with Sparta, and was unlikely to survive the next turn of the Aegean merry-go-round. When that happened, Athens could only hold out its hat to the members of the old Athenian League, offering protection in return for contributions. Surprisingly quite a few of them paid up, although at rates much lower than they had in Athens' heyday. Contributions and commerce together were just about enough to keep Piraeus functioning in something approaching its old style.

In 338 BC, Philip of Macedon imposed his authority on peninsular Greece, and Athens had to place its navy at Macedon's service. It doesn't seem to have been of much use, for although the number of ships was impressive – as many as 400 were said to be available – fighting quality had fallen to depressingly low levels. This was apparent when Athens tried to shake off the Macedonian yoke in 322 BC: two sea-battles went Macedon's way and the Athenian navy ceased to exist as an independent force. From this time on, when Athens built warships, it was at the bidding of another power. Worse still, Piraeus was forced to accept a Macedonian garrison, which was installed on Mounychia Hill at the root of the Piraean peninsula.

The third century BC saw Piraeus in steady decline. Shipbuilding was fitful, and trade was transferring to RHODES. But some life remained in the town through the third and second centuries, and even into the early first century. Then, in 88 BC, the Athenians were unwise enough to welcome the forces of Mithradates VI of Pontus, who had promised to free Greece from Roman domination. Retribution arrived in the person of the Roman general Sulla, and an army of five legions. He wasn't too hard on Athens town, which didn't put up much of a fight, but Piraeus, where the Pontic troops retreated to Mounychia and refused to surrender, aroused his ire. When Mounychia finally fell in 86 BC, Piraeus was deliberately burned to the ground. There was to be no significant recovery: the geographer Strabo, writing at the end of the century, refers to the place as a village. For Piraeus, as for so many other towns that rose and fell in antiquity, the wheel had come full circle.

Topography

Piraeus has a dumb-bell shape, with one end of the dumb-bell, the Akte peninsula, projecting into the sea, and the other, Mounychia Hill, forming its landward root. The town was built on the saddle of land between the two, the Grand Harbour curving in on its north-western side, and the Zea Harbour, much smaller, indenting its south-eastern shore. The third harbour, the Mounychia Harbour, lay east of the Zea, at the foot of the Mounychia Hill.

The layout of the town followed a master plan drawn up by Hippodamus of Miletus 'at the time of the Persian wars', i.e. at the start of the Big Navy programme. The detail of Hippodamus' plan has been lost, but the essence of it was a grid pattern for the residential area; a commercial zone, the Emporion, on the north and east sides of the Grand Harbour;

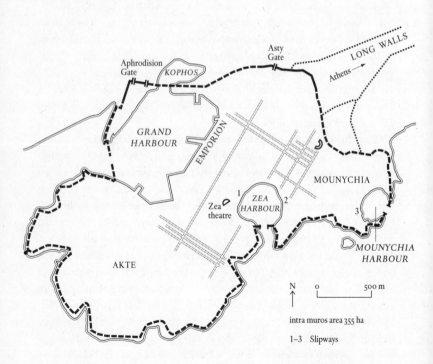

intra muros area 355 ha

1–3 Slipways

a closed-off area around the Zea Harbour for the navy; and an acropolis with combined religious and military functions (as at Athens) on Mounychia Hill. The plan seems to have been considered a great success and was imitated elsewhere, for example at Rhodes; at Piraeus, Hippodamus himself was remembered in the name given to the central plaza of the town, the Hippodameia (also known as the city's agora).

Very little of the classical town survives today, although the hills and harbours conserve its basic shape. Considerable stretches of the sea walls are still visible, and short lengths of the land walls have been excavated, along with three or four gates. Of the 196 slipways for the navy's triremes that ringed the Zea Harbour, some traces remain; one such slipway is preserved under cover by the Maritime Museum on the west side of the port. Similar slipways have been excavated on the west side of the Mounychia Harbour. The Hippodamian grid – its axis only a few degrees different from the modern one – has been uncovered at various points (for which see the map); so has the original theatre, the Dionysian Theatre, at the foot of the Mounychia Hill, although this has since been covered over again. A later, Hellenistic theatre remains on view west of the Zea Harbour.

Population

At Piraeus, purpose and population would have been closely linked, which means that numbers can't have got anywhere near 10,000 before the adoption of the 'Big Navy' policy in 482 BC, or stayed above that level for long after the demise of Athenian naval power in 322 BC. This gives us chronological limits of 450 and 300 BC for the history of Piraeus as a city in the demographically defined sense of the word. When it comes to specifics, the best figure we have is, alas, for the period immediately before Piraeus became important. In Cleisthenes' reform of 507–505 BC the *deme* (district) of Piraeus was allocated nine places out of the 500 in the ruling council (1.8 per cent), suggesting an adult male population of $30,000 \times 1.8/100 = 540$, and a total population of about four times this, i.e. 2,160. And that is for the *deme*; it will have been rather less than that for the village. (This and subsequent calculations have to be read in parallel with the entry for Athens). For the most interesting period, 450–350 BC, we have no data, but for 312–309 BC, the date of the census taken by Demetrius of Phaleron, we have a figure of 10,000 adult foreign residents (metics) for Attica as a whole. Tombstone and similar evidence indicates that 50 per cent of these metics lived in Athens town, which in turn suggests that 50 per cent of the 10,000 households there were metic. Piraeus would have had a higher proportion. If it was 60 per cent, Piraeus would have had 2,000 × 100/60 = 3,333 households in all; if it was 70 per cent, it would have had 2,000 × 100/70 = 2,857 households. Using a multiplier of 3.5 gives us a population range of 10,000 to 11,666. This confirms that at the end of the fourth century BC, Piraeus was about to drop below the 10,000 population mark. That leaves us with the question of how much higher the population got in the town's best days. My vote goes for only a modest increment, a population nearer 12,000 than 15,000, although 15,000 is a possibility.

POMPEII

Campania, Italy

*Town on the Bay of Naples buried by
the eruption of Vesuvius in AD 79*

History

Pompeii is situated near the ancient mouth of the Sarno, a small river that runs along the southern side of Vesuvius. The initial nucleus seems to have been Greek, and dates from the sixth century BC, when this part of the Italian coast was dotted with outposts spun off from the colony

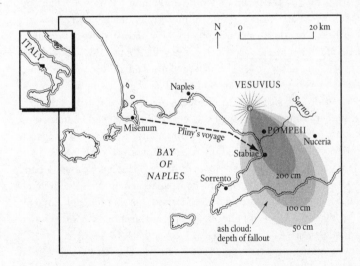

that pioneered Greek settlement in the area, the eighth-century *polis* of CUMAE. A Doric temple on the southern edge of the town, in what subsequently became the 'Triangular Forum', is the sole surviving evidence of this Greek initiative, which may never have amounted to much more than the temple and its surrounding sanctuary. Eventually something more significant in the way of a settlement did appear, centred on a temple of Apollo 300 metres to the west of the Greek sanctuary; the major influence now was Etruscan rather than Greek. This old town – referred to in some archaeological literature as the 'Altstadt' – was very small, covering only about nine hectares, but by the late fifth century it was the focal point of an independent community. If there had ever been Greek or Etruscan political control, this had long since ceased to be effective, and historians consequently classify the town as Campanian (from the region), Sabellian or Samnite (alternative designations of the south-central Italian indigenous people), or Oscan (from the language these people spoke).

In the latter part of the fourth century, the Campanians were drawn into the struggle between the rising power of ROME and the Samnite confederacy of the south-central Apennines. They chose Rome, the winning side, and for the next 250 years – through the third and second centuries BC and the opening decade of the first – Pompeii led an uneventful life as a self-governing community in alliance with (meaning subordinate to) the Roman Republic. This status, shared with many other Italian communities, was less than the Pompeiians thought they deserved, and in 89 BC they joined the anti-Roman uprising known as the Social War (from *socii*, meaning 'allies'). The rising was brutally suppressed, and although the Romans then proceeded to grant the defeated communities many of the legal rights they had been seeking, this was small compensation to the Pompeiians for their loss of separate identity. The victors declared the town a Roman colony in 80 BC and discharged Roman soldiers took over much of the native Pompeiians' property. The upper echelons of Pompeiian society were completely Romanized, with Latin replacing Oscan not just in official documents but in everyday speech. The new Pompeii became, for all practical purposes, a purely Roman town.

It was quite a big settlement. At some stage in the Oscan period a new circuit of walls had been constructed enclosing no less than sixty-five hectares. The street layout suggests that this very considerable area came into use one sector at a time, starting with the area north-west of the Altstadt. The next zone to be developed was the band of territory either side of the road connecting the Vesuvian and Stabian gates, and the last phase of development was the eastern half of the city. The density of housing clearly falls off as you go from west to east, and some of the blocks at the far end remained open ground.

The amphitheatre, built in the years immediately after the Roman takeover, seems to be the oldest surviving example of such a structure. It was dedicated in 70 BC to Gaius Quintius Valgus and Marcus Procius, two Roman military commanders who became magistrates of the town after it was joined to the republic, and it is located at one corner of town on what had presumably been a greenfield site.

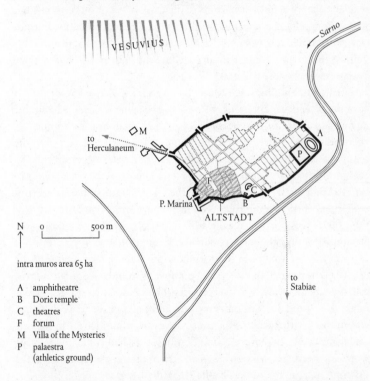

N   0   500 m

intra muros area 65 ha

A   amphitheatre
B   Doric temple
C   theatres
F   forum
M   Villa of the Mysteries
P   palaestra
     (athletics ground)

In its final Roman phase, Pompeii was rarely in the news. The biggest headline it got was in AD 59 when there was a riot in the amphitheatre during a gladiatorial show. Visitors from the neighbouring town of Nuceria were attacked by Pompeiian rowdies; many were injured and some were killed. The Nucerians complained to the authorities in Rome, and the Roman Senate, after pondering the matter, decided to punish Pompeii with a ten-year ban on public gatherings of any sort, a woeful penalty in that era of bread and circuses.

The eruption of AD 79

One clear sign that Pompeii was in some sort of geological trouble came in AD 62 when the town was seriously damaged by an earthquake. We know now that the shock was caused by a plume of magma forcing its way up to a point under the supposedly extinct crater of Vesuvius, but to the Pompeiians it was a one-off event, a disaster certainly, but not one that carried any warning for the future. Their preoccupation was getting the town up and running again, and both public and private energies were bent to this end.

The lists of buildings that were – and weren't – repaired over the next seventeen years is interesting. Most of the housing was made habitable again, and some of the richer citizens had their houses completely redecorated. As regards public buildings, top priority was given to the amphitheatre, theatre and baths, all places that had important roles in the good life as perceived by Pompeiians. Funds were even found to build a completely new set of baths, the Central Baths, in the most up-to-date style. As to temples, there was money for a lavish restoration of the Temple of Isis, a private cult, and work was started on rebuilding the Temple of Apollo, the tutelary deity of the city, but nothing was done to restore the Capitolium in the forum, a grand temple of Jupiter at the centre of the town. Doubtless the Pompeiians would have got around to it in time, but it clearly wasn't a priority. The saddest loss was the earthquake damage to the Alexander mosaic, Pompeii's finest artwork, which was in a house that had been built by a patrician family back in the second century BC. Like most grand families, they had come down in the world in later years, for there was no attempt to repair the damage; the missing segments were simply filled in with plaster.

Such then was the condition of Pompeii in August AD 79. Minor earthquakes still troubled the town, but the Pompeiians had learned to live with them. They had recovered their lifestyle thanks to a generous outlay of self-help, along with the fertility of the volcanic soil that they tilled.

What happened next is described by Pliny the Younger, who was staying with his uncle at Misenum on the other side of the bay from Pompeii. In the early afternoon of 24 August, his attention was drawn to a strangely shaped cloud rising from a mountain in the general direction of Vesuvius. It was like an umbrella pine, says Pliny, with a long vertical trunk and a flat top – what we would call a mushroom cloud, and just as ominous. Pliny the Elder, who had charge of the fleet at Misenum, was sufficiently intrigued to order a warship readied so that he could take a closer look; his nephew, a bookish young man, turned down the offer of a place on the boat, preferring instead to continue making extracts from his copy of Livy. Aided by a northerly wind (specifically north-north-west) and spurred on by a message pleading for help from an acquaintance with a villa at the foot of Vesuvius, the elder Pliny set sail, using the mysterious cloud as his mark.

The same wind that sped Pliny the Elder on his way blew the top of the mushroom cloud directly over Pompeii. As a result, the town received a steadily thickening coat of ash. The pumice stones that were included in this fallout were too light to do significant damage to people or property, but as the accumulated ash reached a depth of 2.8 metres, some roofs caved in. For some, the increasing burden of ash, earth tremors of mounting intensity and the sight of fires burning on the flanks of Vesuvius proved too much and they fled into the countryside. Others decided to tough it out and stay with their property. This was the wrong decision: the nature of the eruption was changing as the throat of the volcano began clogging up, leading to intermittent collapses of the gas-driven column of ash, followed by explosions that temporarily cleared the throat, but also destroyed parts of the volcano's rim. Because of this, each of these explosions launched a cascading mass of searing hot gas, ash and rocks down the sides of the mountain. Early on the morning of 25 August, one of these pyroclastic flows reached the north wall of Pompeii; not long after, another overflowed the wall and tore through the city – flows of this sort can travel at speeds in excess of 100 kilometres per hour (60 mph). Every living thing in the town was killed, near enough instantly. This and a second pyroclastic flow that followed an hour later added another one to two metres to the shroud covering the city, and subsequent airborne ash another metre. By the time it was all over, Pompeii was buried to a depth of five to five-and-a-half metres, and only the tops of the tallest houses were visible, poking up through this mass of volcanic material. Both town and townsfolk had been snuffed out.

Pliny the Elder didn't succeed in his rescue mission, as rafts of pumice prevented him from reaching the shore in the vicinity of Vesuvius. He diverted to Stabiae, where the next morning he died, perhaps coincidentally (he was fifty-five, a good age for the time), but more likely because his lungs failed in the ash-laden, partly poisonous air.

Pliny the Younger, observing events from Misenum, continued his studies undisturbed through the first day of the eruption, but that night there were a series of earthquakes that were alarming even by Campanian standards. At dawn, he and his mother, fearing that the villa was about to collapse, moved on to open ground. From there, Pliny saw a particularly massive earthquake suck the sea back from the shoreline, 'leaving sea creatures stranded on the dry sand' before driving the waters back again. Then a shift in the wind brought the ash cloud over Misenum, plunging the whole northern peninsula into darkness. When an anaemic sun finally broke through, it was early evening and Pliny was left wondering at how 'everything was changed, buried deep in ashes like snowdrifts'.

Rediscovery and excavation

In 1594, the digging of a water channel across the site of Pompeii uncovered frescoed walls, and even an inscription giving the name of the city. Alas, scholars misinterpreted this as a reference to Pompey the Great and decided that the remains were those of a large villa of his. Planned excavations took place in 1748, after enthusiasm for archaeology of a primitive, treasure-hunting sort had been aroused by the earlier discoveries at HERCULANEUM in 1709. Herculaneum, sealed by rock, was very hard to tunnel into. By contrast, Pompeii's shroud of ash and earth was easy to shovel aside. As a result, Pompeii soon became the main focus of the Bourbon monarchy's explorations, and the diggings at Herculaneum were gradually abandoned. That 'Pompey's villa' was in fact a major town soon became apparent. At first it was thought to be Stabiae; then the discovery of another inscription confirmed its true identity.

For the first hundred years, the work done at Pompeii amounted to little more than an ill-organized ransacking of the site, with spoil dumped over areas deemed exhausted, and many finds reburied so that they could be 'discovered' by visiting dignitaries. Records were almost non-existent, the works of art uncovered often sold to foreign collectors. But gradually things improved, and after 1860, when Giuseppe Fiorelli was appointed director, the quality of excavations started to match the unique value of the site. Where possible, finds were left in situ; where that wasn't practical, they were deposited in the Museo Nazionale in NAPLES. Disorder retreated, just as a new threat emerged in the form of mass tourism.

Since the Second World War, the priority has been the preservation of the existing remains; new work has, quite rightly, been confined to the clarification of the existing plan. The unexcavated area (approximately one-fifth of the town) remains for the attention of a future generation.

Population

There seems to be general agreement that the number who died when Pompeii town was overwhelmed is of the order of 2,000 to 2,500. This is based on a body count of 1,000 to 1,500, plus an additional percentage to take account of the skeletons lost or unobserved in the early, erratically recorded excavations, and the size of the area that remains unexcavated.

Unfortunately, this figure is little help in determining the total population, because no one knows how many fled the city before the final disaster. Giuseppe Fiorelli thought in terms of a population of 10,000 to 15,000. The tendency of late has been to lower this, as in Frank Sear's *Roman Architecture* (1982), to 'no more than 10,000'. The most closely reasoned figure is that given by J. C. Russell in *The Control of Late Ancient and Medieval Population* (1985), who reckoned that a town like Pompeii, where almost all the housing was single storey, is unlikely to have had a population density greater than the average for late medieval cities where the houses were generally two storey, and often three. This average is 100 to 120 per hectare, suggesting a population for Pompeii of 6,500 – say 7,000 with suburbs.

PRIENE

Now within Güllübahce Village,
west Turkey

By tradition, the inhabitants of Priene in western Anatolia looked upon ATHENS as their mother city. Priene was a faithful member of the Ionian League and later of the Delian League. At times it controlled the Panionion, a common sanctuary of the Ionian cities. The struggle to control this sanctuary brought both importance and conflict to the people of Priene.

The earliest settlement may have been an acropolis on the high crag above the mouth of the Meander river. In later years, old Priene and its port (Naulochus) must have developed along the riverbanks, but the

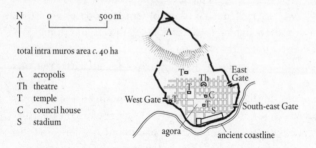

N   0   500 m

total intra muros area *c.* 40 ha

A   acropolis
Th theatre
T   temple
C   council house
S   stadium

ruins of that period are now presumably buried by layers of Meander mud. In the fourth century BC, it became apparent that this rapid silting process would require relocation of the old city. Alexander the Great provided the impetus for a new city when he arrived in 334 BC. He offered to provide funding for construction if he had the right to dedicate the new temple of Athena. His offer was apparently accepted, as evidenced by his dedicatory inscription displayed in the British Museum.

The relocated city of Priene is often regarded as the first and finest example of a planned Hellenistic city. Although constructed on a relatively steep slope of Mount Mycale, the city maintained a systematic grid of right-angled streets by building on a series of parallel terraces. At the top of the town was a conspicuous sanctuary of Athena Polias, reportedly conceived by Pytheus, the same Carian architect who designed the Mausoleum at Halicarnassus (one of the Seven Wonders of the Ancient World).

The city later passed to the control of PERGAMUM, whose last king bequeathed it to ROME in 133 BC. As part of the Roman province of Asia, the citizens of Priene prudently rededicated their principal shrine to honour both Athena and Augustus. Over time, however, Priene gradually sank into insignificance. Its harbour continued to silt up with mud from the Meander river, and it suffered from competition with MILETUS, its larger and nearby commercial rival.

The extensive remains of Hellenistic Priene include a colonnaded agora, a well-preserved council house, a theatre, and a sanctuary honouring Demeter and her daughter Core (Persephone). If one may infer that the council house (seating up to around 640 people) was large enough to accommodate a general assembly of enfranchised citizens, George Bean in his *Aegean Turkey* (1966) suggested that this would imply a total population of around 3,000.

PTOLEMAIS

Present-day *Tolmeita, Libya*

*Capital of Cyrenaica in the Ptolemaic period,
and of the equivalent late Roman province
of Libya Superior; diocese: Egypt*

Ptolemais was founded by one of the Ptolemies of Egypt, probably
Ptolemy III (246–221 BC). Earlier there had been a small settlement on
the site, serving as port to the town of Barca, twenty-four kilometres
(fifteen miles) to the south; this seaside village was now replaced by a
grandiosely planned Greek city with straight streets, an odeon, a theatre, a stadium and an enclosing wall. In the fashion of the time, the wall
took in some of the high ground overlooking the city and, on the flanks,
followed the lines suggested by two wadis running from this escarpment down to the sea. The whole project was carried out with a disre-
gard for cost that suggests it was conceived as an advertisement for the
power of the Egyptian kingdom and a centre from which its Cyrenaican
dependency could be administered.

Ptolemais was certainly big. Its intramural area is of the order of 280
hectares, and even if we discount the third of it that lies on the barren
slopes of the Jebel Akhdar, we are still left with near enough 200 hectares on the plain. In fact only a small part of this was ever built over, and
it is most unlikely that Ptolemais was ever able to challenge CYRENE's
position as the leading city of the region. It may have housed the Ptolemies' governors general (during the periods when the kings of Egypt
administered the province directly) and served as a capital for cadet
branches of the Ptolemaic house (when Cyrenaica was an independent
kingdom), but it would always have been a modest place with a population of no more than a few thousand. Initially, even these few were
present under compulsion, for the nuclear population had been obtained
by enforced transfer from Barca.

Following the Roman takeover of Cyrenaica, Ptolemais received the
usual ornaments of Roman urbanism: an amphitheatre and a Roman-

style theatre. These additions would have been some compensation for a substantial demotion, the Romans' designation of Cyrene as the metropolis of the region. This remained the situation until the end of the third century AD when the emperor Diocletian made 'Libya Superior' into a province on its own account (previously it had been administered in tandem with Crete) and chose Ptolemais as its administrative centre. A triumphal arch of the Constantinian period, with inscriptions honouring Valentinian and, jointly, Arcadius and Honorius, suggests that this official recognition brought benefits to the city, but it remained something of a sham, its citizens surely still too few to man the wide circuit of its walls.

N   0   500 m

intra muros area 280 ha

A present-day village of Tolmeita
B amphitheatre
C late Roman theatre
D odeon
E triumphal arch
F stadium
G Greek theatre
H acropolis

East Wadi

West Wadi

JEBEL AKHDAR

This vulnerability is probably the reason why, in the mid fifth century, the provincial administration was shifted to APOLLONIA. Most of the people followed the governor; the rest would have dispersed when the aqueduct broke down. Later, Justinian claimed to have restored both the water supply and the city's prosperity, but if he got the population back over the 1,000 mark, it wouldn't have been for long. In the Arab period when Barca underwent a revival, Ptolemais, under the name Tolmeita, drew some benefit from its original function as Barca's port, but it was now only a simple village.

RATIARIA

Present-day *Archar, north-west Bulgaria*

Classical *Colonia Ulpia Traiana Ratiaria; capital
of the late Roman province of Dacia Ripensis*

The Roman historian Dio Cassius (*c.* 150–*c.* 235) records that the area of
Ratiaria was already fortified when Marcus Licinius Crassus (grandson
of the triumvir) fought there against the Triballi in 29 BC. Tiberius constructed a military road through the area in AD 33–4. Ratiaria was initially part of the province of Moesia, becoming part of Moesia Superior
when Domitian divided the province in AD 85–6. It received colonial
status and the name Colonia Ulpia Traiana Ratiaria after the emperor
Trajan conquered Dacia in AD 101–6. The town imported Italian colonists, who brought Romanization to the region. The name of the modern village and its adjoining river (Archar) is thought to be derived from
the Roman name.

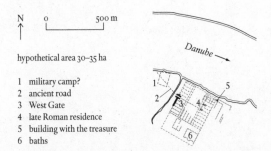

N   0   500 m

hypothetical area 30–35 ha

1   military camp?
2   ancient road
3   West Gate
4   late Roman residence
5   building with the treasure
6   baths

In AD 271, the emperor Aurelian withdrew from trans-Danubian
Dacia. He created a new province north of Dacia Ripensis, in which
Ratiaria was a principal city. It was also a headquarters of the Roman
fleet on the Danube. In 442–3, Ratiaria was sacked by the Huns. Under
Anastasius I (491–518), however, the town was partially restored and

renamed Anastasiana Ratiaria. It appears to have met its end after the Avars overran it in 586.

Roman Ratiaria seems to have been first laid out as a small square, which was later expanded to a rectangle measuring approximately 426 by 284 metres. By around the beginning of the fourth century, a larger city wall enclosed an area in the range of thirty to thirty-five hectares.

Unfortunately, the site has suffered in recent years from looting, and it is difficult to reconstruct a complete city plan.

RAVENNA

Emilia-Romagna, Italy

*Fifth-century capital of the Western Roman Empire
and later seat of the Byzantine exarchate*

History

Ravenna, a modest place on the Adriatic coast of Italy, has an Etruscan name, which suggests that it was founded around 500 BC, the time when Etruscan activity in this area was at its peak. In the course of the fifth century the Etruscan element would have been absorbed by the local folk, the Umbrians; indeed, for the Romans, who didn't think very deeply about it, Ravenna was just another Umbrian town. The region passed under Roman control at the end of the third century. Under the republic it was never more than a minor town, although its situation at the southernmost point of the province of Cisalpine Gaul eventually brought it a moment of fame: it was here that Julius Caesar spent the last night of his governorship of the Gauls, considering whether or not to take his troops south and start a civil war.

Caesar's war went well, and that may have made him look kindly on Ravenna; before the year was out, in 49 BC, he had given its inhabitants Roman citizenship. His successor, Augustus, further boosted Ravenna's position by stationing the Adriatic fleet at Classis, a port facility some five kilometres (three miles) to the south. (At Ravenna itself the sea was too shallow to be navigable.) Later rulers who added to the town's amenities include the emperor Claudius (AD 41–54), who built a monumental gate, the Porta Aurea, at its southern entrance, and Trajan (98–117), who constructed a fine aqueduct. The town had now attained a comfortable position in the urban hierarchy: at the upper end of the common run, but with no claims to special attention.

The extra something needed to boost Ravenna's size was added in the dying days of the Western Empire. In AD 402 the general in charge of the West's defences told the emperor Honorius, then resident in MILAN, that he could no longer guarantee his safety if he and his court remained where they were. He suggested a move to Ravenna. At first sight this might seem a surprising choice because Milan was large and well fortified, whereas Ravenna was small and its walls relatively puny. But other factors made Ravenna the better option. Milan was on the main invasion route, Ravenna miles off it, up a cul-de-sac. Moreover, Ravenna was surrounded by marshes and lagoons, all fed by the waters of the Po. It was almost impossible to bring it under effective siege. Honorius, who was not a fighting man, had no problem accepting the proffered advice. Consequently, as from 404, Ravenna became the capital of the Western Empire and it remained the West's capital until 476, when

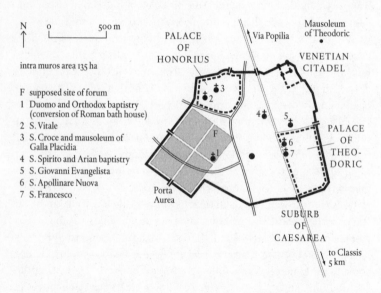

the last emperor was deposed. Subsequently it was the capital of the Gothic kingdom of Italy, and, after Justinian's reconquest of the peninsula in 535–40, the seat of the East Roman governor of Italy, later termed the exarch. During this period the town more than quadrupled in size as Romans and Germans built palaces and churches and spent lavishly on their decoration. All this occurred at a time when there was hardly any building going on elsewhere in Italy, and none at all in the other parts of

the West. As the Dark Ages settled over Europe and urban life contracted, often to vanishing point, Ravenna gleamed like a good deed in a
naughty world.

The East Romans only enjoyed their recovery of Italy for a generation; in 568 a new wave of German invaders, the Lombards, overran
the Po valley, and Ravenna's status was correspondingly reduced. The
exarchs held on to their capital and to the Adriatic coastline, but they
were only marginal players in seventh-century Italy. By the time the
Lombards took the city, in 751, it had lost most of its population and all
of its significance. In the early medieval period it made a brief reappear-
ance, being one of the first Lombard towns to declare its independence
(1177). But it then faded out again and spent the rest of the Middle Ages
being batted about by its more important neighbours before finally
settling down under papal rule in 1509.

Topography

Ravenna's awkward-looking perimeter reflects its history. The early
Roman town was a thirty-hectare rectangle lying to the west of the coast
road, the Via Popilia. The next phase began with the arrival of Honorius
and his court in AD 402–4 and the creation of a new quarter north of the
existing town. Finally, the Gothic king Theodoric (471–526) built his
much larger palace on the east side of the Via Popilia. Theodoric is probably responsible for building the circuit of walls that pulled all three elements together. The walls, with the addition of a Venetian citadel,
survive reasonably well today, and where they haven't, we know where
they ran. We also have a fair number of intact buildings, most notably
one of Theodoric's palace churches (S. Apollinare Nuova), and, in the
area of Honorius' palace, San Vitale, sumptuously decorated by Justinian to celebrate his recovery of Italy. But many other buildings have been
lost and the city plan raises as many questions as it answers. Why is the
Porta Aurea off centre? Could it be that the original Roman town was
built in two stages, a small republican rectangle covering 9.5 hectares
subsequently expanded to cover the full 30 hectares in the imperial
period? Where is the hippodrome, usually said to lie alongside the Via
Cerchio, although this is clearly not long enough to accommodate an

imperial circus? And where in the higgledy-piggledy streets of the north-west quarter is the outline of Honorius' palace? There is much work to be done.

Population

The first secure data for Ravenna's population are from 1371, when the number of taxable hearths was 1,743. Using a multiplier of four, this gives us a figure of 6,972, say 7,000. By 1656, numbers had increased to 12,963, and by 1796 to 16,000, of whom 9,500 lived within the walls. In the course of the nineteenth century the population increased to 36,000, but the number living within the walls only rose to 12,000. This suggests that the Ravenna of the late Roman period never held more than 10,000 people. It would only have had this many on its best days, i.e. from the early fifth century to the late sixth. So although it glowed, its light was small.

REGGIO

Calabria, Italy

Classical *Rhegium; capital of the late Roman
province of Lucania and Bruttii*

Towards the end of the eighth century BC, the Greeks settled on either
side of the Strait of Messina, the narrow channel that separates Sicily
from Italy. The initial settlement was on the Sicilian side, at Messina,
but the Messinians knew that if they were to succeed in their aim of con-
trolling traffic through the strait they needed a matching settlement on
the Italian shore. They found a suitable site at present-day Reggio, on
the tip of the Italian toe, and within a few years a group of colonists from
Chalcis in Euboea was ensconced there, the Messinians providing
whatever backup was needed to make things run smoothly. And
although Reggio was never a very large place, it seems to have been successful enough, the only setback coming in 387 BC when Dionysius I of
Syracuse, who had no intention of letting anyone interfere with his use
of the strait, subjected the town to a bruising sack.

A new era opened for Reggio in 282 BC when the city fathers
requested a Roman garrison, perhaps because they felt threatened
by the local Italic tribe, the Bruttii, but more likely because they saw
the way things were going in this part of the world. Having formed
this alliance, the citizens kept faith with Rome, rebuffing the forces of
both Pyrrhus and Hannibal. Thereafter Reggio settled into a comfortable obscurity until the end of the third century AD, when it became
the seat of the corrector (governor) of the new province of Lucania
and Bruttii. Its walls were still intact, and its population sufficient to
defend them, during the Gothic wars of Justinian's reign (AD 535–52);
subsequently, it is safe to assume that Reggio shared in the contraction
in population and resources experienced by Italy in the Dark Ages,
and that it was during this period that the classical perimeter was
abandoned.

As this account will have made clear, very little is known about Reggio, and this is as true of its layout as its history. The town was built on a strip of level ground between the terminal hills of the Aspromonte range and the sea, its flanks defended by two seasonal rivers, the Santa Lucia in the north-east and the Calopinace in the south-west. The shoreline was straight, as it is today; the town wall ran along the sea-front then inland to take in the summits of the three nearest hills. A short stretch of the wall on the seafront, handsomely built in stone, is still in situ; two stretches of a mud-brick wall survive in the hills. These and the geographical constraints of the site suggest that the intramural

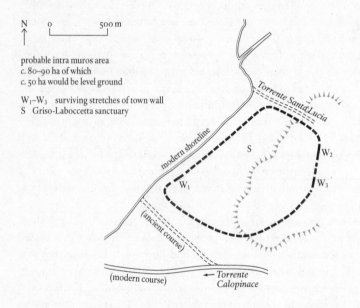

N ↑   0 ⌐_____⌐ 500 m

probable intra muros area
c. 80–90 ha of which
c. 50 ha would be level ground

W₁–W₃   surviving stretches of town wall
S   Griso-Laboccetta sanctuary

Torrente Santa Lucia

modern shoreline

S

W₁

W₂

W₃

(ancient course)

(modern course)   ← *Torrente Calopinace*

area is about eighty to ninety hectares, of which, at the most, fifty hectares would have been built over. Nothing is known of the street plan and although Roman inscriptions mention several public buildings – baths, a basilica, a temple of Apollo and another of Isis and Serapis – none of these structures has been located. The only significant discoveries have been the fragmentary terracotta sculptures found in the 'Griso-Laboccetta sanctuary', which come from an altar or temple of the late sixth century BC.

Reggio was clearly never a large place, being overshadowed by its Sicilian counterpart, Messina, throughout its history. Its population first reached the 10,000 mark in the early nineteenth century. It is unlikely to have come anywhere near this figure before.

REIMS

Marne, France

Classical *Durocortorum Remorum, county town of the Remi;*
capital of the province of Belgica in the early Roman Empire
and of Belgica Segunda in the fourth century

On the eve of the Roman conquest, Reims was one of the more important of the oppida of north-west Gaul. Oppida were tribal meeting
places, not towns, but the Romans were keen to see them develop into
genuinely urban structures, seeing this as part of their civilizing mission. They had a particular interest in this process in the case of Reims,
for the Remi, the Belgic people for whom Reims was the tribal centre,
were both powerful and pro-Roman. Caesar had benefited greatly from
their friendship during his conquest of Gaul, and now that Roman rule
was established it was payback time. In the new order of things Reims –
Durocortorum Remorum to give it its full title – emerged as the capital
of the province of Belgica (north-east Gaul), as well as county town of
the Remi.

Despite this mark of favour, early Roman Reims remained a curiously
unfocused place. To judge by the distribution of the surviving mosaic
floors, there seem to have been almost as many Roman dwellings outside
the rampart of the oppidum as inside, and there is no evidence for the
features characteristic of Roman urbanism: no sign of a theatre, or
amphitheatre, or any baths, public or private. Most of the negativity in
this picture is probably due to the complete rebuilding of Reims in the
medieval period, but it is true to say that the few constructions that do
survive are late rather than early: the town's gates, and the cryptoporticus under the forum are all dated to the period AD 175–250. At the
moment it looks as if the town fathers only decided to make Reims a
truly Roman city at that time. Until then they were apparently content to
let the inhabitants determine the configuration of their town.

Celtic and early Roman Reims had been defined by a roughly circular
rampart enclosing an area of about ninety hectares. Within this, Roman

planners at some stage laid out an orthogonal street grid in a rectangle covering some fifty-five hectares. The north and south gates were sited on the line of the rampart, beyond the edges of the rectangle. The east and west gates were placed within the rampart, at the edges of the rectangle. Aside from the fact that the forum was just north of centre, that is almost all we know about middle period (early third-century AD)

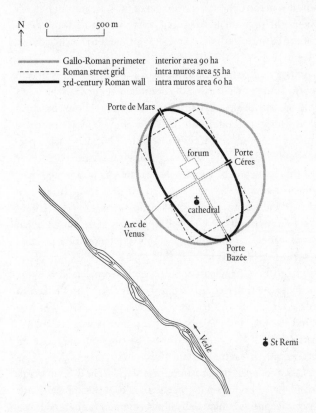

Reims. In the second half of the century a defensive wall was built, probably as a rush job, which completes our picture of the town. It followed an economical, oval course, connecting the four gates while cutting off the corners of the original rectangle. The area enclosed was about sixty hectares.

Long though Roman memories were, there came a time when the

services of the Remi to the Roman state began to seem less important than the town's geographical disadvantages. Its rival, TRIER, was better positioned as regards the administration's main preoccupation, the Rhine frontier, and as the years passed, more and more functions were switched to the city on the Mosel. After the late third-century crises, Trier emerged the clear winner and Reims had to content itself with less exalted status. It remained, however, the seat of the governor of Belgica Segunda, one of the new small provinces created in Diocletian's reorganization of the empire, and, of course, it continued to be the county town of the Remi.

Reims acquired a Christian community by the third century and in the course of the fourth this became the dominant element in the city's life. There are records of several churches, most notably the cathedral dedicated to the Virgin standing on the same site as the present-day building. Although the founder of the cathedral, St Nicaise, was to perish when the Vandals sacked the city in 407, the ecclesiastical organization survived this blow and St Remi, who became bishop in 459, was able to engineer a remarkably successful transition from Roman to Frankish rule. His culminating triumph was the baptism of Clovis, king of the Franks, in 498, the start of a tradition that was to bring French kings to Reims for their coronation for as long as the monarchy lasted.

When St Remi died he was buried in the cemetery to the south of the city. In the sixth century a basilica was built over his tomb and it was this basilica, not the cathedral, that attracted the pilgrims who flocked to Reims to seek intercession of the saint. The result was that Dark Age Reims acquired a second focus, in exactly the same manner as TOURS. Fortified in the early tenth century, this 'Châteauneuf de St Remi' sustained its separate character until the thirteenth century.

Reims was always one of the most important towns in Roman Gaul, and it was to make a good showing in the medieval period too – not quite in the same league as Rouen or Toulouse, but not far behind these pacesetters in the resurgence of urban life. A new, more extensive wall built in 1209–1358 joined the town to the Châteauneuf de St Remi and brought the area between these two and the River Vesle within its circuit. This increased the intramural area to 200 hectares, far more than was needed, but indicative of the resources available to the town fathers of the early fourteenth century. We are fortunate in having a house count for this period; it suggests a population in the 12,000 to 15,000 range, which in turn suggests a Gallo-Roman population of about half this, i.e. something in the region of 6,000 to 7,500. This would only have been achieved in the periods of maximum prosperity, the mid first to mid third centuries AD, and numbers would then have declined in step with ROME's fortunes. By AD 500 the total must have been under, rather than over, the 1,000 mark and it would have stayed there for the remainder of the Dark Ages.

RHODES

Dodecanese Islands, Greece

*From the fourth century BC, the leading town of the
Aegean islands; capital of the late Roman province
of Insulae ('Islands'); diocese: Asia*

History

In the fifth century BC, the island of Rhodes was divided between three
mini-states: Kamiros in the west, Lindos in the east and Ialysos in the
north. In 408 BC the three of them decided to merge and to construct a
federal capital at the northernmost point of the island. From this time
on, island, state and capital town shared the same name of Rhodes.

Rhodes town prospered as the fourth century BC progressed. Its situation was ideal for trade between the Greek archipelago and the
Levant, and in particular for one of the few open sea crossings that
Greek mariners were prepared to undertake, the voyage to Egypt. But
the real take-off came when Alexander the Great conquered Egypt and
started work on a new capital for the country at ALEXANDRIA. The old
capital, MEMPHIS, lay in the interior, below the southern apex of the
delta; Alexandria was on the coast at the delta's westernmost tip, exactly
where ships crossing from Rhodes made their landfall. As soon as Alexandria opened for business in 313 BC, the Rhodes–Alexandria route
became the busiest in the Mediterranean. Ptolemy, the Macedonian
general who took over Egypt on Alexander's death, needed Greek immigrants to underpin his rule: the Rhodians may or may not have shipped
in the new settlers, but they certainly took on the job of providing them
with the goods they needed to make them feel at home. The most important item, to judge from the rubbish dumps of Alexandria, was wine;
indeed, some of the dumps consist of nothing else but broken bits of
Rhodian amphorae. The Ptolemies paid the Rhodians with wheat,
which in the context of the shortage-prone Aegean world was as good a
currency as you could ask for.

The Colossus of Rhodes

The most dangerous moment in the early history of the Rhodian state came in 305 BC, when it was attacked by the Macedonian adventurer Demetrius Poliorcetes. Over the next twelve months Rhodes town was subjected to a series of furious assaults, the last of which came within a whisker of success, but just when the defenders were approaching exhaustion, events elsewhere forced Demetrius to withdraw, and, in doing so, to abandon all the towers and engines he had constructed in the course of the siege. The Rhodians realized 300 talents from the sale of these items, and they decided, understandably enough in view of what they had just been through, that they would use the money to construct a new statue of the city's protecting deity, Helios. Not the usual cult statue – life-size or a bit more – but a real monster, thirty-five metres high. The job was entrusted to a local sculptor, Chares of Lindos, who built the statue up by fixing bronze plates on to an iron armature. After twelve years the work was finished, and in 292 BC the Colossus was dedicated.

Reconstructions that show the Colossus standing astride the entrance to the Great Harbour are, of course, nonsense; as a statue

Rhodes was now a minor power. It had survived a fierce assault by Demetrius Poliorcetes in 305–304 BC, during the wars of Alexander's successors, and this, and its alliance with the Ptolemies, discouraged the major players from attempting a takeover. The third century saw the city-state proudly independent and at the peak of its prosperity. But as the century drew to a close the political situation began to change to Rhodes' disadvantage: Egypt fell into disarray, and the Ptolemies' rivals, the Antigonids of Macedon and the Seleucids of Syria, started moving in for the kill. Rhodes had to look for a new ally, and the obvious candidate was the era's rising power, the Roman Republic. The appeal to ROME worked brilliantly: the Antigonid and Seleucid states were humbled and Rhodes, which already held a segment of the coast of Asia Minor, was given some more as a sign of Rome's favour. Alas, the subsequent euphoria led to the Rhodians misreading the nature of their

of Helios it would have stood, legs together, in the precinct of the Temple of Helios. Whether it was really thirty-five metres high is more than moot, but it was certainly the biggest free-standing statue of the day, and it remained standing long enough to get on the list of the Seven Wonders of the Ancient World. But only just: in 227 BC, less than seventy years after it was put up, the Colossus was toppled in an earthquake. Its legacies are the term 'colossus', which is actually just an Anatolian word for 'statue', and the Statue of Liberty's crown of spikes, which are copied from the rays of Helios as sun god. The Statue of Liberty, incidentally, is fifty metres from her toe to the top of her torch, and thirty-five metres to the top of her head. It is very unlikely the Colossus was more than half as high as this.

Apparently the Rhodians consulted an oracle about what to do with their fallen idol, and were told to leave it where it was. The story goes that it lay there for 900 years, until some Arab raiders loaded the remains on 900 camels and sold the bronze to a Jewish merchant from Emesa. This is the stuff of *Arabian Nights*: any taboo the Rhodians may have observed would not have survived the arrival of Christianity, and if the bronze survived so long, it would have been sold off long before the 900 years were up. Doubtless the Arabs got their plunder, but the Colossus won't have been part of it.

alliance with Rome. In the next regional squabble in 167 BC, instead of immediately placing their forces at Rome's disposal, they offered to mediate between the two sides. This wasn't the behaviour the Romans expected from an ally and they quickly made their displeasure plain. They revoked their earlier territorial grant; more importantly, they declared the central Aegean island of Delos a tax-free haven and made it clear that this was where they expected Greeks to trade in future. Overnight, Rhodes' harbour dues all but vanished, falling from 166 talents a year to a mere 25.

After that it was downhill all the way. With Egypt sliding towards anarchy, the connection with Alexandria was of progressively less value; with Rome hostile, there was little chance of finding compensating markets elsewhere. Rhodes town gently lapsed into obscurity, although it always remained the biggest place in the Greek islands. Diocletian

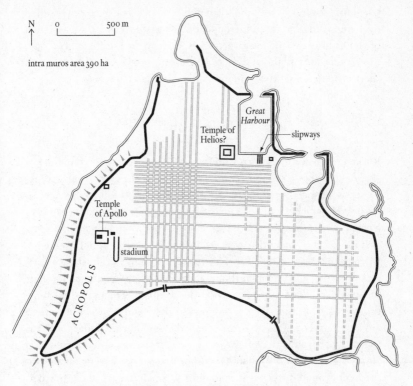

made it the capital of the province of Insulae he created at the close of the third century AD, but that doesn't mean that it had more than 5,000 inhabitants at the time, and it may well have had fewer.

Rhodes did have a period of renewed fame in the late medieval/early modern period. In 1309 the island was purchased by the Knights of St John, a Crusader organization that had been expelled from Palestine and was looking for a new home somewhere on the Muslim/Christian interface. Being a well-funded lot, the Knights were able to provide the harbour quarter of Rhodes town with lavish fortifications, an investment that was to pay off in 1488 when an Ottoman army attempted the conquest of the island. After failing to make any headway in a three-month siege, the Turks gave up and Rhodes remained a Christian enclave, a notable event at a time when Turkish arms were generally victorious. Thirty-seven years later the Turks came back, this time in overwhelming force; even so, the formidable defences of the town enabled the Knights to negotiate a surrender on favourable terms: they, and such of the locals as wished to, were allowed to go free, initially to Crete. From there the Knights moved to Malta, and enjoyed a much-deserved success in their final encounter with the Ottomans.

Topography

Rhodes town occupies the northern tip of its island, so it is triangular in shape, with the sea to either side (harbours on the right) and a transverse ravine forming the base. The Hellenistic walls follow this natural perimeter, which encloses far more space than its inhabitants can ever have needed. Nonetheless, the street grid – still visible in aerial photographs – covers the entire area, so it was obviously laid out in one go, when the city was founded. The urban centre of gravity must have been on the east, by the Great Harbour, and this is where we should look for the major monuments, in particular the Temple of Helios and the huge bronze statue of the god, the famous Colossus of Rhodes. But if there are any traces of these structures left, they are buried under the Crusader city that now occupies this quarter of the town. In fact there is almost nothing left of Hellenistic Rhodes except the street plan and, on the high ground to the west, a stadium, a small theatre and a few columns of a temple of Pythian Apollo.

Crusader Rhodes is only an eighth the size of the Hellenistic city (47 hectares, compared to 388 hectares). It was lovingly restored by the Italians during their occupation of the Dodecanese (1911–45), with results that some find a bit lifeless. But better that than the sort of anarchic redevelopment that would have taken place otherwise.

Population

At its peak the Rhodean state seems to have been about one-fifth the size of mid fifth-century ATHENS. It had 6,000 citizens (compared to Athens' 30,000) and in the third century BC it maintained a fleet that averaged forty ships (compared to Athens' 200). These data would suggest a native population for the island of about 24,000, to which we can add 4,000 foreign residents, making 28,000 in all. This is much the same as the 30,000 living on the island in 1911, the first figure in which we can place any real confidence.

The population of Rhodes town is more difficult to estimate. If it had the same ratio to the state as the Athens–PIRAEUS complex did to the Athenian polis, then it would have had about 45,000/5 = 9,000 people in the period 350–150 BC. Given the uncertainty of all these calculations, it is not unreasonable to push this figure up to the 10,000 mark for the glory years of the third century BC.

A statement that three of the island's thirty-three demes were urban is unfortunately no help in making this assessment. The demes would have been formalized at the time of the union, before Rhodes town was anything more than a gleam in the planner's eye; presumably they refer to the three original towns.

RIETI

Latium, Italy

Classical *Reate; capital of the late*
Roman province of Valeria

Rieti was one of the more important towns of the Sabines, the Sabines
being the people immediately to the north-east of ROME, and 'town'
being used in the sense of hilltop village. As the legend of 'The Rape of
the Sabine Women' indicates, the Romans bullied the Sabines from the
start, and in their habitually dour way they didn't let up until they had
eliminated them as an independent community. The nearer settlements
were added to the Roman state in the course of the fourth century BC,
leaving Rieti, at the far end of the Sabine territory, to be annexed in
around 290 BC by Curius Dentatus. The good news for its inhabitants
was that they were subsequently granted Roman citizenship in 268 BC.

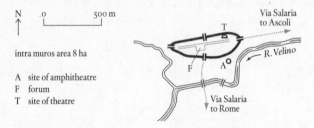

N   0   500 m

intra muros area 8 ha

A   site of amphitheatre
F   forum
T   site of theatre

Via Salaria
to Ascoli

R. Velino

Via Salaria
to Rome

Rieti was built on a bluff overlooking the Velino river (classical
Avens). It was connected to Rome, seventy-eight kilometres (forty-
eight miles) to the south-west, by the Via Salaria, the 'Salt Road'. This
was the route by which salt was brought from the mouth of the Tiber to
the communities of the middle Apennines, a traffic that probably began
as early as the Bronze Age, and certainly antedated the foundation of
Rome. The Romans turned the existing track into a proper road and
extended this first to ASCOLI PICENO, then to the Adriatic. As a result,

Rieti acquired a certain strategic importance. It was, however, always a very small place. Its walls enclosed an area of only eight hectares, which means that it can never have had a population of more than 1,000 souls.

In the imperial period Rieti had two claims to distinction: it was the home town of Vespasian (69–79), founder of the Flavian dynasty, and in the final reorganization of Italy it was made the capital of the minor province of Valeria. The name comes from the Via Valeria, which ran along the southern border of the province – presumably Salaria wasn't considered dignified enough.

Rieti survived the Dark Ages and did well in the medieval centuries. New walls gave the town an intramural area of fifty-seven hectares, a seven-fold increase on the classical figure. Then stagnation set in, with the population in the sixteenth and seventeenth centuries stuck somewhere around the 7,000 mark.

RIMINI

Emilia-Romagna, Italy

Classical *Ariminum; terminus of the Via Flaminia,
starting point of the Via Aemilia*

An Umbrian settlement originally, Rimini succumbed to the Gallic invasion of the early fourth century BC, becoming part of the 'Ager Gallicus', the strip of territory between the central Apennines and the Adriatic that constituted the southern apex of Gallic settlement. As such, it was the first place of significance to fall to the Roman counter-offensive that began in the third century BC, a change in ownership that was marked by the refoundation of Rimini as a Latin colony in 268 BC. Its importance was underlined when it became the terminus of the Via Flaminia, the strategic highway that was built in the 220s BC to support the Roman advance into the Po valley. The next step in this road-building programme, the construction of the Via Aemilia from Rimini to PIACENZA (187 BC), nailed down the entire area south of the Po; the subsequent construction of the Via Popilia from Rimini to AQUILEIA in 132 BC extended the dominion of ROME to the head of the Adriatic.

Rimini joined the majority of the Latin colonies in the revolt known as the Social War (91–89 BC) but was soon recovered by Sulla. Its strategic position meant that it often featured in the Italian civil wars precipitated by Julius Caesar's ambitions; in the subsequent period, *c.* 30 BC, it was refounded as a Roman colony. This time the town was built on a gridded plan that is still discernible at the heart of the city today. The grid covers about twenty hectares, making Rimini a place of middling size by contemporary standards, but as regards public monuments it soon became rather grander than most. Augustus (27 BC–AD 14) built an arch on the southern approach to the town to mark the termination of the Via Flaminia; on the north he began the construction of a bridge across the Marecchia (finished by his successor, Tiberius), which can be taken to mark the start of the Via

Aemilia. Subsequently, Hadrian (AD 117–38) added an amphitheatre.

Rimini prospered in the first two centuries of the imperial period and seems to have hung on to its prosperity when darker times began in the mid third century. When the emperor Aurelian (AD 270–75) refortified the city, he did so on an extended plan that included the amphitheatre as a bastion and raised the intramural area to forty-six hectares. Not long after this, it probably became the capital of the newly created province of Flaminia et Picenum. If so, it would have had to yield up this title in AD 402 when RAVENNA, fifty-two kilometres (thirty-two miles) to

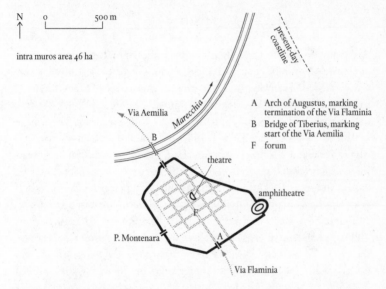

the north, became the residence of the imperial court. Despite the demotion it retained a significant place in the late antique hierarchy of the region, which was to last until the extinction of the exarchate of Ravenna in the eighth century AD.

In the seventeenth and early eighteenth centuries, Rimini's population was in the 8,000 to 10,000 range. As early modern Rimini was larger than the classical town (seventy-eight hectares, compared to forty-six), a figure of 5,000 would seem a generous estimate for classical Ariminum. This would only apply during the period when it was at its peak, say AD 100–400.

ROME

Latium, Italy

History

According to the Romans, their city was created by the union of seven small Latin communities at a date corresponding to 753 BC. Subsequently it was ruled by seven kings, the last three of whom were of Etruscan stock, the Etruscans being the people to the immediate north of Rome. Because of their trading contacts with the Greeks, the Etruscans were more advanced than the other native peoples of Italy, and in the mid sixth century they turned this superior political sophistication to advantage, creating a hegemony that covered their neighbours to the north (in the lower Po valley) and south (in Latium and Campania). There is no evidence to suggest that the Romans put up any resistance to the imposition of Etruscan rule, and the first two Etruscan monarchs, Tarquin the Elder and Servius Tullius, were remembered favourably. Not so the last of the three, Tarquin the Proud, who was said by the Roman author Marcus Varro (116–27 BC) to have been expelled in 509 BC, allegedly for condoning his son's rape of a Roman noblewoman. More probably, his downfall was simply one aspect of the general collapse of Etruscan power over the region following a defeat at the hands of a Campanian-Greek force at the Battle of Aricia, twenty-six kilometres (sixteen miles) to the south of Rome.

Whatever Rome's situation was before its Etruscan period – and the Romans, naturally enough, tended to think that they had been important from the start – it emerged from it as the most powerful of the fifteen mini-states into which Latium was divided. It had one-third of the entire Latin territory, more than double that of its nearest rival, Tibur, and far more than the average, which was a humble 156 square kilometres (as against Rome's 822). The disparity made the other Latins so nervous that they formed a league aimed at keeping Rome at arm's length. The Romans took the bull by the horns and, after winning the Battle of Lake Regillus (493 BC) over the forces of the league, wrote a new set of rules that transformed it from an anti-Roman alliance into an instrument of Roman control.

For the Latins, this setback proved to have an upside. Rome provided the leadership needed to repel a series of damaging invasions by the Volsci and Aequi, hill tribes from the neighbouring Apennines. Indeed, by the end of the fifth century BC the Romans were powerful enough to start nibbling at Etruscan territory, beginning a long war with Veii, the nearest of the Etruscan towns, in 406 and sticking with it until Veii had been captured and its lands incorporated in the Roman state. But only six years after the conclusion of this, Rome's first step outside the bounds of Latium, disaster struck. A marauding army of Gauls fell on Latium, overwhelmed the Roman army attempting to oppose it (at the Battle of the Allia, a stream 17.5 kilometres (eleven miles) north of Rome) and then swept on to Rome itself and put it to the sack. The humiliated Romans had to buy off their persecutors and, summoning all the stoicism for which they would later become famous, begin rebuilding their homes, their city's defences and its political position.

It took the Romans thirty years to re-establish their position in Latium. This done they turned their attention to Campania, the region immediately south of Latium, whose inhabitants were suffering from the same sort of incursions from the local hill tribes – in this case the Samnites – that Rome and the other Latin communities knew all too well. The Campanians appealed to Rome for help, and the Romans, their confidence now restored, agreed to step in and save the situation. This proved a more difficult task than they expected. The Samnites were much more numerous than the Volsci and Aequi; they were also better organized and even harder to get at. On one expedition in 321 BC the entire Roman army (which at this time consisted of two legions of 4,000 men apiece) was trapped in a valley and forced to surrender. The Samnites only let it go in return for a peace treaty that was all in their favour, and the Romans were so discouraged that they kept the treaty's terms for the next four years. Then they came back, more determined than ever.

One method the Romans used to pin down conquered territory was to plant colonies, fortified settlements with several thousand inhabitants, at strategically important points. On average during the fourth century BC they had founded one colony every ten years. Now – counting from 315 BC – they stepped up the rate, to an average of one new colony every two years, and they were to maintain this average over the next twenty-five years. Some were sited for reasons of defence, particularly a cluster in the narrowest part of the corridor between Rome and CAPUA, the leading city of Campania. Others were set up as bases for attack, being right up against the Samnite frontier. The most remarkable were two that were placed on the far side of the Apennines, at Luceria and Venusia. The Romans had made treaties with the tribes on the way to, and along, the Adriatic coast, so they were now able to put the squeeze on the Samnites from both directions. Even so, it was to take the Romans all of twenty-five years to bring the Samnites to heel. The Roman army, now increased to four legions, had to grind its way through the region valley by valley. A second treaty, in 304 BC, was all in Rome's favour; the third, in 290 BC, proclaimed Rome's total victory. Samnium was effectively annexed to the Roman state.

Much to their surprise, Rome's allies were similarly annexed. The obligations they had assumed for the duration of the war, in particular the undertaking to supply contingents to the Roman army (the numbers being decided by Rome), turned out to be permanent. No one could withdraw from an alliance with Rome. What had seemed at first like a reassuring handshake was in fact an iron grip.

The successful conclusion of the Samnite wars meant that Italy south of Rome now contained only one independent power, the Greek colony of Tarentum. The Tarentines, far too few to hold off the Romans on their own, called in Pyrrhus, king of Epirus, a modest state on the Greek side of the Adriatic, to sustain their cause. Militarily Pyrrhus was up to the job, for his army was built on the Macedonian model, and little more than a generation earlier the Macedonians, led by Alexander the Great, had conquered most of the known world. So, as expected, Pyrrhus won his battles – at Heraclea in 280 BC, and at Ausculum the next year. However, the cost of doing so dampened his appetite for continuing the war, which he soon saw was unwinnable. In 275 BC he left Italy for good – although so long as he lived he kept a garrison in Tarentum, which meant that the Romans weren't able to complete their occupation of southern Italy until after his death in 272 BC.

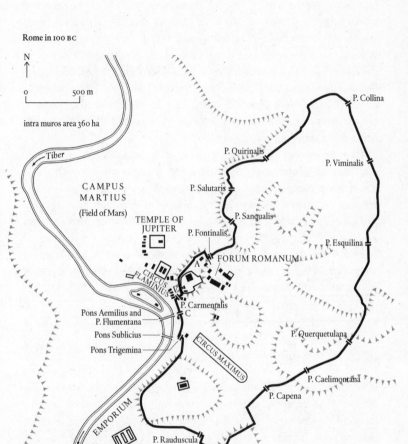

Rome in 100 BC

N

0 ——— 500 m

intra muros area 360 ha

Tiber

CAMPUS
MARTIUS

(Field of Mars)

TEMPLE OF
JUPITER

P. Fontinalis

CIRCUS
FLAMINIUS

Pons Aemilius and
P. Flumentana

Pons Sublicius

Pons Trigemina

EMPORIUM

Horrea
Galbana

P. Collina

P. Quirinalis

P. Viminalis

P. Salutaris

P. Sanqualis

P. Esquilina

A   FORUM ROMANUM

P. Carmentalis
C

CIRCUS MAXIMUS

P. Querquetulana

P. Caelimontana

P. Capena

P. Rauduscula

C   cattle market (Forum Bovarium)
V   vegetable market (Forum Holitorium)
A   Arx, Temple of Juno Moneta

The conquest of central and southern Italy meant that Rome had made the jump from city-state to territorial empire. Nothing like this had been seen before in the Mediterranean world. ATHENS and CARTHAGE had created maritime empires, but they were relatively fragile structures, with little manpower and strictly limited capacities when it came to waging war. Rome, by contrast, already controlled two-thirds of the population of Italy – say 3 million out of a total of 4.5 million – a figure an order of magnitude greater than any of its potential rivals. How had the Romans made this transition from local to peninsular power, the crucial transformation that had eluded all their competitors? What was their magic formula?

Part of it was undoubtedly their attitude towards citizenship. Through the gradual extension of this right, conquered peoples became a part of the conquering power, sharing in the spoils of conquest as the republic acquired an ever-widening circle of colonies at ever-increasing distances from Italy. The Roman administrative system, tied together with an effective legal system and the ancient world's most advanced system of roads, also served to create a sense of unity and stability among peoples who had suffered from wars and despotism before they were folded into the empire.

Topography

The one thing everybody knows about Rome is that it was built on seven hills, the generally accepted implication being that it was founded by the merger of seven adjacent hilltop communities. Three lists of the hills involved have been preserved, but, alas, they don't agree as to the names, or even whether there were six, seven or eight of them. The one that supports the traditional figure of seven is late (fourth century AD) and includes hills that lie outside the republican wall, so it cannot satisfactorily explain Rome's beginnings. The other two are more promising in that they stick to the area inside the wall. That area contains eight reasonably well-defined hills. Three of them overlook the Tiber (the Capitoline, Palatine and Aventine), with a fourth (the Caelian) lying just east of the Palatine. The remaining four are spurs running down from the high ground to the north-east, like fingers reaching towards the first four.

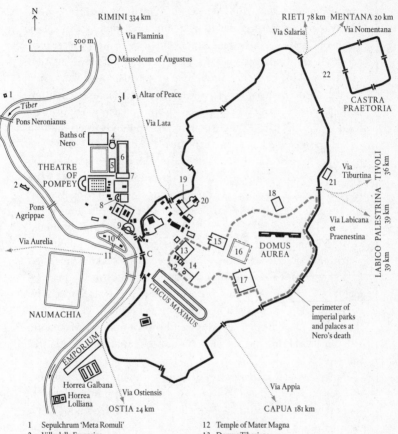

Rome in AD 68

1 Sepulchrum 'Meta Romuli'	12 Temple of Mater Magna
2 Villa della Farnesina	13 Domus Tiberiana
3 Horologium Augusti	14 Domus Augustana
4 Pantheon	15 Temple of Venus and Rome
5 Baths of Agrippa	16 artificial lake of Nero
6 Saepta Julia	17 Temple of Divine Claudius
7 Diribitorium (public voting hall)	18 Portico of Livia
8 Theatre of Balbus	19 Forum Julium
9 Theatre of Marcellus	20 Forum Augusti
10 Tiber Island	21 Market of Livia
11 Pons Sestus	22 Campus Cohortium Praetorium

Founding Fathers

The Romans had two separate stories about their origins. The first traced their descent from Aeneas, a fugitive Trojan prince who, after various adventures including a famous encounter with Dido, queen of Carthage, settled in Latium and became the ultimate progenitor of the Roman people. The second concerned the foundation of the city of Rome, a very different matter, which took place some 350 years after Aeneas' death. As was frequently the case with foundation myths, the city was supposed to have taken its name from its founder, in this case Romulus, or, as we would say, the founding father was given a name that explained the name of the city. The first story is obviously tosh, invented to give the Romans a dignified place in the early history of the Mediterranean as perceived by the Greeks. It was easily linked to the Romulus story by having Aeneas' son found a line of kings that ruled the Latin city of Alba during the three and a half centuries needed to bridge the gap. In the combined version, Romulus was a prince of Alba, cast out as an infant by a usurping uncle but saved, first by a she-wolf who suckled him, then by a shepherd who raised him to manhood. Discovering his true identity, Romulus led a troop of supporters to Alba, deposed the wicked uncle and restored his father to his rightful place on the throne. Then he returned to his youthful haunts on the Palatine Hill and made this the nucleus of a new city that he named after himself.

If that was all that there was to the story, it would be a straightforward example of the sort of foundation myth common to many cities in the Greek world. The unusual feature is that Romulus had a twin brother, Remus. Moreover, the two didn't get on as twins

They are, from north to south, the Quirinal, Viminal, Cispian and Oppian. Marcus Varro, author of one of the two early (first-century BC) lists, seems to have taken geography as his guide, simply omitting the two least obvious hills, the Viminal and the Cispian, to get his total of six. Festus, the author of the other early list, gives a more interesting set of names. Four of his eight, the Palatine, Cispian, Oppian and Cae-

should. According to the most frequently cited version of the legend, when Romulus was ploughing the ritual furrow that was to mark the position of Rome's city wall, Remus poured scorn on the project and on the wall that wasn't a wall, and, in an ill-advised attempt to make his point, hopped over it. So Romulus killed him.

Nobody has ever come up with a satisfactory explanation of why Remus figures in this story. He isn't much of a help, or much of a hindrance; all he does is add a note of ineffectual discord. There was, however, a strong element of duality in Roman political life, and it could be something to do with that. The early years of the republic were dominated by the struggles between patricians and plebs, the later centuries by the alliance between Senate and people. The executive consisted of two equally empowered consuls. But in that case, why wasn't Rome considered a joint foundation, rather than the work of Romulus, with some barracking by Remus?

To round off this precis, it is perhaps worth noting that the modern pronunciations of Romulus and Remus are wrong. Romulus was *Rome-ulus*, as it must be if you think about it. And Remus, unlike Uncle *Remus*, has the 'Rem' rhyming with *stem*. Gore Vidal has remarked that it is lucky the quarrel between Romulus and Remus turned out as it did because otherwise we would be talking about Reme, which would be a sad business indeed. But in fact we know that things would never have been that bad, because in some versions of the myth, Remus did get to found a short-lived city of his own and it was called not Reme but Remoria. It was said to have been on the Aventine, which is where, according to many, the plebs withdrew when they were threatening to secede – a coincidence that provides some small support for the idea that Remus represented the less prominent half of a two-part Roman state.

lian, are straightforward, but his other 'hills' aren't really hills at all. They are the Velia (a saddle connecting the Oppian and the Palatine), the Fagutal (the southern face of the Oppian), the Subura (the valley between the Cispian and Oppian) and the Germalus (the part of the Palatine facing the Velia). The fact that his eight form a tight cluster at the very heart of Rome suggests that what Festus has preserved for us are the sites of the villages involved in the original merger.

The new city would surely have been surrounded by a ditch and palisade, although no trace of either has ever been found. We can be equally certain that a ninth hill, the Capitoline, would have been included in the perimeter, for although it was not a suitable site for a village, it was ideal as a citadel, being small, craggy and easily defended. What the acropolis was to Athens, the Capitoline was to Rome, and like the Athenian acropolis it became the site of the city's defining cult. By the beginning of the fifth century BC, at the time when the Romans expelled King Tarquin, the Capitoline was already adorned with a magnificent Etruscan-style temple housing the image of Jupiter Optimus Maximus, 'Jupiter the Best and Greatest'.

By the start of the fourth century BC, the Romans were beginning to think of themselves as important players in the push and shove of central Italian politics. But, keen as they were to advance at others' expense, they had neglected the defences of the city, and when their army was defeated by the Gauls in 390 BC, the townsfolk of Rome found themselves at the mercy of the victors. There was nothing to be done but buy off the invaders and then set to work on a city wall strong enough to stop anything of the sort happening again. Greek architects were called in to plan the wall, which, in the Greek style, followed the contours of the hills wherever possible. It is always referred to nowadays as the Servian Wall, after Servius Tullius, one of the Etruscan kings of Rome, who, of course, had nothing to do with it. Parts of it still stand, the first significant monument of republican Rome.

In fact, if we are talking significant monuments, the Servian Wall had very few competitors during the republican period. Two hundred and fifty years after its completion, the Romans were masters of the Mediterranean, but their capital remained an undistinguished huddle of housing, with no semblance of a plan to it and very few buildings of scale or merit. Most of the republic's business was conducted in the open air, a great deal of it outside the city, on the Campus Martius ('Field of Mars'). It was on the Campus Martius, the flat floodplain of the Tiber between the city and the river's westward loop, that the Romans assembled for the census that underpinned the call-up. Here too the elections were held that confirmed the Senate's candidates for military command, the consuls and praetors. And of course it was on the Field of Mars that the legions were mustered, and to the same site that victorious armies returned before making their triumphal entry into the city. Elections to legislative and judicial posts, by contrast, were voted on by assemblies that were generally held inside the city, in the Roman forum at the foot of the Capitoline, or on the hill itself, but they were sometimes held outside the city, in the Circus Flaminius, a venue better known for its horse races. Chariot races were held in the Circus Maximus, between the Aventine and Palatine hills, where there was a suitable strip of flat land to act as a track and the hills to either side could act as stands for the spectators. Gladiatorial contests were usually held in the Roman forum, using temporary wooden stands. There was no sign at all of the colossal theatres and amphitheatres, fora and baths that we think of as typically Roman.

The best that the city had to show – apart from the wall and the Temple of Capitoline Jove – was a plethora of small temples, most of them little bigger than shrines. They were built by victorious generals out of the spoils of war. Most of these military monuments were, as you might expect, on the Field of Mars where the army could see them. The few state temples weren't much bigger; the most interesting is the Temple of Juno Moneta ('Juno Who Warns') at the northern end of the Capitoline Hill. The epithet refers to the geese who supposedly honked out an alarm when a party of Gauls attempted to seize the Capitol during the Gallic occupation of the lower town. Because the Romans later minted their coins in the temple precinct, *moneta* became the common term for what we still refer to as money.

The lack of large, showy monuments did not trouble the Roman Republic. The senatorial system of government was collegiate, and no senator was supposed to promote himself above his colleagues by, for example, building a bigger temple than any of his predecessors. No matter how splendid his victories might be, he was expected to return to his accustomed place on the senatorial benches when he laid down his command, and any attempt to keep himself in the public eye with a fancy building programme would be heavily frowned on. 'No kings' was the club motto. There was also a puritan streak that favoured the practical over the merely aesthetic. If there was money to spare in the government's coffers, let it be spent on improving the city's water supply, or Italy's roads. If you wanted something to attract admiration, what about the ten-kilometre-long (six-mile) arcade that carried the Marcian aqueduct across the Campania and into the city? Compare a sight such as this, said Frontinus, curator of the water supply under the emperor Nerva, 'with the Pyramids, or the useless, though famous, works of the Greeks', a sentiment only slightly spoilt by the fact that by his day, Rome had its fair share of useless buildings, including some mini-pyramids.

Population

The geographical growth of the Roman state was first charted in detail by Julius Beloch in *The Population of the Greco-Roman World* (1886). He reckoned that in the first years of the republic, in the 490s BC, it covered some 822 square kilometres and had a population of around 20,000 to 25,000. This population had recently been divided into twenty-one geographically distinct 'tribes', seventeen of which were rural and four urban. On this basis, early fifth-century Rome (the town) would have had about 20,000–25,000 × 4/21 = 3,810–4,760 inhabitants, say 4,250. At the beginning of the next century, after the capture of Veii and the annexation of its territory (traditionally in 396 BC), four new rural tribes were created. The Roman state now covered about twice the area it had a century earlier (1,562 square kilometres, compared to 822) and would have had a population – assuming some population growth in Latium as a whole – in the range 50,000 to 60,000. If we assume that the new tribal distribution still reflected the situation on the ground, the urban population would have been 50,000–60,000 × 4/25 = 8,000–9,600, say 9,000. These numbers – 4,250 in 500 BC and 9,000 in 400 BC – look about right for the period, and suggest that Rome was already the biggest city in peninsular Italy by the start of the fourth century BC.

After 400 BC we run low on useful data. Although the number of rural tribes was increased as the Roman state underwent further expansion, it is clear that the increase didn't match the additions to the rural population. And after 241 BC, the creation of rural tribes stopped altogether. Nor is there anything to be gained from looking at the physical remains of the city. The Servian Wall was built by the Greek architects in their habitual extended manner, following the contours of the ground to get the most defensible circuit: the intramural area is no guide to the size of the population. At the time of its construction, in 375–350 BC,

Rome is unlikely to have had a population of more than 15,000. The 360 hectares inside the Servian perimeter would be sufficient for many times that number. In fact, all figures given for the Roman population between the early fourth century BC and the first century BC are simply guesses, which you can believe or not as you choose.

There is nothing to be done about this except to try to clarify the thinking behind the guesses. One approach is to assume a constant growth rate between the only two reasonably fixed points we have, a population of about 10,000 in 400 BC and 250,000 in AD 1. If we plot this line, we get the following set of figures:

400 BC	10,000
300 BC	22,000
200 BC	50,000
100 BC	110,000
AD 1	250,000

This seems to fit with what we know of the city's increasing requirements as regards food. Up to 300 BC this wouldn't have been a problem except on occasions of unusual dearth, for the Roman Campania would have been able to supply the city's needs until its population was well over the 20,000 mark. And in the third century BC, the conquest of south Italy and, more importantly, Sicily meant that supply kept up with demand even though the urban population reached levels that were well beyond the capacity of Latium to sustain. Sicily's cereal exports, in fact, seem to have been sufficient to keep the Roman plebs fed and happy for the major part of the second century BC too. It was only in the final quarter, as the city's population (on this model) approached the 100,000 mark, that demand outran supply and the matter became an urgent political issue. Meeting this challenge would have taken a massive military and administrative effort, and was surely one of the factors bringing about the change from republican to imperial rule.

In the reigns of Julius Caesar (59 BC–44 BC) and Augustus (27 BC–AD 14), 150,000 and just over 200,000 recipients of wheat rations were recorded respectively in the Roman rosters. Later, in the time of Constantine (AD 306–36), a survey of the city's residences recorded 1,790 houses and 46,000 apartments. Assuming an average of ten persons per house and four in each apartment, one can calculate the city's population at $(1,790 \times 10) + (46,000 \times 4) = 201,900$. Although the population may have been greater during the intervening period of the Antonine emperors, this data suggests that Rome in the fourth century AD had a population similar to the time of Augustus. As a further cross-check, the Renaissance census of AD 1526 recorded 45,178 people living in approximately 220 hectares. If this same density is extended to the entire walled area of the city (1,380 ha), it suggests a population in the range of 283,000. Adjusting for the fact that around a third of the classical city was public space, we return to a figure in the range of 200,000.

Some scholars argue for Rome having a peak population more in the range of 1 million persons. They do this by construing the apartments in the fourth-century survey as referring to apartment blocks, and they argue that the tallied wheat rations may have been distributed only to adult males. If there had been 46,000 apartment blocks in Rome in the fourth century, however, and if it is assumed that each would have covered an average of 300 square metres, they would have filled the entire area inside the Aurelian walls, leaving no room for the well-known and extensive public buildings and gardens. As to wheat rations being distributed only to men, we can see on the Arch of Constantine that women and even children lined up for (and presumably received) such rations. It is therefore reasonable to infer that the recorded total of wheat rations corresponds at least roughly to the population as a whole rather than to men alone.

To support a hypothetical Roman population of a million or more, it is also argued that lists of wheat rations were understated by omitting tens or even hundreds of thousands of slaves. Aside from the problems of physical space to house such numbers, it seems unlikely that masters in the city would use their own resources to maintain large staffs of slaves when they could obtain service from the same individuals as freedmen who qualified for the public dole.

The area enclosed, 360 hectares, is unremarkable by the standards of Magna Graecia (Greater Greece, meaning the Greek areas of Sicily and southern Italy), as witness Agrigentum at 450 hectares, TARANTO at 510 and Croton at 615. It certainly doesn't mean that Rome must have had a large population at this date, although, of course, it doesn't preclude the possibility that it did.

SALAMIS

Cyprus

Legend tells that at the end of the Trojan War, a prince named Teukros from the Greek island of Salamis founded a new city with the same name on the east coast of Cyprus. Archaeology suggests that the city of Salamis was founded around 1075 BC by inhabitants of the nearby town of Enkomi after it was damaged by an earthquake. Cyprus was an important place for Bronze Age traders, in part due to its productive copper mines.

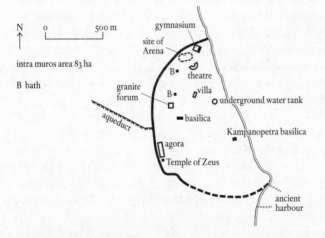

Salamis featured a temple of Zeus, who remained the city's patron deity down to Roman times. The city also had an excellent natural harbour, which helped facilitate its success as a centre for international trade. In 707 BC, Cyprus agreed to submit to Sargon II, the king of Assyria. Rich tombs from that period indicate that the local kings of

Salamis enjoyed sufficient autonomy to accumulate substantial wealth. In the seventh century BC, Salamis was one of the largest and richest cities in the Eastern Mediterranean. The Salaminians traded actively with Greece, Asia Minor, RHODES and Egypt. Their products included bronzes, ivories, painted vases and limestone statuettes.

In 669 BC, following the collapse of the Assyrian Empire, Cyprus fell increasingly under the influence of Egypt. By 570 BC, the Egyptian king Amasis had become effective ruler of the island. Chafing under Egyptian control, however, the Cypriots were willing to switch masters and submit to Cyrus the Persian in 545 BC. By 521 BC, Cyprus became part of the Fifth Persian Satrapy. It seems, however, that the locals came to dislike Persian rule as much as that of the Egyptians. Under Darius I (521–486 BC), a member of the Salaminian royal family named Onesilos led a revolt that attracted support from Greece. When Onesilos was killed, the Greeks withdrew their fleet and Persian rule was reinforced. In 480 BC Xerxes I led a Persian army against Greece, and Cyprus was obliged to send 150 ships to assist the campaign.

In 459–458 BC, the Greeks again sent a fleet for the purpose of liberating Cyprus from Persia. After suffering defeat in Egypt, however, the Greeks withdrew. Again in 449 BC, the Greeks attempted unsuccessfully to conquer Salamis, but they ended up signing the Treaty of Kallias, which left the Persians in control. Under King Evagoras I (410–374 BC), the city enjoyed a Hellenic revival, although he also was ultimately compelled to submit to Persia.

The kings of Cyprus sent ships to support the campaign of Alexander the Great, whose victory freed Cyprus from Persian domination. Upon Alexander's death in 323 BC, Cyprus was disputed between his successors, Antigonus and Ptolemy. Salamis sided with Ptolemy, who sent his brother Menelaos to seize the island. After initial success, Demetrius (son of Antigonus) arrived to besiege Menelaos in Salamis. Even though Ptolemy sent a fleet of ships to assist his son, Demetrius used catapults and various other inventive weapons to prevail in his siege. Demetrius thereafter ruled at Salamis successfully for twelve years. When he was away in Cilicia in 294 BC, however, Ptolemy arrived with a fleet and captured Salamis after a short siege.

Thereafter, the Ptolemies of Egypt ruled Salamis and the rest of Cyprus until it became a Roman province, under Marcus Porcius Cato, in 58 BC. As an example of the balanced Ptolemaic administration, the highest official had the title of *strategos*, while the official in charge of the copper mines was the *antistrategos*. Salamis remained a large prosperous city, minting its own coinage. After being handed back briefly to the Ptolemies in 47 BC, Cyprus resumed its Roman status in 30 BC after the Battle of Actium. At that point, the Roman capital city shifted from Salamis to Paphos, which was restored by Augustus and referred to as Sebaste Augusta.

Although no longer the political capital, Salamis remained the largest city on Cyprus in Roman times. It attracted a large international population, including many Jews. St Paul and St Barnabas (a Cypriot) founded a Christian community there. Meanwhile, the emperor Augustus sponsored construction of a large gymnasium and a theatre that could hold 15,000 spectators. The city also boasted an amphitheatre and stadium. Excavations have uncovered a large reservoir for water that came into the city through a 48-kilometre (30-mile) aqueduct.

In the reign of Trajan, a large segment of the population died or was dispersed during the unsuccessful Jewish revolt of AD 116. The city is unlikely ever to have regained its previous population, which the archaeologist Vassos Karageorghis has (excessively) estimated in the range of 350,000.

In AD 332 and 342, Salamis suffered substantial damage from earthquakes. During the reign of Constantius II (337–61), the city was granted four years' exemption from imperial taxes in order to concentrate on reconstruction. The citizens expressed their gratitude by renaming their city Constantia, and under that name it served as an episcopal see. Salamis gradually declined as its harbour silted in, however, and was finally abandoned during the seventh-century Arab invasions, after which the remaining inhabitants moved to Famagusta.

SALONA

Present-day *Solin, now a suburb of Split,*
on the coast of Croatia

Capital of the Roman province of Dalmatia
from its creation in A D *9 to its fall in the*
sixth century; diocese: Illyricum

Salona was one of the more important places of the Dalmatae, an Illyrian people who lived on the eastern shore of the Adriatic. It was captured by the Roman general Metellus in 117 BC, occupied permanently
following a second conquest by Cosconius in 78 BC and became a
Roman colony in the early years of Augustus' reign, probably around
33 BC. In 11 BC, by which time Augustus had conquered the entire area
between the Adriatic and the Danube, Salona became the capital of the
province of Illyria, newly created to cover this region. Illyria proved too
large a responsibility for a single governor, and twenty years later Augustus split it in two. Salona continued as capital of the south-western half,
initially known as Illyricum Superius and subsequently as Dalmatia.

Salona was to have an uneventful history and remain Roman for
longer than most places in the western half of the empire. In fact, in the
dark days of the fifth century AD, it was home to the last man with a
claim to the western throne, a governor of Dalmatia called Julius Nepos,
who had been briefly recognized as Emperor of the West in 473–5,
returned to Salona after being deposed, and lived on, his title still
accepted by some, until 480.

Salona spent its final years under the wing of the East Roman Empire.
Ceded to the Gothic king Theodoric in 493, it was taken back under
imperial control by the emperor Justinian in 535. Not long after, raids by
Slavs from across the Danube began to trouble the hinterland, but during the sixth century these did not reach the coast, and Salona's inhabitants lived in reasonable security. Then, at the start of the seventh
century, the frontier defences collapsed, and all over the Balkans Slav
tribes moved in and made the land their own. Salona held out until about
614, when its inhabitants, abandoning their homes, fled to Split, where

the palace built for his retirement by the emperor Diocletian offered a more readily defensible haven.

The outline of Roman Salona can be mapped with some confidence. The town consisted of two unequal halves, the old town, covering some thirty hectares, and the new town on its east side, somewhat larger at forty-two hectares. The old town clearly represents the final Roman perimeter; by then, the new town had been abandoned, and the population concentrated within a perimeter that, as was often the case with late Roman town walls, used the amphitheatre as a bastion. The new town equally clearly represents the eastward expansion of Salona

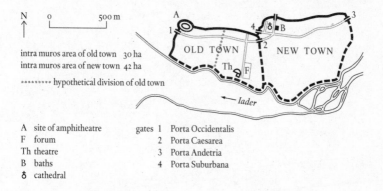

N   o   500 m

intra muros area of old town 30 ha
intra muros area of new town 42 ha

•••••••••• hypothetical division of old town

A   site of amphitheatre   gates 1 Porta Occidentalis
F   forum   2 Porta Caesarea
Th theatre   3 Porta Andetria
B   baths   4 Porta Suburbana
ō   cathedral

during its imperial noon, but the extent of the occupied area in this period would have been less than the seventy-two hectares obtained by adding old and new together, for the old town would not have stretched so far to the west at the time. In fact the current hypothesis is that when the new town was built, the old town was only half its final size, and if this is true, Salona at its peak would have covered no more than fifty-eight hectares. It is consistent with this view that the original nucleus of the colony lies in the eastern half of the old town, an area of some fifteen hectares. As to chronology, we have inscriptions dating the Porta Caesarea, the gate between old and new towns, to the time of Augustus, and the north wall of the new town to the period of the Marcomannic Wars (c. AD 170). The refurbishment of the Porta Caesarea, which can be assumed to mark the moment when the new town was abandoned, is placed in the reign of Constantius II (337–61).

In *Dalmatia* (1969), J. J. Wilkes suggests that Salona could have had a population of 60,000. His calculation is based on the size of the amphitheatre, although this was barely larger than POMPEII's (Salona's had space for 13,380, compared to Pompeii's 12,800), and Pompeii is now considered to have had a population of 10,000 at most. In fact, the underlying premise – that amphitheatres of this class had seats for less than half the city's adult population – seems a bit improbable. It is just as easy to believe that not only was there room for all the urban plebs, but that there was space left over for the country folk, who were equally citizens and would have expected to be able to see the shows put on by the town fathers.

SARDIS

Present-day *Sartmustafa*,
Manisa province, western Turkey

*Capital of Lydia under its native kings and
under the Persian and Roman empires*

Sardis started life as a hilltop citadel, home to the kings of Lydia, a state
that emerged as the dominant political unit in western Anatolia in the
course of the seventh century BC. The country was famous for its gold
deposits: Sardis overlooked a stream, the Pactolus, which was later
remembered as having been the source of a particularly rich strike. Perhaps this was what attracted the kings of Lydia to Sardis in the first
place, although its position at the centre of the kingdom must have been
another positive factor. Whatever their motivation, the kings had made
a good choice: Sardis soon developed into the sort of two-part town so
familiar in the Near East. Its palace was in the royal, or upper, town; the
ordinary folk lived in a settlement that straggled along the banks of the
Pactolus, and constituted the 'lower town'.

According to Herodotus (fifth century BC), the lower town was a
modest place with many of its houses built entirely of reeds from the
river and even those of more solid construction having reed thatching.
There was no surrounding wall, so it could not be defended, nor was any
attempt made to defend the lower town when the Persian king Cyrus
invaded Lydia in 547 BC. Instead, Croesus, the Lydian king, retreated to
the upper town, hoping to hold out until his vassals could come to his
rescue. However, Cyrus found an unguarded spot in the citadel's
defences and stormed the place. Lydia became a Persian satrapy and
remained so for the next two centuries.

These two centuries don't appear to have seen much change in
Sardis. A Persian garrison was installed in the acropolis, while the main
Lydian settlement remained as before, a straggle of housing along the
right bank of the Pactolus. Xenophon (*c.* 435–*c.* 354 BC) mentions an
altar of Artemis, which we can assume to have been at the southern end

of this 'ribbon development', where later on the temple to the goddess was to rise.

In 334 BC Sardis surrendered to Alexander the Great. Subsequently, a new lower town was laid out to the north of the acropolis, and the old lower town was left to decay. An exception was made for the sanctuary of Artemis, where construction was started on a massive temple: a few people continued to live in and around this presumably sanctified area.

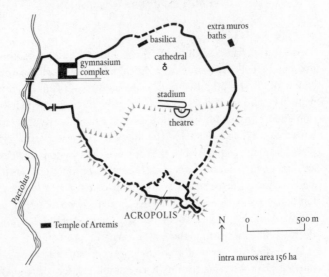

intra muros area 156 ha

Everyone else moved to the new town, which had as its axis the east–west road running from the interior to the coast. It was equipped with the usual Hellenistic public buildings, including a theatre and a stadium, both of which are visible today, although unexcavated. It was also walled, for when the Seleucid monarch Antiochus III took Sardis by assault in 215 BC, it is stated that his troops got across the city wall in the vicinity of the theatre. Although no remains of this wall have been identified, a plausible line for it would give the city an area of 130 hectares, of which about sixty would be on level ground.

Sardis was an important place in the Hellenistic scheme of things, acting as the Seleucids' administrative centre for Anatolia. It remained important under the Romans, who put it at the head of a *conventus* (judicial circuit) and eventually, when Lydia was revived as an administrative unit, made it the provincial capital. During the high noon of empire, in the second and early third centuries AD, the city expanded westwards and possibly eastwards too. The final area can be estimated from the city wall constructed at the beginning of the fifth century, which encloses 156 hectares (of which eighty to ninety hectares is on the level).

In construction terms, this city wall is unimpressive, thrown up without much care or forethought. It is difficult not to see this as a sign of civic decline, but Sardis, so far as we can tell, appears to have preserved its vitality better than most cities of the Asian diocese. The chief architectural glory of the lower town, the gymnasium complex completed in the third century AD, probably remained in use until the sixth century. Among its facilities was a synagogue of handsome proportions, and the repairs to this suggest that the Jewish community remained prosperous as long as the city lasted.

The end came suddenly, in 616, when a Persian army broke through the Roman defence line in the east of Anatolia and brought devastation to the west. Sardis' fortifications failed to save the city, which was sacked so thoroughly that no subsequent attempt was ever made to revive it. A military detachment reoccupied the citadel in 660, but the lower town remained deserted and all subsequent references to Sardis are to the castle on the hill, not to the town at its foot.

Population estimates can only be highly speculative, but given that settlement seems to have been patchy even within the area suitable for housing, something of the order of 5,000 plus seems reasonable for the city's heyday (150 BC–AD 250), and something under 5,000 for the late antique period (AD 250–616).

Since 1958, the site of Sardis has been the object of annual excavations by Harvard and Cornell universities. Only around 10 per cent of the principal area of interest has been investigated at the time of this writing, and there is clearly an immense amount more to do, but what has been done has been done well, including a magnificent restoration of the gymnasium. This shows just how grand Roman public architecture could be even in relatively out-of-the-way places.

SAVARIA

Present-day *Szombathely, Vas province, Hungary*

*Capital of the late Roman province of
Pannonia Prima; diocese: Illyricum*

The colony of Savaria was founded by Claudius (AD 41–54) for the discharged veterans of the legion XV Apollinaris stationed at CARNUNTUM 130 kilometres (eighty miles) to the north. Scanty traces of the street plan survive, suggesting, according to the favoured reconstruction, a rectangular grid covering 38.5 hectares, although no more than thirty hectares in other versions. The town is said to have suffered damage in the Marcomannic War of AD 171–5 and the Gothic incursions of

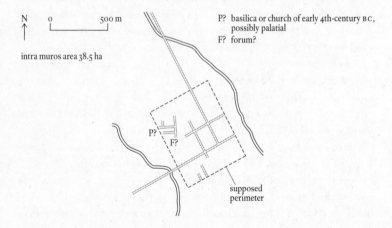

N   0   500 m

intra muros area 38.5 ha

P? basilica or church of early 4th-century BC,
    possibly palatial
F? forum?

P?
F?

supposed
perimeter

the 250s, but it survived well enough to be made the capital of Pannonia Prima when Diocletian divided the old province of Pannonia Superior into northern and southern halves – Pannonia Prima and Savia – in 297. New buildings – what is probably a palace of the Constantinian period, plus an inscription denoting the reconstruction of a granary by Constans' praetorian prefect *c.* 348 – celebrate this promotion and bring Savaria to a new high, although, as is typical of fourth-century embellishments, the prosperity was somewhat artificial, being dependent on the expenditure of central funds, and correspondingly precarious. Included in the package was a permanent garrison, the first we know of. It probably consisted of the Lanciarii Sabarienses, a unit that features in the late Roman army list known as the Notitia Dignitatum.

The financial crisis that followed the reign of Julian the Apostate (361–3) seems to have exposed Savaria's vulnerability. Ammianus Marcellinus, writing of the emperor Valentinian II's visit in 375, says that 'the town was weak, having suffered repeated misfortunes' (30.5.14–17) and gives a telling instance of the low ebb to which its affairs had come. Valentinian, who was on his way to Gaul, wanted to leave by the west gate, but found it so deeply buried in rubbish that he had to send a working party to open it up. Even then, he was thwarted: the portcullis had jammed and the best efforts of his soldiers failed to shift it. The emperor had to leave by another gate.

Savaria lingered on until the fall of the empire in the West, the *coup de grâce* apparently being delivered by an earthquake in 455. It can never have been a very big place, with a population of no more than 3,000 to 4,000 (not counting its garrison), even in its early fourth-century heyday.

SCYTHOPOLIS

Present-day *Beth Shean, north Israel*

The ancient city of Beth-Shean was founded on a natural hill at the intersection of two roads that crossed Israel from north to south and from east to west. It was apparently occupied as early as the Late Neolithic period. The name Beth-Shean ('House of the God Shan') seems to have been first recorded during the Egyptian New Kingdom (1570–1070 BC), when it was mentioned in topographic lists of the pharaohs Thutmose III, Seti I and Rameses II. During the period of Egyptian control, the city seems to have been an unfortified administrative centre in Canaan. There is evidence that the Egyptian dominance ended abruptly during the reign of Rameses IV, V or VI, perhaps because the Canaanites asserted their independence. In 732 BC, however, a layer of ash indicates that the city was destroyed by fire during the conquest by Assyria.

The next clear evidence of occupation comes almost half a millennium later, during the Hellenistic period, when Egypt's Ptolemaic dynasty refounded the city under the name Scythopolis. Pliny the Elder asserts that this name derives from the decision by Ptolemy II Philadelphus to settle a group of Scythians at the site, but that etymology remains debated.

The Greek historian Polybius records that in 198 BC the city surrendered to Seleucid control in the face of military successes achieved by Antiochus III the Great. The city later passed into Jewish control in 107 BC under John Hyrcanus I. Following the conquest of Judaea by Pompey the Great in 63 BC, the Romans rebuilt the city, which became a member of the Decapolis Greco-Roman federation. The Roman proconsul Gabinius (57–55 BC) undertook substantial renovations and apparently favoured renaming the city as Gabinia. Writing around five years after the First Jewish Revolt (AD 66–70), the chronicler Flavius Josephus (who participated in the war) reports that the Greek inhabitants of Scythopolis, after defeating the Jewish rebels in their area, shamefully put 13,000 of them to death. Scythopolis was later attached to the province of Syria Palaestina and thereafter to Palaestina Secunda, and seems to have enjoyed an afterglow of prosperity in the late Roman and Byzantine periods, when the city is likely to have had its largest population.

The city fell to Muslims following the Battle of Pella in AD 635. The city surrendered on terms, after which its name reverted to Beisan

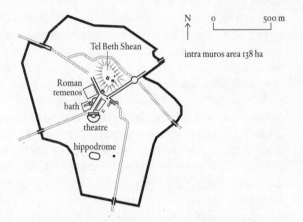

N   0   500 m

intra muros area 138 ha

(Arabic) and the urban infrastructure began a long and steady decline. An earthquake in 660 caused substantial destruction, and the city was essentially destroyed by another earthquake in 749.

Surviving ruins include a fourth-century amphitheatre seating around 5,000 spectators, which was converted from the second-century hippodrome. Visitors can also see sections of several grand colonnaded streets. Building inscriptions allow us to date a number of buildings to the reigns of Anastasius (AD 491–518) and Justin I (AD 518–27).

Around the beginning of the fifth century, the city was encircled by 4.8 kilometres (2.9 miles) of walls, enclosing an area of approximately 138 hectares. Based on this enclosed area, the city's peak population (in the early sixth century) has been estimated in a range of 30,000 to 40,000.

SELEUCIA ON
THE TIGRIS

28 km (18 miles) south of Baghdad, Iraq

Capital of the Seleucid Kingdom

Seleucia was built as a replacement for BABYLON. Where Alexander the Great (336–323 BC) had been content to let Babylon continue as the metropolitan centre for Mesopotamia (and points east), Seleucus, the Macedonian general who took over the eastern two-thirds of Alexander's empire, was determined that this core region should have a Greek-style capital. The position he chose for his new metropolis – which, in the fashion of the time, he named after himself – was some seventy kilometres (forty-five miles) to the north of Babylon, in the 'waist' of Mesopotamia, the region where the gap between the Euphrates and Tigris is at a minimum, and where the two were connected by the Nahrmalcha, or Royal Canal. There was already a settlement here called Opis – on the south side of the Nahrmalcha at its junction with the Tigris – which appears to have been a nodal point in Alexander's itinerary. It marked the point where the road leading north divided, the left-hand fork following the line of the Nahrmalcha and the Euphrates towards Syria and, ultimately, Europe, the right-hand fork staying with the Tigris and its branches and providing access to Media and Armenia. The site was a perfect match for Seleucus' ambitions.

The sources don't say exactly when construction of the town began; it could be as early as 312 BC, when Seleucus first emerged as a lead player in the carving up of Alexander's empire; it was certainly no later than 300 BC, the year after Seleucus defeated and killed Antigonus, his main rival, at the Battle of Ipsus. Work on it will have been essentially complete by 274 BC, the date when Antiochus I, Seleucus' son and heir, had the remaining inhabitants of Babylon forcibly removed to the new capital. From that time on, Seleucia on the Tigris (the extended title is necessary to distinguish it from the dozen or so Seleucias elsewhere in the empire) was counted as one of the major cities of the Hellenistic world. After the city was established, we know very little about its history over the next 400 years.

The pre-existing settlement of Opis bequeathed one monument to Seleucia, a ziggurat dating back to the eighth century BC; everything else was swept aside by the Greek king's surveyors, who laid out a grid of rectangular blocks covering the entire area south of the ziggurat – something of the order of 366 hectares. The exact shape of the city is unknown, but it was compared to an eagle with its wings spread.

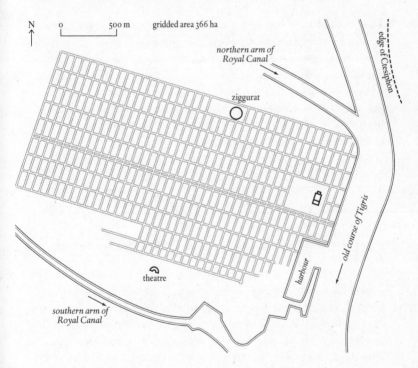

SENS

Yonne, France

Classical *Agedincum; county town of
the Senones and capital of the late Roman
province of Lugdunensis IV*

The Senones were one of the more important of the Celtic tribes of Gaul, with a particularly impressive past: a branch of the Senones spearheaded the Celtic invasion of Italy and, under the leadership of Brennus, put ROME itself to the sack in 390 BC. Three and a half centuries later when Caesar invaded Gaul, the boot was on the other foot. In 53 BC, the Senones resisted Caesar's selection of Cavarinus to be their ruler, leading to two years of hostilities. At the end, they were absorbed like other Gallic territories into the Roman provincial system.

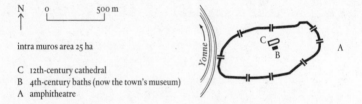

N   0   500 m

intra muros area 25 ha

C 12th-century cathedral
B 4th-century baths (now the town's museum)
A amphitheatre

Despite the prominence of the Senones, their county town, modern Sens, was not recognized as having any particular distinction until the closing decades of the empire. In the first three centuries AD it was merely one of two dozen county towns in the province of Lugdunensis; after the division of the provinces in 297, it occupied a similarly undistinguished position in the roster of Lugdunensis I. But when the emperor Valens subdivided Lugdunensis I in 375, it became the provincial capital of the northern half, Lugdunensis IV, alternatively known as Lugdunensis Senonia, or simply Senonia. Sens now stood above the other towns of the new province, including such ultimately far more famous places as PARIS and Orleans. This rank it retained until the collapse of the

Roman Imperium in Gaul that began in 406 with the invasion of the Suevi from across the Rhine.

Late Roman Sens had a fine town wall dating from the 260s, the period when Gaul first came under attack. It enclosed an area of twenty-five hectares, a considerable area in that era of declining prosperity. Unfortunately, the wall was pulled down in the 1840s and as it was the only significant structure surviving from the Roman period, there is now nothing of Roman date to see in the town apart from one surviving tower (out of twenty-three) and the reconstructed facade of a bath building just to the south of the twelfth-century cathedral. So we don't know if the town was originally bigger, as is often the case in Gaul, or if the late Roman circuit enclosed the entire built-up area. Either way, the population is unlikely ever to have been more than 2,000 to 3,000.

One curious survival is Sens' position in the ecclesiastical hierarchy. The clerical order of seniority held to the Roman model long after it had ceased to be relevant, with the archbishop of Sens still outranking his colleague in Paris until the 1620s, at which time Paris had a population of 200,000, compared to Sens' 5,000.

Presumably because the lack of remains is so discouraging, no one has attempted to publish a connected history of the Roman town.

SEPPHORIS

*Near modern village of
Moshav Zippori, north Israel*

Later *Diocaesarea; capital of
Roman province of Galilee*

In the latter half of the first century AD, the Jewish writer Flavius Josephus described the walled city of Sepphoris as the 'ornament of Galilee'. It was built in the late Hellenistic period in an area of low hills that was well supplied with abundant springs and fertile soil. It lies approximately 6.5 kilometres (four miles) north of Nazareth.

In the second century BC, Ptolemy IX of Egypt attempted unsuccessfully to take the city from Alexander I Jannaeus. In around 57 BC, after the region was conquered by Pompey the Great, the Roman proconsul Gabinius made Sepphoris the capital of the district of Galilee. It thereafter fell under the control of Herod the Great, who is recorded as having attacked the city during a snowstorm in 37 BC. After Herod's death in 4 BC, a local rebel (Judas, son of Ezekias) seized the local armoury and attempted to lead a revolt. Josephus reports that the Roman governor (Publius Quinctilius Varus) punished this disobedience by burning the city and selling its inhabitants into slavery. After this undoubted lowpoint, Herod Antipas refortified the city, which he renamed Autocratoris, and built a royal palace.

When Nero closed the Temple of Janus in ROME (*c.* AD 66) to celebrate peace across the Roman Empire, he rewarded the loyalty of Sepphoris by renaming it as Neronias Irenopolis. During the First Jewish Revolt that followed almost immediately thereafter, the city maintained its peaceful reputation by expelling its rebel commander, Josephus, and opening its gates to Roman troops.

A number of Jewish priests who fled JERUSALEM during the revolt made their new homes in Sepphoris, which later, during the reign of Caracalla (AD 211–17), became the seat of the Sanhedrin. The city seems, however, to have enjoyed reasonably favourable ratings among the

Romans for a considerable time thereafter. Hadrian adorned the city with a temple dedicated to Tyche, and no later than AD 130, he had also given it the new name Diocaesarea (the city of Zeus and of the emperor). It should not be confused with the sanctuary of the same name that Vespasian built at Olba in Rough Cilicia – known in modern times as Uzuncaburç.

In AD 351 a revolt against Constantius Gallus broke out in Sepphoris under Patricius, but it was put down by the Roman commander Ursicinus. The city was heavily damaged by an earthquake in AD 363, although it was rebuilt thereafter. It eventually became an episcopal see, and its bishops are recorded as having attended synods in Jerusalem early in the sixth century.

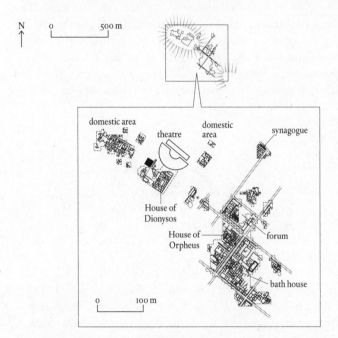

Sepphoris had a Roman-style theatre, built early in the first century AD, that held around 4,500 people. It had an aqueduct too, carrying water from two sources to a reservoir with a capacity of more than 4,300 cubic metres. The site has also yielded fine mosaics, including a large depiction of the Nile festival in Egypt. In the first century AD, Sepphoris and Tiberias appear to have been the two principal cities of Galilee.

339

SIDE

Present-day Selimiye,
Antalya province, south-west Turkey

Second city of the late Roman
province of Pamphylia

Side, a small town on the Pamphylian (south Turkish) coast, was said to have been founded by Greeks in the years immediately after the Trojan War – *c.* 1150 BC. If so, the Greek element was soon absorbed in the native population, for in the early classical period the Sideans had their own language and script (Sidetic), neither of which was comprehensible to the Greeks – or to us. The town first achieved a measure of prosperity

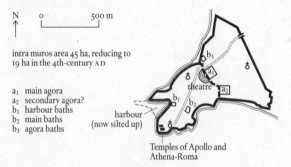

N   0   500 m

intra muros area 45 ha, reducing to
19 ha in the 4th-century AD

a₁ main agora
a₂ secondary agora?
b₁ harbour baths
b₂ main baths
b₃ agora baths

theatre

harbour
(now silted up)

Temples of Apollo and
Athena-Roma

in the late second and early first centuries BC when the pirates of Cilicia, then in their heyday, started using it as a slave market. Surprisingly, when the Romans moved in and put an end to the piracy, Side managed to avoid punishment. Nor did its somewhat raffish reputation prevent it from acquiring the ornaments of Greco-Roman respectability. Most notable among these is an outsize theatre capable of holding 13,000 spectators.

In the third century AD, Side and its neighbour PERGE both claimed the title of 'First City in Pamphylia'. Side's intramural area of forty-five hectares is much the same as Perge's 47.5 hectares and there probably wasn't much to choose between the two as regards population; a figure around the 5,000 mark would probably do for either. But in any event, it was Perge that won the contest when Diocletian made Pamphylia a province and chose Perge as its capital; Side had to wait until Justinian's day (527–65) before the elevation of its bishop to metropolitan status gave it an official mark of distinction. The remains of several large churches attest the wealth of Side's Christian community during this period, although the defended area had been reduced to only nineteen hectares by the building of a new land wall as early as AD 300.

In the seventh century, Side came under Arab attack and although the town survived, its population by this time can't have been more than a couple of thousand or so. Even this number would have been dwindling as life on the eastern perimeter of Christendom became increasingly precarious. Eventually the surviving remnant withdrew to Attaleia (present-day Antalya) seventy kilometres (43.5 miles) to the west, a process that seems to have been completed during the tenth century.

As late as the 1980s, Side was still an idyllic site, lapped by the sea and blessed with a perfect climate. It has, however, been increasingly over-run by tourism.

SILCHESTER

Hampshire, England

Classical *Calleva; county town of the
Atrebates of southern Britain*

Unusually for a Romano-British town, Silchester seems to have had a
significant pre-Roman history. The evidence for this is an inscription on
a coin issued by a chieftain of the Atrebates some time around AD 5–10,
in which he calls himself 'Eppillus rex Callev' (Epillus, king of Calleva).
Not that there is much to say about Calleva in its pre-Roman phase. All
that has been discovered so far is that a bank of earth was built around
the site and then almost immediately replaced by another one enclosing
three times the space (ninety-five hectares, compared to thirty-three).

The larger circuit proved far too ambitious. When the Romans took
over direct responsibility for the region (*c.* AD 80), after a forty-year
period in which the Atrebati continued under the rule of their native

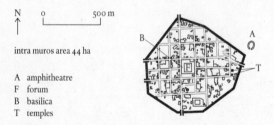

N   0   500 m

intra muros area 44 ha

A amphitheatre
F forum
B basilica
T temples

chiefs, they reduced Calleva's area to eighty-six hectares. When the
Romans eventually fortified the town (*c.* AD 165–95) the area enclosed
was only around forty-four hectares. Something of this order is what
one would expect for a Romano-British county town, and there is no
evidence to suggest that the built-up area of Silchester ever exceeded
this figure. Quite the opposite: the inhabitants of the town always had
plenty of room to spare.

This brings us to the reason for this entry. Silchester has no special historical interest: it simply served its local function for 350 years and then faded away. Nor does it offer the present-day visitor much in the way of sights: the wall still stands, but all that it encloses is a field or two, a farm and a tiny church. But the fact that it has lain open to the sky ever since it was abandoned in the early fifth century has given archaeologists a rare opportunity to excavate a Romano-British 'city' *in toto*. Thanks to the patronage of the local landowner and the energy displayed by the Society of Antiquaries, this opportunity was splendidly taken in the late nineteenth century; as a result we have a plan for Silchester that is essentially complete. It is our best bit of evidence on Romano-British urbanism.

Silchester had a street grid with a forum at its centre. It had a set of baths, an inn and, outside the east gate, an amphitheatre. This is all pretty standard stuff, neither more nor less than one would expect for a town in this class. What Silchester didn't have was many houses – 150 at the most and, for much of its history, probably no more than half this number. Moreover, most of the houses were small so it is unlikely there were more than four or five occupants per house – medieval figures suggest that even this will be a high average. So we are talking about a population of 750 people at a maximum, and very likely only half this number for much of the time. This is very different from the usually accepted picture of Romano-British towns as busy places with crowded streets and a generally urban air to them.

The truth is that Roman Silchester must have been a sleepy place with wide spaces between its buildings. The majority of the houses would have been little more than shacks, and the few public buildings little better than barns. Insofar as it was more than a village, it owes its extra status to Roman administrative formalism; it had no significant trade or industry or function of its own and as soon as the Romans left, it died.

SIRMIUM

Present-day *Sremska Mitrovica, Serbia*

Capital of the province of Pannonia Secunda;
residence of the prefect of Illyricum;
diocese: Illyricum

An oppidum of the Illyrian Amantini, Sirmium was occupied by the Romans during their conquest of Pannonia, probably by Tiberius in 13 BC. It was not, so far as we know, ever a military base but its Roman population must have grown rapidly because it was already sufficient to fend off the natives during the Pannonian revolt of AD 6–9. Subsequently Romanization was carried through to completion, an achievement that was recognized in AD 79 when Vespasian gave the town colonial status.

Sirmium's success must have owed a lot to local factors, in particular to its situation near the Save's junction with the Danube, but its position in the wider Roman world was the key to its real importance. In the later second century AD, the Roman Empire was forced on the defensive as Germanic tribes repeatedly challenged the Danube frontier. Sirmium emerged as a useful command and control centre for the central sector and as such was used by the emperor Marcus Aurelius during his Marcomannic war in 173. Fifty years later, the soldier emperor Maximinus Thrax (235–8) spent most of his brief reign in the town directing operations. It is at this time that we find Sirmium being referred to as 'the largest city in Pannonia' (Herodian VII.2.9). When the Danube line finally collapsed in the 260s, Sirmium was one of the few places that managed to hold out. We have no details of its travails apart from a brief mention of the fate of the emperor Probus, who was murdered by mutinous soldiery in the town's Iron Tower in 282, but when order was finally restored, Sirmium's strategic importance was given formal recognition. As part of the package of administrative reforms initiated by Diocletian in the last years of the third century, Sirmium became the residence of the prefect of Illyricum, one of the half-dozen most important officials in the empire, as well as being made the provincial capital of Pannonia Secunda (the southern half of what had previously been Pannonia Inferior). A few years later the town reached its peak. It served the emperor Licinius as his capital from 308 to 314, and when Constantine the Great chased him out, its metropolitan status was enhanced, not diminished. Constantine, who was in residence from 316 to 321, held the city in the highest esteem, and seems to have seriously considered making it the empire's senior capital. But this was not to be: Constantine moved on to the conquest of the Eastern provinces, and eventually created his New Rome on the shores of the Bosporus.

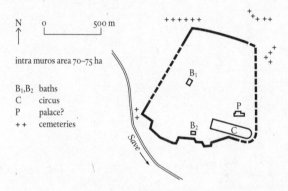

N
0   500 m

intra muros area 70–75 ha

B₁,B₂   baths
C   circus
P   palace?
+ +   cemeteries

Although its days as an imperial city were now over, emperors continued to stay at Sirmium when they were visiting the area. Constantius I was there in 351, and Valentinian I in 374. But Valentinian found the city in a sorry state, its walls crumbling and its moat full of garbage (Ammianus Marcellinus, 29.6.3). Prodded by Valentinian, the prefect cleaned out the moat and used materials collected for a proposed rebuilding of the theatre to patch up the walls. But the root problem, the crumbling of the local economy, was not so easily addressed. Eventually the attempt to hold on to the Pannonian provinces was abandoned, the whole area being ceded to the Huns in 441. After the collapse of the Hun Empire, the region passed to the Ostrogoths (454), the Gepids (474), back to the Ostrogoths (508) and then back to the Gepids (537). After the defeat of the Gepids by the Avars in 567, the East Roman emperor Justin II managed to sneak a garrison into Sirmium, in a move that annoyed the Avars more than somewhat. Eventually, in 582, the Avars took the town; whatever part of it was still inhabited went up in flames the next year.

Some preliminary excavations have uncovered the northern and southern sectors of the city wall, some baths and a circus, all dated to the early fourth century. It seems probable that the main feature of late Roman Sirmium was an imperial palace of the type developed under the Tetrarchy. The intramural area appears to be of the order of seventy-five hectares, suggesting a peak population of about 7,000. Something around the 5,000 mark is a plausible figure for the earlier period (100–250).

SISCIA

Present-day *Sisak, Croatia*

*Capital of the late Roman
province of Savia*

Roman Siscia, like the modern town of Sisak that overlies it, was situated on the left bank of the River Kupa, a few kilometres above its junction with the Save. A pre-Roman settlement called Segestica lay on the opposite bank, but is not mentioned after the Roman conquest of the region in 35 BC. It had a history of resisting Roman interventions in the area, so it is likely that Octavian, the future Augustus, who was masterminding the advance to the Danube that began at this time, destroyed Segestica, replacing it with a new construction, perhaps a legionary camp, where Sisak now stands.

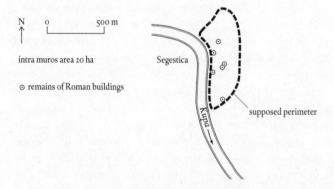

After Augustus and Tiberius had completed their military programme, the army units involved were gradually moved up to the Danube line. They left behind a population of discharged veterans, of which Siscia would have received its fair share – only this can explain the town's recognition as a Roman colony by the emperor Vespasian at the very

347

early date of AD 71. Among the towns of Pannonia – admittedly not a very impressive lot – Siscia had been singled out for special favour.

Further promotion came in the troubled times of the later third century. When the Danube frontier collapsed under barbarian attack, Siscia became an important backup for the new defence line on the Drave. In 262 the embattled emperor Gallienus established a mint in the town to ensure that the defending troops got paid; when the emperor Diocletian restored order in the region, he made Siscia the capital of Savia. This new province had been created by the division of Pannonia Superior into Pannonia Prima (the northern half) and Savia (the south). In terms of status, if nothing else, the early fourth century was to be Siscia's high point.

The town's decline began with a sack by the usurper Magnentius in 351. Thereafter it mirrored the fading fortunes of the Western Empire. In the late fifth century it passed under Ostrogothic control; in the sixth it was part of the Lombard domain, before finally succumbing to the Slav inundation of the seventh century.

Sisak's town wall was mapped in the eighteenth century before being demolished in the nineteenth. Such remains of the Roman town as have been discovered lie within this circuit, which enclosed about twenty hectares, and all the cemeteries lie without, so it is a fair assumption that the same wall served the town throughout its history. On the other hand the deduction is not completely reliable, as witness SOPIANAE, and there is a distinct possibility that there is a smaller Roman circuit inside the eighteenth-century perimeter. Planned excavations are needed to decide the matter, but planned excavations are exactly what Siscia has never had; all of the finds so far are accidental, and as a result next to nothing is known about the Roman town.

The archaeologists Remza Koščević and Rajka Makjanić think the population of Siscia was at a minimum 20,000 to 30,000, and maybe 'much higher'. A figure somewhere around the 2,000 mark seems easier to accept.

SKOPJE

Macedonia

Classical *Scupi, capital of the late*
Roman province of Dardania

Skopje is the key to the Vardar–Morava route connecting Macedonia
with the Danubian lands. As such, its occupation (probably around
13 BC) was the necessary prelude to the Roman conquest of Moesia, a
province that stretched along the right bank of the Danube from its mid-
section to its mouth. The native settlement that the Romans found at
the site of Skopje took the form of a Thracian 'oppidum' on a hill overlooking the Vardar. The Roman town was built at the foot of the hill,
probably utilizing the camp of the legion that spearheaded the advance
into Moesia (tentatively identified as IV Scythica). A legionary camp

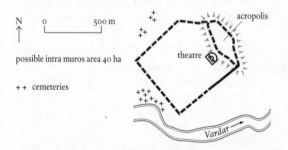

N   0   500 m

possible intra muros area 40 ha

++ cemeteries

acropolis

theatre

Vardar

was normally not much over twenty hectares, but Skopje town was considerably larger than this, probably twice the size. This was because it
took in both camp and hilltop oppidum, the latter presumably as a sort
of acropolis.

Skopje's strategic position ensured that it retained its importance
over time. It was the first town in Moesia to be given the status of a
Roman colony (by Domitian *c.* AD 86), and when the province of Moesia
Superior was divided in two, *c.* AD 300, it became the capital of the

southern half, the province of Dardania (the Dardanians being the local Thracians). It probably became a garrison town again at this time, for there was a regiment of 'Scupenses' in the Roman army list of the late fourth century.

The fifth century saw the end of Roman Skopje in its original form. Under the pressure of the Gothic and Hunnic invasions the population melted away. When Justinian decided to resurrect Roman administration in the region, he ignored the abandoned town and built a new Skopje on the hill now known as Markovi Kuli, some way off and on the opposite bank of the Vardar. This late Roman version of Skopje has walls that enclose an area of only six or seven hectares, making it more of a citadel than a town. A few years later this fortification, and all other traces of Roman rule, were swept away by the Slav migrations that began in the late sixth century AD. Ultimately Skopje did revive in the form of another, even smaller, castle well to the east of the Roman town. This Slav fortress, going by the name of Kale and covering a mere 2.3 hectares, dates to the tenth century. It became the focal point of the modern city.

The archaeological investigation of Roman Skopje has barely begun. All that has been discovered so far is the line of the south-east wall and the site of the town's theatre, which dates to the time of Hadrian (AD 117–38).

Given its size, it seems unlikely that the civilian population of Roman Skopje ever numbered more than a couple of thousand.

SMYRNA

Present-day *Izmir, Aegean Turkey*

History

The eleventh century BC saw the beginning of a trans-Aegean migration that brought Greeks of various sorts from peninsular Greece to the western coast of Anatolia. The Gulf of Smyrna was supposedly settled by Aeolians (Greeks from the sector north of ATHENS), but early on they seem to have been joined by groups of Ionians (Athenians and their immediate neighbours), which led to some confusion of loyalties. The settlement prospered, and by the seventh century BC there was a small town, now known as Old Smyrna, on the north side of the gulf, acting as the focus for a farming community that had spread around the coast to the south side and a short distance – a few kilometres only – into the interior. This was the situation when Alyattes, king of the inland state of Lydia, decided to establish control over the coastal communities that fringed his kingdom. When the Smyrniotes demurred, Alyattes reacted with vigour, storming Old Smyrna, expelling its inhabitants and razing it. The Smyrniotes became a purely rural community, paying taxes to the Lydian king, and subsequently to the power that succeeded him in Anatolia, the empire of the Medes and Persians.

This depressing state of affairs was brought to an end by Alexander the Great in 334 BC, when, as a first step in his invasion of the Persian Empire, he liberated the Anatolian littoral. The Smyrniotes were now able to think in terms of reconstituting themselves as a proper polis, with an urban centre where the business of the community could be conducted with dignity. The site they picked was on the south side of the gulf, some eight kilometres (five miles) distant from the ruins of Old Smyrna. According to later legend it was Alexander himself who decided on this position. One of his hunting expeditions took him to the slopes of Mount Pagus where our hero, exhausted by the chase, decided to take a short nap. While he slept he dreamt that two young ladies – later identified as water nymphs from a shrine nearby – had appeared before him and commanded him to build the Smyrniotes' new city on this very spot. And so Mount Pagus became the acropolis of New Smyrna.

Be that as it may, nothing practical seems to have been done until the Macedonian general Lysimachus took over the area thirty-three years later. He found the resources necessary for the project and by 288 BC, when Smyrna was enrolled as the thirteenth member of the Ionian League, the work must have been far enough along for the city to have become a reality.

Lysimachus clearly hoped that Smyrna would be an important place, and its subsequent history fulfilled his expectations. By the Roman period it was accounted the third city in the province of Asia (the western third of Anatolia), after PERGAMUM, the titular metropolis, and EPHESUS, the de facto capital. By the Smyrniotes' own account, they were really number one; they had no hesitation in proclaiming their city 'First in Asia for beauty and size' and even, more debatably, as 'Metropolis of Asia'. This self-advertisement came a bit closer to the truth with the rapid decline of Pergamum, but Ephesus continued to outrank Smyrna to the end of antiquity. The best the Smyrniotes could do was get the ecclesiastical authorities to confer independent status on their bishop so that he did not have to answer to the archbishop of Ephesus.

The history of Smyrna in late antiquity is an almost complete blank. Its fortifications were apparently maintained in good order: surviving inscriptions commemorate restorations of the east gate by Arcadius in the fifth century AD and by Heraclius in the seventh. So far as we know, no enemies ever gained entry even in the empire's darkest days, and the city appears to have survived the secular decline of the Mediterranean economy much better than most places of which we know. Certainly it was still a significant place in 1076 when, in the aftermath of the imperial catastrophe at Manzikert, it was seized by a Turkish adventurer named Chaka. He made it the centre of a pirate state that included Chios and Lesbos, before being evicted by a Byzantine army in the counter-offensive that followed the First Crusade. The city was a prize worth fighting for, as it was now the only port of significance on the Aegean coast of Anatolia, and this at a time when trade was picking up again. The main trading partners were the Genoese, and when the Byzantine state began to go under in the early fourteenth century, it was the Genoese who took control of the city, hoping to protect it from the encircling Turkish tribes. They didn't succeed: the city fell in 1329 and although a Holy League of Crusaders, put together by the Pope, got half of it back again in 1344, this partial success was the best the expiring Crusader movement could manage. For the next sixty years the town was divided, with the Crusaders holding the harbour and the Turks the citadel, an odd situation that finally came to an end in 1402 when the Great Emir, Timur the Lame, stormed the harbour defences and erased this, the last Christian enclave on the Aegean littoral. As usual, Timur did such a thorough job that nothing much was left of the city, and even a century later Smyrna – Izmir to the Turks – had no more than 1,500 inhabitants. The harbour basin in use since antiquity silted up during this period. Today, it is built over and lies underneath the present-day bazaar. Smyrna's later recovery began at the close of the sixteenth century, and the runaway growth that established Izmir as one of Turkey's major cities began in the seventeenth century.

Topography

Smyrna has a splendid site, and a visitor standing on Mount Pagus in Roman times would have been favoured with a fine urban prospect: a stadium and theatre at the foot of the hill, long straight streets running down to the curve of the gulf and, on an eminence at the southern end of the shoreline, a massive temple of Zeus. In the centre of town and on the same orientation as the street plan there was a spacious agora, while somewhere as yet unlocated was a precinct dedicated to the memory of Homer, reflecting Smyrna's claim to be the poet's birthplace. Ancient authorities allowed that this was one of the better claims of this sort.

Classical and medieval Smyrna are now hidden beneath the vast sprawl of modern Izmir, and there are few remains of either to be seen. Most impressive is the agora, which, in its existing form, dates from a Roman rebuilding of the second century AD but is nonetheless fine for that. The theatre and the stadium were both visible in the nineteenth century; now they have vanished beneath houses constructed from their stones. As for the existing castle on Mount Pagus, this contains, despite reports to the contrary, no Greek work at all: it is a purely medieval structure. This is a disappointingly short list for what was clearly one of the most important cities in the ancient Aegean.

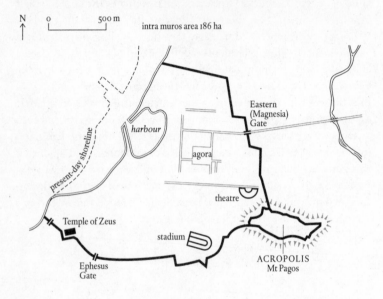

Population

Its size and rank suggest that in its heyday, the second century AD, Smyrna's population was of the order of 20,000. As indicated above, it showed more resistance than most places to the hard times of late antiquity, and probably kept above the 10,000 level until the seventh or eighth century. It is likely that this reflects its durability as a port, although medieval Smyrna was clearly only a minor one.

SOPIANAE

Present-day *Pécs, Baranya, Hungary*

Capital of the late Roman province of Valeria;
diocese: Illyricum

Sopianae seems to have started life as a small Celtic settlement. Annexed along with the rest of Pannonia by Augustus, its Romanization only began with the consolidation of the Danube frontier by the Flavian emperors Vespasian, Titus and Domitian (AD 69–96). It was probably first recognized as a municipium by Hadrian (117–38).

Sopianae was damaged in the Marcomannic War of the late second century, and again in the troubles of the mid third century. Yet the town not only survived, it emerged with its status enhanced, for Diocletian,

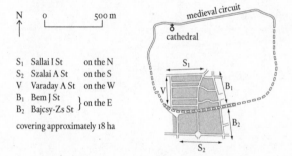

N   0   500 m

S₁ Sallai I St   on the N
S₂ Szalai A St   on the S
V   Varaday A St on the W
B₁ Bem J St   } on the E
B₂ Bajcsy-Zs St

covering approximately 18 ha

c. 295, chose it as the capital of his new province of Valeria. Named for his daughter, Valeria corresponded to the northern half of the old province of Pannonia Inferior. The original administrative centre for this region, the town of AQUINCUM on the Danube, was considered too exposed to continue in this function; Sopianae, set well back from the frontier, seemed a safer bet. In the event it didn't fare much better than Aquincum, lasting only to the later fourth century, when the whole area of Pannonia north of the Drave drifted out of Roman control.

Archaeology has not as yet added much detail to this story. It is safe to assume that the town was walled, but so far no trace of the Roman circuit has been found. It clearly is not coincident with the medieval circuit, for this included the cathedral, a structure built over part of the northern necropolis of the Roman town. Using such finds as have been made, the leading authority on Roman Pécs has suggested that its limits are defined by the modern streets named on the plan. These enclose an area of about eighteen hectares.

STRASBOURG

Alsace, France

Classical *Argentoratum*

The modern city of Strasbourg was once a Roman outpost on an island in the River Ill (previously known as Helella), around three kilometres (two miles) west of the Rhine. The initial settlement may have been founded by Nero Drusus (d. 9 BC), the stepson of Augustus and father of the emperor Claudius. It was named Argentoratum ('Silver Fort'). By AD 12, the legion II Augusta had built a timber-and-earth fort and occupied it until the legion left for Britain in AD 43. The fort covered an area

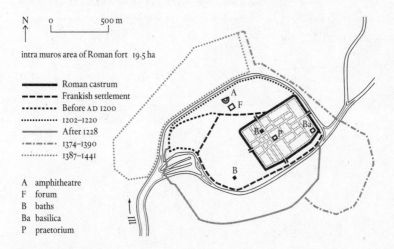

N   0   500 m

intra muros area of Roman fort 19.5 ha

▬▬▬ Roman castrum
– – – Frankish settlement
•••••• Before AD 1200
•••••• 1202–1220
▬▬▬ After 1228
▬·▬·▬ 1374–1390
•••••• 1387–1441

A amphitheatre
F forum
B baths
Ba basilica
P praetorium

of around 19.5 hectares, in which few remains have been found. Argentoratum was part of the military command that later became the Roman province of Germania Superior. The fort was destroyed during the Gallo-German rebellion of AD 69–70, but it was reoccupied by a

357

detachment of the legion XIV from MAINZ. By the end of the 80s, legion VIII had supplemented the earthwork fort with a wall of limestone blocks built on basalt foundations. During the more peaceful years that followed, Argentoratum grew substantially until it covered an area of around 240 hectares.

Ammianus Marcellinus records that in 357, Constantius II sent Julian (later emperor) to defeat a rebellious confederacy of Alemanni. After that success, the Romans built a 3.5-metre-thick rampart in front of the old wall, greatly reinforcing the city's defences. After the Vandals crossed the Rhine in the winter of 406–7, however, soil strata reveal the traces of multiple burnings associated with their attacks. In the later fifth century AD, the city was finally taken over by Franks, who gave it its modern name (meaning something like 'Stronghold on the Road(s)').

Today, the north–south route of Grande Île marks the Roman *cardo,* and the Rue des Hallebardes marks the east–west alignment of the *decumanus.* Excavations have confirmed that the city had an aqueduct bringing water from a spring twenty kilometres (twelve miles) away, and in 1995 archaeologists discovered a mausoleum sixty metres in diameter that is estimated to have stood twenty metres high, indicating the burial place of a very important person who is not yet identified.

SYRACUSE

Sicily, Italy

Greek *Syrakousai* and Roman *Siracusa;*
capital city of the Roman province of Sicily

Just off the south-east coast of Sicily, the island of Ortygia has been
occupied since Palaeolithic times. The island was colonized in around
733 BC by Corinthians, and the colony grew to include the adjacent Sicilian mainland. Harbours were developed on both sides of the artificial
causeway connecting the two parts of the city.

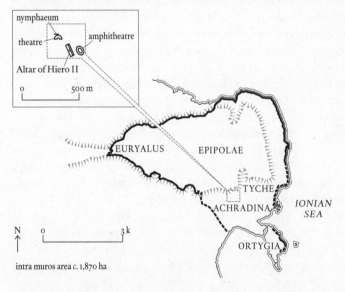

After relocating or enslaving the nearby native Sicels, the Corinthian colony grew to the point where it founded its own colonies and
came into conflict with Carthaginian cities on Sicily, the island that had
been founded by Phoenicians. In 480 BC, the tyrant Gelon defeated a

Carthaginian force at Himera, establishing Syracuse as a great Mediterranean power. Six years later, Gelon's brother Hiero I defeated an Etruscan fleet in a battle off CUMAE, further consolidating the city's power.

During the Peloponnesian War (431–404 BC), Syracuse overcame a massive invasion by the Athenians, a victory celebrated by issuing the famous series of silver decadrachms with Arethusa on the obverse and a four-horse chariot on the reverse. The city extended its influence across more of Sicily under the tyrant Dionysius I (406–367 BC), and its fortifications expanded to an overall length of around twenty-five kilometres (seventeen miles). During its cultural height, Syracuse attracted such distinguished visitors as Pindar and Plato.

Syracusan independence came to an end after the city supported Hannibal in the Second Punic War. In 213–211 BC, the Romans sacked the city after a difficult siege that was reportedly prolonged by the defenders' use of ingenious weapons devised by Archimedes. This ALEXANDRIA-trained mathematician and engineer had mastered the principles of leverage and devised a grapnel that could hoist the prows of besieging ships until their crews fell out into the sea. He was even said to have used mirrors and/or lenses to focus sunlight and burn enemy ships, although this tale seems to have been highly magnified. As capital of the Roman province of Sicily, Syracuse suffered from the rapacious conduct of the governor Gaius Verres (73–71 BC), who was ultimately disgraced after a public prosecution led by Cicero. Even in that time, however, Cicero affirmed that Syracuse remained 'the largest of all Greek cities, and the most beautiful of all cities'. Under Augustus, in 21 BC, the city became a Roman colony. St Paul stopped there for three days while en route to ROME, and the city enjoyed prosperity even after it was attacked by Franks in around AD 280.

The tyrant Gelon reportedly constructed the first stone theatre, where the playwright Aeschylus was invited to open the premier season in 476 BC with a production of *Women of Aetna*. By the time of Hiero (d. 467 or 466 BC), Syracuse could boast a theatre holding around 24,000 spectators. A Roman amphitheatre was added in the first century AD. The city's importance during early Christian times is reflected in extensive catacombs. After the Roman period, however, the city's size and importance declined substantially, although the emperor Constans II chose to live there for several years until his assassination in 668.

TANGIER

Classical *Tingis; capital of the province of
Mauretania Tingitana; diocese: Spain*

History

Established by the sixth century BC at the latest, Tangier was a Phoenician colony with an important strategic function: it guarded the southern side of the Strait of Gibraltar against interlopers. From the late sixth century to the end of the third century BC, it served the Carthaginian cause in this role. Then, when the Carthaginian Empire was dismantled at the end of the Second Punic War (201 BC), it became an independent community allied to ROME, in other words a Roman dependency. During the first century BC, it issued coins with Punic inscriptions.

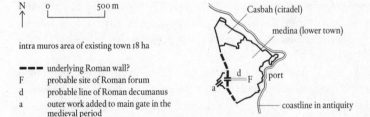

N   0   500 m

intra muros area of existing town 18 ha

▬ ▬ ▬ underlying Roman wall?
F   probable site of Roman forum
d   probable line of Roman decumanus
a   outer work added to main gate in the
     medieval period

Casbah (citadel)
medina (lower town)
port
coastline in antiquity

Augustus confirmed Tingis' status as an independent town standing outside the kingdom of Mauretania, the Moorish state that had developed in its hinterland. He also gave it the rank of a Roman municipium. The reign of Claudius saw the town receive an even more important honour. In the early 40s AD, Claudius decided to annexe the kingdom of Mauretania, split it into two provinces and make Tingis the administrative centre of the western half. This consequently became known as Mauretania Tingitana, in contrast to the eastern half, Mauretania

Caesariensis, named for the original Mauretanian capital of Caesarea. Unfortunately this promotion is the last we hear of classical Tangier until the closing years of the empire, when it fell to the Vandals in 429. The intervening four centuries are an almost complete blank.

After its capture by the Vandals, Tangier's strategic function was usurped by Ceuta, forty-five kilometres (twenty-eight miles) to its east, at the Mediterranean end of the Strait of Gibraltar. When Belisarius recovered North Africa for the Roman state in 534, Ceuta was the only place in Mauretania Tingitania that he bothered to occupy. Tingis seems to have lost all importance, and doubtless nearly all its population too.

Topography and Population

Classical Tingis is buried beneath modern Tangier, and there is nothing to be seen of it today. If, as seems likely, the existing walls follow the Roman circuit, it would have had an intramural area of about twenty hectares. It is also possible that the existing division between the citadel (the Alcazaba, or Casbah) and lower town (medina) reflects an ancient division between the Punic and Roman quarters; certainly the Roman forum was in the lower town, with the main east–west street running straight between forum and main gate. The forum area has provided some inscriptions from Diocletian's day (AD 284–305).

The intramural area suggests a peak population for classical Tangier of 3,000 or so.

Ceuta, situated on a spindly peninsula, was even smaller than Tingis and covered nine hectares at most. In classical times it was known as Septem, a shortened form of Septem Fratres, after the Seven Brothers (meaning hills) that formed the spine of the peninsula.

TARANTO

Apulia, Italy

Greek *Taras,* Roman *Tarentum; capital of the late
Roman province of Apulia et Calabria*

Taranto was one of a cluster of Greek colonies established in the late eighth century BC on the instep of the Italian peninsula. The traditional foundation date is 706 BC, and the original settlement was supposedly a mix of locals (Messapians, also known as Iapygians), Cretan traders and Spartan colonists. Socially and politically, if not numerically, the Spartan element was the dominant one, and it was to Sparta that the Tarentines turned when they ran into trouble with the peoples of the interior.

Initially there were no problems of this sort. Taranto, occupying only the tip of its peninsular site, was simply too small to have ambitions that would put it in conflict with the main Messapian tribes. But in the fifth century BC, when the Greek world experienced a new surge of energy, the Tarentines raised their game. They challenged the Messapians in their hinterland, and they made a bid for the leadership of the Greek cities in south Italy by founding a colony named Heraclea. This was supposed to serve as a meeting place for representatives from all of them, with Taranto taking the chair. Nothing much came of these initiatives: the Messapian war ended in defeat, and the Greek cities, whatever their wishes in the matter might have been, were to become dependants of SYRACUSE, not Taranto. What the period did bring was a massive increase in the size of Taranto town. A new wall was built across the base of the Tarentine peninsula, increasing the intramural area from a paltry sixteen hectares to something of the order of 560–70 hectares. Of course, not all of this was built up; four fifths of it remained open ground, with the roads that passed through it lined with tombs, not houses. But if we assume that around 110 hectares was inhabited (including the 'old town'), that would be comfortably enough to make Taranto the largest community in the heel of Italy, a status that it was to retain for the remainder of antiquity.

The contrast between Taranto's growth as a town and its failure to establish itself as a political force became increasingly obvious in the fourth century BC. To keep the Messapians at bay, the Tarentines decided to call on their progenitor Sparta for aid, but militarily Sparta was fading even faster than Taranto, and three separate interventions by Spartan mercenaries (in 338, 334 and 303) failed to produce any permanent improvement in Taranto's position. Worse still, by the early third century BC, the Tarentines were facing a new and much more serious threat in the shape of the rapidly expanding power of ROME. If they were to preserve their freedom, what the Tarentines needed was a state-of-the-art Hellenistic army of the sort that Alexander of Macedon had used to overthrow the Persian Empire. They found their answer in Epirus, a Macedonian satellite whose young king, Pyrrhus, saw himself as a second Alexander and was eager for a western adventure. In 280 BC, Pyrrhus landed in Italy with enough soldiers to defeat the Romans, first at Heraclea, then, the next year, at Ascoli in Apulia. But there was little profit for Pyrrhus in these successes – won at such cost that the term 'pyrrhic victories' came to be applied to battles that were as damaging to the victor as the vanquished – and he decided to divert to the more promising field of Sicily. In 275 he was back in Italy again for one more battle, claimed as a draw by the Romans; then he left on another adventure, this time in Macedonia. While he lived he kept a garrison in Taranto, but by 272 his short life was over. The Epirote soldiers went home, leaving the Tarentines no choice but to bend the knee to Rome.

The Tarentines were to get one more chance to re-establish their ancient freedoms. In 218 BC, the Carthaginian general Hannibal arrived in Italy; two years later, at Cannae in Apulia, he turned on the Roman army pursuing him and totally annihilated it. For four years the Tarentines dithered over whether to stand by their 'alliance' with Rome, or go over to the Carthaginians, now masters of much of southern Italy. Finally they decided to take their chance with Hannibal. One of the city's gates was betrayed to him, but he didn't move fast enough to prevent the Roman garrison withdrawing to the old town, which had retained its fortifications. The result was a stand-off between the Carthaginian-Tarentine force in the new town and the Romans holding what was now referred

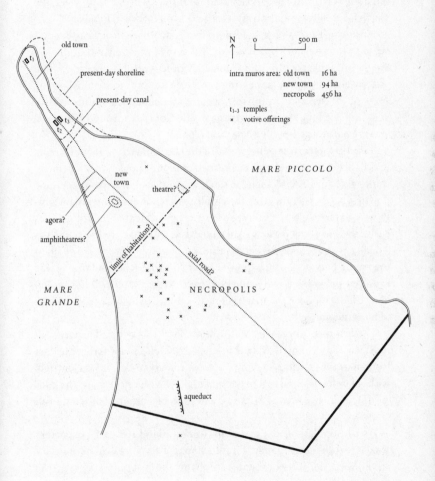

N   0   500 m

intra muros area: old town   16 ha
                  new town   94 ha
                  necropolis 456 ha

t_{1-3} temples
× votive offerings

old town

present-day shoreline

present-day canal

t_1

t_3
t_2

MARE PICCOLO

new
town

theatre?

agora?

amphitheatres?

limit of habitation?

axial road?

*MARE
GRANDE*

NECROPOLIS

aqueduct

to as the citadel. After three years of this, some of the Tarentines, conscious of the slow but steady weakening of Hannibal's position, played the same trick on him as they had on the Romans. A Roman army entered the city by night, linked up with the force holding the citadel and slaughtered the Carthaginian garrison, the Tarentines who had supported the Carthaginian cause and anyone else whose looks they didn't like.

After these excitements, Taranto finally accepted its role as Rome's strong point in south-eastern Italy. A southward extension of the Via Appia brought it within the Roman road network by 244 BC (a final stretch of the Via Appia then ran east from Taranto to Brindisi on the Adriatic coast), and it probably acquired an enhanced administrative standing with the Augustan reorganization of Italy (around 7 BC) and was the natural centre for his second region.

Taranto was certainly the capital of the late Roman province of Apulia et Calabria, the second region's successor in the Diocletianic scheme of things (AD 297). But by then the town was suffering from the economic downturn that was affecting the empire as a whole, and the urban component in particular. In Taranto's case it is possible that the rot set in as early as AD 109, when a new road from BENEVENTO to Brindisi, the Via Traiana, was opened; this cut Taranto out of a loop that carried much of the traffic between Rome and the East. Not that Roman Taranto was ever that prosperous: even allowing for the fact that it still lies buried beneath the modern town, it has produced surprisingly little in the way of monuments.

The last mention of classical Taranto dates to AD 547. The city wall must have deteriorated by then, because Procopius records that the East Roman general sent to occupy the town remarked that it was 'entirely without defences' and had to content himself with refortifying the citadel (*De bello Gothico*, VII.23.12). The tale of Taranto had come full circle.

As to population, the classical Greeks' liking for vast perimeters makes it difficult to gauge Taranto's size. The conspicuous military weakness of the Tarentine state is probably the best pointer; it suggests that the population never topped 20,000, which makes something under 10,000 a probable maximum for Taranto town. On the other hand, it seems unlikely that the town had fewer than 5,000 to 6,000 inhabitants in its best years, say between 350 BC and AD 150.

TARRAGONA

Tarragona province, Spain

Classical *Tarraco; capital of the Roman*
province of Tarraconensis

At the start of the Second Punic War (218 BC) the Romans made Tarragona the base for their operations in the Iberian peninsula. Fortifications on the high ground to the north-east of the native settlement belong to this period; this 'upper town' became the administrative centre for Near Spain some time after the two provinces of Near and Far Spain were set up at the end of the war. Its status as a provincial capital was confirmed in 26 BC when Augustus divided Spain into three; the sector centred on Tarraco subsequently became known as Tarraconensis.

Augustus, who resided in Tarraco in 26–25 BC, gave the city a new plan, centred on the previously undeveloped zone between upper (Roman) and old (native) towns. This 'lower town' was given an orthogonal street grid (we think) and certainly a forum and theatre; it soon became the main focus in the urban life of Tarraco, leaving the upper city free for a grandiose rebuilding programme that, under the Flavian emperors (AD 69–96), turned this area into a purely ceremonial centre. Presumably this was intended to provide a dignified background for meetings of the provincial assembly. The second century AD saw the construction of an amphitheatre to the south of the upper town, near the seafront.

In AD 260, a crisis year for the empire, a band of Franks who had been pillaging their way through Gaul reached across the Pyrenees and put Tarraco to the sack. The damage seems to have been limited: Tarraco remained the provincial capital, and there are notices of continuing building work under the Tetrarchy (a 'Porticus Ioviae') and the Constantinians (restorations of the circus and baths). But Tarraco's area of responsibility had been reduced (by Maximian, who split Tarraconensis

into three in 297) and its prosperity was now on the ebb. By the fifth
century the signs of decline are obvious: the lower town had been abandoned, and in the upper town – all that remained of classical Tarragona
– a huddle of poor houses occupied the remains of the grandiose structures erected under the Flavians. Its metropolitan status was increasingly usurped by Barcelona, a small place, but one whose star was rising
as Tarragona's fell.

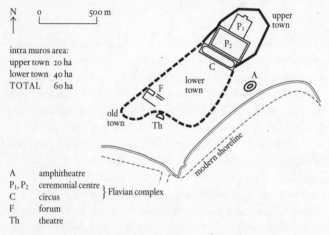

N
0   500 m

intra muros area:
upper town 20 ha
lower town 40 ha
TOTAL   60 ha

A   amphitheatre
P₁, P₂ ceremonial centre ⎫
C   circus   ⎬ Flavian complex
F   forum   ⎭
Th   theatre

In Visigothic hands since 476, Tarragona was finally destroyed by
Arab raiders in 713–14. It was refounded after the Christian recovery of
the area in the twelfth century, and most of the Roman town lies beneath
the modern city. The most visible remains are those of the amphitheatre
and some stretches of the walls of the upper town. There are as yet no
traces of the walls of the lower town, which means that the proposed
intramural area for Tarragona of about sixty hectares (upper town a bit
under twenty hectares, lower town a bit over forty) is only a hypothesis.

It is unlikely that Roman Tarragona ever had a population greater
than the 4,000 recorded for the town in the sixteenth and seventeenth
centuries.

THESSALONIKI

North-east Greece

*Capital of the late Roman prefecture of Illyricum; abbreviated
to Salonika during the Turkish period and up to 1927,
when the original name was officially reinstated*

History

During its glory years the state of Macedon, homeland of Alexander the
Great, was entirely rural, with nothing much in the way of towns and
nothing at all in the way of a capital city. The country's rise from bit
player to top dog had been incredibly rapid, in essence the work of a single king, Philip II, in a not-so-very-long reign of twenty-three years
(359–336 BC). Constant campaigning meant that, even if building a
worthy *Hauptstadt* had been on his must-do list, Philip never had the
time to actually do it. And as his son Alexander left Greece as soon as he
had secured the crown, this situation remained unchanged during his
reign too. The end result was that, after two generations of hegemony
over Greece, the nearest thing Macedon had to a political centre was
whichever country palace the ruler happened to favour – the choice
being between Aigai and Pella.

Not long after Alexander's death his empire broke up, and the governors of the different provinces declared themselves kings. Macedon
became the share of Alexander's brother-in-law, Cassander. In 316 he
decided to celebrate his rule by founding two new towns. One of them
was a refurbishment of Potidaea, a place with a considerable history
that had been destroyed during one of Philip's wars. This was to be
called Cassandreia. The other was a brand-new creation formed by
merging the populations of twenty-six villages on and around the Ther-
maic Gulf. This he named after his wife Thessalonike. Presumably he
thought Cassandreia had the better prospects, but if so he was to be
(posthumously) disappointed. It was Thessaloniki that became the
metropolis that Macedon had hitherto lacked.

The process took a very long time. It was only in the Roman period that Thessaloniki emerged as a place of importance, and the first person to refer to it as the metropolis of Macedonia is the geographer Strabo, at the end of the first century BC. The next step up came another 300 years later, when it became the capital of the diocese of the Moesias, a newly created group of provinces that embraced about a third of the Balkans. A few years later the emperor Galerius made it his official residence (from 305 to his death in 311). None of his successors agreed with his choice, so this particular bit of glory didn't last, but the enhanced provincial status was confirmed when the prefect of Illyricum, the top man as regards Balkan defence, exchanged his post on the Danube for a safer life in Thessaloniki in 441. So long as the empire had a Danube frontier, Thessaloniki would retain responsibility for its central sector.

For a while it looked as if the frontier had been lost to the Huns (which was why the prefect had retreated to Thessaloniki in the first place), but after the death of their king Attila in 453, they withdrew to the Russian steppe and imperial troops were able to reoccupy the line of forts along the river. The next bout of trouble was more serious and lasted far longer. In 586, Slav tribes broke through the defences of the central sector and reached the gates of Thessaloniki itself. Moreover, these were not raiders but migrants. By 615 the entire area between the town and the Danube had been lost to the newcomers, and Thessaloniki had become a Greek-speaking island in a Slav sea. The only way of communicating with CONSTANTINOPLE was by boat.

Recovery was very slow. A land link with Constantinople was reestablished in 783, but it took a further fifty years to make it safe. It was only in the tenth century that things really began to look up. The century hadn't started well – a raid by an Arab fleet in 904 did a great deal of damage – but as the century progressed the town began to share in the general recovery experienced by the Byzantine state at this time. In 1018, when the Danube frontier was restored (for the last time), Thessaloniki seemed to have regained all the advantages it had enjoyed in the late Roman era.

The final phase of the empire's history began with the Battle of Manzikert, a crushing Turkish victory in 1071 that immediately put the Anatolian half of the empire in jeopardy. The subsequent intervention of the Latin West, in the form of the Crusades, brought turbulent times for the

European provinces too. Thessaloniki was sacked by the Normans in 1185 and actually became the capital of a Crusader mini-kingdom in 1204. This was replaced by a Byzantine equivalent, the empire of Thessaloniki, in 1224, before the final reincorporation of the town into the Byzantine Empire in 1246. In the interim the Danube provinces had been taken by the Bulgars, starting in 1186. All this sounds like bad news, as indeed some of it was, but there was an upside. In the wake of the first Crusaders came the Venetians and Genoese, eager for trade and offering new markets. So long as Thessaloniki had a hinterland, it could enjoy the benefits brought by the increase in Aegean traffic. The record of its buildings suggests that it did, that the thirteenth and early fourteenth centuries were Christian Thessaloniki's Indian summer, and that it was only with the loss of the hinterland, first to the Bulgars, then to the Turks, that decline set in. The city fell to the Turks in 1387, briefly returned to Byzantine rule in the aftermath of the Battle of Ankara in 1402, before its definitive incorporation in the Ottoman Empire in 1430. It remained under Turkish rule until 1912.

Topography

As is the case with many Greek coastal settlements, Thessaloniki consisted of a lower town where the people lived, and an acropolis some way inland, which acted as a citadel of last resort. Thessaloniki's lower town was laid out as a rectangular grid of streets and avenues, half a dozen or more avenues parallel with the shore, and more than two dozen cross-streets (a surviving inscription gives an address on 18th Street). Remarkably, much of the grid is still visible in the present-day street plan, a testimony to 2,300 years of continuous habitation. The land walls too, even if much rebuilt, seem to have kept close to the original trace, although at two points there is clear evidence that they had moved out a bit: the early Roman version of the Golden Gate ended up well inside the final version (it was left as a free-standing arch), and, on the opposite side of town, the walls take a jog around the north end of Galerius' palace. Most of the northern half of the circuit survives: the walls and towers of this part are basically late Roman work, although there are some towers with Palaeologan (late Byzantine) inscriptions in and around the acropolis, and other elements are obviously Turkish. The line of the sea wall is unknown, and the reconstruction of this and the harbour works attributed to Constantine the Great is purely hypothetical. Trial excavations in this area could be very rewarding.

N
0   500 m   intra muros area 230 ha

Heptapyrgion
Letaia Gate
6
Arch of Ciad
10
acropolis
Golden Gate
9
8
1
7
forum
4
11
harbour
2
Gate of Archangels
mausoleum
(later Church
of St George)
3
5
Palace of
Galerius
arch
Cassandreia Gate
Octagon
hippodrome

† 1 St Demetrios
  2 Acheiropoietos
  3 St Sophia

† 4 Pauagia Khalkeon
  5 St Panteleimon
  6 St Catherine
  7 Church of the Archangels
  8 Vlattadou Monastery
  9 Prophet Elias
 10 SS Apostoli
 11 St Nicholas the Orphan

The two main building complexes surviving from the Roman period are the forum, of which a corner is visible in the centre of town, and the Palace of Galerius in the south. The palace was preceded by a monumental arch commemorating Galerius' victories over the Persians; north of it was a circular building presumably intended as his mausoleum. Half the arch survives, as does the mausoleum, which by the fifth century had become the Church of St George – ironical considering that Galerius was a determined opponent of Christianity. Other parts of the palace survive as foundations, as does the outline of the hippo-drome, a must-have add-on for an imperial palace of this period.

Aside from these public monuments of the imperial era, Thessalo-niki is known for its many churches. The three most remarkable are the Acheiropoietos of the mid fifth century, St Demetrios, a seventh-century replacement of a fifth-century original, and St Sophia, built some time between the late sixth and the early eighth centuries. After a long gap, church building resumed in the late Byzantine period; half a dozen churches, most of them rather small, represent the final flourish of Christian Thessaloniki. All these churches, early Christian and Palaeologan alike, ended up as mosques following the Turkish conquest of 1430.

Population

The first firm evidence we have for the size of Thessaloniki's population is an Ottoman census of households from 1478. This shows that the town was still more Christian than Muslim at the time – 1,275 Christian households and 826 Muslim. By 1519 the two communities were equal in size (1,387, compared to 1,374), and both were overshadowed by a Jewish community of 3,143 households. Although the Jewish community was swollen by refugees expelled from Spain in 1492, it must already have been in existence in 1478 (indeed, Benjamin of Tudela says the town had 500 Jews in the twelfth century), so the early account needs upward adjustment. If we assume something of the order of 1,000 Jewish house-holds in 1478, the total population for this date will be 1,275 + 826 + 1,000 = 3,101 × 4 = 12,404, say 12,000, compared to 1,387 + 1,374 + 3,143 = 5,904 × 4 = 23,616, say 24,000 in 1519. Interpolating gives us a total population of 18,000 for 1500, and back-projecting suggests that the population is more likely to have been under than over 10,000 in 1450. This fits with the fact that the number of captives taken by the Ottoman sultan Murad II when the town surrendered to him in 1430 was only 7,000.

On this basis it seems reasonable to take 10,000 to 15,000 as the range of Thessaloniki's population in its prosperous phases. There seem to have been two of these: the first beginning with the town's brief promi-nence as a tetrarchical capital in AD 305 and ending with the loss of its hinterland to the Slavs in the early seventh century; the second beginning with the late tenth-century recovery of the Byzantine Empire and lasting until the empire's collapse in the early fifteenth century. To be conservative, we can credit Thessaloniki with a population of 10,000 in the period AD 350–600 and again in AD 1000–1400. If you are an optimist you could raise some or all of these figures to 15,000. The final figure of 18,000 is the only one that is entirely secure.

TOMIS

Present-day *Constanţa, Romania*

Roman *Constantia; provincial capital of Moesia Inferior
and subsequently of Scythia*

Tomis, on the Black Sea coast a bit to the south of the Danube delta, was
founded by Greeks from Miletus at the beginning of the sixth century BC. Like many Greek colonies of the time, it was situated on a small
promontory, and the area covered by the original settlement was tiny, a
matter of a few hectares. It had grown to something like twenty hectares
by the time it passed under Roman control in the first century BC, but
that still left it a small place, situated in inhospitable country at the edge
of the classical world. That is doubtlessly why Augustus chose it as a

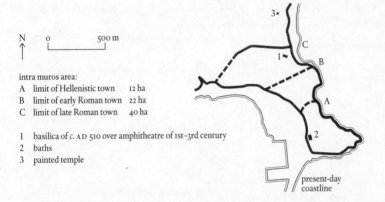

N   0   500 m

intra muros area:
A   limit of Hellenistic town   12 ha
B   limit of early Roman town   22 ha
C   limit of late Roman town   40 ha

1   basilica of *c.* AD 510 over amphitheatre of 1st–3rd century
2   baths
3   painted temple

present-day
coastline

suitable place of exile for the poet Ovid, who had offended him in some
now-forgotten way. Ovid passed the last eight years of his life there
(AD 9–17), bewailing his fate in numerous, self-pitying verses. Tomis'
Greek inhabitants, he had to admit, were kindly enough, but the climate
was loathsome and he was constantly alarmed by the uncouth Getes

and Sarmatians who raided the city's territory and shot arrows over its walls. And it must have seemed a dismal place to one with fond memories of the fleshpots of ROME.

Tomis prospered under Roman rule. When the province of Moesia was split into two in AD 82, it was made the capital of Moesia Inferior. It was also placed at the head of the Pontic Federation, an association of Greek cities on the west side of the Black Sea, some of them beyond the Roman frontier. A new wall ascribed to the late second century took the intramural area up to about forty hectares.

Decline set in during the early fourth century when the town's area of responsibility was restricted to the terminal stretch of the Danube, the province of Scythia in the new order of things. Not long after, it was renamed Constantia after Constantine the Great, who presumably conferred some marks of favour on the city. It survived the Gothic and Hunnic invasions only to be swept away by the Slav outpouring of the late sixth and early seventh century. No more than a village when it was taken over by the nascent Romanian state in 1878, it is now the country's largest port with a population of 350,000. This makes the investigation of the classical town very difficult, and the archaeologists' ideas on the way the city developed, although doubtless correct in outline, lack the detail needed to bring its history to life.

TOURS

Indre-et-Loire, France

Classical *Caesarodunum Turinorum*

Roman Tours was built, apparently on a greenfield site, as a county town for the local Celtic tribe, the Turini. Work probably started in the reign of Augustus (27 BC–AD 14), with the planners laying out a street plan of the usual gridded type on the south bank of the Loire, and the authorities cajoling the better-off Turini into building themselves houses there. The grid probably covered around forty-five hectares and the built-up area forty hectares by the second century AD when the town acquired its sole surviving monument, a massive amphitheatre. This was situated at the eastern end of town and, truth to tell, all we know of the town is that it occupied the area between the amphitheatre in the east and a cemetery in the west; all the rest – the grid, its extent, and the extent of the built-up area – are suppositions with almost no archaeology to back them up.

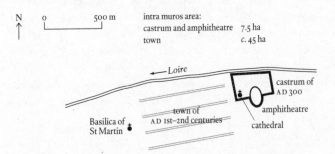

N
0   500 m

intra muros area:
castrum and amphitheatre   7.5 ha
town   *c.* 45 ha

← Loire

castrum of AD 300

amphitheatre

cathedral

town of AD 1st–2nd centuries

Basilica of St Martin

Such prosperity as Roman Tours had enjoyed in the first century began to ebb away in the second, well in advance of the third-century invasions that were to bring more drastic sorts of trouble. With the fourth century came two important consolations: Tours was made the administrative centre of one of the new small-sized provinces, Lugdunensis III, and in consequence of this promotion it became the seat of an archbishop. When the governor arrived, he probably found the town in ruins; more certainly he found what was left indefensible, for there is no evidence that early Roman Tours had ever been walled. His solution was to fortify the amphitheatre and a small area around it and concentrate what was left of the population in this castrum. The enclosed area was tiny, amounting to no more than 7.5 hectares. The archbishop built his cathedral – the predecessor of the current Cathedral St-Gatien – in the south-west quarter of the castrum, and there is no sign of urban life continuing outside of it. Late Roman Tours was not really a town in any meaningful sense of the word.

It was against this unpromising background that Tours acquired its first measure of fame. This came in the form of St Martin, archbishop of Tours in the last days of the empire, a great enemy of pagans and the founder of many churches and monasteries. When he died in AD 397 he was buried in the old western cemetery, which subsequently became a hallowed spot. By 470, St Martin's reputation as a miracle worker – even in death – was attracting so many pilgrims that the church authorities built a basilica over his tomb. As the Roman Empire crumbled away, other buildings were added, including an abbey, and eventually, in 918, after the Normans had burned down the original basilica, the complex was given its own defensive wall. Medieval Tours consisted of two physically distinct mini-towns: the settlement around the basilica of St Martin ('Châteauneuf'), and the old Roman castrum a kilometre (0.6 miles) to the east. Of the two it was Châteauneuf that was to prove the more dynamic.

Roman Tours is unlikely to have held more than a couple of thousand people at best; in its final form it was too small for more than a few hundred.

TRIER

Rhineland-Palatinate, Germany

Classical Augusta Treverorum; county town of the Treveri and capital of the late Roman province of Belgica Prima; seat of the prefect of the Gauls

Trier was built in the reign of Augustus (27 BC–AD 14) as a part of his programme to provide each Gallic tribe with a county town, a focal point for its administration and Romanization. As the Treveri were one of the most important tribes of Belgic Gaul, Trier was always going to be a considerable place, but just as important as its civil role was its location on the Mosel river, the main highway between central Gaul and the Rhine frontier. This gave it a strategic function that reinforced, indeed in some ways transcended, its position in the civil hierarchy and meant that when things turned nasty and most of the Gallo-Roman towns began to dwindle (as they did in the mid third century), Trier defied the trend and got bigger and grander. During the fourth century, under the new dispensation created by Diocletian, it became the imperial capital of the prefecture of the Gauls, a status it held till the start of the final collapse.

Little is known about the Augustan town. It seems to have had the usual playing-card shape and rectangular street plan and to have covered an area of about forty-five hectares, although as there was no defining town wall at this stage – at least none has been found – one can't be too certain about its extent. In fact only one monument has survived from the Augustan period, part of a memorial to Gaius and Lucius Caesar, the emperor's prematurely deceased stepsons. Also remaining, although not usually visible, are the piles for the wooden bridge across the Mosel immediately to the west of the town, which are sometimes credited to Claudius (AD 41–54) rather than Augustus.

Over the next 200 years, Roman Trier acquired the usual weighty apparatus of Roman urbanism: a forum, an amphitheatre, a set of public baths (today known as the Barbarathermen, from a nearby church dedicated to St Barbara) and a new bridge with stone piers a few yards upstream from the original purely wooden structure. The town was clearly prospering, with extensions (following the original street plan) bringing the built-up area to some ninety hectares, double the Augustan

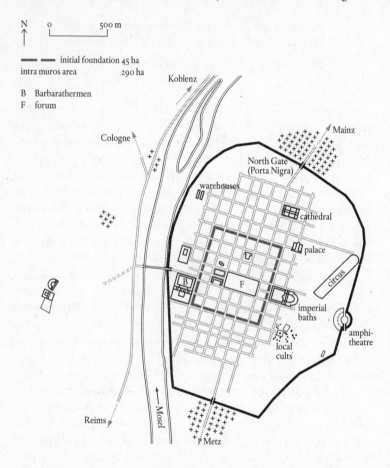

figure. This phase culminated in the construction of a town wall that has two remarkable features: it encloses a huge area of no less than 290 hectares, and it has a north gate, the famous Porta Nigra, of staggering size. At least some of the job of fortification was done by XXII Primigenia, the legion in garrison at MAINZ, for an inscription found there suggests that as a result of the legion's intervention, Trier was able to withstand a siege in the reign of Septimius Severus (AD 193–211). The context of this can only be the civil war between Severus and Clodius Albinus, governor of Britain and unsuccessful contender for the imperial throne. The simplest hypothesis is that the legion constructed the town wall to meet the emergency of Albinus' invasion of Gaul in AD 196 and the unnecessarily colossal north gate was built in a long period of peace that followed Albinus' defeat.

The peaceful years came to an end in the mid third century, which saw trouble on all the empire's frontiers and frequent defeats for the Roman army. From the subsequent chaos, Gaul emerged as an independent empire, with Britain and Spain as dependencies. Three successive Gallic emperors chose Trier as their capital, initiating a new era in the history of the town. After this Gallic empire was reabsorbed by Rome, the administrative grouping of Britain, Gaul and Spain became the prefecture of the Gauls, and Trier continued to function as a capital, this time as the residence of one of the four emperors (two Augusti, two Caesars) who jointly ruled the revived Roman state. As such, it became the seat of the Constantinian dynasty – first Constantine's father, Constantius, then Constantine himself. Constantine the Great was a compulsive builder, and during his reign Trier acquired some impressive new monuments: an imperial palace with a circus attached, a huge new set of public baths (never finished) and a cathedral. Another addition was a pair of large warehouses by the Mosel, doubtless built to ensure the food supply of what must have been a considerably enlarged population.

Constantine left his prefect behind in Trier when he set out on his campaign to reunite the empire, so the town continued to play a quasi-imperial role until the last years of the fourth century, when Stilicho, the generalissimo of the western armies, began stripping the Rhine frontier of its troops and transferring them to Italy. Trier was too close to the front line to be defensible under these circumstances, and the prefect of the Gauls took himself (and his mint) off to Arles. Deprived of the benefits conferred by the presence of the prefectural bureaucracy, Trier went into a rapid decline. There weren't enough men to man the vast circuit of the walls, and the city was taken and sacked by the first wave of invading Germans, the Vandals and Suevi, when they crossed the

Rhine in 406. Sacked again *c*. 440, this time by the Franks, it passed permanently under Frankish rule *c*. 475.

It is not difficult to find very high figures for Trier's population in its imperial heyday; 80,000 is the one most often quoted. Insofar as it is based on anything, it seems to derive from the idea that 250 per hectare is a reasonable density and Trier's wall enclosed 290 hectares, so 250 × 290 = 72,500 (plus a few more for good measure). A more reasonable essay along these lines would be 250 × 90 (the inhabited area) = 22,500, and even that can be criticized on the grounds that 250 per hectare is a very high density – something nearer 100 would fit better with what we know of Roman towns. That would give Trier only 9,000 inhabitants – not a lot by Mediterranean standards, but enough to put it at the top end of the Gallo-Roman hierarchy.

TRIPOLI

Arabic *Tarabalus, capital of Libya*

Classical *Oea; second city of Roman Tripolitania,
chief town of the region in the Byzantine
and Arab periods*

Tripoli takes its name from Tripolitania, the section of the North African coast that in classical times was shared between the three cities of Sabratha, Oea and LEPTIS MAGNA. For most of this period Leptis was the most important of the three, but in the twilight years of the Roman Empire both Leptis and Sabratha were abandoned, and Oea, as the sole surviving urban centre, became synonymous with the province. Hence the metamorphosis into Tripoli, the name by which it has been known ever since.

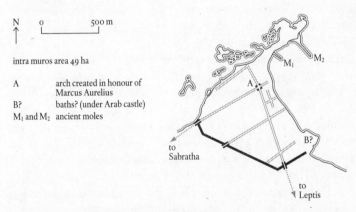

N   0   500 m

intra muros area 49 ha

A   arch created in honour of
            Marcus Aurelius
B?   baths? (under Arab castle)
M₁ and M₂   ancient moles

to
Sabratha

to
Leptis

The fact that Tripoli has been continuously inhabited since antiquity means that archaeology is of little help to us in tracing the city's early history. It is a safe bet that it started life as a Phoenician trading post, probably in the late seventh century BC, that being the date of the earliest traces of settlement at Leptis, for it is more likely that Tripoli, with a much better harbour, was founded at the same time as Leptis, rather than 200 years later as indicated by the earliest *in situ* archaeology. It would also have shared its subsequent political history with Leptis: part of the Carthaginian Empire (to 146 BC), then of the Numidian kingdom (to 46 BC), then of ROME. The emperor Augustus incorporated the two of them, along with Sabratha, in Africa Proconsularis, the province ruled from the newly refounded city of CARTHAGE.

We know of one episode in Tripoli's history in the early imperial period: a war with its neighbour Leptis in AD 69–70. At first the war went Tripoli's way, largely because it had obtained the help of the local nomads, the Garamantes. Then Rome intervened on Leptis' side, and Tripoli was put firmly back in second place in the regional hierarchy. The surviving monuments indicate just how marked the difference between the two became: all Tripoli has to show is a modest four-way arch built in honour of Marcus Aurelius in 163–4 (contrast the many splendours of Leptis). Of course it could be argued that Tripoli's Roman heritage has simply been erased during its sixteen centuries of post-Roman history, although it seems unlikely that buildings on the scale of Hadrian's baths and Severus' basilica at Leptis could have vanished without trace. What is incontrovertible is that the early fourth-century AD intramural area at Leptis is two and a half times that of Tripoli (130 hectares, compared to 49).

In the declining years of the Western Empire, Tripolitania was ceded to the Vandals (455). In the next century it was recovered by the Eastern emperor Justinian (532), but the province, now shorn of its hinterland, was only a shadow of its former self. Of the three towns Tripoli had fared much the best, and as Leptis subsequently faded out completely it assumed the role of chef-lieu for the remainder of the Roman/Byzantine period. The new era that started with the Arab invasions of 643 and 645 confirmed Tripoli's status as capital of the region.

Even at its best the population of Roman Tripoli is more likely to have been under than over 5,000. Medieval and early modern estimates are 6,000 for the fourteenth century and 12,000 for the eighteenth.

TURIN

Italian *Torino, Piedmont, Italy*

Classical *Augusta Taurinorum;*
county town of the Taurini

In 218 BC, when Hannibal launched his invasion of Italy, one of the first places he captured when he debouched from the Alps was Taurasia. This sounds as if it was the tribal centre of the Taurini, a Ligurian people of the upper Po valley, who would have certainly been in Hannibal's path. Subsequently, as the Romans ground their way to victory, the Taurini would have passed under Roman control, although so far as we know, this was not exerted directly before 25 BC, when Augustus decided to shed the full light of Roman civilization on this hitherto backward part of Italy. The core event as far as the Taurini were concerned was the provision of an over-large urban centre named, unsurprisingly, Augusta Taurinorum. It was probably founded around 28 BC, a little before AOSTA, another step in the same programme.

The general run of towns in the Po valley had areas of twenty to twenty-five hectares; the more important (PIACENZA, BOLOGNA, VERONA and PADUA) were laid out at a bit less than double this figure (forty to forty-three hectares). This gives the scale of urbanism in the republican period. Augustus upped the ante: Augusta Taurinorum has a grid that covers fifty-one hectares. The town consists of 8 × 9 = 72 square blocks, with the *cardo* (the main north–south street) offset in the manner seen in military camps. The north-east corner of the town is cut off, so the actual total is 71.5; the reason for this deviation from the otherwise strict plan is unknown. Two of the gates survive, and the northern Porta Palatina is in particularly good condition. The only other public monument found so far is the theatre, two blocks to the east of the Porta Palatina. The intramural area implies a population of the order of 5,000, and at its best, in the first two centuries AD, the actual number may have come close to this figure.

As the seat of one of the more important Lombard dukes, Turin maintained its identity during the Dark Ages better than most. Nonetheless, these centuries saw the town reduced to a huddle of housing that had scant regard for the original rectangular street plan, and suggests that the population was well below its Roman peak. It remained at this low ebb for most of the Middle Ages, to blossom in the early modern period when, as the capital of Piedmont, it shared in the rise of the House of Savoy.

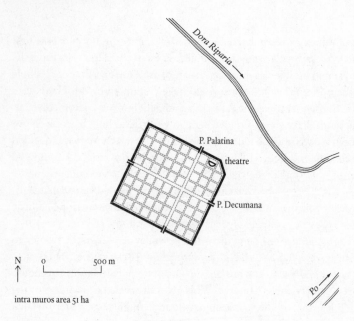

VERONA

Veneto, Italy

*City in the tenth region of Italy, subsequently the
late Roman province of Venetia et Histria*

Little is known about early Verona, except that the Romans found a
native settlement on the site when they moved into the area north of
the Po. There is argument about which natives are meant – the Raeti
to the north, the Gauls (specifically the Cenomani of Brescia) to the
west, the Veneti to the east, or maybe the Euganei, a local Italic tribe.
There is also no certainty as to the first settlement's exact position,
although the consensus favours the San Pietro hilltop on the left bank
of the Adige, opposite the loop of the river that encloses the heart of
Roman (and modern) Verona. The move from the hilltop to the flat area
within the loop is thought to have taken place in the late republican
period, i.e. sometime in the first century BC. This marks the starting
point of Verona's history as a classical town.

Roman Verona was laid out in square blocks of which thirty-two survive in the street plan as it exists today. The implication is that the original city was a square with seven blocks on each side, covering an area of
forty-one hectares. This reconstruction puts several blocks in the current bed of the Adige, but, as regards the eastern corner this isn't a problem: we know that the Adige, until relatively recently, made a wider
swing around the city on this side, the old bed being marked by the
'Internato dell'Aqua Morte' of the present-day street plan. We have no
such evidence for the west side, but the shift required is small and seems
easier to believe in than an incomplete Roman rectangle. There were at
least three gates: preliminary versions of the present-day Porta Borsari
and Porta Leoni, and a gate on the north indicated by a track – fossilized
in the current street plan – leading from the foot of the Ponte Pietra.

Verona occupies a position of considerable strategic importance and
was the site of many battles – between the armies of Vespasian and

Vitellius (69), of Philip and Trajan Decius (249), of Constantine and Maxentius (312) and of Stilicho and Alaric (403). In the imperial crisis of the mid third century AD, it became the command and control centre for the emperor Gallienus' defence of north Italy. A lasting memento of

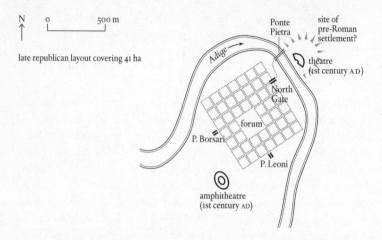

this phase in the town's history is the inscription of AD 265 on the Porta Borsari celebrating the completion of Gallienus' new wall for the city. As the plan on p. 389 shows, this wall took in the amphitheatre, giving a new intramural figure of forty-seven hectares.

Procopius' account of the Gothic War – the reconquest of Italy by the armies of the East Roman emperor Justinian in the mid sixth century – includes an interesting episode involving Verona in 542. A traitor let the Romans into the town by night, and the Gothic garrison was forced to beat a rapid retreat to the San Pietro hill across the river. From this vantage point the Goths could see into the town, where it soon became apparent that it contained only a few Roman soldiers. They could also see that no guard had been posted at the nearest gate. Coming down from the hill they soon swept the Roman force out of the town, which they were to hold on to for the next twenty years. In the end the Romans won, but they had little time to enjoy their victory, Verona falling to the Lombards in 569, the first year of their invasion of Italy. King Alboin made it his capital, and although his successors preferred PAVIA, Verona became the seat of one of the most important Lombard dukes.

Verona obviously had a better Dark Ages than most Italian towns, and may not have lost any population at all. The eleventh century saw the town sharing in the rapid expansion that was a feature of the time, and numbers soon began to build. By 1300, population was approaching

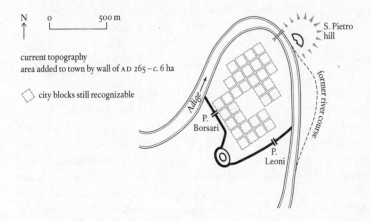

30,000 within a new wall (built 1287–1325) enclosing 365 hectares. At the same density of eighty per hectare, Roman Verona would have had a population of about 5,000, but at its best it may well have done better than this: a peak figure in the area of 6,000 to 7,000 would be fully acceptable.

VIMINACIUM

East of Kostolac, Serbia

*Provincial capital of undivided Moesia,
subsequently of Moesia Superior and, in the
late Roman period, Moesia Prima*

Viminacium is situated near the point where the Morava river (classical
Margus) joins the Danube. This made it the linchpin of the L-shaped
province of Moesia, which was charged with the defence of the right
bank of the Danube between Belgrade and the Black Sea, together with
the line of communication back to Macedon via the Morava–Vardar
corridor. The position must have been held from the start of the Roman
occupation of the area in 15 BC; the permanent camp was built in the 60s
and 70s AD by Legio VII Claudia. The legion was to have Viminacium as
its base for the better part of the next 400 years, a long posting by any
standards.

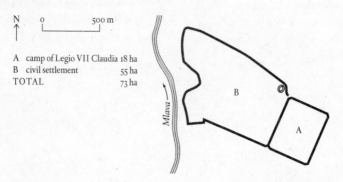

N   0   500 m

A   camp of Legio VII Claudia 18 ha
B   civil settlement   55 ha
TOTAL   73 ha

The legionary fortress, of the usual playing-card shape, covers eighteen hectares, a little smaller than some. Attached to its west side is a
civilian/veteran settlement covering fifty-five hectares, much larger
than usual for such appendages. This settlement was recognized as an
independent town (municipium) by the emperor Hadrian in 117, and as

a Roman colony by Gordian III (238–44). Always the most important place in Moesia, it was the capital of the initial, undivided province, then, when the province was split in two, of Moesia Superior. When Diocletian divided the area into five it became the capital of Moesia Prima, and of the diocese of Dacia, a new collection of provinces of Diocletian's invention.

Viminacium was destroyed by the Huns in 441 and never reoccupied. In the mid sixth century the name was revived for a fortress that the emperor Justinian built on the far side of the Mlava, a loop of the Danube that skirts the western edge of the original town. This fortress, which covered a mere six hectares, acted as the civil, military and ecclesiastical centre for the recovered province until all was swept away in the Slav invasions of the early seventh century. The modern town of Kostolac, whose name is sometimes used as a synonym for Viminacium, lies even further to the west; its name is a Bulgarization of *castellum* ('castle'), and refers to Justinian's fort, not the classical town.

The only certain datum we have regarding Viminacium's population is the size of the garrison, which was in the order of 5,000 in AD 60–250 and 1,200 in AD 350–400. The population of the attached town would presumably have been comparable, which means that, at its best, the complex would have passed the magic 10,000 mark. Of course, that doesn't mean that it qualifies as a permanent city of that size, because half the number would have consisted of soldiers, but it does mean that it ranks among the empire's most prosperous garrison towns.

VIRUNUM

Zollfeld, Carinthia, Austria

*Capital of the Roman province of Noricum, and,
after its division, of its southern half, the Roman
province of Noricum Mediterraneum;
diocese: Illyricum*

Noricum – the equivalent, roughly speaking, of modern Austria – was a Celtic kingdom of some dignity when it was annexed by Augustus in 15 BC. It had a history going back for 100 years or more, and a sort of capital in the oppidum of Noreia, twenty kilometres (12.4 miles) to the north of the present-day city of Klagenfurt. Like all Celtic oppida, Noreia was large – being spread over some three square kilometres (1.8 square miles) – but unfocused, and the scattering of buildings it contained didn't add up to anything that Romans would have called a city. It was also inconvenient, being perched on top of the Magdalensberg. The situation was remedied by the emperor Claudius, who, sometime around AD 48, decided the time had come to give Noricum a proper capital. He chose a greenfield site some ten kilometres away in the Glan valley, had a street grid laid out and began building. The new town was called Virunum; it was to serve as the administrative centre for both the province and the local tribe, the Norici.

Virunum had the public buildings usual for a Roman town – a forum and adjacent capitolium (a public temple honouring higher deities), a set of baths, a theatre, and an oddly shaped amphitheatre that may have doubled as a racetrack. On the east side of town was a palatial villa, which some have seen as the residence of the procurator (governor) of Noricum. The town was never walled, which makes it difficult to judge how big it was. The street grid covered a large area, maybe as much as 100 hectares, but Roman surveyors often laid out more grid than was needed, and probably did so here. The evidence currently available suggests that the settled area was in the forty- to fifty-hectare range.

Virunum had a long and, so far as we can tell, generally uneventful history. Surprisingly, in view of its lack of defences, it emerged unscathed from the Marcomannic Wars (AD 169–75), which did great damage to many other communities in the Upper Danube area. It was not so lucky during the more serious incursions of the later third century, when the fact that the baths were burned down suggests at least one unhappy experience. This was probably of less importance to the standing of the town than the administrative demotion that occurred at the end of the third century when Diocletian recast the provincial structure of the empire. As was the case with many other provinces, Noricum was split in two, into Noricum Ripense (the northern half, bordering the Danube) and Noricum Mediterraneum ('Inland

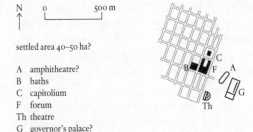

N   0   500 m

settled area 40–50 ha?

A   amphitheatre?
B   baths
C   capitolium
F   forum
Th theatre
G   governor's palace?

Noricum'). Virunum retained its capital role in Noricum Mediterraneum, but Noricum Ripense was given a capital of its own in the shape of the Roman colony of OVILAVA.

The convulsions of the first half of the fifth century finished off Virunum. What was left of its bureaucracy retreated to the hill fort of Teurina, seventy kilometres (43.5 miles) to the west, which, under the title of Metropolis Norici, maintained a semblance of authority over the region during the pitiful last decades of the Western Empire.

The historian Géza Alföldy dismisses claims that Virunum's population was 'at most 50,000', suggesting instead 'at most 5–10,000'. This would apply only to the town's best years, which were probably limited to the second and first half of the third centuries AD.

XANTEN

North Rhine-Westphalia, Germany

Classical *Colonia Ulpia Traiana*

In the Gallo-German revolt of AD 69–70, the rebels conquered and destroyed a Roman camp (Vetera I) that had been founded near the west bank of the lower Rhine by Augustus. The military camp was later reconstructed at a site closer to the Rhine (Vetera II), opposite its confluence with the River Lippe. This second legionary fort remained occupied until at least around AD 260 as part of the province of Germania Inferior.

Near the fort, Tiberius had resettled the German tribe of Sugambri from their former home on the opposite (east) bank of the Rhine. Under the emperor Trajan (Marcus Ulpius Traianus) and in around AD 100, this settlement was raised to the status of a colony under the

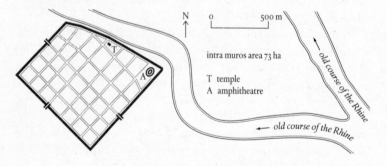

name Colonia Ulpia Trajana. From that time, the Roman fort was occupied by the legion XXX Ulpia Victrix. The colony seems to have enclosed an area of around seventy-three hectares. It was laid out in the traditional Roman grid of streets running nearly at right angles to each other, and was surrounded by a wall with eight gates. Because there was little rock in the area, the walls were built with stone hauled by cargo ships from the 'Seven Peaks' up the Rhine near Bonn.

Systematic excavations began in 1972. They have revealed two temples, a large bath complex, a wrestling school and an amphitheatre. The latter building would have held around 12,000 spectators. Water came from a spring lying eight kilometres (five miles) to the west, and the major streets varied in width from eleven to sixteen metres. It has been estimated that the colony's inhabitants numbered between 10,000 and 40,000 persons, with the most probable figure being in the lower half of that range.

The modern name Xanten derives from 'ad Sanctos' ('to the saints or martyrs'), the name of a monastery founded in around AD 590. The site became a pilgrimage destination during the Middle Ages due to its association with the death of Viktor, a Roman saint killed during a persecution under the emperor Julian II (AD 362–3).

XANTHOS

Antalya province, south-west Turkey

Capital of Lycia from the earliest days of the Lycian Federation to the Roman conquest.

History

Lycia is an alpine land on the south-west coast of Turkey. In antiquity it was inhabited by a people of Hittite (specifically Luvian) stock who had been there since the Bronze Age. In the fifth century BC, they were still using their own language and writing their inscriptions in an alphabet of their own invention, but during the Hellenistic period they were gradually absorbed into the Greek world.

The Lycians had a strong sense of unity. Some sort of federal organization, with Xanthos as its centre, existed as early as the sixth century BC, for in describing the Persian invasion of 540 Herodotus refers

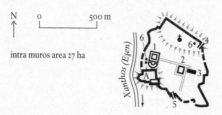

N ↑   0   500 m

intra muros area 27 ha

Xanthos (Eşen)

A Lycian (and Byzantine) acropolis
1 agora and theatre
2 basilica
3 cathedral
4 North Gate
5 South Gate and Arch of Vespasian
6 tower tombs

to Xanthos as 'the city of the Lycians'. And Xanthos was confirmed as the national capital when the Lycian League was given a formal constitution in the second century BC. Nonetheless, Xanthos was a small place: its walls enclose only twenty-seven hectares, and it is clear from the way the Lycians chose to scatter their tombs across the intramural area, that the town had lots of empty space.

Xanthos was brutally sacked on two occasions. The first was in 540 BC, when the Persian general Harpagus stormed the city and massacred

396

its inhabitants. It was said that of the entire community only eighty families escaped and they owed their survival to the fact that they had taken refuge in the hills rather than the town. Five hundred years later disaster struck again, this time in the shape of a Roman army commanded by Marcus Brutus, Caesar's assassin. Brutus wanted money and communicated this desire in no uncertain terms; the elders of Xanthos, knowing that Antony and Octavian were already on the march against him, refused. It was a bad miscalculation. Brutus launched a whirlwind assault, in the course of which Xanthos was reduced to ashes.

Lycia at this time was still technically independent, although of course in reality it had been a Roman client state for more than 100 years. Eventually, in AD 43, it was formally incorporated in the empire, and, either on its own or as one half of the province of Lycia and Pamphylia, took its place in the roster of Roman provinces. It remained there for the next six centuries, i.e. until the collapse of the provincial system in the seventh century AD. Early on in this period Xanthos was rebuilt, and much of what is visible today is Roman work of the first or second centuries. The Roman governors didn't reside at Xanthos, however, preferring PATARA, which had better communications with the outside world.

Topography and Population

Xanthos lies on a hill overlooking the river of the same name in western Lycia. The largest monuments are the Roman theatre and agora; the most interesting are the unique tower tombs, one of which bears the longest known inscription in the Lycian script. The walls are Lycian work of the fifth or fourth century BC, but settlement at the time they were built was apparently confined to the few hectares of the 'Lycian acropolis' in the south-west sector of the city. The Roman town spread over more of the intramural area, but by the Byzantine period the inhabited area had once again been reduced to the south-west corner. By the end of the seventh century the site was deserted.

At its peak, in AD 50–150, the population of Xanthos may have touched 2,500 but for most of its history it would have had far fewer inhabitants than this.

YORK

Yorkshire, England

Classical *Eboracum, capital of the Roman province
of Britannia Inferior; diocese: Britain*

York was originally built as a legionary fortress by IX Hispana in
AD 71. The legion, which had previously been stationed at LINCOLN,
provided the spearhead for the Roman advance into northern Britain
on the route east of the Pennines. It kept York as its base until early in
the second century when it was transferred to the continent before
mysteriously disappearing from the Roman army list – maybe annihilated, more probably cashiered following a culpable defeat. Its place
at York was taken by VI Victrix, which arrived in Britain from Germany in AD 122. This legion was to remain at York as long as the empire
lasted.

The twenty-hectare legionary fortress of York lies on the north bank
of the River Ouse. A civilian settlement soon grew up on the opposite
bank, and this ultimately received official recognition as a Roman colony. The promotion may well have been linked to another cause, the
choice of York as the capital of North Britain (Britannia Inferior) when
the province of Britain was divided in two by Caracalla (AD 211–17).

Roman York now entered its most prosperous phase. The legionary
garrison was at its full strength of 5,000 or so, there were something
like 2,000 civilians in the walled (27-hectare) town on the opposite
bank, plus another 1,000 in the shanty town surrounding the legionary fortress, a total of around 8,000. It seems unlikely that York ever
exceeded a population of 10,000, because it remained what it had been
from the start, a garrison town. It can, however, claim the title of ROME's
northernmost town of significant size.

Little remains of York's Roman glories. On the south side of the
Ouse there is nothing at all to see; on the north bank there are some
stretches of the fortress wall, and the corner tower on the west, referred

to in travel literature as the 'Multangular Tower'. More interesting are the remains of the legionary headquarters building under the cathedral crossing. The amphitheatre has not been found as yet.

The mid third century AD will have marked the peak of York's Roman prosperity. In the fourth century the strength of the garrison will have halved and halved again in line with the reduction in the size of the legions that took place throughout the empire. Similarly, the governor's entourage will have been cut when Britannia Inferior was divided into two, maybe three, smaller provinces. And population trends were down anyway. As an urban unit, Roman York was already dying when the fifth century opened. By the sixth century both the castrum and the colony were deserted.

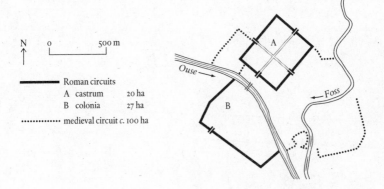

N
0   500 m

——— Roman circuits
A   castrum   20 ha
B   colonia   27 ha
·········· medieval circuit *c.* 100 ha

If York was in ruins in the seventh century, the Catholic Church had not forgotten its previous status, and when the opportunity for a missionary enterprise in the north presented itself, York was given a starter bishop. In 735 the see was elevated to an archbishopric, making it the second most senior ecclesiastical post in the land. As such it was an obvious target for the Vikings when, 100 years later, they began laying the foundations of a kingdom covering the northern half of Britain. York became a capital again, this time of a Scandinavian state standing in opposition to the Anglo-Saxon (English) kingdom of Wessex in the south. It fell to the English in 954, then, after a severe harrying, to William the Conqueror in 1068–9. The Domesday survey indicates a population in the 4,000 to 5,000 range in 1086 (while suggesting it had been nearer 8,000 twenty years earlier). This figure had risen to 14,000 in the fourteenth century when the newly built wall enclosed something over 100 hectares (compared to the two Roman perimeters' total of forty-seven hectares, a figure that could be raised to sixty hectares if the unwalled civilian settlements on the north bank are included).

Sources

and David Winfield's *Byzantine Forti-fications* (Pretoria, 1986). The much larger figures quoted by Liebeschuetz – of the order of 2,000 hectares – include hypothetical suburbs as well as the slopes of Mount Silpius. The aerial photograph of the city can be found in Glanville Downey's *Antioch* (Princeton, 1963).

ANTIOCH IN PISIDIA

See Barbara Levick, *Roman Colonies in Southern Asia Minor* (Oxford, 1967), and Stephen Mitchell and Marc Waelkens, *Pisidian Antioch: The Site and Its Monuments* (London, 1998).

AOSTA

See Francesco Corni, *Aosta Antica* (Aosta, 1989).

APHRODISIAS

See K. T. Erim, *Aphrodisias* (New York, 1986), and the chapter by Christopher Ratte in *Urbanism in Western Asia Minor*, ed. David Parrish, *Journal of Roman Archaeology* Suppl. 45 (Portsmouth, 2001). Ratte's guess is that the city had a peak population of 12,000 to 14,000, but notes in passing (p. 146) that this is double the population of any place in the valley today, which might be taken to strengthen the case for a figure under rather than over 10,000.

APOLLONIA

See R. G. Goodchild, *Cyrene and Apollonia* (Tripoli, 1959).

AQUILEIA

See Raymond Chevallier, *Aquilée et la romanisation de l'Europe* (Tours, 1990).

AQUINCUM

See Janos Szilagyi, *Aquincum* (Budapest, 1957).

ASCOLI PICENO

See Umberto Laffi, *Asculum I* (Pisa, 1975).

ASSUR

The results of extensive German excavations at the site are summarized in Walter Andrae, *Das Wiedererstandene Assur* (Leipzig, 1938; 2nd edn, Munich, 1977).

ATHENS

Although there are probably tens of thousands of books about Athens, the best one to follow the city's fortunes from its classical beginnings to modern times is John Travlos's *Poleodomike Exelixis ton Athenon* (The Architectural Development of Athens) (Athens, 1960). A typescript translation of this by R. E. Wycherley (God bless him) is in the library of the Institute of Classical Studies of London University. It's a great pity it has never found a publisher. Travlos is also responsible for the *Pictorial Dictionary of Ancient Athens* (New York, 1981) and the updates on this in *Bildlexicon zur Topographie des Antiken*

Attika (Tübingen, 1988). For getting around the city, there is no better guide than John J. Freely's *Strolling Through Athens* (London, 1991). See also John Camp's *The Archaeology of Athens* (New Haven, 2001).

The classical references are Herodotus, 5.97.2; Thucydides, 2.15–16; Xenophon, *Memorabilia*, 3.6.14; Dikaiarchos, 20; and, for Demetrius of Phaleron's census, Ktesikles, see Felix Jacoby, *Die Fragmente der griechischen Historiker* (Berlin and Leiden, 1923–58), 245. For the reconstruction of the Council constituencies, see J. S. Trail, *Demos and Trittys* (Toronto, 1986), updating his monumental study *The Political Organization of Attica*, *Hesperia* Suppl. 14 (Princeton, 1975).

AUGSBURG

See Ludwig Ohlenroth, 'Zum Stadtplan von Augusta Vindelicum: Zusammenfassender Vorbericht', in *Germania* 32 (1954), pp. 76ff.

AUTUN

See the chapter on Autun in *Les villes antiques de la France*, ed. Edmond Frézoules, Vol. 3, Part 1 (*Lyonnaise 1: Autun, Chartres, Nevers*) (Strasbourg, 1997).

AVENCHES

For a useful guide, see Hans Bögli, *Aventicum: Die Römerstadt und das Museum* (Lausanne, 1984), and the detailed city map in Walter Drack and Rudolf Fellmann, *Die Römer in der Schweiz* (Stuttgart, 1988), pp. 338–9.

BABYLON

Joan Oates's *Babylon*, revised edn (London and New York, 1986), is an excellent history of the town. A. R. George's paper is to be found in *Antiquity* 67 (1993), pp. 734–46.

BENEVENTO

See Marina R. Torelli, *Benevento Romano* (Rome, 2002).

BESANÇON

See *Les villes antiques de la France*, ed. Edmond Frézoules, Vol. 2, *Germanie supérieure 1* (Strasbourg, 1982).

BOLOGNA

See Francesca Bocchi, *Bologna*, Vol. 1, *Da Felsina a Bononia* (Bologna, 1996).

BOSTRA

See Maurice Sartre, *Bostra: Des origines à l'Islam* (Paris, 1985).

CAESAREA MARITIMA

See *King Herod's Dream*, ed. K. G. Holum (New York, 1988), which is very readable and has excellent maps.

CALAH

We know the exact population of Calah at the time of its official opening in 879 BC because King Ashurnasirpal II gave a mammoth banquet to celebrate the occasion and had a stele erected to commemorate it. On the stele he lists all the people he invited to the banquet: '47,074 workmen and women summoned from all the districts of my land, 5,000 high officials and envoys, 16,000 people of Calah, and 1,500 officials of all my palaces'. The stele is described, transcribed and translated in D. J. Wiseman's 'A New Stele of Assurnasir-pal II', *Iraq* 14 (1952), p. 24ff. The archaeologist who discovered the stele, Max Mallowan, persuaded himself that all but a few of the people it enumerates eventually became residents of the new capital. This despite the fact that Ashurnasirpal specifically says that 'the happy peoples of all the lands, along with the people of Calah, I feasted, wined, bathed, anointed and honoured for ten days, and then sent them back to their lands in peace and joy.' It's a telling example of how entrenched the idea of high populations for ancient places can get. At least Mallowan was consistent. After suggesting 65,000 'as a minimum' for Calah, he went on to characterize Jonah's 120,000 for Nineveh as 'rather a moderate figure' (M. E. L. Mallowan, 'The Excavations at Nimrud (Kalhu), 1951', *Iraq* 14 (1952), pp. 20–22).

Calah's agricultural potential is discussed in David Oates, *Studies in the Ancient History of Northern Iraq* (Oxford, 1968).

CAPUA

See Werner Johannowsky, *Capua Antica* (Naples, 1989). Although basically a coffee-table book, this, the most recent publication on Capua, does have an updated version of the sketch map, which is all that Italian scholarship has managed to produce for the classical town so far, plus a bibliography.

CARNUNTUM

See Werner Jobst, *Provinzhauptstadt Carnuntum* (Vienna, 1983).

CARTHAGE

The best discussion of Punic Carthage is in Gilbert and Colette Charles-Picard, *Daily Life in Carthage at the Time of Hannibal* (London, 1961), p. 61. Appian records that when the city surrendered to the Romans, 'forthwith there came out 50,000 men and women together' (see *Roman History* 8.19). Currently the clearest plan of Roman Carthage is on p. 33 of H. R. Hurst and S. P. Roskams, *Excavations at Carthage: The British Mission* (Sheffield, 1984), Vol. 1.1.

CHUR

See Anne Hochuli-Gysel et al., *Chur in Römischer Zeit* (Basel, 1991), Vol. 2, p. 491, for the conclusion made by the most recent survey, and p. 487 for the map.

CIRENCESTER

See John Wacher, *The Towns of Roman Britain*, 2nd edn (London, 1995).

COLCHESTER

See the article on Colchester by Philip Crummy in *Fortress into City: Consolidation of Roman Britain*, ed. Graham Webster (London, 1988).

COLOGNE

See Gerta Wolff, *Das Römisch-Germanische Köln* (Cologne, 1981).

CONSTANTINOPLE

The best introductions to Constantinople are two guidebooks by John Freely: *Istanbul* in the Blue Guide series (2000), and *Strolling Through Istanbul* (co-authored with Hilary Sumner-Boyd, 2010). Also recommended is *Byzantine Monuments of Istanbul* by John Freely and Ahmet Cakmak (Cambridge, 2004). Judith Herrin's *Byzantium: The Surprising Life of a Medieval Empire* offers a good overview. The scholars' equivalent is Wolfgang Müller-Wiener's monumental *Bildlexicon zur Topographie Istanbuls* (Tübingen, 1977); it's a bit difficult to use, partly because it is in German, partly because it has an odd arrangement (and a very odd index), but everything is there if you look hard enough. The most exciting find of recent times is the church of S. Polyeuktos; the story of its excavation is told by John Harrison in *A Temple for Byzantium* (Austin, Texas, 1989).

Michael Maclagan's *The City of Constantinople* (London, 1968) provides a good summary of the city's history. The standard work on the Byzantine Empire (replacing George Ostrogorsky's classic *History of the Byzantine State* (Oxford, 1968)) is Warren Treadgold's *History of the Byzantine State and Society* (Stanford, 1997); a shortened version (*A Concise History of Byzantium* (New York, 2001)) is available for those who don't need the detail. Penguin has published a translation of Villehardouin's *Conquest of Constantinople*, which contains an eyewitness account of the capture of the city by the Crusaders: Joinville and Villehardouin, *Chronicles of the Crusades* (Harmondsworth, 1963). For the Turkish conquest, see Steven Runciman's *The Fall of Constantinople* (Cambridge, 1965), a masterful evocation of the city's final days as a Christian capital.

For Constantine's 80,000 rations, see A. H. M. Jones, *The Later Roman Empire* (Oxford, 1964), Vol. 2, pp. 695–705, and note 20 in Vol. 3, pp. 215–16. For subsequent changes in this total, see Jean Durliat, *De la ville antique à la ville Byzantine* (Paris, 1990), pp. 250–53. For the figure of 30,000 in 1453, see Steven Runciman, *The Fall of Constantinople* (Cambridge, 1965), p. 85, note 2; Runciman himself is inclined to raise the figure to 40,000–50,000. For Mehmet Fatih's house count of 1477, see the *Encyclopaedia of Islam*, 2nd edn, ed. P. J. Bearman et al. (Leiden, 1960–2005), Vol. 4, p. 222, under 'Istanbul', an entry that also gives the 1927 census figures.

The Description of Constantinople (*Notitia Urbis Constantinopolitanae*) is published in Otto Seek's edition of the *Notitia Dignitatum* (Berlin, 1876), pp. 229–43. There is a translation of sorts appended to John Ball's 1729 version of Pierre Gilles' *Antiquities of Constantinople* (Lyon, 1561), itself a mine of curious information.

CORDOBA

See *Las capitales provinciales de Hispania*, Vol. 1, *Cordoba*, ed. Xavier Dupré Raventos (Rome, 2004).

CORINTH

See *Corinth: The Centenary*, ed. Charles K. Williams II and Nancy Bookidis (Athens, 2003), pp. xxiv–xxviii.

CTESIPHON

There is a useful sketch map of the site in *Syria* 15 (1934), p. 3, and a summary of the observations made so far in *Sumer* (1976), p. 167 (although the article is mainly about Seleucia).

CUMAE

The best current guide is *Cuma e il suo Parco Archeologico* by Paulo Caputo et al. (Rome, 1996). The map is based on Tav. 1 of *CUMA Nuove forme di intervento per lo studio del sito antico* by Bruno d'Agostino and Andrea D'Andrea (Naples, 2002).

CYRENE

See R. G. Goodchild, *Cyrene and Apollonia* (Tripolis, 1959).

CYZICUS

See F. W. Hasluck, *Cyzicus* (Cambridge, 1910).

DOCLEA

See J. J. Wilkes, *Dalmatia* (Cambridge, 1969); the scale of his map is a little generous when compared with the original in *Schriften der Balkankommission, Antiquarische Abteilung* 6 (1913).

DUR-SHARRUKIN

See map by Victor Place in Gordon Loud and Charles B. Altman, *Khorsabad* (Chicago, 1938), part 1, p. 2, and an introductory history in Michael Roaf, *Cultural Atlas of Mesopotamia and the Ancient Near East* (Oxford, 1990), p. 184.

EDIRNE

The main source for the various elements in this account – including the map – is the entry in the *Encyclopaedia of Islam*, 2nd edn, ed. P. J. Bearman et al. (Leiden, 1960–2005), Vol. 4. Aside from that, there is not much of interest. The *Blue Guide: Turkey* by Bernard McDonagh, 3rd edn (London, 2001) is useful if you are visiting, although it has no plan. There is no proper history of the town.

For the 1525 figure, see O. L. Barkan, *Journal of the Economic and Social History of the Orient* 1 (1957), p. 35, table 7. The number of hearths (3,338 Muslim, 522 Christian and 201 Jewish) is wrongly totalled as 6,351, a dittography from the entry above.

EPHESUS

Although you wouldn't think so from the title, much the best introduction to the history of Ephesus is *Ephesus after Antiquity* by Clive Foss (Cambridge, 1979). It's good on the topography too. The official Austrian account, *Ephesus: Der Neue Führer* (1995), sounds like a guidebook, but is a weighty volume. The *Blue Guide: Turkey* by Bernard McDonagh (plans by John Flower) is a very adequate substitute.

For the population figure of pre-Lysimachean Ephesus, see N. J. G. Pounds, 'The Urbanization of the Classical World', *Annals of the Association of American Geographers* 59 (1969), p. 142.

GENOA

See Ennio Poleggi and Paolo Cevini, *Genoa* (Rome, 1981).

HERCULANEUM

The standard guidebook is still Amadeo Maiuri's *Herculaneum*, first published in 1936 but frequently revised and reissued. For the general picture, see the sources quoted in the entry for POMPEII, including (despite its title) *The Natural History of Pompeii*, ed. Wilhelmina Feemster Jashemski and Frederick G. Meyer (Cambridge, 2002), which has a very interesting section on the skeletal material found on the Herculaneum seashore. *Pompeiian Brothels*, by Thomas McGinn et al., *Journal of Roman Archaeology* Suppl. 47 (Portsmouth, 2002), contains an article justifying the relabelling of what has always been considered a basilica, as a monumental portico. For an attractive book with an updated site plan, see Andrew Wallace-Hadrill, *Herculaneum Past and Future* (London, 2011), at pp. 38–39.

HIERAPOLIS

See the chapter by Francesco D'Andria in *Urbanism in Western Asia Minor*, ed. David Parrish, *Journal of Roman Archaeology* Suppl. 45 (Portsmouth, 2001), pp. 94–115, and the same author's excellent guidebook.

IOL-CAESAREA

See Philippe Leveau, *Caesarea de Maurétanie* (Rome, 1984) and T. W. Potter, *Towns in Late Antiquity* (Sheffield, 1995).

JERASH

Rami Khouri, *Jerash* (London, 1986).

JERUSALEM

Much the best synopsis of Jerusalem's history and monuments is the *Blue Guide* to the city by Kay Prag (London, 1989). A multi-author volume edited by K. J. Asali, *Jerusalem in History* (London, 1989), is another good starting point. Both have excellent plans and full bibliographies.

The sixteenth-century figures and the estimate for 1800 are taken from Amnon Cohen and Bernard Lewis, *Population and Revenue in the Towns of Palestine in the Sixteenth Century* (Princeton, 1978).

LAODICEA AD LYCUM

See *Laodicea di Frigia*, ed. Gustavo Traversari (Rome, 2000).

LEPTIS MAGNA

See David. J. Mattingly, *Tripolitania* (Ann Arbor, 1995).

LINCOLN

See John Wacher, *The Towns of Roman Britain*, 2nd edn (London, 1995).

LONDON

There are many good books on Roman London. The one I've enjoyed most is Gustav Milne's *Roman London* (London, 1995).

LUCCA

See Paolo Mencacci and Michelangelo Zecchini, *Lucca Romana* (Lucca, 1982), and for the figure of 15,000 in 1331, M. E. Bratchel, *Lucca 1430–1494* (Oxford, 1995).

LYON

See André Pelletier, *Lugdunum: Lyon* (Lyon, 1999).

MAINZ

There is a good summary of the topography and history of Roman Mainz in the Landesmuseum's *Römische Steindenkmäler: Mainz in Römischer Zeit* (Mainz, 1988). The map is based on the Römisch-Germanisches Zentralmuseum's *Mainz zur Römerzeit Stadtplan* (Mainz, 1989).

MALATYA

See T. A. Sinclair, *Eastern Turkey* (London, 1989), Vol. 3.

MARSEILLE

For the Greek period and maps, see *Marseille Grecque* by Antoine Hermary, Antoinette Hesnard and Henri Tréziny (Paris, 1999). For the Roman period, see *The Roman Remains of Southern France* by James Bromwich (London, 1993).

MEMPHIS

Dorothy J. Thompson's *Memphis under the Ptolemies* (Princeton, 1988) is an excellent summary of what is known about Memphis, before and after the Ptolemies as well as under them. The Egypt Exploration Society's findings are in David G. Jeffreys's *The Survey of Memphis* (London, 1985, with subsequent updates).

MÉRIDA

See *Las capitales provinciales de Hispania*, Vol. 2, *Mérida*, ed. Xavier Dupré Raventos (Rome, 2004). The maps of the town are, alas, very poor – not one has a scale, and the keys are either missing, illegible or just plain wrong. For a scaled plan, see J. M. Álvarez Martínez, 'Roman Towns in Extremadura', in Manuel Bendala Galán (gen. ed.), *The Hispano-Roman Town* (Barcelona, 1993) at p. 141.

MILAN

See *Milano Capitale dell'Impero Romano 1990*, an excellent exhibition catalogue, although suffering from a failure to put scales on maps. For a scaled plan, see Mario Mirabella Roberti, *Milano Romana* (Milan, 1984), at pp. 8–9.

MILETUS

See Vanessa Gorman, *Miletos: The Ornament of Ionia* (Ann Arbor, 2001). Also helpful is the entry in the *Blue Guide: Turkey* by Bernard McDonagh, 3rd edn (London, 2001). The carrying capacity figures are taken from Alan M. Greaves, *Miletos* (London, 2002), p. 100.

MYRA

For a map of Andriace, see Hartwin Brandt and Frank Kolb, *Lycia et Pamphylia* (Mainz, 2005).

NAPLES

The basic archaeology of Naples is lavishly presented in *Napoli antica*, ed. G. Macchiaroli (Naples, 1985). For an excellent, up-to-date account of the history and topography of the classi-

cal and early medieval town, see Paul Arthur, *Naples, from Roman Town to City-State* (London, 2002).

NINEVEH

The classic book is Austen Henry Layard's *Nineveh and Its Remains* (London, 1849), followed by *Discoveries in the Ruins of Nineveh and Babylon* (London, 1853). For a more updated map, see Michael Road, *Cultural Atlas of Mesopotamia and the Ancient Near East* (Oxford, 1990), p. 186.

OSTIA

The classical sources are covered in Russell Meiggs's *Roman Ostia* (Oxford, 1973). The artificial harbour is well described and mapped in Simon Keay, Martin Millett et al., *Portus: An Archaeological Survey of the Port of Rome* (London, 2005). For the population estimate, see John Dominic Crossan, *The Birth of Christianity* (San Francisco, 1999), p. 220.

OVILAVA

See Géza Alföldy, *Noricum* (London, 1974).

PADUA

See Vittorio Galliazzo, *I Ponti di Padova Romana* (Padua, 1971).

PAESTUM

See J. G. Pedley, *Paestum* (London, 1990). The plan is from J. B. Ward-Perkins, *Cities of Ancient Greece and*

Italy (New York, 1974), fig. 30, with additions (and scale) from Emanuele Greco and Fausto Longo, *Paestum: Scavi, Studi, Ricerche* (Paestum, 2000).

PALMYRA

Iain Browning's *Palmyra* (London, 1979) is a readable and excellently illustrated presentation of the city's history and monuments.

PARIS

See James Bromwich, *The Roman Remains of Northern and Eastern France* (London, 2003), p. 79 ff.

PATARA

See George Bean, *Lycian Turkey* (London, 1978), p. 82.

PAVIA

See D. A. Bullough, *Papers of the British School at Rome* (London, 1966), pp. 82ff.

PERGAMUM

Books on Pergamum tend to be either fearfully academic (and in German), or perfunctory, with too many colour plates. The nearest thing to an overall history is *Pergamon: Citadel of the Gods* (Harrisburg, 1998), a very interesting collection of papers edited by Helmut Koester. It has excellent maps covering all phases of the city's history, plus a full bibliography.

PERGE

See George E. Bean, *Turkey's Southern Shore*, 2nd edn (London, 1979), and *Urbanism in Western Asia Minor*, ed. David Parrish, *Journal of Roman Archaeology* Suppl. 45 (Portsmouth, 2001).

PERINTHOS

For a history and the best published map, see Mustafa Hamdi Sayar, *Perinthos-Herakleia und Umgebung* (Vienna, 1998).

PETRA

See Iain Browning, *Petra* (London, 1973). More recently, see Glenn Markoe (gen. ed.), *Petra Rediscovered* (New York 2003), with a good map at p. 153.

PIACENZA

See Francesco Giarelli, *Storia di Piacenza*, Vol. 1, *Dalle origini ai nostri giorni* (Piacenza, 1889), Part 3, tavola 13 for the town plan.

PIRAEUS

Just about everything you need to know is in Robert Garland, *The Piraeus* (London, 1987). The book's one weakness is its maps, which are sketchy; for proper plans, see Klaus von Eickstedt, *Beitrage zur Topographie des Antiken Piraeus* (Athens, 1991).

POMPEII

A splendid and bang up-to-date account of Pompeii's history, and of the nature and course of the eruption, is given in the opening chapters of *The Natural History of Pompeii*, ed. Wilhelmina Feemster Jashemski and Frederick G. Meyer (Cambridge, 2002). My entry follows this magisterial account except as regards the terminal event, the cloud that blanketed Misenum, which is interpreted as a pyroclastic flow in Jashmenski et al. The younger Pliny's account is given in two letters to Tacitus (6.16 and 20); how Tacitus worked the story up is not known because the relevant section of his *Annals* is lost. The best guidebook is still Amadeo Maiuri's *Pompeii*, first published fifty years ago but revised many times since. Also available onsite is a truly marvellous map by Hans Eschebach. The population figure of 10,000 is given in Frank Sear's *Roman Architecture* (London, 1982), p. 105.

PRIENE

See George Bean, *Aegean Turkey* (London, 1966), p. 161.

PTOLEMAIS

See Carl H. Kraeling, *Ptolemais: City of the Libyan Pentapolis* (Chicago, 1962).

RATIARIA

See R. F. Hoddinott, *Bulgaria in Antiquity* (New York, 1975), p. 111, and information published on the Internet by the Bulgarian Archaeological Association (www.archaeology.archbg.net).

RAVENNA

A standard reference is Carla Giovannini and Giovanni Ricci, *Ravenna* (Rome, 1985), a volume in the Laterza series on Italian towns. A useful recent work is *Ravenna in Late Antiquity* by Deborah Deliyannis (Cambridge, 2010). Also worth consulting is an especially good account of Theodoric's building programme by Mark J. Johnson, *Dumbarton Oaks Papers* 42 (1988), pp. 73ff. The best map is in F. W. Deichmann, *Ravenna: Hauptstadt des Spätantiken Abendlandes* (Wiesbaden, 1969), Vol. 2 – in the pocket at the back. The population data are all given in Giovannini and Ricci, cited above.

REGGIO

See *Il Museo Nationale di Reggio Calabria*, ed. Elena Lattanzi (Rome, 1987).

REIMS

See Pierre Desportes, *Histoire de Reims* (Paris, 1983).

RHODES

Richard M. Berthold, *Rhodes in the Hellenistic Age* (Ithaca, 1984) is a detailed account of the rise and fall of the Rhodian state; P. M. Fraser, *Rhodian Funerary Monuments* (Oxford,

1977) is better on the topography. For the 6,000 citizens (and 1,000 resident foreigners of military age) in 305 BC, see Diodorus Siculus, *Library of World History*, 20.84.1–3.

RIETI

See M. C. Spadoni Cerroni and A. M. Reggioni Masarini, *Reate* (Pisa, 1992).

RIMINI

See Grazia Gobbi and Paolo Sica, *Rimini* (Rome and Bari, 1982).

ROME

The precis of Rome's early history uses the chronology devised by the Roman author Marcus Varro (116–27 BC) in the last years of the republic. It puts the expulsion of Tarquin the Proud about five years too early (in 509 BC, rather than a more likely 504 BC) and the sack of the city by the Gauls four years too early (390 BC instead of the 386 BC given by Polybius). After this it is probably as accurate as any other version of ancient history. Dates prior to the expulsion of Tarquin are completely worthless. Rome's seven kings are supposed to have reigned for a total of 244 years, which is far too long; 150 years would be a more reasonable span. If the list has any validity at all, it would suggest that the city was founded in the mid seventh century BC, not the mid eighth, and fell under Etruscan domination not long after. For an excellent guide to the city's ancient layout, see

David Romano Gilman, *Mapping Augustan Rome* (Portsmouth, 2002), and accompanying website http://digitalaugustanrome.org.

SALAMIS

See Vassos Karageorghis, *Cyprus* (London, 1982).

SALONA

See J. J. Wilkes, *Dalmatia* (London, 1969).

SARDIS

See George M. A. Hanfmann and S. W. Jacobs, *Archeological Exploration of Sardis: Report I* (Cambridge, 1975).

SAVARIA

See A. Mocy, *Archaeologiai Értésitő* 92 (Budapest, 1965), pp. 27–36.

SCYTHOPOLIS

See *The New Encyclopedia of Archaeological Excavations in the Holy Land*, ed. Ephraim Stern (Jerusalem, 2008), p. 1,616.

SELEUCIA ON THE TIGRIS

Two groups of archaeologists have worked at Seleucia, an American team in the 1920s and 1930s, and an Italian team in the 1960s and 1970s. The American results are summarized in *Topography and Archaeology of Seleucia on the Tigris*, ed. Clark Hopkins (Ann Arbor, 1972). The best of this book is the account of Seleucia's history; the worst is the maps of the site, which are badly drawn, wrongly scaled and often incomprehensible. The reports of the Italian excavators are to be found in *Mesopotamia* 1–8 (1966–74); the results are summarized in Antonio Invernizzi, *Sumer* 32 (1976), pp. 167–75. The Italian map of the site is fair enough as far as it goes, but this isn't very far; it's more of a map of the surveyor's plan for Seleucia than of the city as it actually existed. This is not a criticism; the truth is that a lot more needs to be done on the ground before anyone can say what Seleucia really looked like.

SENS

See James Bromwich, *The Roman Remains of Northern and Eastern France* (London, 2003), p. 230 ff.

SEPPHORIS

See *The Oxford Encyclopedia of Archaeology in the Near East*, ed. Eric Meyers (Oxford, 1997), Vol. 4, p. 527; and *The New Encyclopedia of Archaeological Excavations in the Holy Land*, ed. Ephraim Stern (Jerusalem, 2008), p. 2,030.

SIDE

See George E. Bean, *Turkey's Southern Shore*, 2nd edn (London, 1979).

SILCHESTER

See George C. Boon, *Silchester: The Roman Town of Calleva* (London, 1974).

SIRMIUM

See *Sirmium: Archaeological Excavations in Syrmian Pannonia*, ed. Vladislav Popović (Belgrade, 1971–9), in particular the article by Miroslava Miković on the town's history (at the start of Vol. 1).

SISCIA

See Remza Koščević and Rajka Makjanić, *Siscia: Pannonia Superior*, British Archaeological Reports, Ser. 621 (1995).

SKOPJE

See Ivan Mikulčić, 'From the Topography Scupi' (*sic*), *Archaeologia Jugoslavica* 14 (Belgrade, 1973), pp. 29–35.

SMYRNA

The story of classical Smyrna is told by C. J. Cadoux in *Ancient Smyrna* (Oxford, 1938). Investigations since then have not added materially to his account. See also Ekrem Akurgal, *Ege ve İzmir* (Izmir, 1993).

SOPIANAE

See Ferenc Fülep, *The History of Pécs during the Roman Era and the Problem of Continuity of the Late Roman Population* (Budapest, 1984), p. 35, end col. 2 for the town's limits.

STRASBOURG

See François Louis Ganshof, *Étude sur le développement des villes entre Loire et Rhin au moyen âge* (Paris–Bruxelles, 1943), pp. 12 and 58, and the map at http://www.diercke.com/kartenansicht.xtp?artId=978-3-14-100790-9&stichwort=Romans&fs=1.

SYRACUSE

For an introduction to ancient Syracuse, see Luca Cerchiai, Lorena Jannelli and Fausto Longo, *The Greek Cities of Magna Graecia and Sicily* (Los Angeles, 2002), p. 202. For a map and information about the city's layout, see 'Urban Planning in Magna Graecia' by Dieter Mertens and Emanuele Greco, in *The Greek World* (New York, 1996), p. 243.

TANGIER

See Noé Villaverde Vega, *Tingitana en la antigüedad tardía* (Madrid, 2001); accessible online at http://books.google.com/books.

TARANTO

See Ettore M. De Juliis, *Taranto* (Bari, 2000). Note that in antiquity Calabria was the heel of Italy, not, as now, the toe.

TARRAGONA

See *Las capitales provinciales de Hispania*, Vol. 3, *Tarragona*, ed. Xavier Dupré Raventos (Rome, 2004).

THESSALONIKI

For a good map of the Roman city, see *Tabula Imperii Romani, K 34* (Ljubljana, 1976) – although the scale is wrong. For the Byzantine buildings, and for getting around the city generally, you can't do better than the *Blue Guide: Greece* by Charles Freeman et al., 7th edn (London, 2005). The census figures can be found in the entry for Salonika in *The Encyclopaedia of Islam*, 2nd edn, ed. P. J. Bearman et al. (Leiden, 1960–2005), Vol. 8. The number of captives taken by the Turks in 1430 is given by John Anagnostes, who was there at the time.

TOMIS

I have been unable to find a connected history of Tomis in any accessible language. Ovid's feelings about his place of exile are summarized in his letter to Maximus (Epistulae ex Ponto 2). The map is based on one in *Pontica* 28 (1995), p. 90, adding a scale taken from a pre-war Baedeker.

TOURS

There is a good account of Roman and Dark Age Tours by Henri Galinié in *The Rebirth of Towns in the West*, ed. Richard Hodgess and Brian Hobley (Oxford, 1988), pp. 57–62.

TRIER

The website www.landesmuseum.de has a list of all the recent publications on its museum shop page. For an excellent – and recent – guide to the

Roman city, see *Das Römische Trier*, ed. Hans-Peter Kuhnen (Stuttgart, 2001). A usable guide in English is Wilhelm Reusch, *Treveris: A Guide through Roman Trier* (Trier, 1977). The best map of Roman Trier is the *Archaologischer Stadtplan Trier* (2002) published by the Rheinisches Landesmuseum Trier.

TRIPOLI

See D. J. Mattingly, *Tripolitania* (Ann Arbor, 1995).

TURIN

See Valerio Castronovo, *Storia Illustrata di Torino*, Vol. 1, *Torino antico e medievale* (Milan, 1992).

VERONA

See I. A. Richmond and W. G. Holford, *Papers of the British School at Rome* (London, 1935), p. 69ff.

VERSAILLES

The figures for Versailles are taken from Bernard Lepetit's articles in *Annales de Démographie Historique* (1977), pp. 49–83, and *Revue d'Histoire Moderne et Contemporaine* 25 (1978), pp. 604–18.

VIMINACIUM

Viminacium remains unexcavated as yet. A good English-language introduction to what is known about the site, and to the Bulgarian literature on the topic, is Dragan Spasić-Durić, *Viminacium: The Capital of the Roman Province of Upper Moesia* (Požrevac, 2002).

VIRUNUM

See Géza Alföldy, *Noricum* (London, 1974), p. 328.

XANTEN

The site is well described and mapped in Werner Böcking, *Archäologische Ausgrabungen in Xanten* (Kleve, 1987).

XANTHOS

A good guidebook to Xanthos is Jacques des Courtils's *A Guide to Xanthos and Letoon* (Istanbul, 2003).

YORK

See Patrick Ottaway, *Roman York*, 2nd edn (London, 2004).

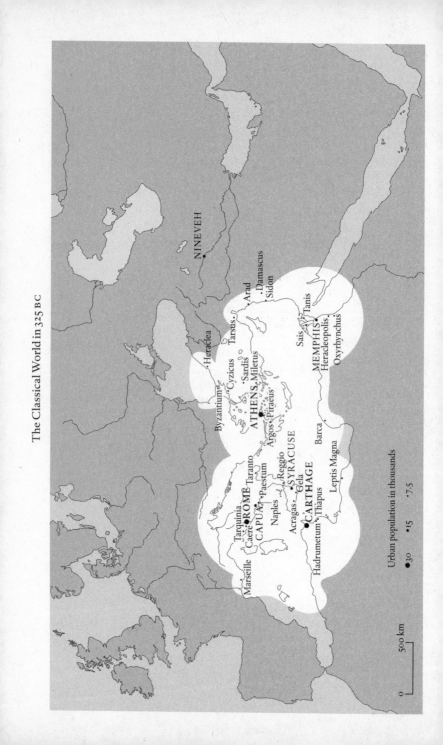

The Classical World in 325 BC

NINEVEH

Heraclea
Cyzicus
Byzantium
Sardis · Miletus
ATHENS · Piraeus
Argos

Tarsus
Arad
· Damascus
Sidon

Tanis
Sais
MEMPHIS
Heracleopolis ·
Oxyrhynchus ·

Marseille
Tarquinia
Caere · ROME
CAPUA · Taranto
Naples · Paestum
Reggio
Acragas · Gela
Hadrumetum · SYRACUSE
Thapus
CARTHAGE
Barca
Leptis Magna

Urban population in thousands
● 30   ● 15   · 7.5

0   500 km

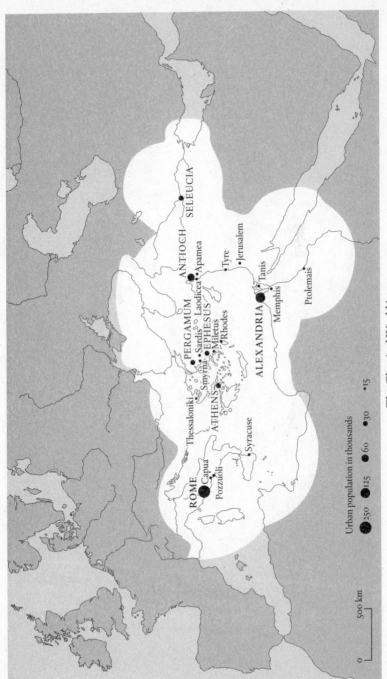

The Classical World in AD I

Urban population in thousands

● 250 ● 125 ● 60 ● 30 • 15

Thessaloniki
ROME
Capua
Pozzuoli
Syracuse
ATHENS
PERGAMUM
Sardis
Smyrna
EPHESUS
Miletus
Rhodes
ANTIOCH
SELEUCIA
Laodicea · Apamea
Tyre
Jerusalem
Tanis
Memphis
ALEXANDRIA
Ptolemais

0   500 km

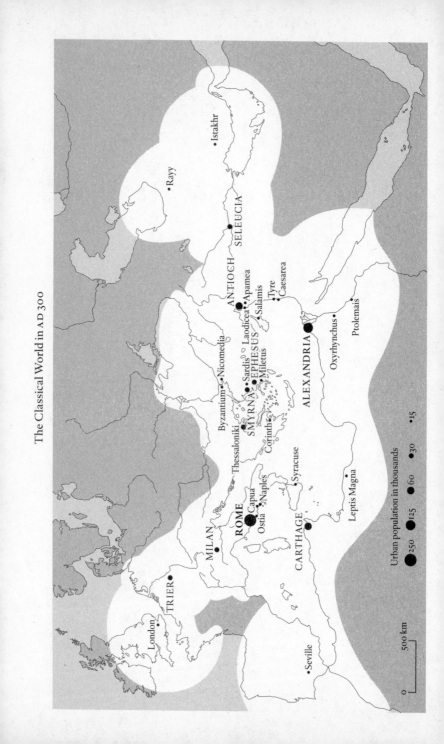

The Classical World in AD 300

Urban population in thousands

250 125 60 30 15

London
TRIER
MILAN
Seville
ROME
Capua
Ostia Naples
Syracuse
CARTHAGE
Leptis Magna
Thessaloniki
Byzantium Nicomedia
SMYRNA
Corinth
EPHESUS
Sardis Laodicea
Miletus
Apamea
ANTIOCH
SELEUCIA
Salamis
Tyre Caesarea
ALEXANDRIA
Oxyrhynchus
Ptolemais
Rayy
Istakhr

0 500 km

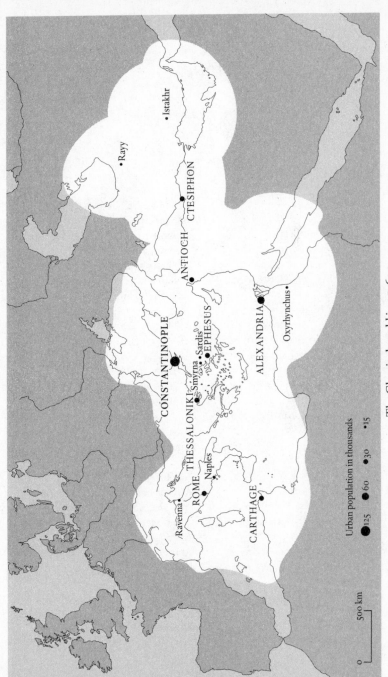

The Classical world in AD 600

Urban population in thousands

● 125 ● 60 ● 30 • 15

Ravenna
ROME
Naples
CARTHAGE

THESSALONIKI
CONSTANTINOPLE
Smyrna
Sardis EPHESUS

ANTIOCH
CTESIPHON
ALEXANDRIA
Oxyrhynchus

Rayy
Istakhr

0   500 km

Index